SEARCHING FOR THE STATE IN BRITISH LEGAL THOUGHT

Janet McLean explores how the common law has personified the state and how those personifications affect and reflect the state's relationship to bureaucracy, sovereignty and civil society, the development of public law norms, the expansion and contraction of the public sphere with nationalization and privatization, state responsibility and human rights. Treating legal thought as a variety of political thought, she discusses writers such as Austin, Maitland, Dicey, Laski, Robson, Hart, Griffith, Mitchell and Hayek in the context of both legal doctrine and broader intellectual movements.

JANET McLEAN is Professor of Law at the Faculty of Law, University of Auckland, and a public and administrative lawyer.

CAMBRIDGE STUDIES IN CONSTITUTIONAL LAW

The aim of this series is to produce leading monographs in constitutional law. All areas of constitutional law and public law fall within the ambit of the series, including human rights and civil liberties law, administrative law, as well as constitutional theory and the history of constitutional law. A wide variety of scholarly approaches is encouraged, with the governing criterion being simply that the work is of interest to an international audience. Thus, works concerned with only one jurisdiction will be included in the series as appropriate, while, at the same time, the series will include works which are explicitly comparative or theoretical – or both. The series editors likewise welcome proposals that work at the intersection of constitutional and international law, or that seek to bridge the gaps between civil law systems, the US and the common law jurisdictions of the Commonwealth.

SEARCHING FOR THE STATE IN BRITISH LEGAL THOUGHT

Competing Conceptions of the Public Sphere

JANET McLEAN

CAMBRIDGE
UNIVERSITY PRESS

CAMBRIDGE
UNIVERSITY PRESS

University Printing House, Cambridge CB2 8BS, United Kingdom

Cambridge University Press is part of the University of Cambridge.

It furthers the University's mission by disseminating knowledge in the pursuit of education, learning and research at the highest international levels of excellence.

www.cambridge.org
Information on this title: www.cambridge.org/9781107022485

First published 2012

A catalogue record for this publication is available from the British Library

Library of Congress Cataloguing in Publication data

McLean, Janet, 1963–
Searching for the state in British legal thought : competing conceptions of the public sphere / Janet McLean.
p. cm. – (Cambridge studies in constitutional law)
Includes bibliographical references.
ISBN 978-1-107-02248-5 (Hardback)
1. Law–Great Britain–Philosophy. 2. State, The–Philosophy. 3. Great Britain–Politics and government. 4. Law–Political aspects–Great Britain. I. Title.
KD640.M39 2012
320.10941–dc23
2012020436

ISBN 978-1-107-02248-5 Hardback

Thus the modern state crept up, in a sense unobserved, upon both politicians and lawyers.[1]

1 J. D. B. Mitchell, 'Administrative Law and Policy Effectiveness', in J. A. G. Griffith (ed.), *From Policy to Administration: Essays in Honour of William A. Robson* (London: George Allen Unwin, 1976), p. 181.

CONTENTS

ACKNOWLEDGEMENTS

Early on in this project I was having lunch with Mike Taggart. We were talking about John Austin's legal theory. Mike stopped me short asking: 'But what impact did his theory have on the real life of the law?' 'That,' he added, 'is the question Brian Simpson would ask.' Neither Brian, who was my teacher, nor Mike, who was my colleague and friend, have lived to see completed this attempt to assess the impact of political and legal theory on common law conceptions of statehood. Had they done so, they would each, no doubt, have pointed out the many cases, counter-examples and discussions I have missed out and should have included, and the misconceptions that have remained. I miss their contributions greatly and no doubt the work is worse for that. I thank them nevertheless for the many ways in which they have each influenced this project.

I owe thanks to numerous other people and institutions. For invitations to present early versions of the work, my thanks go to audiences at the Law Schools at the universities of Auckland, Dundee, Edinburgh, Glasgow, London, Victoria University of Wellington and Yale, to Oxford University's Constitutional Theory Seminar and to the seminar at the Law and Public Affairs Program at Princeton University. I also thank the New Zealand Crown Law Office for the opportunity to discuss what became Chapter 5. I am grateful to Dean Alan Page and my colleagues at Dundee Law School for carrying an increased administrative and teaching burden while I spent two semesters' leave at Princeton University, and to Kim Lane Scheppele at the Law and Public Affairs Program there for a wonderful and stimulating year. For their enthusiasm and support for the project generally I would particularly like to thank Mark Aronson, Nick Barber, Justin Borg-Barthet, Corey Brettschneider, Peter Cane, Robin Churchill, Louisa Cross, Stuart Cross, David Dyzenhaus, Pamela Ferguson, Patrick Ford, Rodger Haines QC, Dirk Hartog, Mark Hickford, Susan Karr, Stan Katz, Sir Kenneth Keith, Melissa Lane, Peter Lindseth, Joanna Manning, Michael Moreland, John Morrow, Aileen McHarg, Campbell McLachlan QC, Geoff McLay, Richard Mulgan,

Alan Page, Dame Alison Quentin-Baxter, Quentin Skinner, Kim Lane Scheppele, Rayner Thwaites and Adam Tomkins. For their inspiration and insights which were the motivation for this project, I particularly thank Stuart Anderson, David Runciman and Quentin Skinner. Paul Rishworth, Hanna Wilberg, Tim Mulgan, Richard Ekins, Margaret Bedggood, Katherine Sanders, Barry Sullivan and Treasa Dunworth gave me written comments on drafts. John Haldane gave me biographical and other details about Viscount Haldane. Alistair Birchall and Anita Wan gave excellent assistance with proofing and references. David Hollander, law librarian at Princeton University, helped with the UK statutory materials. Finola O'Sullivan and Elizabeth Spicer at Cambridge University Press and Kate Ollerenshaw (copy-editor) were incredibly supportive at critical stages. Agnes and Barrie McLean brought me up with the idea that an individual has a duty to the public. Tim Mulgan gave me a room of my own, and my heart's desire.

1

Searching for the state

Lawyers must work forwards as well as backwards. The stream must be traced downwards as well as upwards.[1]

Searching for the state

The orthodox view is that the British do not have a developed concept of the state. Disliking abstractions, they prefer to focus on real people vested with real powers. Consequently, it is claimed, there is no sufficiently distinct body of public law or developed concept of state responsibility in British law. The absence of a developed state concept has also been blamed for the ease with which privatization policies have been able to be effected. There is undoubtedly truth in all of these claims. But what if we were to view these consequences as evidence of a particular state tradition rather than as evidence of its absence? What if we were to view this as Britain's struggle with the same questions as her continental counterparts but reaching different solutions? Then we might uncover a subtle, complex and distinct conception of statehood and one with its own riches as well as blind spots.

This book tests the claim that British legal thought has never had a very robust conception of the state. It identifies ideas of statehood in legal writing and attempts to trace their influence on legal doctrine, and legislative and administrative structures. In doing so, it takes legal thought seriously as a variety of political thought.

At times the common law's own (often older) pre-commitments resist external ideological movements and at others embrace them. Spanning the period 1832–2010, the book traces the influence on legal thought of

[1] F. W. Maitland, 'The Shallows and Silences of Real Life', in H. A. L. Fisher (ed.), *The Frederic William Collected Papers of Maitland*, 3 vols. (Cambridge University Press, 1911), vol. I, p. 493.

intellectual movements such as Utilitarianism, Idealism, Pluralism, Fabian Socialism and public choice theory. Beginning in 1832, with the first Reform Act, the book covers the development of centralized bureaucracy and the expansion of state functions, the rise of administrative law and its new public morality, nationalization and privatization of industry, changing relationships between the state and civil society and changing views about the relationship of the individual to the collective, and the advent of a new era of human rights. This is not a story about Empire, though sometimes the imperial story breaks through into the domestically focused one. At times it is more of an English than a British story and at others a more general 'common law' one.

Searching for the state in the idea of the Crown

Historically speaking the obvious starting place from which to investigate the state in British thought is in the concept of the 'Crown'. But even choosing the Crown as a starting place is controversial among common law scholars. The Crown may be the common law's closest approximation to the state,[2] but at the same time the idea of the Crown is commonly regarded as responsible for inhibiting the development of a state concept.[3] Another school of thought contends that we simply do not need a conception of the state (founded in the Crown or elsewhere) in order to get on with the public law project.[4] There is some truth in each of these propositions. That is why the Crown will sometimes take centre stage and at other times inhabit the peripheries in our search for the state.

It is Blackstone who has been credited with giving expression to a Hobbesian theory of state in English legal thought in his *Commentaries of the Laws of England* (1765).[5] In the introductory essay, Blackstone

[2] See M. Loughlin, 'The State, the Crown and the Law', in M. Sunkin and S. Payne (eds.), *The Nature of the Crown* (Oxford University Press, 1999) where he contends that both of these first two propositions are true. *Rudolph Wolff & Co Ltd and Norranda Inc.* v. *The Crown* [1990] 1 SCR 695 69 DLR (4th) 392: 'The Crown cannot be equated with an individual. The Crown represents the state.'

[3] T. Daintith and A. Page, *The Executive in the Constitution* (Oxford University Press, 1999), pp. 12–13.

[4] J.A.G. Griffith, 'The Political Constitution', *Modern Law Review* 42 (1979), 1, 16. See Chapter 6.

[5] W. Blackstone, *Commentaries on the Laws of England*, 4 vols. (Oxford: Clarendon Press, 1765–9). See Q. Skinner, 'A Genealogy of the Modern State', *Proceedings of the British Academy* 162 (2009), 325–70.

portrays the people, unified through a social contract, as forming the state. The state is a *persona ficta* with a distinct moral personality which is in turn represented by the sovereign which is itself an artificial person. By these fictions, the state as a collective is able to act as if it were 'one man' with 'one uniform will'. Sovereigns may come and go but the state endures.

Blackstone suggests that at the same time as civil society is formed, a superior is constituted with the power to make and enforce the laws.[6] In Britain's mixed constitution, the 'making of laws' is entrusted to three distinct powers – King, Lords and Commons – all of which are independent of each other and balanced.[7] From this we may infer that Blackstone means to suggest that the sovereign that is artificially constituted by law to represent the state in Britain is composed of these three branches of government working together to make and enforce law for the good of the state, and authorized by it.

But Blackstone's account of the state also introduces the early seeds of potential confusion when he attempts to engraft a Hobbesian theory of state onto older medieval ideas of the King's two bodies – 'the disunion of the king's body natural from his body politic'.[8] According to medieval systems of thought, the King simultaneously embodies the body natural, which dies, and the body politic, which is perpetual. The distinction between the King in his natural person and the special qualities which the law assigns to the King in his political capacity is expressed by Blackstone (though not always consistently) as the distinction between the King and the Crown. The King understood in his political capacity is an artificial person (the Crown) which is the product of legal rules.

Confusion arises, however, in the later books, because it is the King *alone* whom Blackstone identifies as the one who unites 'those several wills and reduces them to one' and '[i]n the King therefore, as in a centre, all the rays of his people are united'.[9] But by 1765, it was well established that the body politic firmly resided in the King acting *with* the Commons and Lords. Blackstone's work represents an incomplete synthesis of modern political thought and medieval political theology.

[6] Blackstone, *Commentaries*, above n. 5, vol. I, p. 48.

[7] J.L. De Lolme, *The Constitution of England* another highly influential work of the period, would not be published until 1771 in France, an English version appeared in London in 1775.

[8] Blackstone, *Commentaries*, above n. 5, vol. I, p. 242 referring to *William* v. *Berkley* (1559) Plowden 233a.

[9] Blackstone, *Commentaries*, above n. 5 vol. I, p. 245.

Shortly after the *Commentaries* were published, Blackstone became the target of an 'almost lethal attack'[10] by Bentham, not least because of the absolutist powers he appeared to vest in the King.[11] Bentham suggested that Blackstone's indulgence in fictions involving political compacts and absolutist sounding sovereigns should be avoided altogether in legal thought. For Bentham, what constitutes rulers is not normative and neither is it the product of political theory: it is a fact of power. He urges that we should focus on real powers and on real people, and that we should avoid abstractions, such as King and Crown, which do not do any real work.

While Bentham's approach has tended to dominate British legal thought, a state tradition centred on the personality of the King and Crown would nevertheless survive. At the end of the nineteenth century, Maitland would revive the idea of the Crown. He had an unlikely object. He thought that the concept of the Crown could provide a means by which to capture the modern democratic relationship between citizen and state in the common law. In other words he sought to complete the task that Blackstone had left half done – to incorporate the modern political relation in the old feudal form. In doing so, he suggested we needed to reject the idea of the King as a 'corporation sole' – which treated the King's two bodies and capacities as residing in the one natural person. More fruitful, he thought, would be to adopt the less popular idea of the Crown conceived as a corporation aggregate of the many of which the King is merely the head. He admitted that this interweaving of the old and new, substituting the Crown for the King, was a subterfuge, but it was one he considered to be capable of providing a legal person to serve the role of representative of the state. His aim was to align common law thought and political thought so that the law represented the *real* political relation.

Thus Maitland drew explicit attention to the corporate nature of the state itself, at a time when it was being argued that corporate forms of social life depended entirely on the sovereign for their existence. Viewing the state through a corporate lens would have consequences for broader debates, both legal and political, about the basis of sovereignty, the relationships between sovereignty, civil society and the individual,[12]

[10] Skinner, 'A Genealogy of the Modern State', above n. 5, 355.

[11] J. Bentham, *A Fragment on Government*, W. Harrison (ed.) (London: Basil Blackwell, 1948) (first published 1789).

[12] Chapter 3.

the moral capacities of all corporations and whether sovereigns could be limited by law. The Crown itself, then, was not the simple object of the inquiry – but rather provided a point of entry into these much larger questions.

Since Maitland, there have been other attempts to revive notions of statehood by focusing on the concept of the Crown and once again it is the point of entry into deeper controversies. The object of Kantorowicz's *The King's Two Bodies: A Study in Medieval Political Theology*[13] was not so much to democratize the state but to humanize it after its deification by German nationalists. Like Maitland, Kantorowicz argues that the modern state can develop out of the theological and absolutist beginnings represented in the medieval idea of the King's two bodies. In a work that has been described as 'demythologizing' and 'deliberately ironic',[14] he suggests that out of a shared European medieval heritage, the singular achievement of the English law was in conceiving of the Prince as a corporation sole '– admittedly a hybrid of a complicated ancestry – from which the body politic as represented by Parliament could *never be ruled out*'.[15] (He ignores the controversy about the corporation sole and aggregate that had so exercised Maitland.) This idea of the two bodies, he contends, was much more fully articulated, and closer to its Christological origins, in England. It played a part in establishing a healthier, more 'universal' and 'human' version of the nation state in England than in her continental counterparts.[16]

Kantorowicz suggests that the political theology of the King's two bodies also performs important work not explicitly identified by Maitland. The duality between the King's body natural and the body politic, according to Kantorowicz, also helps to explain the duality that the King is at once above and subject to the law (the source of the laws of man but subject to the laws of nature). The King's two bodies, he suggests, may also help to distinguish not only between the public and private natures of the King's person but between the public and private *within* the concept of rulership – matters affecting individual relations between the King and his subjects

[13] E. Kantorowicz, *The King's Two Bodies: A Study in Medieval Political Theology* (Princeton University Press, 1957).

[14] C. Landauer, 'Ernst Kantorowicz and the Sacralization of the Past', *Central European History* 27(1) (1994), 1–25.

[15] Kantorowicz, *The King's Two Bodies* above n. 13, p. 20 (my emphasis).

[16] J. Mali, 'Ernst H. Kantorowicz: History as Mythschau', *History of Political Thought* 18 (1997), 579–603, 598.

and matters affecting all of his subjects.[17] Kantorowicz explicitly links the idea of the Crown to the distinction between public and private law.

Kantorowicz's contribution is significant to our broader project not least because it reminds us of the crucible in which Western conceptions of statehood have been played out in the twentieth century and just how much it has mattered how the state is conceived. What is noteworthy about Kantorowicz's work is that he contemplates that the state conceived as a distinct legal and moral person does not *need* to embrace the worse kinds of nationalism, and in doing so he uses the Crown as the basis for his argument. In this he is pretty much alone. As we shall see, the same political commitments moved lawyers such as Dicey, Lauterpacht and H. L. A. Hart to reject the idea of the state as a special moral and legal person. Superhuman overtones attach too quickly to such personifications. Kantorowicz's contribution is singular too because later legal theorists, such as Loughlin, would credit the absence of a distinct body of public law in the common law to the *incomplete* separation of the Queen and Crown in the English legal tradition. Once again we shall see that these issues run deeper than questions about the nature of the Crown itself.

Reacting to common law case law in more recent times, Loughlin has also attempted to revive the Crown as a central concept. He urges modern lawyers 'to re-conceptualise the Crown as a symbol of government'[18] as part of a 'continuing project of developing a body of public law and setting in place a more realistic conception of the nature of state power and the conditions under which it may legitimately be exercised'.[19] The Queen, standing for the state, is unable to satisfy the need for a general expression of an institution of rule.[20] Loughlin wants to complete Maitland's project. He argues that the Crown should be conceived as both 'a corporation aggregate standing for the community and as an executive body otherwise known as the government';[21] and for the common law development of a distinct public law 'of official liability for acts of the Crown'.[22]

Maitland, Kantorowicz and Loughlin share in common the view that the medieval concept of the Crown is able to be adapted to reflect the state in its modern political instantiation. They want the law better to reflect the contemporary political relation. They each regard this as

[17] Kantorowicz, *The King's Two Bodies*, above n. 13, p. 172.
[18] Loughlin, 'The State, The Crown and the Law', above n. 2, p. 33
[19] *Ibid.*, pp. 33–4. [20] *Ibid.*, p. 36. [21] *Ibid.*, p. 75 [22] *Ibid.*

necessary but for different reasons. Maitland wants to democratize the state, Kantorwicz to humanize it and Loughlin to hold it responsible.

The responses to these *particular* concerns, however, do not wholly or necessarily depend on how the *Crown* is conceived. While we may argue about how well it works in practice, constitutional convention has enabled the feudal forms of the legal constitution to adjust to modern democratic relationships while preserving a distinction between the legal and the political constitution. Similarly, ideas about the relationships between the sovereign, the state and civil society do not *necessarily* depend on the common law concept of the Crown, though viewing the state as another corporation is a powerful idea which may well shed light on such relationships. Laski, for example, shared many of Maitland's views about the relationship between the state and civil society, and yet rejected personifications of the state.[23] There are various ways to achieve Kantorowicz's object of humanizing and constraining state power as Dicey, Wade, Lauterpacht and Hart each demonstrate.[24] If the object is to create a distinct system of responsibility and public law, as Loughlin contends, then we ought to acknowledge the part already played by the Crown in the *existing* common law systems of Crown liability and judicial review. As I shall argue, in those areas of law the Crown often does represent a version of the state – being the 'collective will' or 'society in a moral guise'.[25] Difficulties occur when the Crown representing the public seeks to hold liable the Crown meaning the *core* political organs of the government apparatus. A separate system of state liability *is* emerging to fill this gap. It does not depend on notions of the Crown and, indeed, circumvents such notions. It depends instead on international law ideas of state which derive from European Union law and international human rights law. There are, then, other ways to argue about the nature of the state in British legal thought which do not necessarily place the Crown at the centre.[26] They involve arguments about sovereignty,[27] civil society and the public–private distinction,[28] and responsibility[29] – all issues which this book will address.

Ideas about the Crown are not necessarily central to these questions about the nature of the state – they can even sometimes get in the way. We can see an early example of this in Bentham's reaction to Blackstone. Given Britain's constitutional history and the fact that absolutist

23 Chapters 4, 6 and 7. 24 Chapters 2, 5, 9 and 3 respectively.
25 Chapter 7. 26 Chapter 9. 27 Chapter 3. 28 Chapters 4, 5 and 9.
29 Chapters 7 and 9.

monarchies were plentiful in Europe at the time, endowing the Crown with the unified will of the people was unlikely to be an attractive proposition. Moreover, in common law thought, as we shall see, it was difficult to imagine quite how the Crown could have come to serve as the focus of unifying public law norms or positive duties. It never represented the whole of the public sphere and over the nineteenth century it came increasingly to be characterized as the repository of immunities and privileges – in contrast to other public and all private bodies.[30] Both private and public law obligations, as they evolved, focused on real officials and their real powers.[31] Another reason why the Crown is potentially problematic as a source of unity is that it has so many different legal guises. It has never been a single *personne morale* but rather it wears different masks in different areas of the law – representing the public and the law, power and authority, the Empire and sometimes represented as a private person. This is not merely a problem of terminology but one that, I shall argue, goes to the heart of the sovereignty debate.[32]

Focusing on the Crown as a *personne morale* may also distract us from more central questions about relationships between sovereignty, state and the citizen. The citizen's relationship to the state has been highly contested in political thought over the nineteenth and twentieth centuries. This book tells a legal version of that historical contest. Dicey's individualism is well-known. Not so familiar is the philosophical Idealists's conception of the individual as socially constituted or the influence of the new liberalism on the administrative lawyers of the early twentieth century and on the law's relationship to the state more generally.[33] The post-War distrust of ideas about the collective will and the new era of human rights continues to present a challenge to traditional common law concepts and I shall consider how the law has responded to these challenges. The legal relationship between citizen and state has been redefined much more through public administrative law (judicial review of administrative action) and the adoption of human rights instruments than through any reinterpretation of how the Crown has been conceived – though of course the question of what constitutes the public sphere continues to exercise scholars, lawyers and legal theorists. The search for the state in the Crown is only a small part of these much larger debates.

[30] Chapter 5. [31] Chapters 7 and 6 respectively. [32] Chapter 3. [33] Chapter 6.

It would be a mistake to suggest that those who avoid focusing on the Crown or any other personification are not interested in the state or in the normative questions associated with it. Indeed, as I shall argue, there is a British state tradition (though with mixed ideological commitments) which treats the common law judges as a representation of the state. This view can be found in Dicey who thought that judges would moderate the excesses of democracy. A different version is to be found in Robson who modelled all official actors on disinterested judges. His conception of the 'judicial mind' approximates to the 'collective will'. In contemporary times the judges have found themselves (perhaps reluctantly) in the middle of an effort to establish how a fragmented government apparatus can be held to a unified set of public law norms. Public law norms and not ideas of the collective will would now be viewed as the means to unify the state. The earlier constitutional neutrality about the functions a state should perform for its citizens has been challenged in the post-privatization era, and the common law judges now find themselves in the role of arbiters of these large questions too. In the process, many of the old issues about sovereignty, the state and civil society are required to be confronted once again. In the context of the European Union, the common law judges are beginning to ask questions about constitutional identity. It is now possible that the contemporary state may comprise a unified set of norms and commitments enforced by judges, rather than be represented as a person. Indeed, that is much closer to Hart's vision of law as a system of rules without a 'person' standing behind it.[34]

And, of course, flowing throughout this narrative is the issue about what is the relationship between the state and the law. Does the law serve the state? I deliberately avoid the issues surrounding terrorism and its potential threat to the state. That particular question has been the subject of important recent work. I am more interested here in what the mundane and commonplace interactions between the law and state may reveal about these issues.

Neither do I engage directly with Loughlin's *Foundations of Public Law*,[35] an important and challenging work that arrived too late for me to do its arguments justice. While I also press on the issue of whether there is a boundary between constitutive and constituted law, the distinctive aim of my project is to explore the *lived* state tradition in British legal thought.

34 Chapter 3.

35 M. Loughlin, *Foundations of Public Law* (Oxford University Press, 2010).

Together the theorists who focus on the persona of the state and Crown and those who seek other ways to conceive of statehood constitute a British state tradition. It is a debate full of contestation, but that makes it all the richer in what is an ongoing search for the state in British legal thought.

The state apparatus

The book begins by examining the development of the state apparatus during the nineteenth century. This is not to equate the state with the government apparatus – a view that Skinner attributes to Weber and describes as normatively impoverished.[36] Rather, as I shall argue, the ways in which the government apparatus has been organized has had very serious normative consequences for the ways in which the state has been imagined as a legal concept. Sometimes the very way in which the government apparatus is organized of itself reflects a representation of the state.

The nineteenth-century development of a centralized bureaucracy challenged older conceptions of authority and came to be connected with an Austinian version of sovereignty.[37] The fellowships of civil society struggled against the notions that all power was delegated from above as opposed to being self-originating.[38] And yet notwithstanding these changes (though for normative reasons) the common law persisted with a system of responsibility designed for an earlier conception of authority.[39] The twentieth-century expansion of the government apparatus and functions was associated with a particular view of the collective will and of the individual understood as socially conceived. This was reflected in much of the administrative law scholarship of that time.[40] The changes to administration giving effect to nationalization and later privatization also had normative consequences for how the state was conceived. Nationalization resulted in the loss of a number of legal resources which had formerly been used to define the public sphere.[41] Later privatization provoked a new urgency to define the public sphere by way of legal norms.[42] In both cases, it was a particular view of the relationship between state and law that allowed the expansion and contraction of state functions without legal impediment. At both points,

[36] Skinner, 'A Genealogy of the Modern State', above n. 5, 326. [37] Chapters 2 and 3.
[38] Chapters 3 and 4. [39] Chapter 7. [40] Chapter 6. [41] Chapters 4 and 5.
[42] Chapter 8.

change was effected by relying on the idea that the individual or the law should not be regarded as in opposition to the state but rather the state should be viewed as serving the individual and the law as serving the state. Despite the version of the state on which it depended for its implementation, privatization brought with it a new conception of the state – and one that has been met with some ideological if not practical resistance from the common law since. In these different ways, the government apparatus and the way it is organized (including in modern times in its relationship to the EU), is central to this narrative of the state and its relationship to law.

Chronological time and law time

This story takes place in three different chronologies: 'real time', 'no time' and 'law time'. Changes in the apparatus occur in real time. I use the government apparatus and changes to it in order to sustain a degree of chronological narrative. And it is these changes which most closely track movements in political thought such as Utilitarianism, Idealism, Pluralism, Empiricism, Fabian Socialism, public choice and human rights. Thus we start with the Reform Act 1832 and end with the operation of the Human Rights Act 1998; we begin with the centralization of the bureaucracy in the nineteenth century and end with the disaggregation of the government apparatus that followed the 1980s.

Analytical jurisprudence, on the other hand, tends to occur in 'no time' or 'every time'. The 'ahistorical moment of general jurisprudence' aims to describe all legal systems over all time. Large issues about the relationship between the sovereign, the state and the law are ever present. I suggest that these ideas are not quite as unaffected by 'real time' as most modern jurisprudes may think.[43]

But, as we shall see, the legal reactions to and sometimes instantiations of political theories of the state do not tend to occur in 'real time' or 'no time' but rather in 'law time'.[44] As we have already seen in relation to our discussion about the Crown, old common law ideas are often sustained and affected by new ideas. So too ideas of common law responsibility, for example, derive from a time long before our period but are able nevertheless to survive even if by fiction and evasion. The common law tends to look both forwards and backwards at the same time: 'the stream

[43] Chapter 3. [44] I am grateful to Stuart Anderson for this expression.

must be traced downwards as well as upwards'.[45] It lurches between making highly contextualized decisions to determining general principles abstracted from their original historical contexts. It always has an eye to the future. This is not a linear narrative and neither is it a Whiggish one of constant progress and refinement of earlier concepts. Legal ideas are sometimes lost, recovered or adapted to incorporate or resist change. Old ideas often endure long after the point of their political salience. That is why this book is not intended *primarily* as a work of history. Rather it adopts Maitland's historical method in order to glean what we can from the past that may be helpful to the present.

Structure

Chapters 2 to 6 are historical in that they attempt to explain where we have been and to revive resources that we may have lost in order to analyse contemporary problems. Chapter 3 places the jurisprudential debates in an historical context (chronological time) but also attempts to identify issues which continue to face us about the relationship between sovereignty, statehood and law. Chapters 7 to 9 have a more contemporary focus.

The book begins by tracing the nineteenth-century development of the state as bureaucracy. Chapter 2 argues that in the nineteenth century greater centralization led to changes in the way authority was conceived. Authority – which had been local, personal and had involved particularized decision-making – became more centralized, bureaucratic and increasingly the subject of general rules. I argue that the Utilitarians provided the critical theoretical justifications for these changes. They were concerned that Parliament should enact general rules, and to make officials with personal legal duties more dependent on the 'sovereign will'. The effect of the changes was increasing centralization and delegation – sometimes explicitly modelled on the French state. The mid-nineteenth-century invention of ministerial responsibility was an attempt to square the circle of a unified authority newly enforced primarily by *political* rather than legal methods. This is the state imagined as a unified, authoritative, administrative apparatus.

There was a strong political reaction against this new centralization. It was seen as an attack on common law method and ideology. Indeed

[45] Maitland, 'The Shallows and Silences of Real Life' above n. 1.

Dicey's work can be seen as a political 'denial' of these developments about which he was undoubtedly aware. This explains why in 1907 he introduces the idea that the closest thing to the state in English law is the 'august dignity of the judges'. The aggregation of power in central political institutions provokes in him a re-imagining of the state in the judges and in the common law which encapsulates for him liberal values of individualism. His reliance on the common law to represent the unified will is much more reminiscent of Blackstone than of Bentham whom he purports to be following.

Lawyers after Dicey would tend to think that the bureaucratic state was born of late nineteenth-century collectivism and the new 'social' legislation. This earlier story of the centralization of power has been almost entirely lost to legal memory. Hence the common misconception that strong governments are necessarily economically interventionist governments. The state was actually built, strengthened and centralized in an earlier era of Victorian Liberalism. The story of the state as government apparatus will be picked up again in Chapter 8 when we consider privatization and deregulation.

Two major currents of thought would follow these developments in the later nineteenth century: one would subsume statehood within notions of sovereignty and authority; the other would react against such mechanistic manifestations of statehood in favour of more organic notions linking the individual to society and to the state. In Chapter 3, I consider these rival philosophical conceptions of the state represented by Austin on the one hand and T. H. Green and the British Idealists on the other, their reception into legal thought and their impact on legal theory or analytical jurisprudence. The reception of Austin is relatively well known but also perplexing. His work was unable to explain the British domestic constitution and the common law – as his contemporaries noted. British Idealism, on the other hand, is regarded as lacking a juristic component.[46] I argue, however, that Idealism was in some respects more compatible with the common law and that central elements of Idealist philosophy can be found in Maitland's thought. Maitland argues that the individual is formed by society and the state is formed by societies. The sovereign is not the source of all law. He argues that it is the task of the law to recognize the 'reality' of social and political life.

The chapter then shifts to the twentieth century and considers the influence of Austinian Positivism and Idealism on analytical jurisprudence

[46] D. Runciman, *Pluralism and the Personality of the State* (Cambridge University Press, 1997).

and ideas of sovereignty. The theory Hart expounds in *The Concept of Law* meets selected concerns of Austinian and Idealist thought while critiquing both. He finds a place for constitutional and customary law (which Austin's theory did not). He maintains the distinction between rulers and ruled that Idealists tended to collapse in the idea of collective will. He ultimately grounds *all law* in social fact (as the Idealists were inclined to do) and not just the political sphere (as Austin did). The sovereign is now constituted by rules and no longer stands behind the law. Hart wants to avoid all personifications of sovereignty. In resolving these issues, however, he leaves us with a new problem. Where is the state? What is the relationship of the state understood as a juristic person and the state understood as a legal system? This is an issue to which I shall return in Chapters 7 to 9.

Chapter 4 turns from legal theory to legal doctrine to assess the impact of Austin, Idealist thought and the political Pluralist movement on legal understandings of the relationship between the state and civil society. Part of Maitland's challenge to the sovereign state was that the state is a variety of corporation and the differences between it and other corporations are matters of degree rather than of kind. As such he is regarded as the founder of English political Pluralism, though his views draw on much older traditions in British thought. Where, then, does the state end and civil society begin? This chapter is in two parts. It begins with Maitland and his analysis of the place of the English fellowships and their relationship to the state. It argues that while Maitland's thought had some limited reception in the case law and in the work of the Pluralists, ultimately his theories about the moral and legal personality of the state and corporation did not contain the resources necessary to protect the English fellowships from the challenges posed by their increasing entanglements with the state apparatus.

In the second half of the chapter I turn to the period in which Britain changed from one of the most voluntarist societies in Europe to its most centralized and bureaucratic welfare state by the mid-twentieth century. For much of this period, the state and civil society indeed look very much alike. They are both vehicles for the public articulation of policy and democratic participation in the moral life of their communities. They both have coercive power. Some aspects of judicial review would be modelled on the working of friendly societies and unions in the operation of the National Insurance Act. This is the age of the 'Big Society'. But what is also evident is that the state and voluntary associations each demonstrate the capacity to undermine the other: the voluntary agencies do so, for example, by undermining the penal practices of the Poor Law regime; the state does so by undermining the self-governing powers of friendly societies – and ultimately by taking over their functions.

Chapter 4 takes us up to the establishment of the welfare state. After the partial dismantling of the welfare state in the 1980s, politicians and judges would once again revisit ideas about the state's relationship to civil society. This chapter anticipates those debates. I do not return to them explicitly until Chapter 9 and only after I have established how and on what basis distinct legal standards came to apply to public authorities.

Up until the middle of the twentieth century there is a gradual aggregation of power to central government and expansion of government functions. In Chapters 5 and 6 I consider whether the Crown could have been capable of personifying the expanding public sphere and public law norms, and if not why not. Chapter 5 considers three possible moments when the Crown could have come to represent the public sphere: mid-nineteenth century as 'public office' was waning; at the turn of the twentieth century as public functions were expanding; and at the point of nationalization. At none of these points did the Crown personify the public sphere or serve as a source of unifying public law norms. Instead, for important legal purposes, by the middle of the twentieth century the Crown would come to be treated as 'private person of full age and capacity'. What had previously been regarded as 'public law' norms actually fragmented at the very time the bureaucratic state was expanding. The chapter considers the explanations that attribute this result to the problematic relationship between the King and Crown. More telling factors include the fluidity of the relationship between the state and civil society and the concern to confine the scope of immunity and privilege.

There were numerous tests of 'publicness' during this earlier period, but these tests tended to be politically rather than judicially enforced. A range of entities qualified, by various mainly political processes, to be included within the public realm. That range included railway companies, public undertakings, trustees and commissioners, municipal trading entities, municipal corporations, the Post Office and central government departments. The degree to which their activities were to the public benefit was commonly assessed at the point at which their powers were conferred. This sliding scale of 'publicness' reflected the diversity of the English fellowships. A body could be avowedly public without attracting immunity or being considered part of the Crown.

Much of this law and practice would be lost to legal memory after nationalization. The new view was that public ownership would be sufficient to invest an activity with concern for the common good. The Crown did not become co-extensive with the state but was instead conceived in a way that restricted the scope of immunity while enabling the government's expansion into new areas with minimal legislative effort.

If the Crown did not come to represent the whole of the public sphere or to unify public law norms, on what basis did judicially enforced distinctly public law norms eventually emerge? In Chapter 6 we shall see that the modern development of public law norms did not depend on the personality of the Crown at all. Instead, public law norms as they emerged as part of the new twentieth-century version of administrative law were modelled on the judge as decision-maker. It would be possible to conceive of the 'state' not as a single *personne morale* but rather as a diffuse and variegated complex of entities whose 'unity' is created by the application of shared 'public law' norms – a new public morality.

We witness for the first time the conscious, if belated, realization by the judges, politicians and practising legal profession that there *is* an administrative state in Britain.

The politics of this new administrative state was initially conceived as antithetical to the common law, its institutions and values. Eventually, however, a new set of administrative law-oriented values come to be enforced by the common law courts in their supervisory jurisdiction.

I argue that prevailing political thought of the time, especially the values of Idealism, Fabian Socialism and the new Liberalism, greatly influenced the 'lawyers of the administrative'. Theirs was a view of individual rights socially conceived, the product of, and not prior to, social and collective life. Such views conflicted with common law constitutionalism and it was for this reason that an explicit debate was required about whether the values of the common law, particularly those associated with laissez-faire, such as freedom of contract and rights of property, should properly apply in the public sphere. Robson's work in particular, is closest to the prevailing civil service thinking of the period. His model of the ideal administrator endowed with 'judicial habits of mind' and whose habits may be enforced by the ordinary courts, was able to be adopted and adapted by the common law prerogative orders. A judicial model of decision making became part of mainstream administrative law and formed the basis of a distinctly public as opposed to private law morality. Public morality has at its core the suppression of self-interest – again in accordance with the prevailing thought of the period. It is these public norms that might possibly unify the state (though in practice they too did not apply across the whole of the public sphere). A number of these ideas, especially about the nature of the individual and of rights as socially conceived would be subject to direct challenge during an era of privatization and deregulation influenced by public choice theory. These are issues we shall visit in Chapter 8.

Chapters 7 to 9 have a much more explicitly contemporary focus. Chapter 7 discusses common law ideas of legal responsibility for government wrong-doing throughout the period and up until the present day. It explains how the structures of common law thought make it difficult for an individual to claim rights directly against the state for its wrong-doing either in tort law or in the law of judicial review. How can the Crown conceived as the government apparatus be responsible for wrong-doing when the Crown also represents the state as society in a moral guise and the source of the common good? This rationale would have to be considered afresh in light of the privatization policies of the 1980s (and their associated views about the individual and state) and the influence of international law – particularly human rights law. Chapter 9 suggests that EU and human rights law and the international law concepts of the state from which they derive have brought into UK law a new kind of state liability. Readers who are primarily interested in issues of legal doctrine should read Chapters 7 and 9 together.

Chapter 8 discusses the political theories underpinning the liberalization and privatization policies of the 1980s. There is no collective will, only individual preferences. The state is no longer to be trusted and the state apparatus has been disaggregated. There are interesting symmetries here. At the point at which the government apparatus centralized, public law norms fragmented. At the point at which the government apparatus has become increasingly disaggregated, part of the law's response has been to attempt to create a new unity through public law norms. There is a new impatience with the idea that the legal personality of the state should be defined by instrument choice. That is, the state's moral and legal personality should not depend on which area of law defines it (as Hart described the position) but should flow from our notions of the state itself as reflected in a separate and distinctive public law. There have been renewed attempts to give priority to public law conceptions of the state and to determine what constitutes the 'truly public' and 'public functions'. There is a renewed (and law-oriented) quest for the state and its moral personality.

Chapter 9 uses the UK Human Rights Act as the lens through which to explore some of these issues in more detail. It examines how ideas about the state which have their source in international law, and particularly international human rights law, challenge traditional common law ideas about government responsibility and liability: if the Crown cannot will wrong-doing, international law concedes that the state can do so. Under this conception the state is part of the problem. But this does not mean that the state is necessarily limited or diminished. Human rights treaties have been interpreted to the effect that the state also has positive obligations to its citizens – a kind of non-delegation doctrine. In the second half of the chapter, I consider the scope of human rights obligations and how far they extend into the 'private' sphere or, as I would prefer to call it, 'civil society'. I attempt to bring some of the historical resources explicitly to bear on this contemporary question. Can Maitland's historical method offer anything new to help us in the present?

2

From state as official to state as machine: unifying political will

Going off to Paris[1]

A unified political will

In the last chapter we encountered an oppositional narrative that associates Blackstone with a normative statist view (the state as a *personne morale*) and Bentham with a normatively impoverished anti-statist view (no state, only real people exercising real power).[2] In this chapter I shall begin to complicate these dichotomies in various ways.

Skinner describes the view that treats the state as synonymous with the government apparatus as reductionist and normatively impoverished. In this and later chapters, I argue that we should not underestimate the effect that changes to the government apparatus can and have had on normative conceptions of statehood and of the public sphere. The nineteenth century saw a shift in the location of public power from individual officials to a collective bureaucracy and from the localities to the centre. Public power, which had earlier been conferred for particular, and often time-limited purposes, gradually came to take more generalized forms. These changes had consequences for conceptions of 'authority' and of 'unified will', and hence for how the state and its representatives were conceived.

The oppositional narrative that pits Blackstone and Bentham against each other obscures an important element which they share in common. They are both concerned with *authority*. Blackstone and Bentham each

[1] S. E. Finer, *The Life and Times of Sir Edwin Chadwick* (London: Methuen, 1952), p. 469 (attributed to Seymour).

[2] Q. Skinner, 'A Genealogy of the Modern State', *Proceedings of the British Academy*, 162 (2009), 325–70.

imagine a sovereign power which is able to effect its will. Blackstone speaks in terms of a *unified* will that resides in the sovereign: he writes of the King in Hobbesian terms as the person who unites 'those several wills and reduce[s] them to one' and as the 'will of the state united in a single person'.[3] Every public act must be traced back to this authoritative source. Bentham, too, is concerned with unifying sovereign will and authority – albeit in much more practical ways. While Bentham is worried about Blackstone's grand abstractions which might license a sovereign to abuse its powers, he is also concerned about the potential for officials to disobey or fail to fulfil the sovereign will. How can the sovereign rely on agents to pursue the greatest good for the greatest number, when 'sinister interests' (especially those of politicians and lawyers) will be wont to pursue their own ends at the expense of the common good? The existence of a unified will, and its faithful execution by agents of the government apparatus, is central to his concerns.

Bentham and Blackstone both give a place to unified authority. Where they tend to part company is in relation to *how* such authority should be conceived and exercised. Blackstone's followers would, for the most part, imagine authority as exercised in a diffuse, tacit, common law way; Bentham's early followers came to imagine authority in a much more *politically unified* way. The joint processes of democratization and bureaucratization helped to promote the latter, *novel*, view of the unified will of the state.

In the mid-nineteenth century, it would be the Utilitarians who would ask the question of how to make dispersed political authority dependent on the sovereign will. In so doing they would be engaged in a defence of a centralized government apparatus drawn along French lines. That accompanying debate was transacted in the language of 'statehood'. As central government self-consciously aggregated power to itself, the accompanying political struggle and resistance would often include direct comparisons with the French state. Centralization challenged, and was seen at the time to challenge, the essential features of the common law system of diffuse and particularized decision-making.

The mechanistic aspects of creating a state machinery in England were not so dissimilar from experiences in France and Germany. It was the intellectual reaction of common law scholars and judges to these developments which represented the more significant legacy for the way in which

[3] W. Blackstone, *Commentaries on the Laws of England*, 4 vols. (Oxford: Clarendon Press, 1765–9), vol. 1, pp. 52, 245.

British lawyers conceived of the state. There would be concerted, apparently self-conscious, collective legal amnesia about these developments and the debates surrounding their meaning. Dicey's late nineteenth-century partial remembering of the century past would become the dominant orthodoxy in legal thought. His approach would be to ignore the new state machinery and to focus once again on real persons and real power. This approach was, however, wholly motivated by normative reasons. He did not treat the government apparatus as a fictional person capable of representing the state or of attracting to itself a distinct body of public law. Indeed, he was suspicious of collective power, 'the exercise of unified will' in all its forms. If there is a personification of the state in his thought, it is the judges who are its representatives.

The chapter will begin by describing some of the major administrative reforms of the nineteenth century. This is not intended to be exhaustive or an attempt to tell in any detailed way the story of a lost administrative law tradition – those books are yet to be written. It aims, instead, to mark out the major directions of change and their wider significance to law and its intellectual traditions. What was left out by the constitutional lawyers writing at the end of the century and why?

Real persons, real power: centralization as state making

We know that by the end of the eighteenth century, Britain had already established a centralized 'fiscal–military state'.[4] Funding the American and French wars had required very high levels of taxation and an efficient centralized customs and excise administration to extract it.[5] The sovereign will to tax, wage war, expand empire and protect the country's economic interests on the high seas (all powers originally associated with the common law prerogatives of the King) was manifest and the envy of Europe. The Treasury, under Sir George Harrison, had already begun to assert its centralized controlling authority and to organize itself in a hierarchical and collective

[4] J. Brewer, *The Sinews of Power: War, Money, and the English State, 1688–1783* (Cambridge, MA: Harvard University Press, 1990). The high levels of taxation for the French wars had been justified as 'the propertied paying most of the bill for a war fought in defence of property', see P. O'Brien, 'The Political Economy of British Taxation, 1660–1815', *Economic History Review*, 41 (1988), 1–32, 13.

[5] Brewer, *The Sinews of Power*, above n. 4.

way – and in so doing had self-consciously borrowed to itself overtly monarchical ideas of the prerogative and royal dignity.[6]

The Treasury would continue to increase its power and control after 1829. And while it would attract some of the critics of the 'new centralization', it would not be their main target. The debate about centralization would be much more vehement in relation to *new* areas and techniques by which the central government claimed greater authority over the localities. The central–local struggle assumed prime importance because so many of the new challenges posed by industrialization were most acute in the localities. There were no systematic mechanisms for dealing with pressing issues spawned by the Industrial Revolution arising in areas such as policing, prisons, Poor Laws, public health, gas, water and drainage, and the regulation of factories. These were not issues in any way associated with royal dignity or prerogative power, or, at that time, with central government.

The issue of centralization would play out differently in different parts of the UK and the Empire. This is an important caveat to all that follows. This narrative is essentially an *English* story. Ireland had often been the experimental canvass for centralizing power. 'The most conventional of Englishmen were willing to experiment in Ireland on lines which they were not prepared to contemplate or tolerate at home.'[7] Reforms to policing, Poor Laws and the like had long been tried out there first. Dispersed Protestant elites in the localities had needed all the centralized authority they could draw on. Scottish local authorities, on the other hand, had been the earliest recipients of general powers of improvement and general policing powers – though they had not been quick to use them. Different parts of the wider Empire would enjoy different degrees of independence over this time. No doubt these colonial experiments informed the English debate (as we shall see in at least one instance), but those important interactions and divergences are not the immediate focus of our attention here.

Before we can understand what the opponents of centralization were reacting against, we need a sense of how executive functions were

[6] J. R. Torrance, 'Sir George Harrison and the Growth of Bureaucracy in the Early Nineteenth Century', *English Historical Review* 83 (1968), 52–88, 86–7. Harrison retired as Secretary to the Treasury in 1826.

[7] O. MacDonagh, 'The Nineteenth Century Revolution in Government: A Reappraisal', *The Historical Journal* 1 (1958), 52–67, 62 (quoting W. L. Burn). See also, e.g., the discussion in O. MacDonagh, *Early Victorian Government 1830–1870* (London: Weidenfeld Nicholson, 1977), pp. 181 ff.

organized in the early part of the nineteenth century. If Bentham was interested in real persons and real powers, it was because, at the time he was writing, both legislation and administration were largely understood in those terms. English domestic government was characterized by a system of personal, localized and dispersed powers in which the King's judges and Justices of the Peace were essential actors as well as overseers. There was no strict separation of powers. Justices of the Peace, for example, decided after hearing evidence whether a local road was needed, where to build it, whose land would be acquired on which to build it, what the owners of such land should be compensated and where best to find the building materials. The particularistic common law style of decision-making provided a model for *all* decision-making – whether legislative or administrative. The emphasis was on determining the matter at hand: processes were not aimed at generating general rules. Private legislation, for example, was formulated out of a process of petition and response before a committee, and costs might even be awarded against those promoters or opponents of legislation who were judged to be unreasonable or vexatious.[8] Even the new 'bureaucrats' – the 'surveyors' and inspectors who would emerge during the century – would initially engage in similar fact-finding processes, except this time bringing to such processes their own expertise, rather than local knowledge and personal standing.

It is difficult to square this highly localized, particularistic and dispersed system of authority with Blackstone's account which places the King or Crown at the centre and as the source of unified 'sovereign will and authority'. Blackstone's account of the sovereign will and authority is a highly abstract and tacit one. He draws on natural law theories of obligation and earlier notions of authority.[9] According to Blackstone, it would be the King's Ministers, the King in Parliament and the King's judges who would do the governing. One of the striking things about the English story is that the Blackstonian version of the constitutional narrative would prove to be remarkably resilient, even as the political facts changed. In his 1886 text, for example, Hearn organizes his chapter headings under the titles 'The Legal Expression of the Royal Will in the Judicature', 'The Legal Expression of the Royal Will in Administration'

[8] 28 & 29 Vict c 27 (1865) (An Act for Awarding Costs in Certain Cases of Private Bills).

[9] P. Hamburger, *Law and Judicial Duty* (Cambridge, MA: Harvard University Press, 2008), p. 73.

and so on.[10] Much of the administrative effort throughout this century, however, would be devoted to making law and administration more rational, efficient and responsive. Officials would become increasingly dependent on 'sovereign will', a term which would become synonymous with 'political will' and that 'will' would come to be located in Parliament and answered for by Ministers.

How was this dispersed power and authority aggregated and how would that impact on notions of a 'unified sovereign will'? I begin with the concept of 'office'. Legal understandings of public office treated obligation and responsibility as personal to the office holder. Power was not conceived as delegated from above, so much as attaching to office and personal standing. Scholars disagree about the extent to which office holders retained real, as opposed to merely formal, independence from a bureaucratic hierarchy into the nineteenth century.[11] There would, of course, have been a patchwork of different types of administrative and legislative organization, and degrees of independence from the centre would have varied. For the moment I shall be dealing in generalities.[12] What is important, for present purposes, is to appreciate the different ways in which 'sovereign will' was conceived at the beginning as opposed to the end of the century.

[10] W. E. Hearn, *The Government of England; Its Structure and Its Development*, 2nd edn (Melbourne: George Robertson, 1886).

[11] While Chester suggests that officers, as opposed to employees, had a more direct connection with the people for whom they performed functions than with the Government on whose behalf they acted, (see D. N. Chester, *The English Administrative System, 1780–1870* (Oxford: Clarendon Press, 1981)) Anderson argues that while their relation to the public may have continued to be characterized by legal notions of office, some offices were already part of a hierarchical employment relationship by the beginning of the nineteenth century (S. Anderson, 'Public Law', in W. Cornish, S. Anderson, R. Cocks, M. Lobban, P. Polden and K. Smith (eds.), *The Oxford History of the Laws of England, Vol. XI, 1820–1914: English Legal System* (Oxford University Press, 2010), pp. 299–523, 343. See also (tending more to Chester's view) B. Selway, 'Of Kings and Officers – The Judicial Development of Public Law', *Federal Law Review* 33 (2005), 187–239; P. D. Finn, 'Public Officers: Some Personal Liabilities', *Australian Law Jounal* 51 (1977), 313–16; P. D. Finn 'Official Misconduct' *Criminal Law Journal* 2 (1978) 307–24. For the contrary view, see J. Brewer, 'Servants of the Public – Servants of the Crown: Officialdom of Eighteenth Century Government', in J. Brewer and E. Hellmuth (eds.), *Rethinking Leviathan* (New York: Oxford University Press, 1999), pp. 127–48.

[12] More detailed inquiry into the Commissioners of Woods and Estates will appear in Chapters 5 and 7.

Real persons

Near the beginning of the nineteenth century, politicians felt the need for reliable agents. Melbourne, Peel, Gladstone and Lincoln each expressed a desire for agents answerable to them.[13] At the time, they had to choose between amateur, but conscientious, Justices of the Peace, who stood between the centre and the localities (and who during this period received an increased criminal workload), oligarchic corporations, semi-literate overseers, unresponsive parishes or statutory commissioners of whom Parliamentarians were jealous and localities suspicious and resistant.[14] There was a limited cadre of salaried civil servants at the centre, but these appointments tended to depend on patronage. Even after a number of reforms to some of the worst abuses of office, Trevelyan would describe the public service in 1854 as attracting 'the dregs of all other professions'.[15]

Many offices were 'for profit' and so were conceived as a form of property. Such offices represented dispersed personal power that was independent both of administrative hierarchy and of Parliamentary appropriation. In formal legal terms, agents were often not answerable in any direct way to political masters.[16] While some officers may have also received a salary, their *main* source of income was usually by way of fee-taking for the services they rendered. Such fees paid their expenses and the salaries of their staff. Fees in surplus could be treated as an officer's own: 'He might use the balance in hand as if it were his own money.'[17] Staff changed with the office holder.

Officers could be made answerable indirectly to the Crown and the public through the common law. The mechanisms that controlled officers were primarily legal rather than political and the way in which these controls operated was to reinforce personal duty and personal responsibility. All public officers, whether or not appointed by the Crown, were understood in law as exercising primary responsibility for the powers and duties conferred on them personally, rather than as delegates of any political superior. They, in turn, were not vicariously liable, being only

[13] J. M. Prest, *Liberty and Locality: Parliament, Permissive Legislation and Ratepayers' Democracies in the Nineteenth Century* (Oxford: Clarendon Press, 1990), p. 14.

[14] Embellishing on Prest *ibid.* p. 3.

[15] C. E. Trevelyan, 'Collected Papers Relating to the Reorganisation of the Civil Service 1854–5' *Parliamentary Papers* Vol. XX 1, p. 413.

[16] Patronage was a very potent source of influence, if not accountability.

[17] Chester, *The English Administrative System*, above n. 11, p. 16.

responsible for those actions of their employees which they had directed or from which they profited.[18] Wilful breach of office could lead to an action for its forfeiture, and failures to act could attract writs of *mandamus*[19] or *quo warranto*. Tort law, and especially the public law torts such as false imprisonment, also played a regulatory role and focused on the person who actually committed the act.

Criminal law was a particularly important means of keeping officials in check. An officer would be answerable in criminal law for abuses of money and power.[20] Indeed, statutes make frequent provision throughout the first half of the nineteenth century for subordinate officers to pay a surety or bond upon appointment to cover any potential fines they might incur for non-performance or negligent performance of their duties. For a time, criminal law, through penalties of fines and forfeiture, seemed to be the preferred means to enforce both sides of the regulatory administrative process.[21] Members of the public could be fined for breaching regulations: officers could be fined for failing to enforce, or wrongly enforcing, regulations. Chester suggests that the use of criminal forfeiture as a punishment declined as office holding was replaced by employee/ employer relationships[22] Certainly these measures seemed to become less frequent as the century wore on, though as late as 1867 a centralized system would be devised for the guaranteeing of such penalties.[23]

Criminal penalties for maladministration or neglect of official duties were not only statutory but were also available under the common law. In the late eighteenth-century case of *R* v. *Bembridge*, Lord Mansfield set out very broad general principles on which a criminal sanction could be based:[24]

> There is another principle, too, and that is this – where there is a breach of trust, a fraud, or an imposition on a subject concerning the public

[18] The sheriff was an exception. See the discussion in Selway, 'Of Kings and Officers', above n. 11, 215.

[19] In 1843 a statute acknowledging an increase in *mandamus* actions was passed to make the writ procedurally easier to obtain (6 & 7 Vict, c 67).

[20] *R* v. *Bembridge* (1783) 3 Dougl 327, 332; 99 ER 679, 681.

[21] So, e.g., a statute regulating Irish linen manufacture in 1835 empowered a committee to make rules to regulate sealmasters of linens. The sealmasters in turn were required to pay sureties upon appointment to cover any subsequent fines they might incur for neglect of such regulations. Breach of regulations by linen manufacturers also incurred fines and forfeiture (5 & 6 Gul IV c 27).

[22] Chester, *The English Administrative System*, above n. 11, pp. 141–2.

[23] 30 & 31 Vict c 108 (1867) (Guarantee of Government Officers Act).

[24] (1783) 22 State Trials 1, 151.

> which as between subject and subject would only be actionable by a civil action, yet, as that concerns the King and the public (I use them as synonymous terms), it is indictable.

It is striking that, in Lord Mansfield's formulation, the Crown does not represent the 'unified political will' of the state apparatus. The unified will of the sovereign here means the will to do right: it is the will to uphold the law. The idea that the King could do no wrong is understood to go beyond mere immunity. The Crown is the moral exemplar ensuring that right be done by his subjects. This is a legal fiction, of course, and the results were almost certainly chaotic, unsystematic and subject to the vagaries of litigation. Even so, it is evident that the common law sometimes imagined the monarch as wronged along with his subjects by the improper actions of his officials. In other words, the monarch does not represent the state apparatus itself, but is above it and simultaneously represents the people. The King is harmed when the people are harmed by public officials. As we shall see, this personification of the state has a variety of manifestations in the common law and performs important work. The state is not personified as a legal person able to be sued, but it is personified nonetheless.

There is no unified 'sovereign will' here in any tangible organizational or political sense. Such controls as existed could only be exercised episodically and after administrative failure. Many controls relied on the actions of individuals (for example, laying an information before a magistrate) rather than on mechanisms of central scrutiny. The concept of office would be a counterweight to attempts to centralize power, especially given that the political authority of office often came from the locality and not from the sovereign, and office was frequently associated with financial and political independence.

Real power

Such personal, independent, particularistic administration would not necessarily have worried the early Victorian. Legislated powers themselves were often personal, particularized and temporarily conferred – also modelled on common law methods of 'rule-making'. Maitland's observation, that in the eighteenth-century age of reason, 'the British Parliament seems rarely to rise to the dignity of a general proposition',[25] remained true for the nineteenth century for some time after the first Parliamentary reform.

The organization and content of the statute book helps us to enter the Victorian mind. Lord Melbourne (1834–46) thought that Parliament's function was primarily an executive one and the statute book still largely reflected this during his time. Both Public General Acts and Private Local Acts contained little by way of general rules. So, for example, power would be given to build a road between x and y as marked in pink on a map deposited in a particular room at a named address. In similar fashion, persons and offices would often be referred to interchangeably. Individuals would be named by statute to official positions.[26] Named individuals would be honoured, receive pensions for service, suffer illnesses which would require their removal from office, become naturalized or obtain divorces.[27] Bentham, that great advocate of general rules, must have had mixed feelings from beyond the grave about the Public General Act that conferred compensation on him by name for non-performance of the contract relating to Millbank Prison.[28]

Though legislation was categorized into Public General and Private Local legislation, the labels were often misleading in both cases. While Public General statutes did contain matters which we would broadly associate with the central government and the prerogative (such as the army (annual mutiny acts), taxation, customs and excise, the colonies, Irish and Scottish matters, treaties (especially anti-slavery measures during this time), appropriation and Crown lands), even Public Acts contained much that was temporary, personal and executive in nature.

The division between Public and Private Acts did not *necessarily* mark the general nature or public importance of the subject matter, but rather where the legislation was initiated and the processes by which it was enacted. Private Local Acts were initiated by local promoters through Parliamentary agents and solicitors who served notice on interested parties and, if opposed, brought petitions to select committees. Select

[25] F. W. Maitland, 'History of English Law', in H. M. Cam (ed.), *Selected Historical Essays of F. W. Maitland* (Cambridge University Press, 1957), pp. 97–121, 114.

[26] See, e.g., 3 & 4 Vict c 104, sections 2 and 3. The office of Secretary of State remained a prerogative position and was exceptional in the sense that different people could share the powers conferred.

[27] E.g., 14 Vict c 4; 14 & 15 Vict c 23.

[28] 6 & 7 Vict c 26 (1843).

committees, chaired by the local Member, would hear evidence from promoters and opponents of the Bills and onerous standing orders had to be observed.[29]

It was these so-called Private Local Acts that dealt with many of the matters that were the most critical to the new industrial economy. They typically conferred powers on particular railway companies, banks, friendly societies, improvement commissioners, municipal corporations and joint stock corporations, effected particular inclosures and concerned the building of particular roads, water works and drains.[30] The preponderance of such legislation is partly explained by the fact that corporations were not automatically considered persons in law and their powers had to be explicitly conferred. Parliament was jealous of these powers and there was money to be made by lawyers and Parliamentary agents from the processes associated with acquiring them. So, for example, when the local government of England and Wales was reformed by the Municipal Corporations Act 1835, the new corporations did not enjoy inherent powers to make by-laws or run trusts as the old common law or chartered corporations had done. If the new corporations needed powers they were required to seek them through a Private Local Act.[31] In many of the localities requiring new infrastructure to meet the needs of industrialization, corporations were increasingly interfering with private common law and especially property rights and needed to be statutorily empowered to do so. 'Private' legislation is a misnomer in the double sense that it was used to create artificial persons and to give them powers over natural persons and their property. If the locality wanted to address pressing social needs, it had to negotiate a costly and expensive legal process. If a locality chose instead to ignore the need for drains and clean water (there were cholera and typhoid outbreaks during this time), there was nothing central government could do about it.

The statutes convey an overall impression that, in the first half of the nineteenth century, most public power was still very much conceived as personal and dispersed, and it was dispensed through patronage (either

[29] Even by 1848 for a Bill to be passed eighteen different motions had to be put each giving an opportunity for debate, Chester, *The English Administrative System*, above n. 11, p. 111.

[30] The King's highways were regulated by Public General Acts.

[31] The Scottish Municipal Act 1833 (3 & 4 Gul IV, c 77) conferred more general and generous powers, though in both Scots and English law it was accepted that a corporation was not a person and could not undertake anything which was not permitted by statute.

central or local) to deal with individual cases. If, later in the century, the superiority of the common law would be asserted against statutes, in the first half of the century many statutes were still themselves the products of particularistic decision-making methods, having been made in the image of the common law.

Centralizing moves

Moves towards centralization came from a number of different political impulses – some conservative and fiscal, some Whiggish and utilitarian, and some pragmatic responses to social needs (often driven by evangelical concerns).

Many of the reforms to the central bureaucracy were prompted by the same tendencies to fiscal conservatism that had developed the fiscal–military state.[32] Good Victorian government should be cheap and efficient government. Government spent less in 1850 than it had in 1780.[33] By reforming the worst abuses of the 'Old Corruption', Tory elites would confirm and defend their fitness to rule, even after Parliamentary reform. Harling describes the reforms wrought between the late eighteenth and the mid-nineteenth century as remaking 'civil service [from] a form of private property to the notion that it was a public trust'.[34] Even before our period, the worst abuses of office had begun to be targeted. There had been commissions as early as the 1780s to enquire into fee taking and the public accounts.[35] A series of legislative measures had been passed to abolish the worst sinecures, the right to grant office in reversion and the right to exercise office by means of a deputy. Statutes also prohibited the buying and selling of offices and the use of office as a bribe.[36] The numerous compensation provisions for lost offices scattered throughout the statutes testify to ongoing reform.

[32] This term comes from Brewer, *The Sinews of Power: War, Money, and the English State*, above n. 4.

[33] P. Harling, *The Waning of Old Corruption: The Politics of Economic Reform in Britain, 1779–1846* (Oxford: Clarendon Press, 1996), pp. 10, 177; E. Hughes and H. O'Brien, 'Sir George Trevelyan and Civil Service Reform, 1853–5', *English Historical Review* 64 (1949), 53–88, 206–34.

[34] Harling, *The Waning of Old Corruption*, above n. 33, p. 14.

[35] Commissioners for Examining Taking and Stating the Public Accounts 1780–87; Commissioners for Inquiries into Fees in Public Office 1786–88 Commissioner for Enquiry into Fees 1786 discussed in Torrance, 'Sir George Harrison and the Growth of Bureaucracy in the Early Nineteenth Century', above n. 6.

[36] See Chester, *The English Administrative System*, above n. 11, p. 131.

It would be a slow process. The *Civil Service Gazette* would carry the offer of a sale of a government position as late as 1855.[37]

The Municipal Corporations Act 1835 was both a Whiggish reform measure (extending the franchise for boroughs beyond that of the 1832 Parliamentary reforms) and part of the project to enhance public trust. It dedicated the corporate funds of the boroughs, which had previously been treated as private in the hands of municipal office holders, to public purposes. Property concepts would linger. The relevant provisions of the Municipal Corporation Act would need to be tested by litigation before the change in status of municipal property would be confirmed as a matter of law.[38]

Statutes by themselves do not change cultures and real change came slowly and often by way of practical administrative and particularly financial reform. Thomas Macaulay and Charles Trevelyan, who had first used the East India Company as a 'staging ground' from which to attack the Old Corruption,[39] would work to increase salaries and pension arrangements, reform the government banking system so that money could be paid in daily and earn interest for the Exchequer rather than the office holder, make more government spending subject to formal appropriation rather than fee-taking and bring the Exchequer account at the Bank of England under tighter Treasury control.[40] By the 1850s, individuals entering the civil service would be required to take entrance exams. A system gradually began to evolve for the appointment of civil servants on merit, who were answerable to a hierarchy and survived changes of government. The legal instrument for reforms of this kind would typically be the prerogative order rather than legislation.

[37] J. Hart, 'Sir Charles Trevelyan at the Treasury', *English Historical Review* 75 (1960), 92–110.

[38] *Attorney-General* v. *Aspinall* 2 My and Cr 613; 40 Eng Rep 773; *Attorney-General* v. *Corporation of Poole* 4 My and Cr 27; 41 Eng Rep 11; *Attorney-General* v. *Corporation of Lichfield* 11 beav 119; S C 17 LJ Ch 472.

[39] T. L. Alborn, *Conceiving Companies: Joint Stock Politics in Victorian England* (London: Routledge, 1998), p. 12. This reform response was not only intended to deflect pressure for Parliamentary reform and not to concede to attacks on aristocratic rule but to reaffirm a belief in aristocratic rule as the natural and best form of government.

[40] In 1835, e.g., Parliament thought it necessary to make clear that the fees taken by a Surveyor of the Highways, on his death became the property of his successor, and that his executor could be sued for them, Preservation of Public Highways Act (5 & 6 Gul IV c 50) section 43. It was still a patchwork at this time but real efforts at rationalization were beginning to occur by the 1850s. By 1850, seven different classes of appropriation were listed in Acts – and we can begin to see more clearly the extent of employment relationships.

The use of prerogative orders would mark an association with Kingly authority. Officials above party politics would claim to represent the 'state above parties' after 1830. The Crown would become a 'symbol less of royalty than of the corporate power and prestige of officialdom'.[41] After 1830, and contrary to the hopes of many of the supporters of the Trevelyan reforms, the Treasury would also become increasingly aristocratic.[42] By 1855, Trevelyan could claim that the Treasury was the 'Chief Office of Government'.[43] There were attempts from within central government to claim that the Crown was synonymous with the state apparatus.

One centralizing trend, then, was contiguous with the forces which had developed the fiscal–military state of the late eighteenth century and had as its primary objects the improvement of efficiency and propriety. Some of the impetus for centralization, however, would also be radical and reformist. Both Whigs and Utilitarians favoured centralized government despite their apparently shared preference for laissez-faire policies. Tories, by contrast, on the whole disapproved of laissez-faire policies, but tended to favour localism which was in practice the surest mechanism for delivering laissez-faire policies.[44] Paradoxically, centralization, forged at a time when laissez-faire was the dominant ideology, would make many social reforms and a paternalistic state possible.

After the first Parliamentary Reform, we begin to see a few but very important legislative examples of the more radical reforms associated with the Whigs and the Utilitarians. This legislation tended to state more general rules and to provide more general empowering provisions. With these general rules came the emergence of more bureaucracy and more systematic regulation. Some measures were necessitated by greater religious toleration requiring secular administrative institutions such as registrars of birth and death. Many were a response to novel social pressures. These included factories legislation, improvement and public health schemes, the regulation of passenger ships, the Alkali Acts using new scientific techniques to

41 Torrance, 'Sir George Harrison and the Growth of Bureaucracy in the Early Nineteenth Century', above n. 6, 87.

42 *Ibid.*, 78. But J. Hart suggests that support for Trevelyan largely came from those seeking to limit aristocratic influence.

43 J. Hart, 'Sir Charles Trevelyan at the Treasury', above n. 37.

44 D. Roberts, 'Tory Paternalism and Social Reform in Early Victorian England', *The American Historical Review* 63(2) (1958), 323–37, 335. Roberts suggests that 'localism was another form of laissez-faire', 335.

reduce air-borne pollution[45] and statutes creating the new tithe and Poor Law commissions. All of these initiatives had a centralizing tendency. They would incorporate new administrative techniques, such as inspection, audit, statistical methods, the use of experts and reporting to central agencies. Political controversies over these new methods were ongoing and some of these experiments would prove to be temporary.[46]

Another aspect of this centralizing tendency was that government gradually acquired more formal control over legislative initiatives in Parliament, after the first Reform Act.[47] At the same time, it also acquired more general rule-making power over the localities – though not as we would understand it today. This more general legislation did not so much *control* local government and administration as *moderate* the central government's relationship with the localities. Permissive legislation became more common – so, for example, Parliament would now pass model sets of improvement powers which individual municipal corporations could adopt by Local Act (lowering the legal cost of local initiatives).[48] It established a system of 'preliminary inquiry' whereby a surveyor, after a local examination of a district, could make a recommendation to Parliament in relation to the district's need for paving, cleansing, waterworks and associated powers.[49] The Public Health Act 1848 (much hated in certain quarters) conferred extensive powers on a central General Board of Health, but these powers were only triggered by an above average death rate, local petition or independent inquiry. The General Inclosure Act[50] empowered Commissioners to make local inquiry and to make provisional orders subject to Parliamentary approval. The cost of such orders was thereafter borne out of the consolidated fund rather than by local agents. Through these different processes we can see that general rule-making was gradually becoming

[45] R. M. MacLeod, 'The Alkali Acts Administration, 1863–84: The Emergence of the Civil Scientist', *Victorian Studies*, 9 (1965), 85–112.

[46] E.g., Public Health Act 1848, Poor Law Act 1834. While the General Board of Health was abolished in 1854, it was turned into a Department of State.

[47] Government would only achieve *formal* priority for its legislative initiatives in 1835 (Anderson, 'Public Law', above n. 11, p. 334) though some commentators put government control of the legislative programme as late as 1870 (Chester, *The English Administrative System*, above n. 11, p. 113). The Parliamentary Counsel Office was not established until 1867.

[48] For example, Town Improvement Clauses Act 1847.

[49] 9 & 10 Vict c 106. [50] 8 & 9 Vict c118.

disentangled from administrative decision-making, and increasingly becoming the product of central government initiative. The establishment of a general registration system for joint stock companies can be regarded as part of the same trend.

Private Local Acts still continued to be significant in terms of their volume and the demands they placed on Parliamentary time, but a new system of central direction and control was beginning to emerge. The processes associated with local Acts themselves began to be the subject of procedural reform. By mid-century, concerns were beginning to be expressed about the expense, time and nature of these procedures. Joseph Hume, a prominent committee member and Utilitarian,[51] suggested that local Bills though private in name, commonly affected the public interest – and that the views of the public were not represented in the existing quasi-judicialized process. This was perhaps one of the earliest critiques of the common law model and of its attempt to instantiate the 'public interest' through the representation of narrow sectional interests. Instead it was to be *bureaucracy* and its processes which would somehow better represent the public – a general public policy preference which was to become a motif of British administrative law for much of the twentieth century. New measures ensured that the procedures for enacting local acts became more public, more bureaucratic, more official and were no longer chaired by the local member.[52] Some categories of Bills would begin to receive prior scrutiny from a central bureaucracy.[53]

One particularly marked trend was the increase in the powers of the Board of Trade.[54] So, for example, Parliament in 1840 gave the Board powers to scrutinize and disallow railway by-laws, powers which had

[51] Hume had made his fortune by way of the East India Company which enabled him to buy a seat in the Commons. 'Having thus profited handsomely from the Old Corruption he made his political reputation by relentlessly attacking it.' Harling, *The Waning of Old Corruption*, above n. 33, p. 172.

[52] The Preliminary Inquiries Act reforms were not entirely successful and those procedures had to be revisited see Anderson, 'Public Law' above n. 11, p. 334.

[53] E.g., Improvement Bills.

[54] The Board of Trade's full title was the Lords of the Committee of the Privy Council Appointed for Consideration of Matters relating to Trade and Foreign Plantations (created by order in council 23 August 1786). The Vice President of the Board of Trade held a junior Ministerial position. Gladstone was the President for a time while a Minister in Peel's government. The Privy Council had about 250 members and did not really meet. The Board of Trade had a number of departments – and performed a lot of real work including in relation to railways.

previously been exercised by local Justices.[55] At the same time the Board acquired from Justices jurisdiction over disputes relating to railway land. Even more striking is the Railways Act 1844 which conferred on government a general option to purchase railways which made more than 10 per cent annual profit, and required as a condition of any company seeking new powers that it offer a cheap daily return fare.[56] The assessment of whether railways had exceeded their by-law making powers was reposed in the Board of Trade inspectors, and the Board of Trade was able to dispense with legislated conditions without being liable for the prescribed penalties.[57] Enforcement no longer relied on an information procedure before Justices, but rested with an inspectorate and the Board of Trade, which advised the Attorney General or Advocate General whether to bring an action.[58] Thus regulation of the railway industry was achieved through centralized inspection, audit, a power of sanction and the threat of ultimate sanction – nationalization of the industry.[59] It would become a model for the regulation of monopoly that would be copied elsewhere. Sponsored by Gladstone (a free trade opponent of the Corn Laws), these are not policies usually associated with a period of laissez-faire – though as measures aimed at ensuring competition they are not necessarily incompatible with it. They also demonstrate that the administrative techniques that so outraged Dicey in *Law and Opinion* (techniques which he regarded as the product of a dangerous new collectivism) had forerunners during what he considered to be the individualistic golden age.[60]

[55] 3 & 4 Vict c 97 (1840).

[56] See, further, I. McLean and C. Foster, 'The Political Economy of Regulation: Interests, Ideology, Voters, and the UK Regulation of Railways Act 1844', *Public Administration* 70 (1992), 313–31.

[57] See, for the detailed discussion of other examples of delegated power, O. MacDonagh, 'Delegated Legislation and Administrative Discretions in the 1850s: A Particular Study' *Victorian Studies*, 2 (1958), 29–44.

[58] By the 1845 Railways Consolidation Act, railways were given general authorization for specified works – along with an obligation to pay damages. Such generalized authorization would not have been possible without an inspectorate.

[59] This is not entirely unlike the way in which the East India Company had been regulated.

[60] A. V. Dicey, *Lectures on the Relation Between Law and Public Opinion in England During the Nineteenth Century*, 2nd edn, (London: Macmillan, 1914). He expresses consternation that under the National Insurance Act 1911, Insurance Commissioners appointed by the Treasury were given wide power to make regulations, p. xl. 'This power to make regulations is probably the widest power of subordinate legislation ever conferred by Parliament upon any body of officials, and these officials namely, the Insurance Commissioners, are appointed by the Treasury.' However, in 1844, e.g., the Board of Trade was

MacDonagh describes the 'progress'of centralization and systematization as stuttering – as a matter of advance and resistance, and by no means inevitable.[61] Many legislative interventions were provoked by public opinion and *cause célèbres* and often the administrative responses proved ill-judged or inadequate and had to be revisited.

There was, nevertheless, a significant shift from personal and particular power, to hierarchical and bureaucratic power and to the use of experts. But the move from personal power, associated with office, to delegated power, associated with bureaucratic hierarchy, leaves a legal responsibility gap. The shift from a Parliament primarily devoted to issues of administration, to one now concerned with general rules, leaves a political responsibility gap. How then to square the circle? How to unify will in both political and legal senses?

Legal responsibility for office did indeed change. At the apex of government, legal notions of liability would for most practical purposes be replaced by *political* notions of responsibility. The Crown and its servants would enjoy immunity from legal liability, including for those wrongs the Crown or its servants directed or ordered. Officials would continue to be personally liable for unlawful actions they personally performed – and even now in cases when they were exercising *delegated* power rather than powers legally reposed in them personally. We shall discuss this in more detail in Chapters 5 and 7. The important point for now is that the effect of these rules was that it would be impossible as a matter of law to locate a 'unified sovereign will' that intended to commit an *unlawful* act. Legal responsibility would continue to focus primarily on 'real persons' rather than abstract ones.

What of political responsibility? If the partially reformed Parliament was no longer to have a role in executive functions, how was it to scrutinize or influence an administration over which it seemed to have little or no control? If hierarchical controls were to be put in place, what should be the proper connection to Parliament? Perhaps these ways of asking these questions make a system of individual Ministerial responsibility to Parliament seem almost inevitable. It was not.

Indeed, when Earl Grey stated the principle of responsible government in 1858 it was very far from the system that uniformly operated in

empowered to make regulations for the form of returns required of Joint Stock Companies. These were to have 'like force as if contained in an Act' so long as they applied to 'all companies alike'.

61 MacDonagh, *Early Victorian Government 1830–1870*, above n. 7, pp. 8–9.

the UK Parliament. It is likely that in this instance the UK's colonial experience informed its domestic constitutional law. In 1839 Lord Durham, for some time Governor-General and Lord High Commissioner of the British North American Colonies during a period of near rebellion, had presented to the UK his Report of the Affairs of British North America.[62] In it he urged acceptance of the principle of responsible government for the colony: that is that the administrative as well as the legislative function ought to be entrusted to Ministers who maintain a majority in the Parliament – and that the administrative function ought not to reside in the hands of the Governor acting in accordance with his instructions from the UK. The idea was taken up in 1854 by the new General Assembly of the New Zealand House of Representatives, who requested of the acting Governor that he consider the resolution of the House that Ministerial responsibility in the conduct of legislative and executive proceedings should be established without delay.[63] The British government's response was affirmative. In 1858, Earl Grey (who had recently held the post of Secretary of State for the Colonies) stated that the situation in the UK Parliament was the following:[64]

> [T]he powers belonging to the Crown [are] to be exercised through Ministers who are held responsible for the manner in which they are used . . . and who are entitled to hold their offices only while they possess the confidence of Parliament, and more especially the House of Commons.

This is an example of imperial government learning public administration from the colonies – or rather transplanting a solution to a colonial problem into a domestic setting. It is, perhaps, significant that the first 'English' constitutional law texts to mention responsible government were written in Australia and Canada.[65] There was, in fact, no uniform or consistent system of Ministerial responsibility for the bureaucracy in the UK

[62] He had been assisted in Canada by his Chief Secretary the reformer Charles Buller and Edward Gibbon Wakefield, who coincidentally was the chief force behind the New Zealand Company emigration scheme. I am grateful to Dame Alison Quentin-Baxter for drawing this to my attention.

[63] Extract from the Minutes of the proceedings of the House of Representatives, 6 June 1854.

[64] Quoted in Chester, *The English Administrative System*, above n. 11, p. 81.

[65] A. Todd, *On Parliamentary Government in England: Its Origin, Development and Practical Operation* (London: Longmans Green, 1867); Hearn, *Government of England*, above n. 10. See further, O. Hood Phillips, 'Constitutional Conventions: Dicey's Predecessors', *Modern Law Review* 29 (1966), 137–148.

Parliament in 1858 and a mixed pattern would continue until at least the 1880s. Even as the centre was becoming increasingly bureaucratized, a range of new offices, boards and commissions had been created by statute especially during the 1830s and 1840s. They took a hybrid form – having some of the characteristics of independent officials and some of the characteristics of officials in a hierarchy. In many cases, the members of such commissions or boards were excluded by statute from holding a seat in the Commons.[66] In other cases one of the commissioners would be a Minister but power and responsibility would be shared equally between the commissioners. The board as a whole may have had an obligation to report to Parliament, but that was all.[67] Far from being answerable for the whole, Ministers would sometimes use their Parliamentary position to criticise the actions of fellow commissioners. The 'mid-century reaction against the Whiggish notion that executive power was best vested in multi-member boards and that there should be a move to "single-seatedness"' (Bentham's expression) was still very much in progress in 1858.[68] Autonomous statutory commissioners would survive into the 1880s and 1890s – though they would be 'invisible to the constitution writers'.[69] Varying degrees of independence from central control would come to characterize English administration, in contrast with the French.

At the time Walter Bagehot was explaining the centrality of ministerial responsibility to the British Constitution in 1867, he was advancing a justification for an evolving practice, rather than (as he claimed to be doing) explaining a well-established orthodoxy.[70] It was, in truth, a new idea that was as often observed in the breach. The political failures of the Poor Law Commission, controversies over the inclosures of Crown land, and problems connected with the General Board of Health, could all now be accounted for, not because of a struggle for central control and local resistance, but because these boards and commissions were too

[66] The idea that officers for profit appointed by the King should not be allowed to sit in the House of Commons goes back to the Act of Settlement. Various statutes during the early nineteenth century allowed and disallowed commissioners and board members to sit in the House. The practice appeared to be unsettled during this time.

[67] Parliament could and did set up some commissions of limited tenure and used that as a measure of accountability, e.g., the General Board of Health.

[68] Anderson, 'Public Law', above n. 11, p. 345.

[69] *Ibid.*, p. 359 citing B. B. Shaffer, 'Idea of a Ministerial Department', *Australian Journal of Politics and History* 3 (1957), 60–78.

[70] W. Bagehot, *The English Constitution*, 2nd edn (London: Chapman and Hall, 1873), preface.

independent from Parliament: there was no politically responsible Minister. The problem was not too much 'centralization', but rather, not enough. He says of the Poor Law:[71]

> Independent, unsheltered authority has often been tried, and always failed . . . The most remarkable is that of the Poor Law . . . [The] whole of its goodness has been preserved by its having an official and party protector in the House of Commons.

Significantly, Bagehot proclaims that the great success of the English Constitution is '"unity"– that in unity the sovereign power is "single, possible, and good"'.[72] Centralization of the sovereign will – understood in a political sense – appears to be complete and has been made compatible with Parliamentary government. It is now Ministerial responsibility (and collective Ministerial responsibility) that brings 'unity'.

Backlash: a debate about the state

These developments – associated at the time primarily with Whig reformers, and to a lesser extent with Utilitarians – met with instant and vehement resistance. The political backlash was robust and expressed in statist terms. English attempts at centralized administration would be compared to the French state by contemporaries on *both* sides of the debate. John Walter in *The Times* protested against the Utilitarian Edwin Chadwick's 'French centralization' in the organization of the Poor Law Commission.[73] Chadwick himself compared his administrative techniques with those of the French.[74] His Board of Health was described as 'going off to Paris' and 'UnEnglish'.[75] Trevelyan, in a letter to Gladstone in 1854, suggested that one of his own reforms to the Treasury would 'bring the office into a more intimate relation, according to the French system'.[76] Podsnap simply said 'Centralization. No. Never with my consent. Not English'.[77] Such comments suggest that attempts

[71] *Ibid.*, p. 194. [72] *Ibid.*, p. 222.

[73] Finer, *The Life and Times of Sir Edwin Chadwick*, above n. 1, p. 99.

[74] *Ibid.*, p. 91 – unlike the French system his system would not destroy local administration, and neither would it direct such bodies in detail.

[75] *Ibid.*, p. 469 (attributed to Seymour).

[76] 9 February 1854 Notes and Documents Sir Charles Trevelyan and Civil Service Reform 1853–5.

[77] C. Dickens, *Our Mutual Friend* (London: Chapman and Hall, 1865), quoted in K. T. Hoppen, *The Mid-Victorian Generation* 1846–1886 (Oxford University Press, 1998), p. 104.

to aggregate power to the centre were conscious and born of explicit comparisons with other state models.

Much of the resistance is stated in passionate language. The Births, Deaths and Marriages Registration Bill is described as the 'Devil's parchment'.[78] 'Centralization is Despotism' reads another headline in an article that complains that centralization lends 'aristocracy to functionaries'.[79] A satirical song about measures to protect public health describes centralization as an 'infection'.[80] An 1870 article in the *Examiner* compares centralization to Bonapartism: 'if works of public improvement and public health went on tardily, officials, mon-eyed men, and club politicians told us that London, too, wanted a Haussmann to trample down all resistance, and to put his hand in the pocket of the future'.[81]

There were very serious arguments at stake. The independence of the local magistracy was being undermined. Patronage now centred almost entirely on central government and this threatened to undermine liberty.[82] 'Unified will' is much safer when understood in the abstract rather than when it is practically 'fetter[ing] John Bull to the chariot wheels of the Minister'.[83] More temperately, a letter to the editor of the *British Magazine* in 1832 recognized that centralization 'is plainly requisite for the well-being of the state'.[84] But the letter goes on to express Skinner's concern:[85] 'hitherto the Nation was the principal and the government but an adjunct to it'. There is a reaction to the 'state' and 'the government apparatus' being used now as synonyms.

While most lawyers thought of statutes as beneath their notice, some commentators, such as Toulmin-Smith, recognized the centralizing trend as a direct attack on the common law:[86]

> The fundamental principles of the Common Law . . . are altogether set at nought by the Public Health Act [1848] . . . [A] central Board having no possible knowledge of circumstances, presumes to arrogate power to

[78] *The Age*, 6 November 1836. [79] *The Age*, 5 November 1837, 36.
[80] *Fun* 4, 'A Song About Centralization', 25 April 1863, 58.
[81] *Examiner*, 10 September 1870, 578.
[82] See, e.g., *The Leader* 2:56, 19 April 1851, 370 commenting on the decay of local influence.
[83] *The Age*, 26 July 1835.
[84] Letter to the *British Magazine*, 6 November 1832, 514.
[85] Skinner, 'A Genealogy of the Modern State', above n. 2.
[86] J. Toulmin-Smith, *Local Self-Government and Centralization* (London: Chapman, 1851) pp. 338–9 quoted in D. Fraser (ed.), *Municipal Reform and the Industrial City* (Leicester University Press, 1982), p. 127.

> dictate as to all those things which . . . can only be well understood and ordered by those immediately interested.

And in the debate on the Public Health Bill, Urquhart suggested that the common law had already solved these issues:[87]

> Anyone who would take the trouble to refer to *Blackstone's Commentaries* would find that the common law provided ample means for putting down all the nuisances to which this Bill referred.

These critics are not wrong in recognizing that the new legislative mechanisms threatened both common law method and ideology. The common law indeed represented an older rival means by which the unity of the sovereign will could be achieved. It was diffuse particularistic decision-making and its tacit acceptance and adoption by the sovereign that conformed to the general principles of the ancient constitution. Not only did these new legislative examples eschew common law method and challenge its ideas about interest representation, they often showed little respect for property rights. The legislation made famous by *Cooper* v. *Wandsworth Board of Works*[88] conferred broad powers (without notice) on sewering authorities to demolish and remove dwellings that posed a risk to health in a time of cholera. The analogy with Baron Haussmann's sweeping powers to rebuild Paris begins to look apt.

The most robust and coherent intellectual defence of centralization came from the Utilitarians. The degree to which the development, albeit incremental, of centralized administration during this period was a *direct* consequence of Bentham's thought and of the efforts of his influential Utilitarian admirers[89] has been the subject of much scholarly debate.[90]

87 Urquhart for Stafford speaking to the Public Health Bill 1848 *Parliamentary Debates* 1848 section 3, 98:710713, 711 12, cited by R. Cocks, 'Statutes, Social Reform and control', in W. Cornish, S. Anderson, R. Cocks, M. Lobban, P. Polden and K. Smith (eds.), *The Oxford History of the Laws of England, Volume XIII, 1820–1914. Fields of Development* (New York: Oxford University Press, 2010), pp. 465–720.

88 (1863) 14 CB (NS) 180.

89 These included Edwin Chadwick, Southwood Smith, Sir James Kay Shuttleworth, John and Edward Romilly, George Grote, Charles Buller, Arthur Roebuck, Sir William Molesworth, Joseph Hume, Henry Warburton, Edward Strutt, Albany Fonblanque, John Black and John Bowring. See, further, D. Roberts, 'Jeremy Bentham and the Victorian Administrative State', *Victorian Studies* 2:(3) (1959), 193–210.

90 Roberts, 'Jeremy Bentham and the Victorian Administrative State', above n. 89; MacDonagh, *Early Victorian Government 1830–1870*, above n. 7. Cocks, Statutes, Social Reform and Control', above n. 87, pp. 465–720; L. J. Hume, *Bentham and Bureaucracy* (Cambridge University Press, 1981).

We should, of course, be careful not to claim too much for the influence of any single political theory. Bentham's *Constitutional Code* was certainly not treated as a blueprint, but equally it cannot be an accident that it was his acolytes who would carry out many of these ideas in the most prominent and controversial legislative examples of the day such as the new Poor Law, inclosure, factory inspection, public improvement and public health legislation. The legislation would incorporate Benthamite methods of audit, inspection and statistical inquiry – though it is impossible to prove that these inclusions were the direct consequence of Utilitarian philosophy. Key figures in the implementation of such laws, such as Edwin Chadwick, would certainly be motivated by the principle of utility. For Chadwick, the idea that private interests should be forced into alignment with the public interest formed the basis of his version of *res publica*. One of the biggest contributions Bentham and his followers may have made to these developments is their emphasis on general laws,[91] long before the need for, or efficacy of, such legislative techniques had been recognized by Parliament.

What can be said is that Bentham was not only concerned about sovereign entities overreaching or abusing their powers but also about the potential for officials to disobey or fail to fulfil the sovereign will. Up until this time, the solutions to these problems had been left almost entirely to the common law and its remedial writs for the performance of duties of office. Such remedies did not operate in any systematic way and were always controls after the event. The Utilitarians were interested in other, potentially more reliable, methods of diagnosis and control.

It is Austin who would deliver the most sustained defence of the reforms to public administration from a Utilitarian perspective. In a forty-eight-page article entitled 'Centralization', which appeared in the *Edinburgh Review* in 1847, Austin defends centralization against the charge that it is necessarily synonymous with 'over-government'.[92] At the same time, he makes clear that *utility* and not *freedom* should be the more fundamental norm: [93]

> [S]ome of these maxims (as for example, the celebrated *laissez-faire*) are plainly false and absurd, since they plainly imply an assumption which would prove the inutility of law and government.

[91] Austin also argues for the removal of private legislation as a category.

[92] J. Austin, 'Centralization', *The Edinburgh Review* 85 (1847), 221–58. [93] *Ibid.*, 241.

The article reads today like an introduction to an early twentieth-century defence of administrative law. The issue of how the administrative apparatus should be organized, he claims, may be more important to a government than how its constitution is arranged. Civilized societies, he urges, need a centralized administration that makes dispersed authority dependent on the sovereign will – but one that also allows for discretion and delegation. Unsurprisingly, given his earlier views about general jurisprudence, for Austin, the details of administrative arrangements making functionaries dependent on the sovereign will are part and parcel of sovereignty itself. In the 1847 article he defends an *idealized* version of sovereignty rather than the more abstract and universal notion which appeared in his *Province of Jurisprudence Determined* in 1832. It is a version of sovereignty for the civilized nations. His 'control view' of administration is remarkably similar to what we would now think of as a 'classic transmission belt theory' of administrative law.[94] The will of the centre should be accurately and completely conveyed to its agents who execute it. The judges should supervise the faithful transmission of the sovereign will. This is novel thinking which modern lawyers now take for granted.

Despite the novelty and importance of Austin's essay, it is not any part of the received canon of modern administrative law.[95] It tells the almost forgotten story of 'state' building: how the substitution of a unified *political* will, for an older less reified version of will moderated through common law processes and practices, made the nineteenth-century state.

Lawyers, on the whole, did not engage in these discussions. As we shall see in the next chapter, the *only* aspect of the Benthamite inheritance that *would* attract broad interest within the legal profession in the nineteenth century was Bentham's account of the highly abstracted sovereign aspects of statehood (the ability to command). It is this account, as retold by Austin, that would become the centre-piece of analytical jurisprudence in the later nineteenth and twentieth centuries. Lawyers would know little about statutes and still less about administration. No one would study them. Techniques of 'good government' would be eclipsed by government *per se*. 'Good government', as understood by the early Utilitarians, would become part of a suppressed legal tradition. Arguments against 'centralization' would, however, continue to feature

[94] A description coined by R. B. Stewart, 'The Reformation of American Administrative Law', *Harvard Law Review* 88 (1975), 1667–1813, 1675.

[95] Roberts, 'Jeremy Bentham and the Victorian Administrative State', above n. 89, 207.

in the periodical press until at least the 1870s.[96] Later in the century the target of resistance would shift from centralization to 'officialism' or 'red-tapism'.[97]

And Dicey?

Lawyers around the Empire received these new ideas about the state apparatus and the practical remaking of the notion of unified will with what appears to be very little self-consciousness. Of the constitutional text book writers, it is only Hearn who even recognizes the *existence* of a civil service. He suggests that: 'men trained to the work [of public service] and skilled in its execution' and 'with security of tenure' have been 'steadily recognized throughout our political history'.[98] The fact that Professor Hearn grew up in Ireland and wrote his book in Melbourne may have contributed to this sense of the inevitable. It appears that the administrative apparatus arrived towards the end of the nineteenth century 'ready-made' at least as far as constitutional law was concerned.

The most famous of the constitutional textbook writers, was, of course, Dicey. For many of the same reasons as he did not recognize an English administrative law, Dicey did not recognize the civil service or 'state building' during this period – the affixing of the Great Seal was administrative 'mechanism' enough for him.[99] In his *Lectures Introductory to the Study of the Law of the Constitution* (1885)[100] he would emphasize the differences between the UK and the French systems of administrative *adjudication* (the sections exploring the differences expanding as the work appeared in new editions). For Dicey, *droit administratif* was about the position and liabilities of officials relative to the civil rights and liabilities of private individuals. It was not about the *powers* of officials and neither was it about the distinctive organs of government and their relationships to each other, as Dicey's French law counterparts would have understood it. While he acknowledged the

[96] I disagree with Roberts about Austin's defence of centralization coming after the fact.

[97] C. Stebbings, '"Officialism": Law, Bureaucracy, and Ideology in Late Victorian England', in A. Lewis and M. Lobban (eds.), *Law and History* (Oxford University Press, 2004), pp. 317–43.

[98] Hearn, *Government of England*, above n. 10, pp. 259–60.

[99] A. V. Dicey, *Lectures Introductory to the Study of the Law of the Constitution* (London: Macmillan, 1886), p. 330.

[100] The third edition onwards was renamed *Introduction to the Study of the Law of the Constitution*.

latter to be a core part of the study of *droit administratif* for the French lawyer, he *deliberately* chose not to discuss it.[101] He certainly would not have been prepared to recognize that the British state apparatus could have been built on a French state model. We (the UK and US), he claims, derive our civilization from English sources, and hence administrative law is unknown to us.[102] There is no state to be found in England, even understood in the most reductionist, Weberian sense of an administrative apparatus.

The debates about, and developments in, the administrative apparatus are, even today, better known to historians of the nineteenth century than they are to lawyers.[103] In legal thought, by contrast, the early nineteenth century is almost universally regarded as a period of unrivalled laissez-faire. Government would not interfere with the economy and the free market would reign: collectivism would be unknown until after 1870. If we know of 'legislation' from that period, we tend to think of the repeal of the Corn and Usury Laws, reform of divorce laws and of free trade. Utilitarianism would mean the political dominance of the view that individuals should be free to pursue his or her own self-interests, not the necessity of subduing 'sinister interests' or of squaring personal interests with the public interest.[104] So we were told by Dicey in his 1905 *Law and Opinion.*[105] Dicey simply fails to take account of the most important legislation passed during the earlier part of the century.[106] His narrative has dominated legal thinking ever since.[107]

101 A. V. Dicey, *Introduction to the Study of the Law of the Constitution*, 10th edn (London; Macmillan, 1959), p. 333.

102 A. V. Dicey, *Introduction to the Study of the Law of the Constitution*, 3rd edn (London: Macmillan, 1889), p. 304.

103 Among the areas regulated were foodstuffs, slaughterhouses, passenger carrying ships, ill treatment of animals, weights and measures, trade quality (wool, flax, gold) and licensing.

104 Ideas which are present in both Adam Smith's and Bentham's works.

105 A. V. Dicey, *Lectures on the Relation Between Law and Public Opinion in England During the Nineteenth Century* (London: Macmillan, 1905) based on lectures given at Harvard Law School 1898. A. V. Dicey, *Introduction to the Study of the Law of the Constitution*, 1st edn, (London: Macmillan, 1885), p. 1.

106 See also Cocks, 'Statutes, Social Reform and Control', above n. 87, p. 604.

107 See, for historical critiques, J. V. Orth, 'The Trade Union Acts of 1824 and 1825: Dicey and the Relation Between Law and Opinion', *Anglo-American Law Review* 5 (1976), 131–53; J. B. Brebner, 'Laissez-Faire and State Intervention in Nineteenth-Century Britain', *The Journal of Economic History* 8, Supplement: The Tasks of Economic History (1948), 59–73, 61.

As the archetypal 'administrative law denier', Dicey has been the favourite whipping-boy of administrative lawyers for so long that it is difficult now to do him justice. We know that he knew about the changes to the central bureaucracy – not from *Law and the Constitution* but from the later *Law and Opinion.*[108] Indeed, in Lecture IX of *Law and Opinion* there is a passage that not only acknowledges that the 'English administrative machinery was reformed and strengthened' during the period he describes as a 'Golden Age' of Benthamite Liberalism, but that 'the machinery was thus provided for the practical extension of the activity of the state.'[109] He also credits Bentham with the invention of the 'new system of centralisation', inspection and central control of local government but laments that:[110]

> The English collectivists have inherited from their utilitarian predecessors, a legislative doctrine, a legislative instrument, and a legislative tendency pre-eminently suited to socialist experiments.

These points are rather hidden in his larger narrative which tells a story associating Bentham almost entirely with laissez-faire, and the first half of the century with policies of limited government intervention. And while in these three sentences he acknowledges that the collective state was built on these earlier reforms, he is not always accurate when describing how powers were actually used in earlier, and allegedly less interventionist, times. For example, in the 1914 edition of *Law and Opinion*, he describes the power delegated to the Insurance Commissioners appointed by the Treasury under the National Insurance Act 1911 as 'probably the widest power of subordinate legislation ever conferred by Parliament upon any body of officials'.[111] We know, as presumably he did, that the Board of Trade had enjoyed equivalent or greater powers as early as the 1840s. On the other hand, he *does* acknowledge what it has taken many modern administrative lawyers a long time to notice: that the existence of strong centralized state power can be as important during a time of laissez-faire or 'more market policies' as it is during a time of welfare intervention. Later, lawyers such as Lord Hewart, in his *The New Despotism* (1929) would almost entirely associate delegated power and bureaucracy with the 'new' collectivist welfare state. Nineteenth-century experiments in administrative regulation, part of a suppressed tradition of administrative law, would only be

[108] Dicey, *Law and Opinion*, above n. 60. [109] *Ibid.*, p. 310.
[110] *Ibid.*, p. 306. [111] *Ibid.*, p. lx.

partially recovered by Carr, Robson, Jennings, Willis and Laski, writing in defence of the welfare state and in reaction to Lord Hewart in the twentieth century (as we shall see in Chapter 6).

Of a 'unified sovereign will' there is, of course, much in Dicey's *Law of the Constitution.* As every constitutional law student knows, according to Dicey, Parliament, or technically the Queen in Parliament (and not the Crown or Queen) is the full repository of legal sovereignty. For Dicey though, political sovereignty or will, as opposed to legal sovereignty remains in 'the people'. Public opinion is to act as a check on Parliament – at the same time as he acknowledges that law can lead as well as follow public opinion. He is plainly concerned about the dangers of a *too unified* sovereign will.

Dicey was, of course, not alone among Utilitarians in approving the 1832 extension of the franchise 'to the middle classes' but recoiling from the later attempts to extend the franchise still further and in deploring the 'collectivist' and 'socialist' legislation which was promised and followed after 1870. Austin, too, opposed any further advancement toward democracy in his pamphlet 'Reform' in 1859.[112] Dicey reads Mill's *On Liberty* (1859)[113] as placing freedom rather than utility at the heart of utilitarian creed (and thus he directly disagrees with Austin's 1847 view without ever having to refer to it).[114] There is a sense in *Law and Opinion* of a Mr Brook 'having looked into a thing' and 'knowing when to pull up, you know'.[115]

In terms of how the law should protect liberty in the face of this new collectivism, however, Dicey finds himself in a quandary. As a Benthamite lawyer, he is thoroughly committed to the view that the 'doctrine of innate rights' is 'logically unsound'.[116] And yet he looks wistfully to the Declaration of Independence and its 'faith that the obligations of contract are sacred'[117] as a limit upon the 'despotism of the majority' (again likely influenced by Mill).[118] He notes that democratic reform in the US, in contrast to the UK, had been accompanied by rights protections.[119] In the

[112] J. Austin, *A Plea for the Constitution*, 2nd edn (London: Clowes, 1859).

[113] J. S. Mill, *On Liberty* (London: J Parker, 1959).

[114] I take no position here about whether this is the 'correct' reading.

[115] George Eliot, *Middlemarch: A Study of Provincial Life* (London: William Blackwood and Sons, 1871–2).

[116] Dicey, *Law and Opinion*, above n. 60, p. 309. [117] *Ibid.*, p. 309.

[118] *Ibid.*, p. 309.

[119] W. Novak in *The People's Welfare: Law and Regulation in Nineteenth-Century America* (Chapel Hill: University of North Carolina Press, 1996), p. 244 suggests that the legal

absence of any Declaration of Rights through which to defend rights, the only recourse would be to the common law – meaning now private law. It is the closest thing to a liberal creed of 'individualistic common sense' he can find. These common law rights, such as the freedom of contract, are for him the *basis*, and not the *result*, of the constitution.[120] This is not merely a political preference: for him self-reliance and 'self-help' are *moral* imperatives and flow out of his version of Utilitarianism.[121] The state harms us if it takes away our personal responsibility to protect our own interests. For an avowed Benthamite, it is ironic, to say the least, that he should discover the Utilitarian dogma to be now best expressed in the common law.

What has largely escaped notice is a sentence that does not appear until the seventh edition of the *Introduction to the Study of the Law of the Constitution* (1908). There Dicey suggests that the closest approximation to 'the state' or the 'Crown' in English thought is the 'august dignity of the judges'.[122] The significance of this can only be appreciated if one recognizes the fundamental nature of the project on which Dicey was embarking in *Law and the Constitution* in the first place. He was very much reacting *against* legal fictions. Hearn's text, while similar to his own in very many core respects, is still tied to Blackstone. Hearn states that: 'In our political system the Crown always has been and still is the sun. Whatever be its merits, democracy has no place in English law.'[123] Dicey explicitly joins Bentham's attack on Blackstone (and by implication on Hearn) for placing the Crown so much at the centre. He also joins Bentham in attacking legal fictions.[124] Dicey's and Bentham's shared method is to '[discern] the facts of the law'.[125] Dicey is also reacting against the historical accounts of constitutional law written by his contemporaries (such as

centralization of state power in the US (which came later than in the UK) was not accompanied by 'the expected enhancement of *salus populi* common good rhetoric, but by its repudiation, and an offering in its stead of a heightened regard for individual right and liberty'. Maine too, flirted with the idea of some kind of formal Bill of Rights as a safeguard against democracy. See Chapter 9.

120 Dicey, *Law of the Constitution* 1st edn, above n. 105, pp. 216, 220.

121 See Dicey's example of the shipping safety certificate in *Law and Opinion*, above n. 60, p. 257.

122 A. V. Dicey, *Introduction to the Study of the Law of the Constitution*, 7th edn (London: MacMillan, 1908), p. 389. The 'august dignity of the judges' is first used here in comparison with *droit administratif.*

123 Hearn, *The Government of England*, above n. 10, p. 17.

124 Dicey, *Law of the Constitution*, 3 edn, above n. 102, p. 11.

125 *Ibid.*

Freeman)[126] – and claims to be telling the constitution as it is today rather than how it was yesterday or how it will be tomorrow.[127]

It is surely noteworthy, then, that in 1908 he reintroduces the notion of the Crown, meaning the state, and suggests that now it is best represented by the 'august dignity of judges'.[128] That is a much more accurate account of the legal position as it had been at the beginning of the nineteenth century than it would be at the end. He appears to be seeking refuge in an earlier, more Blackstonian, version of the unified will – in which sovereign will is neither delegated nor centralized. Is Dicey really so far from Hearn who says 'the will of the King is that which is displayed in his court not in his chamber'?[129] Dicey, with Hearn, is seeking something to stand apart from the governors and governed, that is not the people, society or the bureaucracy. Elsewhere, Dicey acknowledges the dangers of transforming abstract principles into practical maxims (such as the idea that all property belongs to the nation).[130] Arguably here too, he is expressing an emerging appreciation that realizing sovereign will in a unified political will could be dangerous. Judges are now responsible for defending the liberal creed: it is they who must protect the constitution from the worst excesses of democracy – even though, ultimately, they have a duty to obey Parliament.

It is likely that by 1908 Dicey was also concerned about continental theories of sovereign will that had been making ground in Britain through the later nineteenth century in the work of T. H. Green and the Idealists. These theories were also reactions against centralization, but this time against its more mechanistic aspects. Man, viewed not as an individual, but as the product of a larger social organism that was the state with its own organic will, was, for Dicey, much to be feared. He was worried about sacrificing the individual to all forms of the social or collective.

Why did Dicey gloss over the important changes to official liability which at the time were relatively recent? It was Hearn who first suggested

126 E. A. Freeman, *The Growth of the English Constitution from the Earliest Times* (London: Macmillan, 1872).

127 Dicey, *Law of the Constitution*, 3 edn, above n. 102, p. 11.

128 There are earlier indications of this thinking even in the first edition of *Law of the Constitution* (above n. 105) where he suggests: 'Moreover, of the powers ascribed to the Crown, some are in reality exercised by the government, whilst others do not in truth belong either to the King or the Ministry', p. 11.

129 Hearn, *The Government of England*, above n. 10, pp. 18–19.

130 Dicey, *Law and Opinion*, above n. 60, 248.

that one of the great strengths of the English constitution was that the officers of the civil service should be personally responsible for unlawful acts to ordinary tribunals (though Hearn, unlike Dicey, would also recognize a role for criminal law as well as 'ordinary' private law).[131] Dicey never even acknowledges the *public* law controls on officials via the prerogative writs (such as *quo warranto*, *mandamus* and *prohibition*) and the criminal law, which had been so important throughout the century.[132] He insists that it is only the ordinary *private* law that applies to government officials. He ignores the special immunities from vicarious liability that apply only to the Crown after the 1850s and the inconsistencies and problems created by those changes. All of this avoidance is in the cause of emphasizing the importance of ordinary law (in opposition to the French system). The same thing really matters to Dicey and to Hearn, though they express it in different terms. Hearn explains the law in these terms:[133]

> Every official act of the Crown must be done in the manner prescribed by law. Every act so done is lawful. Every act done under colour of royal authority, but not in the proper manner, is not an official act of the Crown.

Hearn is attempting to capture the 'true meaning of the King can do no wrong'.[134] 'Since no unlawful act is the act of the Crown, no command to do any such act can be the command of the Crown'.[135] Dicey says almost the same thing, though he states it more directly and scrupulously avoids any mention of the Crown:[136]

> With us every official from the Prime Minister down to a constable or a collector of taxes is under the same responsibility for every act done without legal justification as any other citizen.

Both are concerned that there should not be a unified will to do wrong. Disaggregating the state for liability purposes, and at the same time denying the existence of a bureaucratic hierarchy and administrative unity, is absolutely central to Dicey's version of the rule of law.

[131] Hearn, *The Government of England*, above n. 10 pp. 101, 109.

[132] Dicey, *Law of the Constitution*, 3 edn, above n. 102, 1889, p. 181 does recognize that soldiers and clergymen may be exceptions.

[133] Hearn, *The Government of England*, above n. 10, p. 20. [134] *Ibid.* [135] *Ibid.*

[136] Dicey, *Law of the Constitution*, 3rd edn, above n. 102, p. 181. He appears to know or care nothing for quasi-commissions. Compare this with the very similar passage in Hearn, *The Government of England*, above n. 10, p. 109.

Dicey is much more subtle than is usually acknowledged. These omissions, evasions and late additions are significant and often destabilize the text in important ways. There is perhaps, even here, another suppressed version of a state tradition. We shall have to return to the question of why the orthodox version of the Diceyan narrative has continued in the legal imagination for so long, and how he was read after World War I, in Chapter 6.

Summary

In the first part of the chapter, I traced the administrative and political changes that turned a highly abstract notion of unified sovereign will into a much more practical and political notion. We can now see that one of the major differences which divided Blackstone and Bentham was how they imagined sovereign authority should be executed. But as the new administrative apparatus emerged neither of their theories would match the facts: Blackstone because his older notions of authority were being replaced by newer political notions and Bentham because power was becoming more collective and corporate. We have also encountered several attempts to personify the state in the Crown: by the centralized Treasury as government above party politics, by the common law as a personification of the public, and by Dicey as the 'august dignity of the judges'. I will return to those issues in Chapters 5 to 7.

Having charted this mechanistic and practical realization of statehood in the first half of the nineteenth century, we are now better placed to understand the two major intellectual currents that would follow in the later nineteenth century: one would subsume statehood within notions of sovereignty; the other would react against such mechanistic manifestations of statehood in favour of more organic notions linking individual to society to the state. It is to these issues that we now turn.

3

Sovereign, state and corporation: political theory and analytical jurisprudence

English lawyers were not good at work of this kind; they liked their persons to be real[1]

Moral and juristic theories

If the political story of state building in the early nineteenth century would be largely forgotten, reactions to the new state mechanisms would provoke important philosophical, jurisprudential and legal debates in the second half of the nineteenth century. For the Positivists, exemplified by Austin, the state as machine would become synonymous with the state as sovereign. His opponents would react against this mechanistic and centralizing conception of statehood and the individualism with which it had come to be associated. Of those offering an alternative conception of the state, it would be T. H. Green who would come closest to engaging directly with Austin's thought. Austin famously argues that the basis of sovereignty is a habit of obedience by the bulk of the people to a determinate superior which is illimitable. Green rejects this view. Instead, he argues that the basis of the state is the unified will and common consciousness of society, which is something separate from sovereignty and does not and could not rely solely on coercion. Instead, social groupings and the bonds that they create are essential to statehood. Green suggests that '[a] state presupposes other forms of community, with the rights that arise out of them, and only exists as sustaining, securing or completing them'.[2] He puts it in these terms:[3]

[1] F. W. Maitland, 'The Crown as Corporation', in H. A. L. Fisher (ed.), *Collected Papers of Frederic William Maitland*, 3 vols. (Cambridge University Press, 1911), vol. III, pp. 244–70, 246.

[2] T. H. Green, *Lectures on the Principles of Political Obligation* (London: Longmans Green, 1941), p. 139 (lectures first delivered in 1879 and published after his death in 1882).

[3] *Ibid.*, pp. 136–7.

> [The] mischief of beginning with an inquiry into sovereignty before the idea of a state has been investigated, is that it leads us to adopt this abstract notion of sovereignty, as merely supremely coercive power, and then, when we come to think of the state as distinguished by sovereignty, makes us suppose that supreme coercive power is all that is essential to a state, forgetting that it is rather the state that makes the sovereign, than the sovereign that makes the state.

Broadly speaking, Austin and Green would, in the later nineteenth century, represent two rival approaches to the idea of the state. Green would provide *some* of the basic premises for other schools of thought such as the Pluralists and even, at times, the Fabian Socialists. The idea of the 'sovereign will' would once again play an important role in the debate about the nature of the state but this time Rousseauian ideas of the general will, Hegelian ideas of freedom and Idealist ideas of the 'real will' would be included as part of the vocabulary. These conceptions of statehood go well beyond the state apparatus.

Runciman argues that in Austin and Green we witness a new schism between the legal and moral aspects of statehood that had not previously existed in political thought. Austin's legal theory of sovereignty contains little by way of a moral conception of statehood and Green's Idealist version of statehood contains few, if any, juristic elements.[4] This observation is striking and suggests that the later nineteenth century was an important moment in the British intellectual history of the state. The legal aspects of statehood have been cleaved from the moral and political for the first time.

The way that Runciman presents the apparent bifurcation between legal and moral theory tends to suggest that it was Austin's version of the state that was received by, and came to dominate, legal thought. We should not be too quick to reach that conclusion. It is not obvious which of these theories was more thoroughly received into legal theory and doctrine. Neither is it immediately obvious which of these theories is the more juristic. As this chapter shall argue, *both* theories had a contribution to make to the re-conception of legal positivism in the middle of the twentieth century.

Runciman is certainly correct in saying that neither Green, nor the Idealists who followed him, directly considered the juristic basis of their moral order. The purpose of Idealist philosophy was to transcend such

[4] D. Runciman, *Pluralism and the Personality of the State* (Cambridge University Press, 1997), p. 78.

legalistic notions.[5] Though Bosanquet, among the Idealists, imagined the state as enjoying a distinctive morality and as serving distinct ends – as a *personne morale* – he never descended into the legal details of what that might mean.

The following extract from Bosanquet's *Philosophical Theory of the State* gives something of the flavour of his thinking (as well as of the prose style):[6]

> But the ideas involved in mere legality, though they bear emphatic testimony to the conscious and artificial aspect of the social whole, have always been regarded with some justice as the type of what is empty and formal . . . [and are] obviously very far short of the whole truth. . . . But yet as we pass beyond these everyday working conceptions, we are beginning to leave the central ground of Jurisprudence, and to move towards a point of view which deals more completely with life and culture.

Despite Bosanquet's evident lack of interest in 'mere legality', Idealist and associated challengers to the Austinian state were in a relatively strong position to influence legal thought. First, they were much more open to common law reasoning and methodology than was Austin. Austin's view of the law, as the commands of the uncommanded commander who owes allegiance to no other, does not obviously allow much of a role for the practices and methodologies of the common law, or indeed of constitutional law. Green allows a greater place for the common law and constitutional law more generally. He challenges Austin's contention that law is of its nature a command of the sovereign on the basis (*inter alia*) that: 'customary or "common" or "judge-made" law does not proceed from any determinate person or persons'.[7] Green argues that the law may itself reflect or express the common good. He defends a role for a written or unwritten constitution and suggests that in order to be considered a proper agent of the state, the sovereign must obey the constitutional order.[8]

Even more significantly, some of the major premises of Idealist thought would have an important juristic interpreter in Maitland. He would become a conduit for the reception of at least some aspects of Idealist thought into legal thought and help provide the undeveloped

[5] *Ibid.*, discussing Bosanquet, at pp. 77–8.

[6] B. Bosanquet, *The Philosophical Theory of the State*, 4th edn (London: Macmillan, 1958), p. 37 (first published 1899).

[7] Green, *Principles of Political Obligation*, above n. 2, p. 97.

[8] *Ibid.*, pp. 137–8.

juristic dimension. Of course Maitland is more commonly associated with Pluralism than with Idealism but the two schools had important commitments in common. The third reason why Austinian Positivism would not be completely received or dominate legal thought was a consequence of Austin's conception of a general jurisprudence. His theory purported to relate to legal systems generally and not to the content of the law of any particular legal system. Unless we are prepared to look at the *content* of the law, we should not too readily conclude that Austin's conception of statehood affected the way British law came to conceive of the state or that the Idealist's moral conception of order failed to achieve any juristic impact. Of course, an undertaking to investigate the *content* of British law is in itself a rejection of the 'scientific' standards of Austinian analytical jurisprudence. To meet the requirements of Austinian 'legal science', theory has to be general and apply to all legal systems. But unless we are prepared to investigate the content of a particular body of legal rules, we are allowing the positivist distinction between the juristic and the moral to penetrate the very nature of the legal scholarly endeavour. Maitland and those who followed him, by contrast to Austin, were part of the older tradition that did not separate the legal from the moral and the political. Indeed, part of Maitland's project was explicitly to bring those different strands of thought into closer relation – in the style of German legal science.

This chapter will assess the significance of Positivist and Idealist thought on British lawyers' abstract theoretical conceptions of sovereignty and the state. I shall argue that both Idealist and Austinian thought had an influence on H. L. A. Hart's ground breaking contribution to the analytical jurisprudential tradition, *The Concept of Law*, published in the middle of the twentieth century. But thanks to the contributions of Austin and Hart, issues to do with the legal personality of the state would no longer be treated as the concerns of legal, moral and political theory but would be reduced to the lowly status of parochial legal doctrine. I argue that theoretical issues do, indeed, remain. And even if one does not accept my arguments that the doctrine impacts on the theory, the *doctrinal* conceptions of the state are worthy of study in their own right as examples of political and legal thought.[9] The remainder of the book will be devoted to those normative doctrinal debates. Indeed, it would be the particulars of

[9] See R. Dworkin, 'Hart's Postscript and the Character of Political Philosophy', *Oxford Journal of Legal Studies* 24(1) (2004), 1–37, 37.

legal *doctrine* that would help keep the debate about the nature of the state alive as a matter of legal thought.

Sovereignty and the corporation debate

I begin by briefly outlining Austin's theory of law and sovereignty, in order to understand what it was that Green and the Idealists and Maitland and the Pluralists were reacting against. I then discuss why it is surprising that Austin's work achieved the currency it did and examine the extent to which it was received. Three aspects of Austin's work would prove most provoking: his portrayal of the relationship between sovereign and subject as one of command and submission; his conception of the sovereign as prior to other forms of association and as the source of all law; and his contention that legal persons, such as corporations aggregate, are merely collections or aggregations of physical persons – 'persons by figment' and 'for the sake of brevity'. For him the basic unit for rights and duties remains the individual.

Surprisingly, it would be the rejection of the last of these propositions that would provide the focus for Maitland's criticisms and for his partial reception into legal thought. Through ideas of legal personhood, Maitland would address the other, larger, questions about the nature of the state's relationship with citizens and with the law. He would base his critique on the premise that the state and the corporation are analytically similar concepts. The state imagined as a kind of corporation would challenge both an absolutist version of sovereignty and an individualistic version of society. A focus on the 'real will' of the corporation *qua* corporation (as distinct from the individual wills of its members) would raise questions about its moral personality. Maitland never directly engaged with Austin's work in the course of *these* arguments. When writing purely as a legal historian, however, he emphasizes the historical contingency of sovereignty theories. He describes, for example, how Hobbes's theory 'shocked mankind' at a time when 'Law had been conceived as existing independently of the will of any ruler, independently even of the will of God; God himself was obedient to the law'.[10] As for Austin, 'before the Reformation

[10] F. W. Maitland, *The Constitutional History of England: A Course of Lectures by Frederic William Maitland* (Cambridge University Press, 1908), p. 101.

Austin's doctrine would be impossible'.[11] In his private correspondence he is much more frank: 'J. A. = 0'.[12]

Austinian sovereignty

In this section we shall expand more fully on the three aspects of Austin's theory which attracted particular controversy later in the nineteenth century.

The relationship between the 'sovereign and the subject'

Austin's general theory of sovereignty contains two important elements: a determinate superior authority which wills *commands* (backed by threat of sanction); and habitual obedience by the bulk of the people. The determinate superior is the sovereign or state (he uses the terms as synonyms).[13] The bulk of the people who submit are subjects. The relation between sovereignty and subjection applies to *all* legal systems, independently of whether the system of rule is a monarchy, an aristocracy or a democracy. Thus the separation of ruler and ruled appears to be central to his general theory.

Not only was this idea of the coercive state–subject relationship unattractive as a sociological portrayal of the political relation (as Green contended), it did not work well on its own terms when applied to the democratizing constitutional systems of the US and the UK. Indeed, when Austin attempts to apply his general formulation to the UK system, he begins to dilute and to undermine some of his apparently fundamental premises.

His first task is to define who would comprise the determinate superior in the British Constitution. According to Austin there are two ways to do this.[14] The first is by specific and appropriate description of the components of the sovereign (A, B, C). The second is by a *generic* description of the persons who compose the determinate body. He suggests that the British Parliament is a determinate body of the second

[11] *Ibid.*, pp. 529–30.

[12] Letter to Pollock, 4 December 1899 in C. H. S. Fifoot (ed.), *The Letters of Frederic William Maitland* (London: The Selden Society, 1965), p. 204.

[13] J. Austin, *Province of Jurisprudence Determined*, W. Rumble (ed.) (Cambridge University Press, 1995), p. 95, fn.

[14] J. Austin, *Lectures on Jurisprudence*, R. Campbell (ed.), Student Edition (London: John Murray, 1875), p. 94.

kind – comprising the King or Queen answering to the generic description in the Act of Settlement, the peers entitled to vote in the Upper House and the commoners entitled to vote in the Commons. The combination of the three parts must be capable of corporate conduct – issuing commands, appointing deputies or receiving obedience from others. When trying to describe a system of electoral representation as part of his scheme, however, the project begins to unravel. He says:[15]

> In our own country, for example, the *commons* (a name specifically applied to those commoners who share the sovereignty with the King and the Peers) exercise through representatives the whole of their sovereign powers, except their sovereign power of electing and appointing representatives to represent them in the British Parliament.

What happens then to the undelegated portion of this power – the power periodically to vote in elections? Austin tells us: 'When Parliament is dissolved, or the period for which a member is elected expires, the delegated share in the sovereignty reverts to the delegating body, so far at least as regards the choice of new representatives.'[16] Further, he suggests that since the members of the House of Commons only exercise their delegated powers on trust and as representatives of the electoral body, sovereignty resides in the 'king and the peers with the electoral body of the commons'.[17] At this point then, the conceptual separation of the ruler(s) and ruled (sovereign and subject) seems to break down. He attempts to rescue his general theory by saying that the 'same person may be sovereign seen from one aspect but subject when viewed from another'.[18] (In relation to the US, his approach is even more perplexing: according to Austin, in the US sovereignty resides in the complex body that has the power of altering the Constitution.)[19]

In the sixth lecture he begins to redefine his ideas about sanction and submission to render them less coercive. Obedience, he says, must be voluntary, free or 'willed': 'Acquiescence which is purely involuntary, or

[15] *Ibid.*, p. 96. [16] *Ibid.*, p. 138.

[17] *Ibid.*, p. 227. The King, lords and electoral body of the commons is also ultimately where sovereignty would reside for the self-governing dominions, given that their legislative powers were also dependent on the British Parliament.

[18] *Ibid.*, p. 132. Contrast Roger Cotterrell's more sympathetic reading of Austin to the effect that he is only interested in where *ultimate* sovereignty lies. See R. Cotterrell, *The Politics of Jurisprudence: A Critical Introduction to Legal Philosophy* (London: Lexis-Nexis, 2003), p. 66.

[19] Austin, *Lectures on Jurisprudence*, above n. 14, p. 103.

which is purely the consequence of physical compulsion or restraint, is not obedience or submission.'[20]

For all its claims to be a general theory which applies to different political systems, Austin's theory is at its least convincing when applied to a parliamentary democracy.[21]

The relationship between the sovereign and the law

The second aspect of Austin's work to draw sustained reaction was his portrayal of the relationship between the sovereign and the law. For Austin, the sovereign determinate body or person is prior to law, is the source of law and cannot be defined or limited by law (and is independent of all others). He does not consider constitutional law to be law at all but rather treats it as an example of positive morality, which is unenforceable as against the sovereign itself. Hence a law made by the sovereign is not required to meet any moral standards before it can be properly called a law.

When one looks more closely at Austin's theory, however, there are more limits to sovereign power than might at first appear. He is explicit that in the British system of constitutional monarchy the monarch is not sovereign but is only a *part* of the sovereign body. Only a very careless reader would view his work as justifying, for example, personal immunity for the monarch herself. Austin is particularly clear on this point. Parts of the sovereign body may be defined and limited by positive law. His point is that it is only the sovereign body *as a whole* understood as a corporate entity that cannot be so defined or limited:[22]

> Considered collectively, or considered in its corporate character, a sovereign number is sovereign and independent: but, considered severally, the individuals and smaller aggregates composing that sovereign number are subject to the supreme body of which they are component parts. Consequently, though the body is inevitably independent of legal or political duty, any of the individuals or aggregates whereof the body is composed may be legally bound by laws of which the body is author.

20 *Ibid.*, p. 126.

21 A common criticism has been that it works better for autocracy. See, e.g., J. C. Smith, *Legal Obligation* (London: Athlone Press, 1976), p. 10: 'Just as traditional English positivism is teleologically and morally neutral it is also politically neutral. If slanted at all, it would probably be towards a totalitarian state rather than a democracy, since it is easier to locate the sovereign in the former.'

22 Austin, *Province of Jurisprudence Determined*, above n. 13, p. 218.

Types of juristic persons

The third aspect of Austin's work to attract attention (though it is not given much prominence by Austin himself) was his discussion of the nature of legal persons and, more precisely, his contention that legal persons, such as corporations aggregate, are merely collections or aggregations of natural persons – 'persons by figment' and 'for the sake of brevity'. As such, they merely aggregate the wills of individuals rather than exercise a real will of their own. They are the product of law, and by the law they are allowed to wear the mask or '*persona*' of personality or legal identity. Austin contends that legal personality has no bearing on sovereignty, being 'simply a technical matter, related to certain issues in private law, and belonging therefore to the detail rather than generalia of the science'.[23]

The paradox of Austin's success

Given these bold outlines of Austin's theory, it is not self-evident why it should have achieved the prominence that it did. Austin's *Province of Jurisprudence Determined* (*PJD*) was first published in 1832, and reviewers of the first edition focused primarily on his discussion of Utilitarianism rather than on his ideas about the nature of law and sovereignty.[24] It would not be until after the posthumous publication (by his assiduous widow) of the second edition in 1861 and of his *Lectures* in 1863[25] that his reviewers would '"see" Austin as the Definer of Law, Separator of Law and Morality, or Theorist of Sovereignty'.[26] Importantly, it would be Mill's review of Austin's *Lectures on Jurisprudence* in the *Edinburgh Review* in 1863 which would draw attention to the work as a *general* description of the nature of law that purported to transcend historical contingency.[27] In this later period, the Utilitarian aspects of the work (which were the subject of lectures 2, 3 and 4) would be criticized and effectively excised from the *study* of a general

[23] J. Austin, *Lectures on Jurisprudence, or the Philosophy of Positive Law*, R. Campbell (ed.), 2 vols., 3rd edn, (London: John Murray, 1869), vol. 1, p. 362.

[24] W. E. Rumble, *Doing Austin Justice: The Reception of John Austin's Philosophy of Law in Nineteenth Century England* (London: Continuum, 2005), p. 65.

[25] He died in 1859. In 1849 Austin had refused to republish *Province* owing to his views about its imperfections.

[26] Rumble, *Doing Austin Justice*, above n. 24, p. 70.

[27] J. S. Mill, *Essays on Equality, Law and Education*, J. M. Robson (ed.) (University of Toronto Press, 1984).

theory of jurisprudence that separated law from morals.[28] Austin's reputation would reach its zenith in the years 1863–85.[29]

In many respects it is surprising that Austin's work and reputation should have achieved the attention it did in the later nineteenth century and so quickly after the publication of the second edition of *PJD* (1861). Maine's *Ancient Law*, published in 1863, was much more in the historical evolutionary style popular during the period. It was also much better written and more accessible. More perplexing still would be Austin's rise to prominence given that his work paid little attention to, and could scarcely explain, the common law and the common law method – which was very much the stock in trade of the legal profession. It is difficult to conceive of common law reasoning as a species of 'command' delegated from the sovereign to the judges (particularly in Scotland given that its private law and judicial system were protected by the Treaty of Union). Indeed, as we saw in the last chapter, common law decision-making was, at the time, seen more often as a way to diffuse and distribute power, rather than as a means by which to delegate it. Not surprisingly, Austin preferred a civilian code stating general rules based on Roman law principles over the method and substance of the common law.

Perhaps most perplexing of all is that Austin's reputation should achieve its height during the time of the second Reform Act. As we have noted, his work is *least* convincing when it attempts to describe legal systems approximating democratic self-government or even the British Constitution as at 1832. We know, from his pamphlets, that early in the nineteenth century Austin had been opposed to *any* kind of Parliamentary reform.[30] He had feared the prospect of the Commons becoming the repository of sovereignty and had thought that the role of the Crown and the House of Lords was to restrain the Commons and to prevent it from becoming tyrannous.[31] He was against socialism which he described in the following terms: 'Control of the economy by a joint stock company . . . consisting of the entire population . . . worked for the equal benefit of all, under the supreme

[28] See, e.g., W. Markby, *Elements of Law: Considered with Reference to General Jurisprudence* (Oxford: Clarendon, 1871), p. 4 suggests that Austin's theory of law does not depend on his theory of utility.

[29] Rumble, *Doing Austin Justice*, above n. 24, p. 106.

[30] W. E. Rumble, *The Thought of John Austin: Jurisprudence, Colonial Reform, and the British Constitution* (London: Athlone, 1985), p. 197. Austin says 'Even before the Reform of 1832, I had rejected his [Bentham's] radical politics' (*ibid.*, p. 207).

[31] *Ibid.*, p. 198

direction of some narrower body and leading to a habitual disposition to insubordination and revolt: whether it comes from addiction to social theories, or from a lust for pillage'.[32] He was politically opposed to democratic government and his theory was weakest when he tried to explain it.

Austin's inability to explain the domestic UK constitution drew criticisms from within his own tradition – most compellingly by Henry Sidgwick. Sidgwick devoted a section of *The Elements of Politics* to a critique of Austin.[33] Sidgwick suggests that as a theory 'intended to represent the relation of what has been commonly recognized as Law to Government in human societies always and everywhere, it [is] . . . quite unacceptable'.[34] He cavils at Austin's characterization of the law as applied by the judges as 'delegated' commands and reminds us of the ancient legal distinctions between the true monarch and the tyrant. For all that his admirers praised Austin's precision, Sidgwick points out the 'contradictions' and 'embarrassments' in Austin's arguments about where supreme political power is located in the British constitution.[35] Sidgwick credits 'my friend Dicey', rather than Austin, with providing a solution that maintains a distinction between the governors and the governed. According to Dicey, in a Parliamentary democracy, Parliament may be legally sovereign but the people are politically sovereign.[36] Though some aspects of Dicey's theory are consistent with Austin's theory (such as the role Dicey gives to constitutional conventions as an example of how 'positive morality' can help shape a constitution), it is Dicey's version of sovereignty that would become the received explanation for the internal British constitution and not Austin's.

Despite these defects, Austin's work became part of the canon of legal texts. In what respects, then, could Austin be taken as speaking for his age? How can that be explained? How, and to what extent, was Austin received by the intellectual community, the legal profession and the doctrines of British law itself?

[32] *Ibid.*, p. 202.

[33] H. Sidgwick, *The Elements of Politics*, 2nd edn (London: Macmillan, 1897). The first edition (1891) included this critique in Chapter 2, editions thereafter in an appendix.

[34] *Ibid.*, 2nd edn, p. 652.

[35] *Ibid.*, 2nd edn p. 656–8. See also J. W. Harris, *Legal Philosophies*, 2nd edn (London: Butterworths, 1997), p. 37.

[36] Sidgwick, *Elements of Politics*, 2nd edn, above n. 33 p. 658.

The reception of Austin

Austin died in 1859 and '[w]ithin a few years of his death it was clear that his work had established the study of jurisprudence in England'.[37] His theory would dominate analytical jurisprudential thinking well into the twentieth century. There is now a great deal of scholarship explaining how Austin's work was received and came to found the analytical school of English jurisprudence.[38] Some of the very people who helped to propagate and popularize the work, such as Maine, Holland and Markby, were also among Austin's harshest critics.[39] Of these, the most important was Maine. His *Ancient Law* (1863) and *Village Communities* (1871) helped provoke a more widespread debate about the very nature of the philosophical approach to the study of law.[40] In 1863, *PJD* became the examination book for both Oxford and Cambridge, though students were more likely to read Holland's *The Elements of Jurisprudence* (1880)[41] or Markby's *Elements of Law: Considered with Reference to Principles of General Jurisprudence* (1871).[42] Both of these latter works summarize and endorse important parts of Austin's theory but also include discussion of Maine's contribution and critique.[43] Both struggle to bring the common law and custom more fully within Austin's

[37] H. L. A. Hart, 'Introduction' in J. Austin *The Province of Jurisprudence Determined* (London: Weidenfeld Nicolson, 1954), pp.vii–xviii, xvi.

[38] See, generally, Rumble, *Doing Austin Justice*, above n. 24; N. Duxbury, *Frederick Pollock and the English Juristic Tradition* (Oxford University Press, 2004); W. L. Twining, *Globalisation and Legal Theory* (London: Butterworths, 2000), pp. 26–7. Student works were not available until 1863. Campbell's student text (above n. 14) appeared in 1875, Clark's in 1874 (E. C. Clark, *Practical Jurisprudence: A Comment an Austin* (Cambridge University Press, 1883)), Holland's *The Elements of Jurisprudence* in 1880 (Oxford: Clarendon Press) (and ran to 13 editions until 1926). Later *Salmond on Jurisprudence* (London: Stevens) (12 editions between 1902–1966) would fill the same niche.

[39] Others included Harrison, Buckland, Bryce and later Salmond.

[40] See generally Rumble, *Doing Austin Justice*, above n. 24, Chapter 7 and S. Collini, *Public Moralists: Political Thought and Intellectual Life in Britain, 1850–1930* (Oxford: Clarendon Press, 1991), p. 761.

[41] Holland, *The Elements of Jurisprudence*, above n. 38, appeared in ten British editions up until 1910.

[42] Collini, *Public Moralists*, above n. 40, pp. 267–8. six editions of Markby, *Elements of Law*, above n. 28 appeared between 1871 and 1896 inclusive.

[43] H. Maine *Ancient Law: Its Connection with the Early History of Society and its Relation to Modern Ideas* (London: John Murray, 1863) was also widely used in law schools by 1871, appearing in eleven editions over twenty-five years. See Cotterrell, *The Politics of Jurisprudence*, above n. 18, p. 45.

frame.[44] It helped too that Austin's discussion of the principles of private law, drawing as it does on Roman law ideas, was much more relevant to the study and practice of law than his discussion of public law (though Austin himself denied the distinction and regarded all law as in a sense 'public').

Austin's theory would be welcomed, particularly during this period, as a contribution to 'legal science'. Here, at last, was a general theory of law that would give academic respectability to the reinvigorated study of law at the English Universities and Inns of Court. It would make a British contribution to continental and US debates about the nature and study of law.[45] Holland, for example, discusses 'the formal science of positive law' and explains that 'like the science of geology' or as 'grammar' is to language, it has of its nature to be focused on the general rather than on the particular.[46] The early twentieth century was to witness this analytical turn in philosophy more generally.[47] Any gap between how Austin described the world and legal systems as were known to exist could be dismissed by an appeal to the general nature of the theory and in the interests of legal science.

Two elements are commonly left out of the standard explanations for the widespread reception of Austin's ideas. As Chapter 2 suggested, Austin's views about sovereignty and authority had lent themselves to the defence of the newly centralizing state. The idea that all public power is delegated from the centre, the importance (and consequences) of his rule Utilitarianism and his suspicion of independent (and potentially rival) sources of political authority all fit within the broader framework of his views of sovereignty as command, and the sovereign as the uncommanded commander who is independent of all others. He seats power at the centre of his theory of law at the very time that power was indeed centralizing.[48] A related aspect of his theory which was 'received' was the state's monopoly on coercion.

[44] For example, Markby, *Elements of Law*, above n. 28, p. 3 concedes that the orders made by ordinary tribunals are not laws. He suggests that they are 'the pre-arranged consequences of other commands that are general'. Holland, *Elements of Jurisprudence*, above n. 41, p. 47 suggests that it is the state which gives custom the force of law.

[45] See also Rumble, *Doing Austin Justice*, above n. 24 Chapter 6. Langdell's approach to the teaching of law as science was gaining popularity and attention in the US at this time.

[46] Holland, *Elements of Jurisprudence*, above n. 41, pp. 6, 8.

[47] T. Rockmore, *Hegel, Idealism and Analytic Philosophy* (New Haven, CT: Yale University Press, 2005).

[48] See also Cotterrell, *The Politics of Jurisprudence*, above n. 18, Chapter 3.

These ideas very much lent themselves to the British colonial enterprise. The idea that to be truly sovereign meant that a sovereign had to be independent of all other sovereigns quite accurately described the sovereign relationship of the UK Parliament to the subordinate legislatures and administrations of various parts of the Empire over which it retained ultimate law-making power. It is not surprising, then, given that *The Elements of Law* began as a series of lectures given in India, that Markby emphasizes this aspect of Austin's theory. It is the UK Queen, Lords and Commons that is sovereign, according to British colonial law, and not any local system of government or representation. The issues, raised by Sidgwick, surrounding who forms part of the sovereign determinate body as the electorate is increasingly enfranchised, simply do not arise for the colonies as far as either colonial law or Austin's theory is concerned. Colonial institutions were not fully sovereign or independent but maintained 'a habit of obedience' to the mother of Parliaments. This is sovereignty viewed from a British imperial vantage point rather than from the inside of the UK – and *this* is where the congruence between theory and practice really mattered for the Empire.

The warmth of Austin's reception by international lawyers may initially seem surprising given that he famously excluded international law from law properly so called (thinking it a variety of positive morality).[49] At the time, however, a new more positivistic movement was emerging from within international law. These lawyers were prepared to look past Austin's view that there could be no law as between sovereigns and instead were prepared to source international law in sovereign will and command. Westlake, a leading British international lawyer writing at the turn of the nineteenth and twentieth centuries, summed it up in this way:[50]

[49] Importantly too, in terms of the reception of Austin's ideas, Austin's disciples were not as sceptical about the possibilities of international law being considered as law as he had been. Pollock and Holland, in particular, took international law seriously and accepted that international law could be analogized to municipal law, even if municipal law remained the primary focus of their legal study. For a sketch of how international lawyers of the time attempted to refute Austin's views about international law's status as law, see A. Anghie, *Imperialism, Sovereignty and the Making of International Law* (Cambridge University Press, 2005), pp. 45–6. As for the will theory, this was not something that Hobbes's or Spinoza's schemes could have contemplated – they both regarded international society as in a state of nature. For a discussion see Green, *Principles of Political Obligation*, above n. 2, p. 51.

[50] J. Westlake, *The Collected Papers of John Westlake on Public International Law*, L. Oppenheim (ed.) (Cambridge University Press, 1914), Preface, p. xxi.

> [W]e are fortunately able to retain most of the fruits of [Austin's] labour, unaffected by the doubt that has at last arisen about [Austin's definition of law].

Austin and the Positivist international lawyers shared a framework that was based on determinate sovereigns and distinguished between law and justice. European powers were expanding into new colonial territory by a variety of means – fiat, command and violence amongst them. International law at that time allowed for the acquisition of new territory by both conquest and Treaty. In what was a break from earlier approaches to international law,[51] these international lawyers would not explore the constitutional or other origins of such power to expand territory but would emphasize instead the fact of supreme coercive power (with 'legal' measures of 'civilization' thrown in). Westlake puts it in these stark terms: it is 'irrelevant to international law, as to where in any political body the Austinian sovereignty lies'.[52] Austin's theory, that in order to be sovereign, states must behave in a *habitually* independent fashion, better explained modern state relations than either Hobbes or Grotius, and united the legal and political in international relations in a way that was descriptively compelling.

Austin's conflation of statehood with sovereignty then suited British colonial ambitions. Indeed, Sorley, writing in 1916 of the British position, claimed that the 'state did not exist except for foreigners'.[53] It also suited the increasingly centralized *administration* of domestic British rule. Where his theory was the least successful, however, was in explaining newly democratized institutions of self-government within the mother country and the potential for self-governing settled colonies.

We should be cautious then when assessing the extent to which Austin's theory of law was 'received' in terms of affecting the content of the law or even certain aspects of legal theory. It had greater

[51] See, e.g., Vattel's treatment of the representative nature of the monarch and its connection through the constitution to the body politic. E. Vattel, *The Law of Nations, or, Principles of the Law of Nature: Applied to the Conduct and Affairs of Nations and Sovereigns* (London: Robinson, 1797) pp. 8, 14. In other respects, Vattel may be considered a pivotal figure in the shift to positivism, see A. Anghie, *Imperialism*, above n. 49, p. 42.

[52] Westlake, *Collected Papers*, above n. 50 p. xxiii.

[53] W. R. Sorley, *The International Crisis: The Theory of the State* (Oxford University Press, 1916), quoted in M. Francis, 'Nineteenth Century Theories of Sovereignty and Thomas Hobbes', *History of Political Thought* I (1980), 517–40, 519.

explanatory force in some areas than others and was the subject of serious critique even among his contemporary admirers.

I turn now to the more indirect critiques of Austin's theory of sovereignty. What unifies these commentators is that they sought to critique Austin's theory through questions about the nature of legal personhood. Does a corporation have a legal personality that is distinct from the personality of its members and, if so, on what basis? Is the state itself an example of a corporation differing only in degree rather than in kind from other forms of collective life? And if so, why should these lesser corporations depend on the state and the law for their existence? As we shall see, this debate drew on philosophical, political, moral and legal frameworks. It was also, for a time, a debate to which both public and private lawyers contributed.

The critique of Austin from legal personality

It may initially appear surprising that ideas about legal personality should have been the gateway through which to mount a challenge to sovereignty, to attack some of the central tenets of positivism and to investigate the moral personality of the state. But set against the larger currents of the Victorian period there is a certain degree of inevitability about this. As I signalled in Chapter 2, Bentham's focus on real persons and real power would not serve fully to explain the bureaucratization of the public and private spheres, or the proliferation of collective and voluntarist organizations which occurred throughout the nineteenth century. In his *Fragment on Government*, Bentham himself acknowledges that 'corporate or collective forms of action in which different people have a different share in issuing commands and ideas of representation too, may require more by way of explanation'.[54]

Austin too assumes, in his definition of the sovereign, a 'determinate body or person' which is able to exhibit a 'corporate character'[55] but does not examine in any direct way how the component parts of the many would be able to constitute a unity or 'determinate' whole. This is a serious omission given that the *determinacy* of the sovereign is central to his theory. And, even if one accepts the Austinian explanation, that the state exists as a pre-legal political fact, why is the same not true for other group entities? On what basis can we accept the reality of the 'state'

[54] J. Bentham, *Fragment on Government*, W. Harrison (ed.) (London: Basil Blackwell, 1948), pp. 42–3.

[55] Austin, *Province of Jurisprudence*, above n. 13, p. 218.

and its will and not the reality of the will of other forms of group life? As Maitland asks of Sidgwick: 'why do political and legal theorists so readily credit the sociological existence of the political realm and not of other groups that make up society?'[56]

Sidgwick, for his part, recognizes that voluntary groups could have a continuous life rivalling and even threatening the state, but thinks of that as a reason for the state to control them.[57] He also worries about the nature of the 'unity of supreme control' and the need for the 'supreme direction of one person or body'[58] and admits that supreme power is likely to be distributed in a much more complex way than Austin imagines.[59] He stops short, however, of identifying the state as a moral person. As Maitland notes with enthusiasm,[60] Dicey too acknowledges the reality of group life. Dicey says that when 'a body of twenty, or two thousand, or two hundred thousand men bind themselves together to act in a particular way for some common purpose, they create a body, which by no fiction of law, but by the very nature of things differs from the individuals of whom it is constituted'.[61] Sidgwick, Dicey and Maitland all agree, for example, that something which may be lawful if done by an individual, may be unlawful if done in concert with others.

Dicey recognizes something else that is novel and important for the later nineteenth century. The new proliferation of joint stock companies signals the passing of management from private persons to corporate bodies. In the case of joint stocks, such as the railway companies, this inevitably brings with it legal privileges and monopoly. He says: 'The characteristics of modern commerce, looked at from this point of view, make for socialism'.[62] 'Hence the antithesis between the individual and the state is with difficulty maintainable'.[63] How much more difficult would it be to maintain an

[56] F. W. Maitland, 'Body Politic', in H. A. L. Fisher (ed.), *The Collected Papers of Frederic William Maitland*, 3 vols. (Cambridge University Press, 1911) Vol. III, pp. 285–303.

[57] *Ibid.*

[58] Sidgwick, *Elements of Politics*, above n. 33, p. 411.

[59] *Ibid.*, p. 638.

[60] F. W. Maitland, 'Moral Personality and Legal Personality', in H. A. L. Fisher (ed.), *The Collected Papers of Frederic William Maitland*, 3 vols. (Cambridge University Press, 1911), vol. III, p. 306.

[61] A. V. Dicey, 'The Combination Laws as Illustrating the Relation between Law and Opinion during the Nineteenth Century', *Harvard Law Review* 17 (1903–4), 511–32, 513. Dicey was a member of the Old Mortality Society with the leading Idealist T. H. Green.

[62] Dicey, *Lectures on the Relation Between Law and Opinion in England during the Nineteenth Century*, 2 edn (London: Macmillan, 1914) p. 340.

[63] *Ibid.*, p. lv.

antithesis between the individual and state if the state were itself to be conceived as a kind of corporation? The blurring of the distinction between the state and other manifestations of civil society is an issue to which I shall return in the next chapter.

There was another philosophical development that emerged in British thought in the later nineteenth century that meant that followers of Bentham could no longer avoid questions about the corporate or other nature of the state by focusing on 'real' persons and 'real' power. The British Idealists lent their metaphysics of the 'real' to the debate about the corporation. Idealism assumed 'that there is no such thing as matter apart from mind, that what we commonly call things are not self-subsistent realities, but are only real when taken in connection with mind – that they exist for mind, not for themselves'.[64] Boucher paraphrases the Idealist position thus: the 'real is that which is in conformity with the unfolding reason of the whole'.[65] Green gives an example of some of the consequences of such a view: 'Nothing is more real than a right, yet its existence is purely ideal, if by "ideal" is meant that which is not dependent on anything material but has its being solely in consciousness. It is to these ideal realities that force is subordinate in the creation and development of states.'[66] A Benthamite focus on real persons rather than fictions of the common law could no longer be used to avoid a debate in which *the* central question came to be whether the personality of the corporation was real, artificial or fictitious. My object is not to explore these metaphysical arguments on their own terms but we need to acknowledge that underlying the *legal* arguments were controversial *philosophical* commitments about 'what is real'? It is this debate which brings us back to Maitland, who sought through ideas of legal personality to challenge much of what Austin said about sovereignty and positive law.

Maitland and the Crown as corporation in context

Maitland writing at the turn of the twentieth century was insistent that the Crown should be conceived in its 'suppressed' medieval form as a corporation aggregate rather than as a corporation sole. Maitland

[64] H. Randall, 'Personality: Human and Divine', in H. C. Sturt (ed.), *Personal Idealism: Philosophical Essays by Eight Members of the University of Oxford* (London: Macmillan, 1902), pp. 369–93, 370 quoted in D. Boucher (ed.), *The British Idealists* (Cambridge University Press, 1997), p. xii and see surrounding discussion.

[65] Boucher (ed.), *The British Idealists*, above n. 64, p. xxviii.

[66] Green, *Principles of Political Obligation*, above n. 2, pp. 140–1.

identified the corporate Crown as a possible manifestation of the state. We need to set his discussion in its wider context in order to understand its ambitions and to demonstrate the extent to which it relied on, and departed from, central commitments of Idealist thought. Using corporate conceptions to imagine the public realm would, Maitland thought, better represent the political relation between people and sovereign than prevailing jurisprudential thought and also provide real practical guidance about how to theorize and frame the law. He denies any separation of legal, political and moral frameworks and credits the 'English addiction to ethics as a by-product of the specifically English history of the English law'.[67] After all, he acknowledges, it would not be the first time that political theorists had looked to law for their ideas.[68] Maitland cites as earlier examples Rousseau's social contract theory and the trust theories used by Locke. He dismisses social contract theories as too individualistic.[69] And while he acknowledges that the English trust has allowed corporations to flourish 'behind a screen',[70] he argues that trust concepts now need to be 'renovated'[71] to enable a more open and straightforward approach.[72] The state imagined as a corporation, he contends, would contribute to political thought by challenging both an absolutist version of sovereignty and an individualistic view of society. It would also directly raise questions about the qualities that the state does and should exhibit as a moral and legal person. Attempting to define the state as a corporate legal person would also force a deeper explanation of the government's relationship to the legal system itself. In the idea of the corporation, Maitland would (*contra* Austin) seek to bring juristic and political thought together. For a time, there would be a significant connection between the legal and political debates.

Why then was Maitland so insistent that the Crown should be conceived as a corporation aggregate rather than as a corporation sole? A corporation sole connotes an office that exists in perpetuity which attaches to a series of natural persons. This idea, as one commentator

[67] Maitland, 'Moral Personality and Legal Personality', above n. 60, p. 305.

[68] F. W. Maitland, 'Introduction', in O. Gierke, *Political Theories of the Middle Age*, F. W. Maitland (tr.) (Cambridge University Press, 1958), pp. vii–xlv, xxiii (citing Gierke), first edition published in 1900 ('Introduction to Gierke').

[69] 'Introduction to Gierke', p. xxiii. [70] *Ibid.*, p. xxix. [71] *Ibid.*, p. xxxv.

[72] Skinner and Runciman would argue that Hobbes's was the first significant theory to think of the state as a kind of corporation. See Q. Skinner, 'A Genealogy of the Modern State' *Proceedings of the British Academy* 162 (2009), 325–70; Runciman, *Pluralism and the Personality of the State*, above n. 4.

put it, 'was constructed primarily not to represent the oneness of the corporation of the several, but, on the contrary, merely as a "feigned substratum for rights"'.[73] What is important about the corporation aggregate, by contrast, is that the oneness of the group enjoys a life that is distinct from its individual members. The whole is observably more than its parts and can exercise its own will. Maitland goes further to suggest that the corporation is a *real* moral and legal person capable of exercising a collective will (a *real* will) that is separate from (but not unrelated to) the will of the individual members. This is not simply the result of some artificial or fictitious device of positive law: *all* groups (including the state itself) are distinct moral persons because that reflects the very nature of things and is of their essence.

Philosophical underpinnings

While Maitland denies any direct engagement with the philosophical debates of the time suggesting that '[a]s to philosophy it is no affair of mine',[74] he goes some way to acknowledging his philosophical sources. He does not, however, refer to any particular philosophical school or philosopher directly by name. In the introduction to his translation of Gierke he admits that:[75]

> Finally we are among the summits of philosophy and observe how a doctrine which makes some way in England, ascribes to the State, or, more vaguely, to the Community, not only a real will, but even 'the' real will, and it must occur to us to ask whether what is thus affirmed in the case of the State can be denied in the case of other organised groups.

This must be a reference to the British Idealists in general and almost certainly to Bernard Bosanquet in particular.[76] The British Idealists dominated the philosophy departments at Oxford and the Scottish Universities at the end of the century. It is their concept of the 'real' to which we have already referred. They, in turn, drew on Rousseau for

[73] R. L. Raymond, 'The Genesis of the Corporation', *Harvard Law Review* 19 (1905–6), 350–65, 361.

[74] Maitland, 'Moral Personality and Legal Personality', above n. 60, p. 318.

[75] Maitland, 'Introduction to Gierke', p. xi.

[76] Bosanquet's *Philosophical Theory of the State* (London: Macmillan) was first published in 1899, the year before Maitland's translation of Gierke. Runciman explores the similarities between Gierke's and Bosanquet's thought in *Pluralism and the Personality of the State*, above n. 4, p. 77.

ideas about the general will or the *volonté générale*[77] but, like Hegel, rejected the social contract as too individualistic to be the basis of social life.[78] Instead, the British Idealists shared with Hegel the older Aristotelian view that the individual is morally and ethically formed by his *membership* in the family, civil society, the corporation and the state.[79] And as we shall see in more detail in Chapter 6, they also adopted and adapted a Hegelian version of individual freedom.

It is, of course, Gierke, and not the British Idealists, who is commonly recognized as inspiring the Anglo-American Pluralist tradition of which Maitland is viewed as a major protagonist. From this historical distance it may seem strange that both Gierke and the British Idealists should exert an influence on Maitland's thought. Gierke's discourse on medieval political theory was motivated by his desire for a unified Germany 'in which the Germanic [as opposed to the Roman] laws of association applied'.[80] Gierke's concern was to ensure that other forms of associative life maintained an independent existence within a unified state. Maitland appropriated some of these ideas for the very different circumstances of the UK. He opposed the centralizing trend in the UK domestic system of government and expressed a desire for more power to and trust in local government and officials beyond 'mere registering of orders of the central bureau'.[81] He and his followers would attack the idea that all power is delegated from the central state apparatus. He also sought

[77] See Green, *Principles of Political Obligation*, above n. 2, p. 95. Green attempts to reconcile the general will with Austin's theory saying 'Let this sense or desire – which may properly be called the general will – cease to operate, or let it come into general conflict with the sovereign's commands, and the habitual obedience will cease also' (p. 97). He also thought customary law was an expression of the general will (p. 101) and sometimes used the term 'general will' as a synonym for 'law', e.g., (p. 102) 'impartially or according to a general will or law'.

[78] See A. Patten, *Hegel's Idea of Freedom* (Oxford University Press, 1999), Chapter 4; Green, *Principles of Political Obligation*, above n. 2, pp. 68 ff., 93 ff.

[79] Rockmore, *Hegel, Idealism and Analytic Philosophy*, above n. 47, argues that some of the British Idealists rejected Hegel, and many of the Idealists used Hegel merely as a launching pad for their own philosophies.

[80] Runciman, *Pluralism and the Personality of the State*, above n. 4 pp. 71–2. For a full discussion of the context of Gierke's thought and how it became increasingly conservative as the century wore on, see R. Harris, 'The Transplantation of Legal Discourse on Corporate Personality Theories: From German Codification to British Political Pluralism and American Big Business', *Washington and Lee Law Review* 63 (2006), 1421–78.

[81] Maitland, 'The Shallows and Silences of Real Life', in H. A. L. Fisher (ed.), *The Collected Papers of Frederic William, Maitland*, 3 vols. (Cambridge University Press, 1911), vol I., pp. 467–79, 475–6. He also supports extension of the franchise 'frankly and courageously', p. 475.

the recognition of distinct parts of the Empire as separate bodies politic. In the distinctive English turn Maitland gives to Gierke's work, we begin now to see the extent to which Maitland's and Austin's views are diametrically opposed – and why Maitland should have been so privately damning about Austin's contribution.[82] The British Idealists, by contrast, would be accused (mainly by the Pluralists)[83] of promoting an 'all-absorptive' 'Hegelian' style state that would restrain other forms of associative life and of being accomplices in Prussian militarism.[84] In this, both Hegel and the British Idealists have been misunderstood.

Hegel's theory about the relationship of civil society to the state is notoriously complicated and remains controversial to this day.[85] He considers civil society and the state to be rival conceptions of state serving, respectively, particular ends and universal ends, and thus representing different relationships that the state potentially has with its citizens. Of these, it is the state serving universal ends which, according to Hegel, has the greater potential to actualize freedom. Whether, and how, the British Idealists read Hegel on this question is unclear.[86] Bosanquet, the most Hegelian of the British Idealists,[87] would certainly not have allowed the state to subsume other forms of social life. (In fairness neither would Hegel who suggests, for example, that the corporation may be a transitional institution between the market economy and state).[88] Bosanquet may have located sovereignty and the common will in the 'organized whole' but he was unclear about whether 'the whole' meant society, community or the state apparatus (as Maitland himself recognizes).[89] At the same time, Bosanquet championed the role of voluntary associations as serving distinct functions from those of the

[82] See text accompanying n 12.

[83] For example, H. J. Laski, *Studies in the Problem of Sovereignty* (New Haven, CT: Yale University Press, 1917), p. 1.

[84] D. Boucher 'British Idealism, the State, and International Relations', *Journal of the History of Ideas* 55 (1994) 671–94. See especially the criticisms of Hobhouse and Hobson.

[85] See Patten, *Hegel's Idea of Freedom*, above n. 78 Chapter 6. This is complicated further by the fact that Hegel assigns the functions of the administration and the police to civil society, p. 168.

[86] Bosanquet and Richie made more of the distinction between the 'real' interests of citizens (which were not in conflict) and their immediate 'felt' private interests (which did tend to be in conflict) according to K. H. F. Dyson, *The State Tradition in Western Europe: A Study of an Idea and Institution* (Oxford: Martin Robinson, 1980), p. 192.

[87] Bosanquet translated Hegel into English.

[88] Patten, *Hegel's Idea of Freedom*, above n. 78, p. 187.

[89] See the quote above in text accompanying n. 75.

government apparatus. In relation to the relief of poverty, for example, he viewed the improvement of moral character through the work of charitable organizations as preferable to state intervention.[90] The other common allegation, that Idealists were implicated in supporting the expansion of the Prussian state, is even less well-founded. The British Hegelians, including Bosanquet, universally condemned German aggression, were much more internationalist than Hegel himself and, among other things, consistently argued that a citizen had a *duty* to resist a bad state.[91]

The central conviction that the Idealists and Gierke shared in common was that the individual is formed by society and the state is formed by societies. They sought to provide an alternative to the extreme individualism, which the British Idealists and Maitland (sometimes unfairly) associated with Utilitarianism.[92] The state is much more than a mere aggregation of individuals. It is rather 'a totality of the common consciousness of a people or nation and the purposes it embodies'.[93] The dichotomy, on which Austin's theory depends, between the sovereign on the one hand and the individual (or 'bulk' of individuals) on the other, ignores the social. The Idealists used 'the state' to refer to all of a single society's institutions and collectivities *unified* in some mystical form of relationship.[94] Both Bosanquet and Gierke used organic language to describe group life – a usage which had resonance in the popular evolutionary ideas of the time.[95] Bosanquet, in particular among the

[90] This aspect of his work may reflect the Hegelian dialectic that a person is both a member of civil society and citizen of the state and has to strike a balance between the two aspects of existence – see further S. Avineri, *Hegel's Theory of the Modern State* (London: Cambridge University Press, 1972), pp. 103–5. See also Runciman, *Pluralism and the Personality of the State*, above n. 4, p. 76. For Bosanquet's views about the role of the Charity Organisation Society, see J. Lewis, 'The Boundary Between Voluntary and Statutory Social Service in the Late Nineteenth and Early Twentieth Centuries', *The Historical Journal* 39(1) (1996), 155–77.

[91] The significant differences between the British Idealists and Hegel when it comes to international relations can be found in Boucher 'British Idealism, the State, and International Relations'. Though many of the criticisms subsequently levelled at the British Idealists were unfair, they were likely caused at least in part by the highly abstract quality of much of their prose – a quality that often rendered their meanings unclear, even to each other.

[92] *Cf.* Sidgwick's version of utilitarianism in *The Elements of Politics*, above n. 33.

[93] Boucher, *The British Idealists*, above n. 64, p. xxi.

[94] Jones criticized Bosanquet on this score. See Boucher, *The British Idealists*, above n. 64, p. 672 at fn. 3.

[95] See, further, on the use of organic language, J. Morefield, 'Hegelian Organicism, British New Liberalism, and the Return of the Family State', *History of Political Thought* 23 (2002), 141–70.

Idealists, explicitly conceived of this unity or 'state' as a real person, which enjoyed a distinctive moral character from that of individuals.[96] He, with Bradley and Henry Jones, attributed 'a reality to the social organism or state that is not merely metaphorical or fictitious'.[97] Jones went even further to argue that 'we can only attribute a moral character to the state if we regard it as a person'.[98] In terms of their core commitments, Bosanquet, Gierke and Maitland shared the view that the state is the greatest corporation of all, is capable of manifesting a common will and is a moral person. Importantly, however, in likening the state to any other ordinary corporation, Maitland wished to portray the state as a moral and legal person subject to and limited by the ordinary common law.

While the British Idealist movement had a practical and reformist political agenda,[99] unlike its Hegelian counterpart it did not contain an explicitly juristic element. Its proponents' use of language and concepts was in stark contrast to analytical styles of thinking. It was partly because, for example, they used the term 'the state' in such a loose and inconsistent manner – sometimes to refer to all the institutions of a society (the community) and at others to refer to the apparatus of government through which individuals act as part of the nation – that their work did not seem able directly to engage with legal notions of sovereignty which presupposed a sharp distinction between rulers and ruled.[100] Crucially, what Gierke, and Maitland in his turn, *added* to the thought of the British Idealists was an explicitly juristic dimension.

Gierke argued that sovereignty is an attribute not of some part of the state but of the whole organized community with the consequence that it is impossible to make the state logically prior to the law or to make law

[96] B. Bosanquet, *The Philosophical Theory of the State* (London: Macmillan, 1899).

[97] Boucher, 'British Idealism, the State, and International Relations', above n. 84, 671, 676.

[98] *Ibid.* Maitland, 'The Crown as Corporation', above n. 1, reports a variation of this – that until they are convinced that states can sin, many people will refuse to accept that they are real people with a real will.

[99] Adherents included Ramsey MacDonald, Asquith, Haldane, Milner, Beveridge and Toynbee. See, further, Dyson, *The State Tradition in Western Europe*, above n. 86 pp. 187, 191. For arguments about how progressive their politics were, see J. Harris, 'Political; Thought and the Welfare State 1870–1940: An Intellectual Framework for Social Policy', *Past and Present* 135 (1992), 116–41.

[100] Some commentators suggested Bosanquet and Austin could be read together – something Bosanquet himself strenuously denied. See B. Bosanquet, *The Philosophical Theory of the State*, 2nd edn, (London: Macmillan, 1910), p. lv.

logically prior to the state. Each exists, in, for and by the other.[101] Law is neither prior to, or the command of, the state, but is part of the organism that makes the state as a whole. Law's role is to recognize and support the 'real'. In Gierke's work these views did not manifest themselves only as abstract legal theory, but were instead closely connected to doctrinal disputes.[102]

For Maitland too, these were not merely abstract theoretical concerns but conceptions with practical legal doctrinal applications and consequences (albeit different from those which concerned Gierke). Among the practical juristic issues for which Maitland sought to apply these theories was the question of who owed the public debt in the self-governing colonies, and the moral and legal responsibility of the Crown for its torts. In answering these questions, he too suggested that the law's role is to recognize and support the 'real'. His aim was not to exalt the Crown but rather to acknowledge its moral, political and sociological similarities with other forms of group life and thus to undermine its legal privileges, as we shall see in later chapters.

Maitland's views of the state did not, of course, begin and end with the Crown. His claim that other groups in society, while inferior to the state, essentially belong to the same genus would also have important juristic consequences. As such, groups of individuals are neither fictional (as Austin contended) nor dependent on the state for their existence (as the concession theory would have it). Instead they are 'real' in some important sense and should be entitled to organic self-originating life. The state should not be regarded as the source and delegator of all power. He suggested that the UK legislature's parsimonious grant of legal powers to local government, for example, effectively robbed local authorities of their 'moral personality'. In similar vein, he was concerned that the law should support the self-governing life of churches, trade unions and other examples of the English 'fellowships'. It was this last aspect of Maitland's work which would later inspire Laski, Cole, Figgis and Barker of the English political Pluralist movement. They would differ among themselves about the relationship between the state and other groups. (Laski and Cole would even deny that the state is a 'person'.)

[101] Maitland, 'Introduction to Gierke', above n. 68, p. xliii and p. 74 of the Gierke text.

[102] Harris, 'The Transplantation of the Legal Discourse on Corporate Personality Theories', above n. 80, 1427 ff.

The next chapter discusses in more detail how these theories influenced and were used to critique the doctrinal content of the common law. It also identifies important respects in which Maitland's vision was not realized. The point for now is that Maitland shared some of the core commitments of Idealist thought. With the help of Gierke and of some of the contemporary legal debates, this gave Idealist thought something of a juristic dimension. How did these debates contribute to the reconceptualization of legal positivism and the problem of sovereignty in the twentieth century?

The sovereignty debate in the twentieth century

Idealism fared rather better than we might have expected in the first quarter of the twentieth century, given its German associations.[103] The 'bottom-up', societal, more common law friendly account of statehood that Idealism suggested continued to have many adherents, and so much so that there were attempts to *blend* Idealist accounts of statehood with an Austinian account. Bosanquet regarded this as a misreading of his theory and in the second edition to his *Philosophical Theory of the State* (1910) sought to correct this attempt, emphasizing (*contra* Austin) how much his view 'prohibits the separation between positive law, and will, custom or sentiment'.[104] Later, the Idealist philosopher Lindsay would again ask whether the two theories of sovereignty could be read together. In an article that anticipates Hart's *The Concept of Law*, he ends up rejecting both. Lindsay begins by asking whether it is possible to reconcile Austin's view that in order for there to be law there must be a distinction between sovereign and subject (those who command and those who obey), with Austin's concession that in a democratic system it would be possible for everyone (or nearly everyone but children and the disenfranchised) to command. The answer Lindsay offers (long before Hart) is this:[105]

103 Hobhouse's critique is the most well-known – but see S. Collini, 'Hobhouse, Bosanquet and the State: Philosophical Idealism and Political Argument in England 1880–1918', *Past and Present* 72 (1976), 86–111, who suggests that Hobhouse, in fact, had a lot in common with Idealist thought.

104 B. Bosanquet, *The Philosophical Theory of the State*, 2nd edn (London: MacMillan, 1910), pp. 259, 261.

105 A. D. Lindsay, 'Sovereignty', *Proceedings of the Aristotelian Society* 24 (1923–4), 235–54, 243.

> It is surely obvious that the main fact about all modern constitutional governments is not that the bulk of the society obey certain persons, but that they accept a certain constitution and that they obey the commands of certain determinate persons, because they have got into authority through the working of the constitution and in so far as their commands are within the limits of the constitution.

This looks close to saying that the 'law is sovereign'. This is not a solution available to Austin himself because he is wedded to the idea that the sovereign is illimitable, and pre-legal, and that constitutional law is not law but only positive morality. Once one allows constitutional rules to be law, Lindsay argues, we are able not only to resolve deficiencies in Austin's theory, but also in the Idealist account of the state. The problem with the collective will is its indeterminateness: 'Bosanquet supplies no link between this common life of society and the political machinery'.[106] Lindsay, by contrast, argues that we must think of the political machinery of society as having the common life behind it. Sovereignty is not *inherent* in persons or personhood[107] – it is determined by constitutional rules:[108]

> [T]he persons who constitute government, be they few or many, cannot act as a government except as in so far as they conform to certain principles – constitutional principles that are not the command of the sovereign.

Here we see the beginnings of a critique of Austin based on the different kinds of rules that exist in a complex system. In the meantime, a sometimes related debate continued in the Anglo-American legal literature about the nature of legal personality of the corporation and the group and whether it was based on a concession theory, a fiction theory or a real entity theory (the US debates also included the contractual theory). At the beginning of the twentieth century, many of these discussions were overtly political and informed by the ideas of the Maitland-inspired, political Pluralist movement. Their commitments differed in emphasis and changed radically over time. What joined them as a movement were shared concerns about freedom in the face of growing power and authority in the state. They saw group associations such as churches and trade unions, and even the League of Nations, as bulwarks against the sovereign state, and as a means by which to defend individual liberty. In his early work, Laski, a prominent lawyer and

[106] *Ibid.*, 253. [107] *Ibid.*, 250. [108] *Ibid.*, 235.

Pluralist, would go further than Maitland to suggest that power is distributed rather than delegated (an argument which both reprises the anti-centralization debates of the earlier nineteenth century from the Left, and anticipates the anti-delegation critique from the Right after World War I). He imagined the world as comprised of small, autonomous and self-sufficient communities, sometimes transcending territorial boundaries. Law's role was to reflect these institutions. The existence of law did not depend on a particular source but rather on the level of acceptance it acquired.[109] At first highly suspicious of the sovereign state and its absolutist claims, in the 1930s, however, he would take up the cause of 'capturing' it for the Left.[110]

Much of the discussion of these ideas in the legal literature took the form of expositions of the historical bases of church and other forms of group life and their independence of the state. Other articles asked questions about the basis of the state's personality alongside questions about legal personality more generally.[111] As the century wore on, however, more analytically-oriented theorists, who would emphasize the artificiality of legal personality as a concept, would come to dominate the debate.[112] By 1930 two important contributions threatened to end the discussion. Dewey suggested that the different theories of group personality served different purposes in different historical contexts[113] and Berle and Means noticed that in business corporations, power had

[109] H. J. Laski, *Studies in Law and Politics* (New Haven, CT: Yale University Press, 1932), p. 247.

[110] L. Jaffe, 'Law Making By Private Groups', *Harvard Law Review* 51 (1937–8), 201–53, 210.

[111] E.g., W. Brown, 'The Personality of the Corporation and the State', *Law Quarterly Review* 21 (1905), 365–79; A. W. Machen, 'Corporate Personality', *Harvard Law Review* 24 (1910–11), 253–67; W. Geldart, 'Legal Personality', *Law Quarterly Review* 27 (1911), 90–108; H. J. Laski, 'The Personality of Associations', *Harvard Law Review* 29 (1915–16), 404–26; H. J. Laski, 'The Responsibility of the State in England', *Harvard Law Review* 32 (1918–19) 447–72; W. W. Willoughby, 'The Juristic Conception of the State', *American Political Science Review* 12 (1918) 192–208; Z. Chafee, 'The Internal Affairs of Associations Not For Profit', *Harvard Law Review* 43 (1929–30), 993–1029, but see more recently A. J. Jacobsen, 'The Private Use of Public Authority: Sovereignty and Associations in the Common Law', *Buffalo Law Review* 29 (1980) 599–666.

[112] G. Deiser, 'The Juristic Person III', *University of Pennsylvania Law Review* 57 (1909), 300–14; P. Vinogradoff, 'Juridical Persons', *Columbia Law Review* 24 (1924), 594–604; M. Wolff, 'On the Nature of Legal Persons', *Law Quarterly Review* 54 (1938), 494–521; E. Merrick Dodd, 'Dogma and Practice in the Law of Associations', *Harvard Law Review* 42 (1928–9), 977–1014.

[113] J. Dewey, 'The Historic Background of Corporate Legal Personality', *Yale Law Journal* 35 (1925–6), 655–73.

shifted from shareholders to managers.[114] But as Twining acknowledges, the theory of legal personality remained a staple in classic analytical jurisprudence texts and continued to be taught and examined into the 1950s.[115] Classic puzzles would include questions about whether a corporation could exist without any members or only a single member, about the legal personality of a Hindu idol or Caligula's horse, about whether a corporation could enjoy nationality[116] and (in a US variation), about whether a prohibition on selling land to an African-American could apply to a church corporation composed entirely of African-American members.[117]

Post mortem on the body politic

Given the currency of these debates in the jurisprudential literature of the first half of the century, it is not surprising that Hart should choose the topic of legal personality as the subject for his inaugural lecture. We can see in that presentation many of the ideas which would later come to inform his work *The Concept of Law.* At the time he gave the lecture, he reported that it would be 'said by many that the juristic controversy over the nature of the corporate personality is dead. If so we have a corpse and the opportunity to learn from its anatomy.'[118] Hart's use of the body metaphor is deliberate. The article attempts to lay the bodily metaphor – associated at least since medieval times with the state – finally to rest. Hart sets out to analyse, as a general matter, the method by which the debate had lately been transacted, to suggest why the debate has not been helpful in answering lawyers' questions and to make some general observations about the relationship between legal concepts and the 'world of fact'.[119] 'What is a corporation?' or 'what is a state?' are not

114 See W. L. Twining, *General Jurisprudence: Understanding Law From a Global Perspective* (Cambridge University Press, 2009), Chapter 15, 'Some Basic Concepts' on-line resource p. 4.

115 *Ibid.*, especially at fn 13 where different jurisprudential texts are compared in detail.

116 *R* v. *Arnaud* (1846) 115 ER 1485.

117 *People's Pleasure Park Co* v. *Rohleder*, 109 Va 439, 61 S E 794 (1908) – the Court held that this did not violate a condition that title should never vest in 'persons of African descent': referred to in B. Smith, 'Legal Personality', *Yale Law Journal* 37 (1928) 283–99, 297.

118 H. L. A. Hart, 'Definition and Theory in Jurisprudence', reproduced in H. L. A. Hart, *Essays in Jurisprudence and Philosophy* (Oxford: Clarendon Press, 1983) (first published 1953).

119 *Ibid.*, p. 23.

proper questions for lawyers to ask, he claims, without reference to the sentence in which the concepts are being used. Better to ask: 'Under what types of conditions does the law ascribe liabilities to corporations or the state?' Hart explains that no legal terms have strict counterparts in the world of fact. He rejects the 'realist' method as an unreliable means of explaining the world as it is. We should not begin by defining an abstraction such as the corporation or the state and from that deduce what its powers and liabilities should be. The process of analogizing about the liabilities of corporations from the liabilities of individuals does not yield eternal or universal truths about identity – it is simply an analogy which should be evaluated against an independent standard of justice. Legal personality is defined by the application of particular legal rules in particular legal contexts, not by some inquiry into the moral character of a particular kind of legal person. There is nothing inherent about it.

In making these arguments, Hart calls in aid of ordinary language philosophy – statements are not the representations of a social reality: statements are themselves constitutive of the social reality.[120] In the process, Hart goes out of his way to suggest that the great Maitland never explicitly accepted the Realist doctrine of Gierke, as others, such as Barker, have suggested.[121] According to Hart, while Maitland thought that the concession and fiction theories did not properly describe the facts, he left the question of the method of analysis under which the corporation could be thought to be 'real' ultimately unanswered. Adopting Maitland's example,[122] Hart seeks to identify the relevant legal rules under which a sentence like 'Nusquamia[123] owes you money' is true as a conclusion of law. Hart rejects Realist metaphysics and offers an alternative method by which to ascertain what is true or real *as a matter of law*. In his emphasis on legal rules in complex relation to social fact, and in his distrust of realist metaphysics, he anticipates some of the central themes of *The Concept of Law* which would appear seven years later.[124]

120 Cotterrell, *The Politics of Jurisprudence*, above n. 18, p. 87.

121 Hart, 'Definition and Theory in Jurisprudence', above n. 118, p. 37. He calls in aid J. A. Mack, 'Group Personality – A Footnote to Maitland', *Philosophical Quarterly* 2 (1952), 249–52.

122 F. W. Maitland, 'Moral Personality and Legal Personality', above n. 60, pp. 304, 318, 319.

123 Latin for 'never-never land'.

124 See also N. Lacey, *A Life of H. L. A. Hart: The Nightmare and the Noble Dream* (Oxford University Press, 2004), p. 157.

The theory Hart expounds in *The Concept of Law* meets selected concerns of both Idealist and Positivist thought. He provides a place in a theory of law for constitutional law and for customary law (for which Green, Bosanquet and Lindsay had argued). Through the idea of the secondary rules of recognition, he maintains a distinction between the government and the governed that was so important to Austin and which the Idealists tended to collapse in the idea of the collective will. He ultimately grounds *all* law in social fact as Maitland as well as the Idealists were inclined to do, and not in a limited set of social facts as Austin did. In so doing he explicates some of the complex varieties of legal rules and their relationships to each other. At the same time, he also rejects Kelsen's views about legal systems ultimately being grounded by purely legal norms. While he later regretted his description of the concept of law as an exercise in 'descriptive sociology' and has been much criticized for it, one can discern here an attempt to provide an analytical approach to such a descriptive project. Through secondary rules of recognition, he simultaneously allows constitutional limits on power, while giving officials collectively a crucial role in determining those limits. This is an attempt to suggest that the law's role is to recognize the sociologically real, as Gierke would have it – but one that substitutes a more analytical methodology for Idealist metaphysics.

It is Austin (and not the Idealists) who is Hart's putative target in *The Concept of Law.*[125] One of Hart's criticisms of Austin is that a habit of obedience may explain the sovereign nature of Rex I but gives no basis for the obligation of obedience to the successor Rex II on the death of Rex I. Habits are not normative and do not render obedience to future legislators likely.[126] There must be a place in any system of law for the rules that govern who can be the rule maker. There needs to be room in a *theory of law* for those rules that constitute the sovereign itself. Such rules not only determine questions of succession in the case of Rex I and II but also help to distinguish when a monarch is acting in the character of a monarch and when he is 'giving private orders to his mistress'.[127] Hart suggests that the analytical shorthand technique of referring to the sovereign or Rex as a personified entity leaves little room for identifying officials in complex political systems. Once one moves from the simple

[125] H. L. A. Hart, *The Concept of Law* (Oxford: Clarendon Press, 1961).
[126] *Ibid.*, p. 58. [127] *Ibid.*, p. 68.

case of sovereign Rex to that of a democratic state, greater elaboration of the rules that constitute the 'sovereign' are required and a place must be found for those rules in one's concept of law.

Hart attributes much misunderstanding to the very idea of the sovereign Rex: 'Whenever the word 'sovereign' appears in jurisprudence, there is a tendency to associate with it the idea of a person above the law whose word is law for his inferiors or subjects.'[128] He also rejects the idea that standing behind a limited legislature, the ultimate repository of sovereignty is 'the people'. If that were the case, he argues, there would be nothing to distinguish between 'revolution and legislation,'[129] constitutional change and rebellion. There can be no personified sovereign standing behind the limited legislature: the sovereign cannot be identified with the electorate, the legislature or the officials of a modern state. He explicitly rejects the idea that a complex democratic legal system ought to be conceived as a personified sovereign at all. What gives a modern legal system unity is not a personified notion of sovereign but a complex system of primary rules and secondary rules about which officials and others hold a shared (internal) view.

We shall take Hart's characterization of the problem and his proffered solution in turn. The personification of the sovereign is not as central to Austin's theory as Hart alleges. After all, Austin himself considered personifications to be a form of shorthand betokening fiction – rather than as representations of 'the real'. Indeed, Austin's theory not only allows for a sovereign Rex but also for a 'conceptual' sovereign defined by generic description.[130] Parts of the determinate body can be defined by law: it is the whole that is undefined by law and illimitable. Austin explicitly mentions the Act of Settlement (which determines succession) as a constitutional rule that would qualify as law rather than positive morality.[131] He even discusses irregularities in the succession of the Roman Emperor and the maxim that the King never dies.[132]

Others have also noticed the puzzling emphasis that Hart gives to Austin's 'error' of personification.[133] One plausible explanation is that Austin is not, in fact, Hart's sole, or even true, target. While it is Austin

[128] *Ibid.*, p. 221. [129] *Ibid.*, p. 78.

[130] See, e.g., Cotterrell, *The Politics of Jurisprudence*, above n. 18, p. 69; M. D. Bayles, *Hart's Legal Philosophy: An Examination* (Dordrecht: Kluwer, 1992), pp. 36–7.

[131] Austin, *Province of Jurisprudence Determined*, above n. 15, p. 218.

[132] *Ibid.*, p. 132.

[133] See Cotterrell, *The Politics of Jurisprudence*, above n. 18, and Bayles, *Hart's Legal Philosophy*, above n. 130.

whom Hart accuses of personifying the sovereign, there are much more obvious offenders – the Idealists in particular. We now know from sources outside of the writing itself that Hart was reacting to the metaphysical versions of statehood associated with continental theorists, and more latterly with Fascism. Everything German, especially theories of statehood, fellowships and groups would become blighted after World War II. These Hegelian-derived theorists may well have been his primary target. This is consistent too with the general efforts of Oxford philosophers at the time to substitute 'common sense' for continental metaphysics.[134] Hart later stated that his aim had been to:[135]

> [puncture] claims that the state was really reinforcing the real will of its citizens, and therefore they must obey, and they are obeying themselves which is in Rousseau and is a travesty perhaps of Hegel – but it is there.

He sought to endow analytical jurisprudence with a 'healthy immunity'[136] to this kind of metaphysics. By substituting a system of rules for a personified sovereign, he may not only have (as Leslie Green puts it in the very bodily metaphor that Hart rejected) 'chopped off the King's head'[137] but also buried the body where it could not be found. It is the final break from a political tradition that 'bodified' the 'common wealth' and which had its beginnings in medieval theology.

Hart's solution is to substitute an 'ultimate rule of recognition which provides a system of rules with its own criteria of validity' for Austin's 'habit of obedience to a legally unlimited sovereign'. For a complex legal system to exist, it is a minimum requirement that the bulk of the *citizens* must generally obey the primary rules, and *officials* must accept as common public standards the secondary rules specifying the criteria for legal validity and for legal change and critically appraise their own and others' actions against such criteria.[138] Hart creates a place in legal theory for the rules that constitute the sovereign and in so doing he creates the possibility that the sovereign can be limited by law.

[134] Lacey, *A Life of H. L. A. Hart*, above n. 124, p. 139 ff.

[135] D. Sugarman, 'Hart Interviewed: H. L. A. Hart in Conversation with David Sugarman,' *Journal of Law and Society* 32 (2005), 267–93, 292.

[136] *Ibid.*

[137] L. Green, 'General Jurisprudence: A 25th Anniversary Essay', *Oxford Journal of Legal Studies* 25 (2005) 565–80, 575.

[138] Hart, *The Concept of Law*, above n. 125, pp. 116 ff.

A solution and some new problems

Hart appears, then, to have solved a number of problems of legal theory. As an explanation of democratic constitutional systems, it is more compelling than Austin's and the Idealists'. The state has now been made the subject of legal rules. Hart tells us that public power is constituted by a set of rules and that sovereignty may be limited. Moreover, he tells us that *all* legal persons are constituted by rules, being the subjects of particular rights and duties. There is no sovereign (whether Rex or the electorate) standing behind the law or the legislature.[139] The rules are instead constitutive of the sovereign – whether or not it is legally limited.[140]

In terms of our particular inquiry into the nature of the British state, Hart's theory has important explanatory force. It is no longer an attribute of a legal system per se that the sovereign is unlimited by law. Hart also offers an explanation of how the Crown in the English common law is able to enjoy distinct 'personalities' and can on different occasions represent: the state as a whole in international law; the public; the executive government of the day; and even sometimes the law itself. The Crown can also be manifest as an entity lacking legal personality or be likened to an ordinary private person. There is, then, no single *personne morale* that is the state. The moral qualities that the state enjoys are not inherent in the definition of statehood itself but are themselves the product of rules. The state as a legal person has no inherent moral qualities from which its capacities and liabilities can be deduced. It enjoys different relationships with its citizens in these different legal guises. The essential personality of the Crown/state is no longer a central matter for political and jurisprudential theory as Maitland had thought.

While Hart's approach to legal personality describes the law better than Idealist abstraction or Austinian reductionism, questions about the relationship between the state, the law and the citizen remain. Hart does not explicitly offer us any account of the state at all. He never distinguishes between the state as juristic person and the state understood as legal system. All is left to the secondary rules and the internal point of view. The unity of the legal order presupposes the prior unity of the state as a matter of social fact – and is the product of the internal point of view of officials. Legal rules are a form of social rules and their legal validity is ultimately grounded in observable social facts.

139 *Ibid.*, pp. 70–6. 140 *Ibid.*, p. 75.

Where we are meant to look for these social facts creates something of a conundrum as Bayles explains:[141]

> The rule of recognition is identified in the practice of officials. Yet, who are officials is to be determined by secondary power-conferring rules of the system and these rules must be valid by the rule of recognition. Consequently, one determines the rule of recognition by considering the practice of officials, but one can only determine who are officials by using the rule of recognition.

This means that once officials have been recognized as officials, it is left to officials to determine whether they are acting as organs of the state. Not only is the question of 'who decides who decides' a matter for political (or social fact), but as we shall see, in certain circumstances officials are also able to choose how the state should be manifested *as a legal subject* and hence which legal constraints apply to it. We are not here primarily interested in the 'state of the exception' – involving the Schmittian spectre of a sovereign acting above or apart from the law – but in the much more routine and 'ordinary' case of officials deciding which legal personification should attach to the state and hence which laws should limit and control its actions and its relationship to the public. This suggests that legal systems are not just *ultimately* self-constituting but are much more routinely so.

Consider some examples that arise from the common practices of governments. A government wants to do X. It could enter into an international treaty setting up an international body to do X (which would be binding in international law, whether or not the treaty complied with a nation's domestic constitutional law), it could contract with B to do X or it could use its own property to do X. In each case the government pursues its policies under a distinct set of power-conferring rules which simultaneously confer on its organs a distinct juristic personality and a distinct relation with its citizens. According to Hart, such power-conferring rules are akin to the secondary rules and confer on persons the ability to change their positions under primary rules. In each of these guises the 'state' or government acts as a kind of law or rule giver.[142] It is not only the case that under Hart's theory it is the internal

[141] Bayles, *Hart's Legal Philosophy*, above n. 130, 81.

[142] Hart treats rules of property and contract as a special class of power conferring rules, pp. 116 ff. He says that many of the features that puzzle us in the institutions of contract and property are clarified by thinking of the operations of making a contract or transferring property as the exercise of limited law-making powers by individuals.

practices of officials which as a minimum give the primary rules generated under treaty, contract or property their force, it is a subset of those officials who decide which power-conferring rules to choose when pursuing their policies. While strictly, it is secondary rules of recognition that give rules generated under contract, property and treaties their force, it looks, superficially at least, as though it is the government or officials who are able to choose the power-conferring source of those rules – the very relationship Hart was trying to avoid in relation to the sovereign and the law. And if the government apparatus may enjoy different rights and duties of personhood in different contexts, for example, in the diplomatic sphere, in contract, tort, administrative, constitutional or human rights law – is there a hierarchy between these in the event of conflict? If it is continuity that defines the state as a legal system, does that suggest that constitutional and administrative law should take precedence over, say, contract or tort law, when defining juristic personhood, as Raz speculates?[143] And what about the exercise of power-conferring rules by private associations in making their own rules and constitutions. Where do these rules fit within a legal hierarchy? In other words where does legal instrument choice fit within this analysis?

The question of what the relationship should be between the state as a legal system and the state as a juristic person is, of course, not 'new' and neither has it necessarily always been treated by legal theorists as a matter best left to 'parochial jurisprudence' or legal doctrine. By the time that Hart was writing, Kelsen had identified this as a central issue.[144] Kelsen absolutely rejects 'dualist' views about the law and the state – especially those associated with the German constitutional theorist Georg Jellinek who was writing at the turn of the century.[145] Dualist theories allow the state to be manifested as a *pre-legal* person standing behind the legal system, and, *simultaneously*, as a legal subject within that legal system. According to Jellinek, the state is essentially different from law, is contrasted with law and is *at the same time* essentially legal in character. This

[143] J. Raz, *The Authority of Law: Essays on Law and Morality* (Oxford: Clarendon Press, 1979), p. 100.

[144] H. Kelsen, *Introduction to the Problems of Legal Theory* B. Paulson and S. Paulson (tr.) (Oxford University Press, 1992). He says: 'The assumption that the legal person is a reality different from individual human beings, a reality, yet curiously imperceptible to the senses, or a supra-individual organism made up of individual human beings – this is a naive hypostatization of a thought, of a heuristic legal notion', p. 49

[145] G. Jellinek, *Allegmeine Staatslehre* (1900) discussed in L.Vinx, *Hans Kelsen's Pure Theory of Law: Legality and Legitimacy* (Oxford: Clarendon Press, 2007), pp. 15–19.

is exactly the kind of analysis, a version of which is more famously associated with the work of Carl Schmitt, that Kelsen sought to discredit by his identity thesis.

Kelsen's solution is to regard the state and the law as identical. Law is not the servant of politics: instead the political authority of the state is derived from law itself. He denies the capacity of the sovereign to create the exception or to suspend the law. For Kelsen the state can personify the comprehensive legal system or, in a different guise, the organs of a legal subsystem. What we refer to as the bureaucracy or the organs of the state is merely a subsystem of the law whereby the actions of particular individual officials are attributed to the sub-part of the whole, for example, for liability or act of state purposes. The personification merely expresses the unity of certain rules *within a legal hierarchy.*[146] The question of whether an act is performed by a collective legal person is one of imputation: can the acts of an individual person be attributed to that legal person? That answer also relies on legal rules and norms. Validity derives from a hierarchy of norms which ultimately depends on the basic norm. Kelsen assumes a hierarchy of legal rules which would determine which personification should prevail *as a matter of law.*

Kelsen's theory does not include an account of the political. Hart, by contrast, would leave these issues ultimately to be resolved by rules of recognition. His response would be that these are not questions legal theory can answer: they must ultimately be resolved as questions of political and social fact. Or he would simply say that it is a matter for the parochial law of a particular jurisdiction to evolve rules of recognition which can resolve the question of how the state is manifest as a legal person. But Raz is correct to suggest that in doing so Hart's theory leaves out something important. Moreover, regardless of whether or not we agree about the importance of such matters within a *general* theory of law, these are questions that the common law *is* being asked to answer. If that requires us to look to the content of particular law – so be it. It is only when we look at the *content* of legal controversies that we can begin to see more clearly the more general issues at stake.

In examining the moral content of the laws that define and constrain sovereigns we are forced to confront once again issues about states and their moral personalities. Should international legal commitments that the state as a unity has entered, prevail over domestic human rights and

[146] *Ibid.*, p. 48.

constitutional understandings of statehood? Should judges be treated as the state for the purposes of human rights obligations when separation of powers rules would protect them under domestic legal systems? Should public law constraints of procedure and rationality apply to government contracts? To what extent is the government entitled to a private life when it uses private legal instruments? How the state is conceived as a juristic person affects citizens in different ways.

Summary

In this chapter, we have seen that attempts to conceive of the state as a legal person contributed to the sovereignty debate. By the mid-twentieth century, theory had caught up with the facts – the sovereign could be limited by law, and constitutional law has a recognized place as law. The issues of what constitutional rules a legal system should adopt, how the relationship between the state and the citizen should be reflected in law, and whether and how the state should be held responsible in law, previously treated as matters of political and legal theory, now tend to be relegated to the detail of parochial legal doctrine. If it is now accepted that the state should be able to be limited by law, how then should we go about constructing the state as a moral and legal person? The following chapters turn to those matters of doctrine and attempt to take those doctrinal discussions seriously as a variety of political thought.

4

Civil society: the English fellowships, the state and the origins of welfare

[T]he incurably clubbable spirit of the English character[1]

'[D]emocratic pioneers of mutual insurance' and 'channels for the spirit of voluntary service'[2]

The clubbable English character

In the last chapter we saw how the legal and moral personality of groups was used to challenge the distinctiveness and sovereignty claims of the state in analytical jurisprudence. In this chapter, I investigate in more detail how the relationship between the state and civil society was conceived as a matter of legal doctrine in British thought and administrative practice up until the establishment of the welfare state.

Exactly who or what comprises 'civil society' is the subject of much debate among contemporary political theorists. Does it refer to institutions in the public sphere, arrangements in the private sphere or to the area of intersection and interaction between the two?[3] Is it the same thing as David Cameron's 'Big Society'? The British tradition, going back to Hobbes, has tended to regard the state *itself* as a fundamental institution of civil society.[4] While Hobbes, for example, insists that every 'lesser Commonwealth' or association should be regarded in law as a

1 E. Macadam, *The New Philanthrophy: A Study of the Relations Between the Statutory and Voluntary Social Services* (London: Allen & Unwin, 1934), pp. 28–9.

2 W. Beveridge, *Voluntary Action: A Report on Methods of Social Advance* (New York: Macmillan, 1948), p. 23 describing friendly societies.

3 Paraphrasing J. Harris, *Civil Society in British History* (Oxford University Press, 2003), p. 5.

4 Harris argues that British writers (such as Hobbes, Locke, Adam Ferguson and Henry Maine) have tended to regard the state itself as a fundamental institution of civil society. There is an argument that the German theorists treat the matter differently and think of civil society as something distinct from the state (including markets, vocational corporations and organs of municipal government). See *ibid.*, at pp. 5, 24–5.

creature of or licensed by the state, that is precisely for the reason that the state too is a Commonwealth – it shares the same genus. He would not allow such lesser Commonwealths to compete with the state for power, but Hobbes nevertheless recognizes that both the state and the group are able to generate their own personalities and to compete for the loyalty of their members. Centuries later Maitland may have disagreed with Hobbes about what the law's role should be in regulating these lesser corporations, but he shared with him important starting premises: the state and the association are of the same genus; they are both corporations; they have competing moral claims on their members;[5] they exist in the public sphere. These shared premises tend to suggest that the British state has been conceived as much more 'embedded' in the structures of everyday life than the more 'abstract' state of continental Europe.[6] The other characteristic of British, as contrasted with continental, thinking is an ambivalence toward conceiving of civil society in primarily economic terms.[7] These two themes have a particular resonance in the early twentieth-century legal story.

The question that this chapter attempts to address is how British law and public administration imagined and mediated the relationship between the state and other parts of civil society up until the advent of the welfare state. Where does the state end and civil society begin? This is not intended solely as an historical account. It anticipates the debates in contemporary law about the nature and operation of so-called 'public function' tests which, after privatization or so-called 're-privatization' and the partial dismantling of the welfare state, have been used to determine whether public law obligations should attach to a 'private body' or voluntary association. The historical account contains resources with which to challenge a number of presumptions made in the contemporary application of public function tests, which tend to assign 'public function status' only to entities vested with duties delegated from central government and subject to central government control.

In this chapter, we shall see how the voluntary sector bequeathed much by way of functions, democratic engagement, initiative, expertise

5 See, further, the argument in D. Runciman, *Pluralism and the Personality of the State* (Cambridge University Press, 1997).

6 Harris, *Civil Society in British History*, above n. 3, pp. 35–6. Policing, public administration and the enforcement of law would be considered part of overarching political authority and not matters for civil society, as they were in Hegelian thought.

7 E. Barker, *Political Thought in England from Herbert Spencer to Present Day* (New York: Holt, 1915), p. 67. This point is further explored in the next chapter.

and even nascent public law principles to the centralizing state. Despite the best efforts of Maitland and others, the independent activities of 'not for profit' corporations came increasingly under central control as they progressively became the subject of delegated rather than self-originating power. Moreover, in their entanglements with the state, associations were often robbed of their independence and democratic life. This was not a contest between public and private norms – both civil society and governmental agencies very much occupied the public sphere. The contest was about authority and democracy. As we shall see, the 1980s concept of 're-privatization' – that functions performed by public agencies were *returning* to the private sphere – is an anachronism.

In Chapters 8 and 9, we shall return to the contemporary debates but only after we have established how, and on what basis, *different* legal standards (immunities, public law obligations and private law obligations) came to apply to different areas of the public sphere, distinctions which only fully emerge later in our story.

This chapter is in two parts. It begins with Maitland and his historical analysis of the place of the English fellowships and their relationship to the state. While his was also an historical account, it was not without relevance to legal developments taking place at the time he was writing. His views achieved some, limited, reception in the legal doctrine and in the work of the political Pluralists. Ultimately, however, his historical and theoretical contributions about moral and legal personality would not contain the resources necessary to protect the English fellowships from the challenges wrought by their increasing entanglements with the state. In the second half of the chapter, we turn to the period in which Britain went from being one of the most voluntarist societies in Europe to its most centralized and bureaucratic welfare state. What joins these two stories is that they both tend to reinforce the view that the state and civil society share important characteristics.

Maitland: the state genus

As we saw in the previous chapter, Hegel distinguishes between the state and civil society in a way which appears to be counter-intuitive to British thought. He views the state in a very abstract way, and counts among the functions of 'civil society' administration, policing and the enforcement of law – functions we would also associate (though not necessarily exclusively) with the state and Crown. British thought has tended to reject a fundamental distinction between the state and civil society.

Hobbes, Locke, Adam Ferguson and Henry Maine, 'portrayed the state itself as the fundamental institution of civil society'.[8] At the end of the nineteenth century, Maitland attempted to instantiate that relationship juridically: the state and other forms of group life are essentially of the same genus. Here too he was drawing on a much older British tradition going back to Hobbes: the state and the English fellowships (Maitland's term) are corporations. The lesser commonwealths share important elements in common with the greatest.

The idea that the state and the corporation are joined concepts had a general currency in Anglo-American legal thought at the end of the nineteenth and the beginning of the twentieth century. In the US, Freund's *The Legal Nature of Corporations* appeared in 1897. Carr's *General Principles of the Law of Corporations* appeared in England in 1905. Both discuss state and government institutions as a variety of corporation – and it is probably no coincidence that both authors go on to contribute to the emerging field of administrative law (which will be discussed in Chapter 6). Legal scholarship did not divide corporate law from public law in ways it does today. If it were accepted that the state and corporation shared important legal aspects in common, however, commentators tended to differ on the question of what should follow from this shared genus. As we have seen, for Hobbes and Sidgwick, the similarities between state and other forms of civil society were a reason for the state to control such other forms. For Maitland and his followers, by contrast, the fact of their shared genus meant that the state should not be viewed as the source and delegator of corporate power. Corporate status should not be considered the gift or grant of the state, as the concession theory presumed.[9] In the previous chapter, we saw how Maitland's claims about the moral and political life of the lesser Commonwealths posed a challenge to Austinian sovereignty. In this chapter, we will focus on the more doctrinal aspects of that challenge.

[8] Harris, *Civil Society in British History*, above n. 3, p. 5.

[9] Maitland seemed to allow that the concession theory had been accepted by the English canonists, but suggested it had never really been entirely 'taken to heart' by the common law and that the trust had allowed English law to avoid its worst consequences: F. W. Maitland, 'Introduction' in O. Gierke, *Political Theories of the Middle Age* F. W. Maitland (tr.) (Cambridge University Press, 1958), p. xxx (first edition published in 1900) ('Introduction to Gierke'). Pollock, by contrast, spiritedly argued that the concession theory had never been accepted into the common law of England (F. Pollock, 'Has the Common Law Received a Fiction Theory of Corporations?', *Law Quartely Review.* 27 (1911), 219–35, 228).

The Roman law-derived concession theory treated corporations as artificial or fictitious creations of the state. As such they were capable of enjoying proprietary rights but incapable of knowing, willing, intending or acting. According to Maitland, such a conception reduced every corporation to a mindless inert group of individuals: 'no subject for "liberties and franchises" or "rights of self-government"'.[10] The theme of self-government can be found throughout Maitland's writing – he raises the issue in relation to the colonies, local government and other forms of English fellowship such as friendly societies and guilds. Unlike Austin, Maitland supported the enlarged franchise and this gives his historical work more political salience. And it is this particular aspect of Maitland's work that attracted the interest of his Pluralist adherents in the early decades of the twentieth century. Corporations, he argued, should be the crucible where participation and democracy is learned. This was not an idea foreign to Victorian culture. Participation in the whole range of institutions of public life was proof of one's respectability and character.

Maitland went further to contend that given that associations do not depend on the state for their existence, the law (meaning here the common law rather than legislation) should recognize their *real* existence. The English fellowships should enjoy both powers and responsibilities like other persons.[11] For Maitland, and for many of the British Idealist movement as well, this is part of having a real moral and legal personality. The controversial legal question should be why *some* groups, which are undeniably real (partnerships and unincorporated associations for example) are *not* recognized in law as having a separate corporate existence.[12] Power should be viewed as distributed rather than delegated, and customary authority defended. There is a strong reprise here to what was described in Chapter 2 as a

[10] Maitland, 'Introduction to Gierke', p. xxi. This provoked Barker to declare Roman law, to be 'the law of an unassociative people – absolutist in its treatment of the state, and individualistic in its treatment of its members'. E. Barker, 'Introduction' in O. Gierke, *Natural Law and the Theory of Society*, E. Barker (tr.) (Cambridge University Press, 1950), p. lix.

[11] Laski would go further to later argue that they ought not to be treated to the strait-jacket of *ultra vires* doctrine.

[12] This is still a question in contemporary Scotland. See Scottish Law Commission, Discussion Paper on Unincorporated Associations, Discussion Paper No. 140 (Edinburgh: The Stationery Office, 2008), p. 2 quoting from N. MacCormick, *Institutions of Law* (Oxford University Press, 2007), p. 84.

Blackstonian view of unified will – that is, sovereign will is dispersed, fragmented and regulated by the common law.

What is immediately striking is that the emphasis on moral allegiance and democratic engagement, when viewed from this historical distance, seems to have little to do with what we tend to think of as the typical corporation – that is the corporation for profit. Where does the corporation for profit fit within Maitland's analysis? Is it part of his civil society? What indeed are the problems motivating his enquiry into the relationship between the state and other forms of civil society?

Corporations for profit: the joint stock company

As others have shown,[13] the adoption of the corporate form for the business enterprise for profit was by no means inevitable, and came rather late in the history of the corporation. By the time Maitland was writing, however, one might have thought that the struggle for legal 'recognition' of the 'for profit' joint stock corporation had been mostly won, at least in Britain.[14] Prior to the nineteenth century, the partnership and unincorporated company had been much more popular, but these forms began to decline in popularity in favour of the publicity, respectability and legal certainty associated with the Parliamentary grant of a Private Act of incorporation.[15] During 1825, near its zenith, Parliament received 438 requests for Private Bills of incorporation of new companies.[16] Practically speaking, the issue of whether incorporation was a privilege that could only be granted by the state had taken up a huge amount of parliamentary time in the earlier nineteenth century. How free Parliament should be with the power to incorporate had been a fiercely contested matter. Lord Eldon, a major figure in the debate, consistently resisted the claims for power by unincorporated bodies, in his judicial capacity,[17] and objected to the liberal grant of the corporate

[13] R. Harris, *Industrializing English Law: Entrepreneurship and Business Organization, 1720–1844* (Cambridge University Press, 2000).

[14] The common law of Scotland was more willing to recognize corporate existence independently of actual registration. The partnership or joint venture does enjoy some elements of separate legal personality. See further P. Ford, 'Supervising Charities: A Scottish Civilian Alternative', *Edinburgh Law Review* 10 (2006), 352–85.

[15] See *Joseph* v. *Pebrer* 3 B & C 639 (1829) and *Kinder* v. *Taylor, Law Journal Reports, Old Series 3, Cases in Chancery 68 (1824–5)* discussed in R. Harris, *Industrializing English Law*, above n. 13, p. 255.

[16] *Ibid.*

[17] *Lloyd* v. *Loaring* (1802) 6 Ves. 773, 778 (involving a Lodge of Freemasons).

form, in his political one. He argued instead for a return to the royal charters of the previous century in which trading companies (such as the East India Company) were closely related to the state and were explicitly required to serve public purposes. A half-way house was established in the Trading Companies Act 1834. It empowered the Crown, by administrative act, rather than Parliament by deliberation, to grant the privilege of suing and being sued in the name of the principal officers of an unincorporated association, without granting formal incorporation.[18]

Eventually, and despite determined resistance, the Registration Incorporation and Regulation Act 1844 was passed, opening the way to a new liberalized era of the corporate form for joint stock companies.[19] It allowed the incorporation of most enterprises merely through registration.[20] Corporate formation would be subject to and regulated by statute, but 'for the first time in at least 500 years corporations could be formed without explicit, deliberated, and specific State permission'.[21] The central government's new role would indeed be largely to *recognize* but not to *create* the corporate form. Parliamentary and executive control would, for the most part, cede to judicial control. There would be a *quid pro quo*. Corporations would no longer be treated as having common law powers to contract, for example, but would have to enumerate their powers in their Memorandum of Association.[22] Nevertheless, the political battle for the more liberalized availability of the corporate form had been mostly won by mid-nineteenth century at least for corporations 'for profit'. The political contest between rival business enterprises which had been part of the petition system for incorporation would, from now on, find a new *locus* in the competition for licences. Incorporation of 'for profit' enterprise was no longer under the state's lock and key: 'for profit' corporations were pushing on an open door.

[18] An 1837 statute empowered the Crown to grant limitation of liability to principal officers.

[19] It would be copied in France, Germany and the US.

[20] Limited liability would not be available until the Joint Companies Act 1862. Different regulatory regimes applied to railways, banks and public undertakings.

[21] R. Harris, *Industrializing English Law*, above n. 13, p. 284. Banks and railways had been separately regulated before then and the degree of regulation was enhanced in 1844.

[22] In *Ashbury Company* v. *Riche* (1874–5) LR 7 HL 653, it is evident that at least two of the judges took a strict interpretation because the corporation had limited liability and in order to protect future shareholders and company creditors.

Given these hard won legislative achievements, we need an explanation of why Maitland regarded the issue of whether the corporation depended on the state for its existence as one of more than historical interest. Harris is correct to suggest that Maitland was not primarily concerned with business associations, even if his theories about real entities continue to survive most prominently in the corporation, as opposed to public law, literature today.[23] Maitland did not, for example, directly engage in debates about the contractual theory of business incorporation which had already achieved traction in the US literature (though he dismissed contractual explanations of the corporation as too individualistic).[24] He did not, for example, use real entity theory to resist and critique the result in the most notorious English company law case of all time *Salomon* v. *Salomon*[25] (which allowed a sole proprietor to avoid liability by assuming a separate corporate personality).[26] What then was he worried about? One has to read in the contemporary context in order to deduce what his concerns may have been. In so doing we need to view the joint stock company as just one of a variety of examples of collective life in Britain during the same period.

One explanation for Maitland's concern is that state recognition of *for profit* joint stock companies was becoming increasingly permissive at the same time as *not for profit* corporate life was increasingly being brought under central government and judicial supervision and control. This seemed an inversion of historical understandings about the nature of the corporation. For, as Maitland recognizes, the joint stock company is in reality much closer to a partnership, or the more individualistic Roman *societas* (in German, the *Gesellschaft)* than to a corporation or *universitas* with its own artificial personality or juristic personhood.[27] By contrast, *older* forms of collective life, the 'fellowships of English history' (to adopt

[23] R. Harris, 'The Transplantation of the Legal Discourse on Corporate Personality Theories: From German Codification to British Political Pluralism and American Big Business', *Washington and Lee Law Review* 63 (2006), 1421–78. See, e.g., M. J. Phillips, 'Reappraising the Real Entity Theory of the Corporation', *Florida State University Law Review* 21 (1994), 1061–123; D. Millon, 'Theories of Corporation', *Duke Law Journal* (1990) 201–62; M. H. Hager, 'Bodies Politic: The Progressive History of Organizational 'Real Entity' Theory', *University of Pittsburgh Law Review* 50 (1989), 575–654.

[24] V. Morawetz, *A Treatise on the Law of Private Corporations* (Boston, MA: Little Brown, 1882), p. 11 discussed in R. Harris, 'The Transplantation of Legal Discourse', above n. 23, 1468 ff.

[25] [1897] AC 22 (HL).

[26] See also R. Harris 'The Transplantation of Legal Discourse', above n. 23, 1465.

[27] Maitland, 'Introduction to Gierke', above n. 9, pp. xxii–xxiii.

Gierke's terminology)[28] seemed to have much stronger claims to corporate status, being examples of *universitas* rather than *societas*. The towns, villages and boroughs, churches, inns of court, universities, colonial trading companies, companies that had become countries, trade unions, friendly societies and the stock exchange were groups which could much more readily claim both real and juristic existence and an existence that did not depend exclusively on state grant. Yet in the same period as the joint stock corporations were being given freer rein to incorporate, these older and more 'state-like' corporations were being brought steadily under centralized legislative and governmental control. This is a striking turn in administrative organisation and it signals important changes in the legal forms adopted by the newly emerging public realm.

That said, it is important not to view the differences between the 'for profit' sector and other forms of corporate life through too much of a modern lens. They often had common political antecedents. Alborn's study of the nineteenth century politics in joint stock companies in the banking and the railway sector suggests that such associations played important *political* as well as economic roles in the nineteenth century. [29]

The potential of the corporation to serve as a vehicle for self-government had been discovered in the late eighteenth century by middle class free traders who had found that 'they had a better chance to get what they wanted by buying their right to vote in [the East India Company] than by lobbying a Parliament which excluded them'.[30] In the first half of the nineteenth century, new middle class voluntary associations proliferated. Initially they adopted the form of 'subscriber democracies', which took as their administrative and organizational models the joint stock company, the non-conformist chapel and the public house.[31] 'Designed to achieve their aims without reference to government aid or authority',[32] such associations would serve a range of functions

[28] *Ibid.*, p. xxv, where Maitland suggests that 'fellowship' is 'our least inadequate word' for the *Genossenschaft*.

[29] T. L. Alborn, *Conceiving Companies: Joint Stock Politics in Victorian England* (London: Routledge, 2003).

[30] *Ibid.*, p. 24.

[31] R. J. Morris, 'Voluntary Societies and British Urban Elites, 1780–1850', *The Historical Journal* 26(1) (1983), 95–118, 104. For later interactions between the voluntary sector and the state, see J. Lewis, 'The Boundary Between Voluntary and Statutory Social Service in the Late Nineteenth and Early Twentieth Centuries', *The Historical Journal* 39(1) (1996), 155–77.

[32] Morris, 'Voluntary Societies and British Urban Elites', above n. 31, 96.

including pooling funds and manpower, furthering the economic security of their members and responding to typhoid outbreaks and urban economic distress.[33] The subscriber democracy model, then, was used for both philanthropy and mutual assistance.[34] By the middle of the nineteenth century these voluntary associations began to take a variety of different legal forms according to the functions they served. Some of these self-governing clubs and societies subsequently became joint stock banks under legislation enacted in 1844.[35] Others served as a blueprint for provincial reform and improvement associations such as Local Boards of Health created under the Public Health Act 1848 and for local trading enterprises such as gas, lighting and waterworks companies.[36] Even so, remnants of their shared local and voluntarist ideals would *initially* remain apparent. In offering the middle classes a form of democratic participation, security and social services hitherto denied them, for example, the early joint stock banks at first explicitly adopted the language of representation and democracy.[37] Both banks and railway companies would also be at the forefront of pioneering efforts in public administration generating an 'expert' class of officials. And railway and mines companies, in their turn, frequently adopted the role of patron to friendly societies by contributing to the insurance schemes for their worker members.[38]

In Alborn's words: [39]

> As companies evolved [like the state itself from the local and the voluntarist organization] joint-stock politics became part of the very language

[33] Other purposes included educational, benevolent, friendly society, charitable, medical and literary functions.

[34] W. Beveridge suggests that this was even true in societies offering aged care but that it sometimes involved the buying of votes. See Beveridge, *Voluntary Action*, above n. 2

[35] It is not clear exactly why that happened (see Alborn, *Conceiving Companies*, above n. 29, p. 98) but it may have been that increasing regulation of joint stock banks and friendly societies encouraged the embrace of different legal forms.

[36] Alborn, *Conceiving Companies*, above n. 29, p. 96.

[37] Alborn explains that they did not live up to these democratic ideals and the state-run Post Office Savings Bank had to step in to provide gaps in services to the poorer members of society.

[38] D. Weinbren and B. Jones, 'Getting a Grip: the Roles of Friendly Societies in Australia and Britain Reappraised', *Labour History* 88 (2005), 87–103, 91.

[39] Alborn, *Conceiving Companies*, above n. 29, p. 259. See further J. F. Wilson, *Lighting the Town: A Study of Management in the North West Gas Industry 1805–1880* (London: Paul Chapman, 1991); J. Sheldrake, *Municipal Socialism* (Aldershot: Avebury, 1989). Austin used the joint stock metaphor in a derisory way: see W. Rumble, *The Thought of John Austin: Jurisprudence, Colonial Reform and the British Constitution* (London: Athlone, 1985), p. 202.

of state formation. Walter Bagehot prefaced his conservative celebration of the English Constitution by remarking:

> '[The] board of directors of the political company has a few slight changes every year and therefore the shareholders are conscious of no abrupt change.'

The local and voluntarist society was seen in the Victorian era as a place where democratic engagement was learned, character was formed and respectability proven. These goals went beyond the pecuniary and the 'cash nexus'. Given these shared *political* foundations of much of nineteenth-century corporate life, it is plausible to view even joint stock companies as part of the same genus as the state. Maitland was right to understand the difference as one of degree rather than of kind. But as we have indicated, the legal forms and incidents of these different associations were already beginning to change according to the functions they performed. This was particularly true for local government, one of the older forms of corporation.

Local government

Harris suggests that in Germany and England, the work of Gierke and Maitland had no bearing on local government – unlike in the US where it was used to strengthen the localities.[40] There are, however, clear indications that Maitland was concerned with what he called the 'moral capacity' of English local government. While he tends to be elliptical and suggestive in relation to the contemporary significance of his historical findings, Maitland directly argues in at least two places that local government ought to be entrusted with greater self-governing power. Not only does he argue that local officials should 'go beyond the mere registering of the orders of a central bureau',[41] he also suggests in *Township and Borough*[42] that in denying municipalities' self-governing power they are being denied 'moral personality'. This too reflects one of the central preoccupations of the late Victorian era. This was part

[40] R. Harris, 'The Transplantation of legal Discourse, above n. 23, 1426.
[41] *Ibid.*, fn 73.
[42] F. W. Maitland, *Township and Borough: The Ford Lectures 1897, With an Appendix of Notes Relating to the History of Cambridge* (Cambridge University Press, 1898), p. 95. Maitland relied extensively on Gierke's ideas in this work.

of a reaction against the 'mechanical state' and an attempt to reimagine it as an organic and explicitly moral force.[43]

It is tempting to read the liberalization of the joint stock form and municipal government reform at either ends of the same decade as part of the same general political and economic shift of power from the traditional land-owning elites to the new middle class entrepreneurs.[44] There were, of course, important links between the joint stock companies and the reforms of the English boroughs. The expansion of the franchise, which the Municipal Corporations Act 1835 effected, provided new avenues for political participation for many of the same middle class entrepreneurs and radicals who had already been active in joint stock politics. Some local authorities too would later engage in municipal trading enterprises using the same skills, techniques and business structures as joint stock utilities – and in competition with them. But despite their similarities in terms of their people and politics, there was a very important difference in the trajectory of the joint stock companies and the municipal corporations. Paradoxically, municipal corporations would exercise much less by way of organic, or self-originating, power as they were becoming increasingly democratized. Their ability to respond to social needs would, even more than before the reforms, depend on explicit legislative authorization. The functions of the earlier subscriber democracies, and of the vilified pre-1835 corporations, would increasingly be exercised by legislatively mandated bodies.

The reform of local government is a complicated story which has received full treatments elsewhere.[45] Our focus is on the corporate aspects of these changes. Much of the scholarly writing about corporate personality at the end of the Victorian era is devoted to uncovering the ancient corporate existence of towns and boroughs. Since the fifteenth century,[46] the borough had been recognized as a corporate body with its own rights and duties. It is from this time that the practice began of granting corporate status by Charter and recognizing ancient boroughs

[43] See, e.g., the discussion in A. McBriar, *An Edwardian Mixed Doubles: The Bosanquets Versus the Webbs; A Study in British Social Policy, 1890–1929* (Oxford University Press, 1987).

[44] How big that political shift actually was is likely to be quite hard to assess and to have varied according to the locality.

[45] M. Loughlin, *Legality and Locality: The Role of Law in Central–Local Government* (Oxford: Clarendon Press, 1996), pp. 20–1.

[46] Laski disputes the date. See H. J. Laski, 'Early History of the Corporation in England', *Harvard Law Review* 30 (1916–17), 561–88, 578.

as having acquired corporate status by prescription.[47] The courts treated many borough powers, such as the making of by-laws, as *inherent* and the product of local custom.[48] In practice this amounted to allowing the boroughs a great deal of local autonomy. This is especially so given that the local Justices, who were the main source of oversight, were effectively enforcing their own decisions, and suits in the courts at Westminster were rare and expensive.[49] Corporations, which could have 'as many as five thousand members or as few as a dozen members', 'exercised the same rights as individuals over the corporate property'.[50] The corporate property and funds were provided for the benefit of the corporators who were the social leaders of the community[51] and held such offices as 'property'.

In making the case for the 1835 reforms, the commissioners had been damning in their assessment about how these powers had been exercised. They found that 'the corporate bodies exist independently of the communities among which they are found' and that 'mismanagement of corporate property is manifold'.[52] Maitland too described the municipal corporation prior to 1835 as 'hardly better than a Tory dining club',[53] though it is likely that the performance of the boroughs actually varied widely and some used charitable trusts in order to deliver considerable local improvements.

The Municipal Corporations Act 1835 brought major and radical reforms. The new corporations would be elected by households of freemen. The Act effectively confiscated the property from 179 of the existing towns and transferred it to wholly elected councils.[54] Towns 'ceased to be forms of property and became instruments of

47 Loughlin, *Legality and Locality*, above n. 45, p. 19.

48 See, e.g, C. T. Carr, *The General Principles of the Law of Corporations* (Cambridge University Press, 1905).

49 Loughlin, *Legality and Locality*, above n.45 pp. 20–1. J. Willis, 'Parliament and the Local Authorities' in H. J. Laski, W. I. Jennings and W. A. Robson (eds.), *A Century of Municipal Progress* (London: Allen & Unwin, 1935), p. 405.

50 W. I. Jennings, 'The Municipal Revolution', in H. J. Laski, W. J. Jennings and W. A. Robson (eds.), *A Century of Municipal Progress* (London: Allen & Unwin, 1935) ibid, quoting Lord Eldon, p. 55.

51 *Ibid.*, p. 56. See R. Gneist, *The History of the English Constitution*, P. A. Ashworth (tr.) (London: William Clowes, 1886).

52 *Ibid.*, p. 58 quoting from the report. We now know that, like the report on the Poor Law, the report painted the corruption and abuses of borough government in the worst possible light in order to achieve reform.

53 Maitland, *Township and Borough*, above n. 42, p. 94.

54 Jennings 'The Municipal Revolution', above n. 50, p. 55.

government'.[55] The Act recognized this by providing for compensation to be paid to those office holders who had lost their offices at election.[56] It reformed the law by providing that municipal property could not be alienated and that municipal funds could only be 'applied for the public benefit'.[57] The Lord Chancellor Cottenham subsequently interpreted these provisions as creating a trust for charitable purposes.[58] The reform changed who was running the borough, for whose purposes and the legal constraints on their powers.

But while the Municipal Corporations Act established some general machinery for the newly structured corporations, it did not initially entrust them with very extensive powers. By-law making power was no longer treated as inherent but was now conferred by statute. By-laws were now subject to disallowance: first by the Secretary of State[59] and later by the Local Government Board as well as to *ultra vires* rulings by the courts (which became more strictly enforced by the end of the nineteenth century).[60] The Attorney General acted as guardian of their funds and enjoyed powers to intervene. Admittedly, the Act was permissive in that it empowered the transfer of the many ad hoc powers which had been vested in Commissioners and trustees to the Boroughs. However, ad hoc bodies continued and the more radical, centralizing and Benthamite reforms such as the administration of the Poor Laws and Public Health Act created legal and institutional frameworks that were separate from elected local governments (even if some of the personnel would be shared) for most of the nineteenth century.

Democratization, then, did not bring organic self-government to the municipal corporation. Even more than prior to the reforms, if they wanted or needed powers, municipalities had to seek them from Parliament. Willis, writing in 1935, described the Municipal Corporation Act as beginning a process that would continue over the next century:

[55] W. I. Jennings, 'Central Control' in H. J. Laski, W. I. Jennings and W. A. Robson (eds.), *A Century of Municipal Progress* (London: Allen & Unwin, 1935), p. 420.

[56] Section 57 Municipal Corporations Act 1835.

[57] Section 93 Municipal Corporations Act 1835.

[58] *Attorney-General* v. *Aspinall* 2 My & Cr 613, 619; *Attorney-General* v. *Corporation of Poole* 4 My & Cr 27, Jennings 'The Municipal Revolution', above n. 50, p. 422.

[59] Later they were subject to 'confirmation' by the Local Government Board (Section 184 Public Health Act 1875).

[60] Jennings suggests that the challenges by way of common law actions alleging *ultra vires* would not come until much later in the nineteenth century, 'The Municipal Revolution', above n. 50, pp. 422–5.

'modern local administration is the still unfinished product of a long series of private Acts, obtained by local authorities on their own initiative and at their own expense: that in passing a private Act, Parliament does not command, but merely adds one new power to the armoury already possessed by its petitioner.'[61]

It was not the municipal corporation but the local Board of Health created under the Public Health Act 1848 that would become the agency in the best position to respond to new urban needs.[62] Local Boards of Health largely replaced improvement commissioners and became the leading agents for urban renewal. By 1870, 700 local boards had been formed especially in places where local government had otherwise been ineffective.[63] Often these boards also became the agents for the municipalization of gas and water undertakings. As we have seen in Chapter 2, they were the products not of local self-government but of Benthamite experiments in centralized administration. In *Township and Borough* (1898), Maitland describes the position thus:[64]

> Parliament fostered the notion that the property of the corporation was morally the property of the corporators, by entrusting to other bodies, groups of commissioners and the like, those new powers and duties that were to answer new urban needs. The watching, paving, lighting of the town, these matters were no affairs of the corporation; with the relief of the poor it had nothing to do. There was a vicious cycle; the corporation was untrusted because untrustworthy, untrustworthy because untrusted . . . Morally the Town loses its personality; for it loses the sense of duty.

Maitland was concerned about the self-governing life of local government and other associations and conceived of the absence of such power as an issue of *moral personality.* Local government had effectively been 'denatured' by the piecemeal 'delegations'[65] of power and functions from Parliament and central government. Local institutions would not be allowed to enjoy the capacity to be spontaneous, voluntarist or self-originating. At the same time, the 'for profit' corporation *gained* self-orginating power in its memorandum of association and were subject only to a registration scheme. The business enterprise would progressively appear more natural and organic, while local authorities

[61] J. Willis, 'Parliament and the Local Authorities', above n. 49, p. 400.
[62] Wilson, *Lighting the Town* above n. 39. [63] *Ibid.*, p. 204.
[64] Maitland, *Township and Borough*, above n. 42, p. 95.
[65] They were not strictly delegations but more often model provisions to which local government could opt in.

were progressively being treated as artificial, defined and constrained. Despite their often shared origins, they would no longer appear as the same genus. As a diagnosis of a problem at least, Maitland's analysis was typically acute: how to protect customary authority in the face of new legislation and the centralization of power?

But the past would prove to be no reliable predictor of the future. Jaffe would attribute the limited impact of Maitland's scholarship on the doctrine to characteristics associated with the historical school movement as a whole: it considers all law as validated from its past but 'at the moment of its present it can evolve nothing new.'[66] As the nineteenth century came to an end, arguments about local government powers would not be treated as issues of inherent corporate power but rather as a matter of *vires*. Ironically, in defending the 'lesser corporations' by arguing that the fiction theory has never been part of the common law, it is Pollock who clearly draws attention to this distinction for the first time. The doctrine of *ultra vires*, he suggests, is not founded on 'any ultimate conception as to the nature of a corporate body. It is a doctrine, to use a convenient American term, of constitutional limitations.'[67] This proved to be an accurate prediction of how the matter would be treated. Of course, such an analysis also fits the Positivist account of delegated power described by Austin in Chapter 2 better. The difference is that the facts were now a much better fit for the theory than they had been when Austin first expounded it. This is likely the very conclusion that Maitland had wanted to forestall in his conception of the corporation.

Legal controversies about corporate life would increasingly focus on whether a particular body was *ultra vires* its parent statute or its own rules and not on the basis of whether it was a corporation per se. If the democratic nature of local government corporations was to be taken into account at all, it would be in the operation of those *ultra vires* tests. Legislative power would be consolidated in the Public Health Act 1875, Municipal Corporations Act 1882 and Local Government Act 1888. The second of these conferred a general power to make by-laws for 'good rule and government'.[68] In an 1898 decision the Queen's Bench distinguished for the first time between by-laws made by corporations for profit (which the majority suggested deserved strict scrutiny) and local

[66] L. Jaffe, 'Law Making by Private Groups', *Harvard Law Review* 51 (1937–8), 201–53, 208.

[67] F. Pollock, 'Has the Common Law Received a Fiction Theory of Corporations?', *Law Quarterly Review* 27 (1911), 219–35, 222 discussing the railways by-laws cases.

[68] Section 23. Local Government Board approval was still required.

government by-laws which were made by way of a public decision-making process by democratically elected officials (and which the judges thought should be viewed more generously).[69] Judges were not yet routinely engaged in frustrating experiments in municipal socialism, though *ultra vires* challenges would later become more frequent and successful – attracting the criticism that the judges were unable to distinguish between local authorities in need of powers in order to provide public services, and joint stock companies for private profit.[70] There would also be judicial and legislative controversy about what counted as a 'for profit' undertaking for the purposes of public authority liability, as we shall see in the next chapter. Maitland did not foresee, either, that the major administrative law controversy in the first quarter of the twentieth century would be prompted by concerns that public bodies (albeit now centralized) were receiving *too much* power by way of such delegations, and not about whether they should be treated as delegates per se. Dicey had been correct in predicting that Bentham would bequeath the legislative doctrines and tendencies that would lend themselves to socialist experiments.

One might have thought that, given these changes in the legal forms of different types of 'corporation', Maitland's work would have remained of mainly historical interest. In both method and substance, however, it continued to have influence. We can fairly speculate about the reasons. Idealism and its emphasis on moral personality continued to be an influential public philosophy within policy circles at least until 1930. And a series of *causes célèbres* affecting churches and unions attracted attention to Maitland's analysis and spawned the Pluralist movement.

Churches and trade unions

It was in relation to churches and trade unions that Maitland's theories about the real personality of associations attracted the greatest attention both in the case law and scholarship – although the analysis was also more generally applicable to other English fellowships.[71] Three *causes célèbres* ignited the scholarly reaction. We focus on them for two

[69] *Kruse* v. *Johnson* [1898] QB 91, 99.

[70] A view attributed to Robson by Loughlin, *Legality and Locality*, above n. 45, p. 45.

[71] Laski would, for example, describe local authorities in Britain as 'the anaemic reflex of the central power' in H. J. Laski, *Studies in the Problem of Sovereignty* (New Haven, CT: Yale University Press, 1917), pp. 279–80.

purposes. First, they are evidence that aspects of Maitland's thought, including some of the premises he shared with Idealists, gained a certain amount of traction in the common law doctrine. Second, and more importantly, they betray the limits of corporate doctrine as a tool of analysis and as a means of achieving decentralized public power.

The first case in time was *Free Church of Scotland* v. *Overtoun.*[72] It concerned a challenge to the power of the Free Church of Scotland to amalgamate with the United Presbyterian Church to form the United Free Church. The question was whether such an amalgamation was consistent with the Free Church's core tenets and fundamental doctrines as set down in the body's 1843 trust deed.

The Idealist philosopher and lawyer Haldane KC, representing the Free Church in the House of Lords, used the case as an opportunity to emphasize the self-originating, organic and *real* personality of the church. He argued that: 'A Church does not depend for its identity on its doctrines. It is an organization on a democratic basis which, like a living organism, preserves its form amid the changes of its material.'[73] The majority of the House of Lords, however, did not agree that the Church was free to change its self-understandings in this way. It found that the Free Church's 1843 trust deed did not give it power to alter its interpretations of what (the *Lords* determined) were matters of *fundamental* doctrine – particularly where such understandings affected property concerns. It vested the entire property holdings of the Church in the twenty-four congregations which had voted against Union, depriving the remaining 1,100.

It is easy to imagine the kind of reaction such a result would provoke. Ultimately a Parliamentary Commission was required to resolve the controversy. It took to itself the task of redistributing the property – further compounding the offence of treating the matter as one for *central* government and not one to be determined by self-governing bodies. Haldane's arguments, however, did not entirely fall on stony ground and would live to see another day. Lord Macnaghten, who with Lord Lindley dissented, acknowledged Haldane KC's argument that there were mysteries here into which the judges ought not to intrude,[74] and himself adopted the organic metaphor. He asked: 'Was she [the church] from birth incapable of all growth and development? Was she (in a word) a dead branch and not a living church?'[75]

[72] [1904] AC 515. [73] *Ibid.*, 609. [74] *Ibid.*, 641. [75] *Ibid.*, 631.

The two other controversial cases to reach the House of Lords involved trade unions. The first was *Taff Vale Railway Co* v. *Amalgamated Society of Railway Servants.*[76] It was a case in which the statutes deliberately withheld corporate status from trade unions and yet the House of Lords effectively recognized the union as having a distinct moral personality and life 'of its own'. The House of Lords recognized that a tortious action could be brought against a trade union as a legal entity separate from its office holders and members, and even though the statutes under which trade unions were registered appeared deliberately to withhold corporate status.

The reasoning in the Lords merged real entity theory (the view that groups have a life of their own that should be recognized by the law) with grant theory (the view that groups derive their corporate existence from the state): the result was based partially on the real capacity of trade unions and partially on implications drawn from the statute.[77] Given that the unions had successfully objected to being given explicit corporate status in the 1871 Act, real entity theory provides the better basis for the analysis.[78] The Trade Union Acts of 1871 and 1876 required unions to be registered, and gave them the capacity for owning property and for acting by way of agents. Given that Parliament had deliberately granted unions two of the essential qualities of a corporation proper, the Lords concluded that they should be recognized as having full legal personality – and hence be held responsible in tort. The House of Lords agreed with the judge of first instance that it should not draw the implication that the 'legislature had in fact legalised the existence of such irresponsible bodies with such a wide capacity for evil'. They must be able to recognize a trade union's full legal personality in order to hold it responsible in law. Any successful claim could be satisfied out of trade union funds.

These conclusions represented a potential disaster for the Union cause. The effect of the decision was to make strike action too expensive and thus practically unavailable. And yet in many ways the decision did exactly what the advocates of real entity theory had been asking. It 'recognized' the capacity of the unincorporated group to enjoy a corporate existence, even if such existence was drawn by implication from a reading of the statute rather than from the general operation of law, as

[76] [1901] UKHL 1.

[77] I adopt the approach of R. Harris 'The Transplantation of Legal Discourse', above n. 23, 1448.

[78] *Ibid.*, 1446.

they would have preferred. And it allowed them the 'capacity to sin' (an aspect of moral personality which Maitland considered essential) and held them morally responsible for such sins.[79] This, it transpired, was not what the unions themselves thought would secure them independence and self-originating power. They fought for and won renewed protection in the Trade Disputes Act 1906 which limited the possibilities of suing trade unions in tort.

In the last case to provoke particular controversy, the application of real entity theory would have led to a result that *was* in the unions' interests. In this case, however, judges reverted to the grant or delegation approach as an explanation of legal personality. *Osborne* v. *Amalgamated Society of Railway Servants*[80] involved the challenge by a union member to the use of trade union funds to support a Labour candidate for Parliament. The allocation of funds had been agreed by the union through its voting procedures. The union had existed as an unincorporated body for a long time serving both benevolent and trade purposes. It had eventually become registered under the Trade Union Act 1871 in order to immunize some of its activities from legal attack as being in restraint of trade. This time, Lord Macnaghten, who had taken the real entity self-governing approach to churches in the *Overtoun* case, treated the union as the creation of the state. He viewed the 1871 Act as a device not merely for the *recognition* of the body but as the *source* of all its objects and powers. Regardless of the long-term existence of the union, he said, it should be treated as created and restricted by the statute. The legislation did not grant any power to support politicians in this way. It was Lord Shaw (in dissent) this time, who was prepared to use the organic metaphor that had earlier attracted Lord Macnaghten. He suggested that it was not the purpose of the trade union statute to define or restrict the 'natural movements of the living organism'.[81]

The cases show that real entity theory achieved some traction in the case law, some of the time. As these cases illustrate, however, legal recognition of the real personality of the group is not necessarily the same as unlimited self-government, and in one case undermined the legislative concessions extracted from Parliament by the unions.

[79] F. W. Maitland, 'The Crown as Corporation', in H. A. L. Fisher (ed.), *The Collected Papers of Frederic William Maitland*, 3 vols (Cambridge University Press, 1911, vol. III, p. 263.

[80] [1910] AC 107. [81] *Ibid.*, 108.

Maitland's twentieth-century Pluralist followers, who were a diverse movement in any event, did not necessarily share all of his premises and often had a larger agenda which theories of real personality did not necessarily advance. In particular they disagreed about whether the state was the greatest corporation of all, what the state's role as a corporation should be vis-á-vis other corporations and on the juristic implications of their theories.

Laski was the most juristically engaged member of the Pluralist movement.[82] In his earlier writings, Laski is much closer to Maitland. Despite his left-wing politics, Laski approved of the decision in the *Taff Vale* case for its recognition of the real life, identity and *responsibility* of associations – though he urged that tortious responsibility should apply to *all* associations including the state. He was in good company. Sidney Webb, appointed as a member of a Royal Commission into the *Taff Vale* decision, reported in 1906 a similar view that unions should accept legal responsibility for their actions.[83] While we might applaud Laski for his principled approach, the result surely did not further his larger causes of more decentralized and distributed power. Neither is it exactly clear, from a case like *Taff Vale*, how the real personality of the group would be able to protect the individual from the state, or challenge its authoritarian claims, which was also one of Laski's central concerns.[84]

What does seem clear is that the early Laski viewed the individual as having more to fear from the state than from organized capital, and he viewed the common law rather than Parliamentary legislation as the primary means to protect forms of group life. When he talks about the state he does not seem to include the judges, and when he talks about the law he means judge-made law and not legislation. Where he seemed to differ from Maitland is that he is loath to concede that the state (used here presumably in a political sense) can exercise a will of its own. While there is evidence in his writings that he read Green and Bosanquet with profit and that he accepted that it is only through group life that the individual is able to flourish (one of the core tenets of Idealist thought), he considered the idea that the state could represent the collective will of

[82] Laski's own central commitments changed significantly over a relatively short period. See, e.g., M. Stears, *Progressives, Pluralists and the Problems of the State: Ideologies of Reform in the United States and Britain 1909–1926* (Oxford University Press, 2002).

[83] Beveridge, *Voluntary Action* above n. 2, p. 90.

[84] See, e.g., the Defence of the Realm Act 1914.

the whole to be a threat to freedom. Such a view would not allow for genuine ideological conflict within a society or for the rival claims to the loyalty of individuals from other corporations. His was a direct assault on both Austinian sovereignty and Bosanquet's Idealism. According to Laski:[85]

> Moral inferiority between the church and state there can hardly be; legal inferiority is either an illegitimate postulation of Austinian sovereignty, or else the false identification of the state and society.

In juristic terms, these commitments led him to conclude that the *same common law* should apply to the state as to other forms of group life. Not only should the law of tort apply to groups such as trade unions in the same way as it does to individuals (as a mechanism of control and accountability as well as to ensure responsibility) but the state should be treated on the *same* basis. As we shall see in Chapter 6, he objected to the emergence of distinct public law rules of obligation.[86] There could be no separate 'public law' under Laski's legal framework. But, as we shall see, that is exactly the direction in which the common law was heading.

These views were not necessarily shared by other members of the Pluralist movement.[87] While all the members tended to view the state and other associations as performing functionally distinct roles, they did not agree about what those distinct roles should be. Figgis saw social life in terms of an ascending hierarchy of groups (which also included the varieties of social life throughout the Empire). He regarded group life as 'public' as far as its members were concerned and 'private' in relation to the state. He conceded, however, that the state should have the power to ensure that groups did not overstep the bounds of justice, to secure the rights of groups and to protect groups from each other.[88] Cole did not recognize real personality at all, wanted to eliminate private capital and suggested that it was the task of 'society' (and not law) to assess whether the state and the group were performing within their proper spheres. His plans for the nationalization of the coal mining industry demonstrate that, unlike the early

[85] H. J. Laski, *Authority in the Modern State* (New Haven, CT: Yale University Press, 1919), p. 66.

[86] *Local Government Board* v. *Arlidge* [1915] AC 120.

[87] The Pluralist movement is discussed in Chapter 3.

[88] J. N. Figgis, *Churches in the Modern State* (Bristol: Thoemmes, 1997) (first edition 1913).

Laski, he was not so much concerned about the prospect that the state would absorb other forms of group life but rather was willing to embrace corporatism as a means by which to establish worker controlled industry and to eliminate the role of private capital. The state, he suggested, should be demoted from father to elder brother.[89] We shall see in Chapter 8 that this programme had an important legacy in the corporatism which would come to regulate industrial and economic life in the UK up until privatization. An important element of Cole's legacy, and a critical departure from Maitland's thinking, was that law (whether in the form of legislation or the common law) would have an extremely marginal role to play in such areas. By the 1930s, Laski too would join Cole in seeking to capture the state for the Left. Barker eventually conceded to the state the role of co-ordinating group purposes through law. In other words, the Pluralist movement got stuck on the question of what it was exactly that made the state and other forms of group life part of the same genus.

Real personality doctrine could not serve as a unifying method of analysing the state and other forms of group life. By itself it did not help to resolve emerging issues such as the proper functions of the state, whether public law principles should be distinct from private law principles or to whom they ought to apply. Statute, not the common law, would become the dominant form of legal recognition for voluntary agencies. Moral personality was unable to capture the variety of new relationships between the state and voluntary associations which were emerging as the twentieth century progressed. If Laski was later to suggest that the state and all forms of group life should be democratic and self-governing, he did not anticipate that in the competition between the state and other groups for democratic approval, the state would often win (and something too would also be lost).

In order to explain one thread of that larger story I will now turn to two other examples of the 'state genus': the friendly society and the philanthropic association. They provide two strands of a complicated story as it emerged in the first half of the twentieth century. How did recognition by the law and the state affect such organizations? What was the result of such entanglements? As we shall see, some kinds of state recognition could prove fatal.

[89] G. D. H. Cole, 'Conflicting Social Obligations', *Proceedings of the Aristotelian Society NS* 15 (1914–15), 140–59, 157.

The road to welfare: mutual aid and the Poor Law

The UK changed from being one of the most voluntarist societies before World War I, to the most centralized bureaucratic society in Europe after World War II. What explains this? Was it, as Laski feared, that the all absorptive Hegelian state would take over the voluntary sector? Or was it, instead, that the state and voluntarist movements were too much alike? The history is, of course, disputed and complicated. Wartime experiments in centralization and corporatism for the production and distribution of food and armaments may have provided important precedents – though some of those experiments were subsequently dismantled. The 'social solidarity' engendered by war may have played a part but the degree of solidanty may have been exaggerated in hindsight: many said they would never have another house guest after their experience of wartime evacuees.[90] An established system of income taxation (compared to other European countries) was probably one important practical factor,[91] and the urgency of social reconstruction another. But how was it thought about?

What is striking is that there was no single dominant public philosopher or philosophy during this period. Idealism, Fabian Socialism, Guild Socialism, Pluralism and Utilitarianism all played a part (and were by no means always distinct from each other). They all emphasized the importance of collective action, and tended to view the individual as 'socially conceived' (an issue to which we shall return in Chapter 6). But there was no leading theoretical figure. The other striking feature is that the change from voluntarism to the centralized welfare state has been largely ignored, both in the legal scholarship of the period and since. That is likely the product of some of the features of the British constitutional system that we have already identified. In particular, the belated emergence of a field of administrative law scholarship, in the French sense of the study of how administration is organized and how the different parts relate to each other, is significant. The insularity of the legal profession is another factor. The very fact that the changes were not the subject of legal debate may tell us something about the absence of a firm pre-existing demarcation line between public authorities and civil society:

[90] J. Harris, 'War and Social History: Britain and the Home Front during the Second World War', *Contemporary European History* 1(1) (1992), 17–35, 28.

[91] M. J. Daunton, 'Payment and Participation: Welfare and State Formation in Britain 1900–1951', *Past and Present* 150 (1996), 169–216.

shifting that line was not self-consciously thought of as a matter of great moment (though as we shall see in the next chapter, more fixed lines were beginning to be drawn between for profit and not for profit enterprise). Unlike today, there was no discussion of 'public' as opposed to 'private' functions. Given that the welfare state adopted the functions of the voluntary sector, such a distinction would not have made sense. While it is true that reference to the 'public service state' emerged – almost certainly borrowed from Duguit[92] – that expression was used to refer to a new state of affairs and did not operate as an *a priori* principle of division. Neither was the public–private distinction used, as we do today, to distinguish between the realm of the personal and the realm of the public and democratic. Voluntary associations were highly *public* forms of participation and aspired to democratic principles. Voluntary did not mean amateur either. For much of this time voluntary welfare agencies, such as the Charity Organisation Society, were the more professional in terms of their training, experience and systems of investigation than the civil service.

Of course, the relationship between the public authorities and voluntary agencies was incredibly variegated and any attempt to make a generalized analysis is a complex and daunting task. We shall resort to broad strokes but concentrate on the story of how the Poor Law Act 1834 (narrow, punitive, selective and administered in local units) became the National Insurance Act 1946 (broad, national in scope for most purposes and relatively generous). It is a story in which path dependency plays a part. The British welfare state is the shape it is because of what it inherited from the past. An important part of that inheritance is the Poor Law.[93] The Elizabethan Poor Laws (1601) imposed *obligations* on local communities to support the destitute and conferred a *right* on the destitute to that support. Another part of that inheritance is the even older English institutions of the ancient guilds and fellowships for mutual aid and assistance which had their origins in the public house and chapel and provided an early form of social insurance.[94] Though the term includes a wide variety of types of association, we shall call these

[92] Duguit was translated by Laski. See also L. Duguit, 'The Law and the State', *Harvard Law Review* 31 (1917–18), 1–186.

[93] This is a point suggested by J. Harris, 'Enterprise and Welfare States: A Comparative Perspective', *Transactions of the Royal Historical Society* 40 (1990), 175–95, 182.

[94] Some of the earliest of these were founded by Huguenots who were not eligible for Poor Law assistance. See Beveridge, *Voluntary Action*, above n. 2, p. 23.

'friendly societies'. They had long been subject to some regulation and by the early twentieth century, some, but by no means all, were registered and enjoyed particular privileges.[95] They were said to be 'the democratic pioneers of mutual insurance' and 'channels for the spirit of voluntary service'.[96] Given those distinct beginnings, how could the law co-ordinate and regulate a system of Poor Law entitlement based on public obligations and rights alongside a system of mutual aid based on membership and reciprocal obligations? We shall see that the form that the UK welfare state eventually took was the product, in large part, of policy choices and not of any principled line drawing between the public and the private or the state and civil society. If anything, the changes were driven by empiricism and functionalism. In the process, the state adopted the functions and methods of the voluntary society, and, at the same time, the voluntary society became more bureaucratic. Indeed, each increasingly came to resemble the other.

Given that empiricism and functionalism were the main drivers of change, the focus of our narrative will be on the policy problems as they were identified and the attempts at their resolution. We take up the story with the workhouse regime established in the Poor Law Act 1834. It was infamous for its harsh treatment of those who were unable or unwilling to work. To qualify for support, an individual was required to be destitute rather than poor or even at risk of descending into destitution. Workhouses took in lunatics (sic), mental defectives (sic), the sick, the old, the able-bodied unemployed and their dependents. The poor, and those at risk of the workhouse (including the 'respectable' poor), did not qualify for relief and were the province of the mutual aid and philanthropic societies. Trade unions and friendly societies provided avenues of mutual aid for low paid workers by way of sickness insurance, and some trade unions provided unemployment insurance for their members. Charities and distress committees also played important roles in relation to relief. It is estimated that the income of the London charities in 1875 equalled the expenditure under the Poor Law. By 1908 it had far exceeded that amount.[97] Already, by

[95] E.g. tax exemptions, exemptions from the Unlawful Societies Act 1799, priority in bankruptcy. See *ibid.*, Chapter one for a comprehensive history including the Inquiry of Lord Northcote in 1874.

[96] *Ibid.*, p. 60.

[97] McBriar, *An Edwardian Mixed Doubles*, above n. 43, p. 41.

that time, central government taxation was supplementing local Poor Law rating for at least 20 per cent of the Poor Law budget.[98]

By the twentieth century there was a broad consensus that the policies, methods and administration of the Poor Law relief needed to be rethought. The Royal Commission into the Poor Law was duly established. It included among its members Helen Bosanquet, a central figure in the Charity Organisation Society, and wife of the Idealist philosopher Bernard Bosanquet, and Beatrice Webb who, with her husband Sidney Webb, was one of the leaders of the Fabian Socialist movement. In the 1909 Report[99] Bosanquet and Webb famously split on how best to deliver relief to the poor. Though they agreed on a wide range of matters, their public disagreement came to symbolize an ongoing contest between 'old-fashioned' voluntarism and 'modern' public (state and local government) provision (and possibly, though not entirely accurately, a contest between Idealism and Socialism).[100]

While they both agreed that the Poor Law commissioners should be abolished and that their duties should be transferred to county councils and county borough councils, Helen Bosanquet, for the majority, advocated greater co-operation between voluntary charities and the new Poor Law authorities. Voluntary charity should be regularized and systematized, given official recognition and status, and co-ordinated by a new 'Voluntary Aid Organisation'. Case workers should be professionally trained, 'harmful' charities should be removed and other selected charities given greater responsibility. In some ways these recommendations reprised earlier squabbles between the Charity Organisation Society and other charities which it considered to be philosophically unclear in their objectives (such as Barnado's, the Salvation Army and the City Missions). The Charity Organisation Society was focused on self-help, independence and the development of character. It did not see its role as augmenting the help offered by the Poor Law guardians but as

[98] H. Bosanquet, *The Poor Law Report of 1909: A Summary Explaining the Defects of the Present System and the Principal Recommendations of the Commission, so far as Relates to England* (London: Macmillan, 1909)

[99] *Ibid.*; B. P. and S. Webb, *The Public Organisation of the Labour Market: Being Part Two of the Minority Report of the Poor Law Commission* (London: Longmans Green, 1909).

[100] Jose Harris argues that Beatrice Webb was more sympathetic to Idealist thought than is often supposed. See J. Harris, 'The Webbs, The Charity Organisation Society and the Ratan Tata Foundation Social Policy from the Perspective of 1912', in M. Bulmer, J. Lewis and D. Piachaud (eds.) *The Goals of Social Policy* (London: Unwin Hyman, 1989), pp. 54–5.

preventing others from the 'moral' slide into destitution.[101] It emphasized character over circumstances. Citing unsound friendly societies and clubs as one of the causes of poverty among the able-bodied poor, Bosanquet also recommended that these entities should be subject to greater regulation. But, she conceded, voluntary societies should not be subject to so much regulation that it would rob them of their special character.[102]

Beatrice Webb, in her minority report, was concerned that too many different types of cases, (for example the sick and the able-bodied unemployed) were being dealt with by the same institutions.[103] She recommended separate policy-making committees, staffed by salaried officers, to make rules for the different circumstances of need. The non-able-bodied poor should be transferred to health authorities and workhouse education to the ordinary education authorities. This policy of separately dealing with different classes of destitution was not new. It was in Bentham's and Chadwick's original proposals for the nineteenth-century reforms. What had changed was that there were now specialized *public* institutions in existence which had jurisdiction over the different subject areas. In other words, these recommendations do not *necessarily* represent an ideological preference for public provision.

More interesting are her recommendations for able-bodied relief. The policy of the 1834 Poor Law had been strictly to limit 'outdoor' relief. The able-bodied poor, for example, were only entitled to relief if they succumbed to the workhouse. 'Outdoor' relief was unavailable to them. Relief was meant to be hard to get and punitive. Webb found that the philanthropic agencies were undermining the penal policies of the Poor Law, by providing outdoor relief from starvation and shelter. She did not blame them for these strategies and did not think that voluntary agencies should or could be punished or persuaded not to offer such assistance, as Bosanquet recommended. 'It is for the State not to lay its heavy hand on the efforts of the charitable, misdirected as these might be, but to find a

[101] For a discussion of internal debates within the Charity Organisation Society about its proper role see J. Lewis, 'The Boundary Between Voluntary and Statutory Social Service, above n. 31.

[102] Not all 'voluntary agencies' were treated alike in the majority's report. Trade unions (who were an important avenue for mutual aid) were cited as one of the moral causes of poverty through employers' liability claims and minimum labour standards. See discussion in McBriar, *An Edwardian Mixed Doubles*, above n. 43, p. 300.

[103] Webb, *The Public Organisation of the Labour Market*, above n. 99.

more excellent way.'[104] No amount of 'co-ordination' of the voluntary sector would be likely to solve this problem, she argued. Neither was it a local problem – but rather a national problem which was also linked to vagrancy as the unemployed sought work further afield. Instead, a rethink of the Poor Law and its penal policies was required, the labour market causes of poverty should be tackled and labour exchanges should be established on a national basis. For the minority, welfare design and policy ought to be the province of local or central government agencies. Voluntary societies should be limited to the establishment and management of institutional relief and their contributions to 'home relief' (at least where financial assistance was concerned) ought to be discontinued. The state and charitable provision could not be co-ordinated until there was a co-ordinated policy.

Both Bosanquet and Webb approved of incentives to encourage workmen to insure against unemployment and both were sceptical about compulsory state insurance.[105] For Bosanquet, a state subsidy would be necessary to provide for the long-term disabled. Webb gave qualified support to the suggestion of a compulsory unemployment insurance system administered through trade unions or friendly societies for particular sectors of workers or specified industries. But she could not see how a compulsory insurance scheme could apply to 'bad risks' as well as those with the 'work habit', and thus how to preserve trade union funds from potentially significant financial losses. 'Moreover, the trade union can, and constantly does exclude from its membership men who have not obtained a certain degree of skill, or regularity of conduct; exactly as a Friendly Society excludes men suffering from syphilis or phthises [consumption], or any mortal disease.'[106] How exactly could voluntarism and selective membership be combined with compulsion?

The differences between Webb and Bosanquet were not about collectivism as opposed to individualism but about how much assistance to give the able-bodied unemployed and which form collectivism should take. The public reception to the report was mixed. The Charity Organisation Society group in the majority won the politicians, but the Webbs won the popular support of the socially conscious. As a result, 1909–11 saw a serious decline in charitable contributions to the Charity Organisation Society.[107]

[104] *Ibid.*, p. 110. [105] McBriar, *An Edwardian Mixed Doubles*, above n. 43, p. 302.
[106] Webb, *The Public Organisation of the Labour Market*, above n. 99, p. 291.
[107] J. Harris, 'The Webbs, The Charity Organisation Society and the Ratan Tata Foundation', above n. 100, p. 38. See also Lewis, 'The Boundary Between Voluntary and Statutory Social Service' above n. 31, 174.

It would take until 1929 for the major part of the Report to be implemented.[108] But, even as the report was being written, Lloyd George was investigating how to establish a system of compulsory state insurance to help address the problem of the able-bodied poor.[109] The resulting National Insurance Act 1911 spelt the 'beginning of the end' for the Poor Law as the primary vehicle for welfare provision.[110] It provided a government- and employer-subsidized compulsory contributory sickness scheme for workers in certain occupations, a voluntary scheme for those earning under £160 a year[111] and an unemployment scheme for specified trades especially susceptible to cyclical fluctuations. In the form in which it was enacted, the National Insurance Act 1911 avowedly adopted a model of co-operation between voluntary and state sectors. This was certainly the announced intention of Lloyd George, who, after investigating the German system of social insurance in 1908, proposed that Britain should adopt a more 'self-governing' model.[112] The Liberals' intention was to build 'upon strong British institutions' rather than to create a centralized bureaucratic system of welfare provision. Friendly societies and other non-profit organizations, managed through the participation of their members, could become 'approved societies' for sickness insurance. Trade unions would do the same for unemployment insurance. The compulsory system would be administered by the voluntary sector, through the pre-existing system of membership societies. This was, then, intended as an early incarnation of some version of the 'Big Society'.

The statute gave significant power to the insurance committees – and to other public bodies including the Treasury and the Local Health Board. The insurance committees were constituted for every county and county borough and they were made up primarily of appointees with some elected representatives. There was limited provision for

[108] Local Government Act 1929.

[109] Though neither the majority nor minority campaigners were satisfied with the 1911 Bill it seems closer to the majority's recommendations. On 9 October 1908, the Webbs were invited to Downing Street to meet with Lloyd George, Haldane and Churchill. They were asked whether they would be prepared to endorse the Bill in their forthcoming minority report – they refused to do so. See McBriar, *An Edwardian Mixed Doubles*, above n. 43, p. 313.

[110] The Old Age Pensions Act 1908 gave pensions without contributions at the age of seventy, subject to a means test.

[111] Or who had already been in a scheme for five years.

[112] Daunton, 'Payment and Participation', above n. 91, 182.

approved society representation.[113] In practice it was the Health Insurance division of the Ministry of Health and the Government Actuary which directed the scheme and implemented the rules.

The promised, more stringent, financial regulation of friendly societies was also an aspect of the 1911 Act. Friendly societies became subject to financial reporting and audit, had to give security against maladministration and could not be dissolved without the consent of the insurance commissioners. Provisions facilitated pooling arrangements for small societies. The Act recognized, regulated and systematized voluntary associations for mutual aid. But, in this particular mix of voluntarism and state administration, the voluntary sector lost a great deal of ground.

The approved societies had limited powers to vary benefits,[114] they needed consent from the insurance committees at every turn, including to change their own rules,[115] and while they did not administer sanatorium or medical benefits,[116] they bore the cost of administering the latter.[117] They were empowered to forgive arrears at their discretion and yet had relatively little control over measures to increase their own funds – especially as they had to compete with each other to attract new (and preferably low risk) members. Indeed, as the scheme evolved the government would impose a drain on their reserves.[118] Shortly before their demise, approved societies were given the further task of regulating the public bodies responsible for employment and sanitation conditions in areas which generated excessive cases.[119] This was all against the backdrop that typically a working man and his employer made seven-ninths of the contributions against the Treasury's two-ninths.[120]

Approved societies were even less able to resist the pressures from central government to restrict expenditure than the local authorities which, by now, administered public health services. Politically the approved society units were small and they were unable to speak with one voice. Government was able to use them as a political buffer for its own policies. The vaunted democratic qualities that they were required to exhibit for statutory designation as an approved society were often

113 Section 59(2)(i). 114 Section 13. 115 Section 14(2). 116 Section 14(1).

117 National Insurance Act 1922.

118 E.g., in requiring the forgiveness of arrears see Daunton, 'Payment and Participation', above n. 91, 185.

119 Section 104 National Health Insurance Act 1924. These measures were ineffective, due to societies lacking the necessary expertise and their members tending no longer to be geographically defined.

120 For women the respective contributions were three quarters, one quarter.

frustrated when they could not meet the demands of their members for extended benefits. Indeed, legislation in 1913 gave the commissioners power to circumvent societies' rules,[121] and approval by the insurance commissioners could be used to cure irregularities in internal procedures.[122] The fraternal rituals associated with the ancient friendly societies were threatened – the insurance committees disallowed club nights and the consumption of profits which had been part of that fellowship.[123] Friendly societies themselves were declining in number and becoming more bureaucratic before World War I with the growth of bodies such as Heart of Oak, which was a centralized collecting society that operated by post (the tradition had been that members brought their contributions in person to local meetings). The friendly societies had become increasingly mechanistic[124] and greater entanglement with government further encouraged that tendency.

What of their 'moral personality'? In order to become an 'approved society' for the sickness scheme, a society could not be carried on for profit, had to be genuinely member controlled and had to be approved by the insurance committees.[125] An approved society could retain control over its membership. It could choose who to include and expel on any basis, except age.[126]

Control over membership was crucial to the operation of members' schemes, as Beatrice Webb's report had suggested. Families suspected of tubercular 'tendencies', women and those with a reputation for immorality or indolence would find it difficult to gain membership of friendly societies and unions. There was a great deal of competition between the different approved societies for members of good standing. Once a member, there would be a large measure of local and personal control over one's conduct and expulsion if it were to fall short. The reported case law reflects this. In one case, for example, an attempt is made to expel a member who has been seen out of doors after 9 pm while in receipt of a sickness allowance. Mutuality brought with it surveillance, control and coercion.[127] Surveillance did not necessarily begin with the state.

[121] See Section 17 Insurance Act 1913.

[122] E.g., *R Quinn* v. *National Catholic Benefit and Thrift Society's Arbitration* [1921] 2 Ch 318.

[123] N. Whiteside, 'Private Agencies for Public Purposes: Some New Perspectives on Policy Making in Health Insurance Between the Wars', *Journal of Social Policy* 12(2) (1983), 65–94.

[124] See generally, D. Weinbren and B. Jones, 'Getting a Grip', above n. 38, 99.

[125] Section 23. [126] Section 30(2).

[127] *Andrews* v. *Mitchell* [1905] AC 78.

Friendly societies, in particular those founded in the chapel, were an expression of respectability and shared morality. The rules of association would commonly allow the expulsion of members for 'immoral or other serious personal misconduct'. The operation of these rules was an important aspect of the self-governing life of the association. But this could come into conflict both with the compulsory nature of the scheme and government policies associated with it.[128] One reported case involved the denial of a married women's maternity benefit under her husband's scheme. The husband was away at war and the child was plainly not his. The Court, disagreeing with the society, (Darling J dissenting) took a literal view of the statutory reference to 'wife' and allowed the benefit.[129]

The New Tabernacle (Old Street Congregational) Approved Society features in two reported cases relating to similar themes. In the first, they refused to pay ordinary (member-based) benefits to a woman.[130] She had given up employment the day before her marriage because she was no longer able to work due to pregnancy-related complications. She intended to be employed again 'as soon as I can leave the little one'. The society claimed that she ceased to be an insured member upon her marriage. Atkin J allowed her claim in the High Court but the Society won on appeal to the Court of Appeal. A later case showed she may have been damned whether married or not. By the time *Sutton* v. *New Tabernacle (Old Street Congregational) Approved Society*[131] was decided, there had been an amendment to the National Insurance Act stating:[132]

> Notwithstanding any provision to the contrary in any rule of any approved society or branch of such society, an insured unmarried woman who is pregnant shall not on the ground that her pregnancy was due to misconduct be deprived of any sickness benefit to which she would but for that provision have been entitled.

Miss Sutton had been a member for ten years and was, at the time, single, pregnant and engaged to be married. She claimed a sickness

[128] I have only for these purposes looked at the reported cases, but a more in-depth study of cases being brought to arbitration would be useful and interesting.

[129] *Scott* v. *Northumberland and Durham Miner's Relief Fund Friendly Approved Society* [1920] 1 KB 174.

[130] *Davidson* v. *New Tabernacle (Old Street Congregational) Approved Society* [1916] 2 KB 80.

[131] *Sutton* v. *New Tabernacle (Old Street Congregational) Approved Society* [1924] 1 KB 494.

[132] Section 12(3) National Insurance Act 1918.

benefit unrelated to her pregnancy. When the society's sick visitor noticed her condition, the visitor notified the society who determined to terminate her membership under its rules for immoral conduct. Lord Hewart considered that the society's rule was not *ultra vires*, and allowed the society the right to expel its members under such rules, but 'not to deprive her of any sickness or disablement benefit to which she would have, but for that provision, have been entitled'.[133] She would lose future contingent benefits but not those which had already been accrued.

Where does someone such as Miss Sutton, who has been expelled by her approved society, then go? And what of the 7 million people who at the time of the coming into force of the National Insurance Act 1911, were too poor, too ill-equipped or too 'unacceptable' to already be members of an approved insurance society?[134] This question exposes another area of controversy created by the Act. And there are two very different versions of its nature.

The National Insurance Act 1911 required approved societies to be 'not for profit' and to be representative of their membership. Under pressure from the 'industrial insurance societies' such as Prudential Assurance and Pearl, a proviso was added to section 23 of the Bill during its passage. It made it possible for societies or companies set up for other (profit) purposes to establish separate sections as approved societies. The industrial assurance societies were loathed by social activists at the time. They offered thousands of illegal and unenforceable schemes especially for life and burial insurance (some of which achieved such notoriety that Parliament was compelled to give them retrospective validity). They allowed people to take what amounted to 'bets' on the life expectancies of their friends or relations. Life insurance policies over young children were prohibited when they became associated with early child mortality.[135] Sickness benefits were not part of this core business but some of these societies sought out approved society status as a way to further these other branches of their business.

The Labour Party consistently argued that the inclusion of the industrial assurance societies undermined the democratic basis of the scheme. Beatrice Webb urged the 1913 Labour Party conference that societies

[133] [1924] 1 KB 494, 501.

[134] Beveridge estimates that 5 million were already members, Beveridge, *Voluntary Action*, above n. 2, p. 76.

[135] See, further, *ibid.*, pp. 54 ff and, for a different perspective, T. L. Alborn, *Regulated Lives: Life Insurance and British Society, 1800–1914* (University of Toronto Press, 2009).

which make a profit ought to be excluded from approved status. The Labour Party reprised these arguments from democracy in their representations to the 1925 Royal Commission on National Health Insurance. It argued that given the presence of the industrial assurance societies, the ambition 'that the scheme was to be democratic, controlled by the insured for the insured . . . is almost a dead letter' and argued that local authorities rather than self-governing friendly societies should be the preferred administrators of the scheme.[136] According to Daunton:[137]

> Frustration at the subversion of self-governing approved societies led to a greater acceptance of the state providing democratic accountability.

But the issues were even more complex than Daunton would suggest. Without the involvement of industrial assurance schemes the state would likely have had to have become involved a lot earlier. The answer to 'where did the people whom the ordinary approved society would not have accepted go?', seems to be 'to the industrial assurance society'. There were provisions in the Act for the transfer of contributions to another society on expulsion. Industrial assurance societies were more willing to accept members and not as concerned about social control.

Like the state, a democratic voluntary society is able to decide if one is a friend or a stranger. The state does this all the time in terms of its own borders. But a compulsory scheme, within those borders, has to provide a place for both the 'good' and 'bad' risks alike. The state is not able to withdraw its obligations as readily as a mutual society. It is not simply a contest between which of the friendly society, the state or the industrial assurance society, is the more democratic, but of what one comprehends by democracy. Beveridge argued, after the fact, that had the state introduced its own administration for those who would not or could not join a friendly society the 'position of the friendly society as a select body in the community qualified for self-government would have been clearly marked'.[138] It is hard to see, however, how this course would have necessarily preserved the democratic practices of the approved societies given the other pressures they were under.

Despite this emerging disquiet, forms of voluntarism intensified over the inter-War years. Relations between statutory and voluntary social services had become so entwined that Macadam described the phenomenon as the 'New Philanthropy'.[139] In many ways Macadam was still very

[136] Daunton, 'Payment and Participation', above n. 91, 183. [137] *Ibid.*
[138] Beveridge, *Voluntary Action*, above n. 2, p. 295.
[139] Macadam, *The New Philanthropy*, above n. 1, pp. 28–9.

much writing in the Maitland tradition. She makes numerous references to the voluntarist and self-help tradition as a uniquely British one and even as late as 1934, she extols the virtues of the National Insurance Act 1911 as representing the 'incurably clubbable spirit of the English character'. While she applauds the Charity Organisation Society for its 'character' (as if it were a 'person'), she laments that it has become somewhat old-fashioned. On the connection between the public and private she finds this quotation of Sidney Webb the most helpful. He:[140]

> deprecates what he calls the parallel bars theory of the relationship between the public and the private . . . The better analogy is that of the extension ladder that draws out length after length to enable the worker to reach greater heights . . . The public authority and the salaried official can only work in gross; they are apt to be blunt and obtuse; to have no fingers but only thumbs . . . We need the voluntary worker to be the eyes and the fingers of the Public Authority . . . as the circumference of Public Authorities is extended, the greater becomes the periphery.

She gives examples of a wide variety of intersections between the public and voluntary sectors in philanthropic enterprises on this periphery. These include the use of voluntary unpaid service in local committees, royal commissions, statutory committees and the magistracy. Forms of 'recognition' of voluntary agencies include registration of charitable homes for children regardless of whether they receive a state subsidy,[141] systems of matched government funding for voluntary donations,[142] the ability of voluntary associations to compete with local authorities for new housing subsidies[143] and even (in areas of 'sexual hygiene' which might be too politically unpopular for the public authorities themselves to provide the service) the conferral of block grants in aid.[144] In many cases it is the voluntary sector that is providing leadership and innovation, and is first to recognize need – as was the case, for example, with the Personal Service League, which provided clothing to the poor.

The Local Government Act 1929 was the next major reform. It was intended to help resolve the multiple problems of co-ordination that still prevailed. There were problems of co-ordination between different

140 *Ibid.*, at pp. 28–9.

141 Regulation of Charities Children Act 1908 (registration became compulsory in 1933).

142 Macadam, *The New Philanthropy*, above n. 1, p. 41.

143 Public Utilities Housing Authorities.

144 See, e.g., the National Council for Combating Venereal Disease and the work of the National Birth Control Association.

agencies for public provision; between voluntary agencies and public authorities; and between voluntary agencies themselves. The Local Government Act 1929 brought Poor Law hospitals and public authority medical services under the same administrative control for the first time. Local government was empowered to fund voluntary society provision for named services (such as to the blind).[145] Issues undoubtedly remained. Though the Act gave local government a duty to 'consult' voluntary hospitals, much of the charitable fund raising effort continued to be devoted to those who were already best served.[146] Attempts to establish registers of 'cases helped' to avoid the duplication of aid and to help identify the most needy cases were often undermined by churches, missions and other voluntary bodies who resisted 'red tape'.[147] Like Helen Bosanquet, Macadam accuses many of the voluntary societies of the time of 'unregulated benevolence', 'wastefulness' and 'generous impulses rather than calculated policy'.[148]

In 1946, the National Health and National Insurance Acts enacted a new centralized bureaucratic welfare state. The National Insurance Act 1946 would centralize and extend the unemployment and insurance schemes. All that would be left of voluntarist effort in the National Insurance Act 1946 would be the requirement of trade union and friendly society representation on the National Advisory Committee (one member each). This striking change of direction would have a devastating effect on the friendly societies. Beveridge had originally recommended in his 1942 report that friendly societies should retain administration over the sickness benefit while the state took over the administration of benefits from the industrial life assurance companies.[149] His regret at damage done to the voluntary fellowships is palpable. As he later remarked, the state effectively 'divorced' the friendly societies: 'The State, like a Roman father, has sent the friendly society to live back in their own house.'[150] They had been robbed of 'the

[145] See Sections 101 and 102 Local Government Act 1929 which refers to maternity and child welfare services, non-institutional care of 'defectives', tuberculosis sufferers etc.

[146] For some of the problems of associated with voluntary hospitals, see A. Digby and N. Bosanquet, 'Doctors and Patients in an Era of National Health Insurance and Private Practice 1913–1938', *Economic History Review* 41 (1988), 74–94; J. Mohan, 'Voluntarism, Municipalism and Welfare: The Geography of Hospital Utilization in England in 1938', *Transactions of the Institute of British Geographers* 28(1) (2003), 56–74.

[147] Macadam, *The New Philanthropy*, above n. 1, p. 96. [148] Ibid, pp. 61, 63.

[149] W. Beveridge, *Social Insurance and Allied Services* (New York: Macmillan, 1942).

[150] Beveridge, *Voluntary Action* above n. 2, p. 80.

intensity of their inner life' and turned from 'organs of good fellowship into being organs of the state'.[151] The state had then cast them off. The future of such societies was in real doubt. They had been effectively denatured. The state had taken over their functions – or as much as it could do without attempting to replicate the system of reciprocal surveillance and social control that was an essential part of the mutuality principle. It would later attempt to replicate this too.

What general lessons then can we glean from this period? The state and voluntary society do look very much part of the same genus. They are both vehicles for the public articulation of policy and democratic participation in the moral life of communities. They both control their membership and are capable of exercising coercion over their members. They each demonstrate an ability to undermine the other: the voluntary agencies by undermining the penal practices of the Poor Law regime and the state by undermining their self-governing powers and – in the case of the friendly societies – ultimately their public functions by taking them to itself.

But the decline and absorption of the voluntary association during this time was not intentional, or at least was not the focus of intention. Regardless of their politics, everyone initially thought that social insurance should be self-governing. Everyone also agreed that the voluntary agency – whether for mutual aid or philanthropy – was better able to know and assist the 'whole person'. The evolution of the British version of the welfare state was predominantly policy driven. It was not without its institutional casualties. Jose Harris argues that both the local institutional and democratic controls that had applied to the Poor Laws were lost along with the market and actuarial constraints that had applied to the compulsory national insurance system.[152] We might also add that the latter also lost the constraints associated with fellowship. Political pressures were all that remained.

And the common law?

The law's role in this process was mostly legislative and instrumental. Lawyers were not thinking about the public–private distinction during this time or about institutional design. Given the state of the law, many of the sources of conflict between approved societies and the government

[151] *Ibid.*, p. 295.
[152] J. Harris, 'War and Social History', above n. 90, 183.

would not have been susceptible to litigation in any event.[153] But the common law did have an important area of contribution to make during this time – though again a largely unconscious one. Figgis had said that the association should be regarded as public to its members and private from the state. The common law judges were beginning to take the first of those propositions seriously. Courts were increasingly hearing and intervening in cases involving expulsions from membership of associations. These cases would produce some of the forms of analysis and basic principles of the new and emerging administrative law. Once again the state would borrow from civil society – this time in the form of nascent public law principles.

Expulsions were usually at the behest of the 'domestic tribunal' applying the rules of the association. These decisions were made by the association's officers and not by outside lawyers or judges. In other words, these decisions look less like the decisions of courts (requiring the highest standards of impartiality, evidence and due process) and more like the decisions of ordinary officials. They are more similar to the decisions made by civil servants. So it is in this context that we find the early cases about what is required by way of natural justice in an administrative setting (such as what due notice and impartiality means), and even whether a privative clause in a society's rules is effective to deprive the courts of jurisdiction.[154] In *Andrews* v. *Mitchell*,[155] for example, the House of Lords said no to the last question. The society's rule that the expulsion decision was final and conclusive and could not be subject to appeal did not stop the Lords from declaring the decision itself to be a nullity. Sixty-three years later, *Andrews* would be cited in argument in the Court of Appeal in the landmark administrative law case of *Anisminic Ltd* v. *Foreign Compensation Commission*.[156] The House of Lords would, on appeal, adopt similar reasoning for core public authorities.[157]

[153] Challenges were brought between the insurance committees and the insurance commissioners under the National Insurance Act 1911. In *Insurance Committee for the Burgh of Glasgow* v. *The Scottish Insurance Commissioners* 1915 S C 504, the Lord President ruled that regulations made by the Commissioners could not be challenged for *vires* in the Courts but only in Parliament.

[154] See, further, D. J. Mullan, 'Administrative Law at the Margins', in M. B. Taggart (ed.), *The Province of Administrative Law* (Oxford: Hart, 1997), p. 134.

[155] [1905] AC 78.

[156] [1968] 2 QB 862 [CA].

[157] [1969] 2 AC 147 [HL].

The exact basis of intervention in the decisions of domestic tribunals would not be clear or self-conscious until long after it had been established.[158] In the late nineteenth-century cases the expelled member's property interests would sometimes be used as a basis for the court's jurisdiction.[159] In cases such as *Andrews* itself the Court merely asked if there was a 'sufficient interest at stake'. One of the earliest textbook treatments of administrative law, Robson's, *Justice and Administrative Law* (1928) devotes an entire chapter to 'Domestic Tribunals'.[160] In other words, he treats them as a mainstream topic of administrative or 'public' law. The rationale he offers for judicial intervention does not depend on the existence of monopolistic or coercive powers, but on the potential for members acting in a judicial capacity to mistake their own interests for that of the common good.[161] Importantly, according to Robson, the power to intervene should not depend on the association's legal status – including whether they have a contractual, statutory or (recognized) corporate basis. 'Voluntary associations' (broadly construed), he suggests are subject to too limited supervision by the courts on the narrow grounds of natural justice, bias and jurisdictional issues only. His view of the 'state' appears, in normative public law terms, to be an organic one that includes the voluntary association.

By the mid-twentieth century, however, the standard basis for judicial supervision was that the member had a contractual relationship with the association, which could be found in the society's rules.[162] The voluntary association was beginning to be thought of much more as a part of the 'private' realm. Even so, this was a variety of contract quite unlike any other. Such rules could be express or *implied* and it was the latter that gave scope for judicial creativity and the interpolation of 'public law like' norms. Motivations such as malice could be treated as relevant (motivation is treated as irrelevant in the 'ordinary' common law of contract). And, the Courts suggested, contractual terms purporting to exclude natural justice obligations would not be treated by the courts as

[158] See, e.g., the various bases for judicial supervision described in R. Forbes, 'Judicial Review of the Private Decision Maker: The Domestic Tribunal', *University of Western Ontario Law Review* 15 (1976), 123–50 and Z. Chafee, 'The Internal Affairs of Associations Not for Profit', *Harvard Law Review* 43 (1929–30), 993–1029.

[159] E.g., *Rigby* v. *Connol* (1880) 14 Ch D 482, 487; *Baird* v. *Wells* (1890) 44 Ch D 661.

[160] W. A. Robson, *Justice and Administrative Law: A Study of the British Constitution* (London: Macmillan, 1928), Chapter 4.

[161] *Ibid.*, p. 222.

[162] *Lee* v. *Showmen's Guild of Great Britain* [1952] 2 QB 329.

enforceable.[163] In truth, domestic tribunals came to occupy an intermediate space between the private realm where the ordinary law of contract applied and the space occupied by public statutory bodies for whom the full range of the prerogative writs were available. This is yet another example of how much the state and civil society appeared to be similar as a matter of legal thought. At least in this limited area, Maitland's faith in the incurably clubbable spirit of the English character and the capacity for the common law to recognize it, would be borne out.

By the time the welfare state was being rethought in the 1980s, however, the public and private law spheres had been increasingly prised apart. 'Public power' would be regarded as delegated from above and private power would be considered a consensual and more 'natural' matter. This earlier story suggests that we need not think of the state and civil society in such starkly different terms. They may indeed be considered part of the same genus. There are other lessons to be learned here too. A major question during this time was not 'what rights does the individual have against the state' but rather what rights does the individual have against the 'collective'? We need not always think of rights in statist terms. Moreover, we have seen that the state and civil society each have the potential to undermine the other. That should pose a warning for enthusiasts for the 'Big Society'. I will consider contemporary issues about the relationship between the state and civil society in Chapters 8 and 9. But before we do so, we need to consider how 'for profit' activities were coming to be viewed over the period we have just covered, and whether the Crown would be capable of personating the expanding public sphere and public law norms. Those subjects will be addressed in the two chapters that follow.

[163] *Ibid.*, 342.

5

The private life of the state: the Crown and the public sphere

'[T]he Crown, though it remained a corporation sole with many extraordinary qualities, did not become coextensive with the state.'[1]

Private King, Public Crown

In the last chapter we saw how Britain's transformation from a highly voluntarist polity to one of the most centralist states in Western Europe was largely driven by empiricism and functionalism rather than by any particular theories about the state. In this chapter, I ask whether by the middle of the twentieth century or, indeed, at earlier points in our period, the Crown could have become an entity by which to 'personate' this increasingly centralized state or 'Commonwealth'[2] and thus become the focus of a distinct public law. As it happened it did neither. Instead, for important legal purposes, the Crown would come to be treated as a 'private person of full age and capacity'.

There were a number of legal 'moments' when the Crown might have become the legal personification of the public sphere as a whole: mid-nineteenth century as the bureaucracy was forming and public office waning; at the turn of the twentieth century as the public realm was rapidly expanding its functions; and at the point of nationalization. At none of these points did that happen. The Crown would not come to personify the public sphere and neither would it serve to unify distinctly public law principles. The Crown and the public sphere were never coterminous. Instead the Crown would be more narrowly defined.

[1] W. S. Holdsworth, *Essays in Law and History*, A. L. Goodhart and H. G. Hanbury (eds.) (London: Oxford University Press, 1946), p. 214.

[2] 'Commonwealth' was Maitland's preferred term see F. W. Maitland, 'The Crown as Corporation', in H. A. L. Fisher (ed.), *Collected Papers of Frederic William Maitland* 3 vols. (Cambridge University Press, 1911), vol. III, pp. 244, 246–7.

And that definition would be almost exclusively associated with immunities and privileges, rather than obligations, until the 1980s. Defining the Crown narrowly in this way enabled the spread of *private* law norms into the public sphere as the range of public functions was expanding.

This chapter covers the period up until nationalization and the enactment of the Crown Proceedings Act 1947. How the private life of the state was re-imagined as part of privatization policies will be the subject of separate consideration in Chapter 8.

One standard explanation for why the Crown did not come to represent 'the public realm' or to unify 'public law' principles in British legal thought concerns the problematic character of the King or Crown as a legal person. According to this argument, the King in his personal manifestation has never been properly separated from the Crown in its public capacity. The first part of this chapter suggests that this critique attributes too much to the problems associated with the King's two bodies. While the Crown understood as a legal person is certainly a *part* of the story of the public–private law divide, legal characterizations of the Crown have often served to mask other more significant and historically contingent factors.

The remainder of the chapter suggests some of these. The relationship between the state and civil society was, and remained, too fluid for the Crown to come to represent the whole. The judicially enforced norms that could have served to unify the public sphere were too much in the nature of privileges and immunities to have been allowed to spread as state and local government functions expanded. These norms denoted the absence of law rather than notions of public duty or constraint. The underlying ordinary law constitution with its presumption that private law norms should apply was too strong. It is also difficult to imagine how such nascent public law norms of immunity and privilege could have developed through the common law into public law norms of duty and special obligation. More duty-based notions of 'publicness' did exist throughout this period but they tended to be *politically* rather than *judicially* enforced – especially in the Special Act processes. As such, many of these more nuanced conceptions of the public (invoking notions of public trust) would later fade from legal memory (or be restricted to specialist areas such as charities law). By the mid-twentieth century, legal conceptions of the Crown would again be restated and for new purposes. By that time, a number of political purposes were served by treating the Crown as far as possible as a private person. The private person account of the state was a repudiation of Idealism, of the 'god state', and absolutist claims to sovereignty: it was also a proactive strike against the new and emerging administrative law. Treating the Crown as a natural and private person appeared symbolically to constrain the state and was, at the same time, *empowering* of the state – enabling its expansion into new activities with minimal legislative effort.

The Crown as distraction

Kantorowicz connects the public–private distinction *within* government with the separation of the King in his natural person from the Crown in its public capacity.[3] In a similar vein, Loughlin suggests:[4]

> [T]he Crown has, in practice, provided a poor substitute for the idea of the state. The main reason for this is that the monarchical structure of our system of government has frustrated any attempt systematically to unravel the 'public' from the 'private' aspects of the Sovereign's responsibilities . . . the King could not be separated from his Crown.

He goes further to connect the failure to conceptualize a separate public law to a tendency to conceive of the Crown as a corporation sole (an office residing in a single person) rather than as a corporation aggregate (an entity distinct from its individual members). The latter, he argues, has inhibited lawyers from recognizing both a modern state apparatus and an associated and distinct public law. He also attributes the British tendency to analogize from private law to the public sphere ('the private law model of public law') to this incomplete separation of King and Crown. In this section I assess these arguments.

One important respect in which King and Crown had still not been completely separated by the middle of the nineteenth century was as a matter of high politics. The law was blind as to whether the monarch actually exercised the legal powers conferred on her, and it was by no means clear how much real political power she was capable of exercising. We know that earlier, prior to the first Reform Act, the Treasury had self-consciously invoked an abstract idealization of the Crown – exalting ministers and the bureaucracy at the expense of Parliament – and in that way had attempted to 'dignify an insane, then a profligate

[3] E. Kantorowicz, *The King's Two Bodies: A Study in Medieval Political Theology* (Princeton University Press, 1957), p. 172.

[4] M. Loughlin, 'The State, the Crown and the Law', in M. Sunkin and S. Payne (eds.), *The Nature of the Crown* (Oxford University Press, 1999), p. 33.

King'.[5] The reigns of William IV and Victoria presented different challenges. Cannadine catalogues that, in just seven years, William IV thrice dismissed a Ministry, twice dissolved Parliament before its time, thrice proposed a coalition between opponents and once used his influence in a controversial vote in the Lords.[6] Victoria artificially prolonged the life of Melbourne's government in 1839, and all but sacked Palmerston from the Foreign Office in 1851.[7] If these were the *public* manifestations of royal influence, one could only have guessed at their *private* manifestations. We now know that Victoria only very reluctantly signed an Order in Council in 1870 creating a sub-Commander in Chief in the Secretary of State for War and that Prince Albert used his influence in the appointment of the controversial figure Edwin Chadwick to the (equally controversial) Public Health Commission.[8] It perhaps did not help that Prince Albert professed to wanting the Crown to represent the state above party politics.

As late as 1879, the Commons debated whether 'the influence of the Crown has increased, is increasing and ought to be diminished' (this is also evidence that 'the Crown' was still sometimes being used to refer to the monarch at this time).[9] Bagehot's 1867 claim that 'the monarchy has increased its strength', by becoming representative of the 'dignified' rather than the active 'efficient' parts of the Constitution, was not a description of the current practice but rather advice as to the course that the monarchy should take. For Bagehot, it was constitutional convention, and not law, that would have to do the work of controlling royal power – and of separating the dignified from the efficient parts of the constitution. Cannadine concludes that at the time Bagehot was writing, monarchy was 'neither impartial or above politics, nor Olympian and above society, as it was later to become, but was actively part of both'.[10] It would take the whole of Victoria's reign before she would accept that the sovereign could no longer take any part in party politics. One explanation, then, was that Royal power was too personal, too unpopular and

5 J. R. Torrance, 'Sir George Harrison and the Growth of Bureaucracy in the Early Nineteenth Century', *English Historical Review* 83 (1968), 52, 86.

6 D. Cannadine, 'The Context, Performance, and Meaning of Ritual: The British Monarchy and the "Invention of Tradition"', in E. Hobsbawn and T. Ranger (eds.), *The Invention of Tradition* (Cambridge University Press, 1983), pp. 101–64, 109.

7 *Ibid.*

8 S. E. Finer, *The Life and Times of Sir Edwin Chadwick* (London: Methuen, 1952), p. 321.

9 Cannadine, 'The Context, Performance, and Meaning of Ritual', above n. 6.

10 *Ibid.*, p. 110.

too interfering for lawyers and politicians to want to vest grandiose ideas of statehood in the Crown. This was particularly so at a time when Britain was one of the few non-absolutist monarchies in Europe.

Holdsworth sets these fears in broader historical perspective:[11]

> If the Stuart Kings and the prerogative lawyers had had their way King and State would have been identified. The result of Parliament's victory was that the Crown, though it remained a corporation sole with many extraordinary qualities, did not become co-extensive with the state.

As a matter of high politics there is certainly force in the argument that King and Crown were not sufficiently separated through the first half of our period.

Another set of arguments, also linked to the incomplete separation of King and Crown, seeks to explain why the Crown is not associated with a distinct public law. Because the King is a natural man, he has all the powers of an ordinary person, and hence there is an incomplete separation between public and private legal norms. These arguments have also been linked to the distinction between the Crown as corporation aggregate and corporation sole. They too require further and more careful analysis.

According to seventeenth-century common law authority, the Crown is a corporation sole.[12] But, the argument goes, the Crown conceived as a corporation sole does not do any 'real work'. The idea that the office of the Crown is perpetual and survives changes of monarch ('the King is dead: long live the King') was famously criticized by Maitland. He contended that the Crown's existence as a perpetual legal person had never been fully taken to heart by nineteenth-century lawyers.[13] On the passing of office from William to Victoria, for example, lawyers thought it necessary to enact legislation continuing military and other commissions signed by her predecessor,[14] authorizing Victoria to carry into

[11] Quoted by D. N. Chester, *The English Administrative System 1780–1870* (Oxford: Clarendon Press, 1981), p. 95.

[12] *Case of Sutton's Hospital* (1612) 77 Eng Rep 960 per Coke CJ.

[13] Maitland rejected the notion of the Crown understood as a corporation sole (an office residing in a single person). That, he said, 'may have described Henry VIII when the King's lands were not yet severed from the nation's lands, the King's wealth from the common wealth or the King's power from the power of the state, but it was unable to describe the modern state apparatus'. See F. W. Maitland, 'The Crown as Corporation', above n. 2, pp. 246–7.

[14] Demise of the Crown Act 1837 (7 Gul VI & 1 Vict c 31) (military commissions to continue). It was not until 1862 that the Queen's personal signature for the renewal of

effect treaties for the suppression of slavery entered by William IV[15] and to transfer obligations to pay pensions out of the civil list.[16]

The important case of *Viscount Canterbury* v. *Attorney General*,[17] decided in Chancery in 1843, also appears to provide evidence of a connection between the Crown conceived as corporation sole and the private law model of public law. That case, brought by Petition of Right against Queen Victoria, involved a fire in the Speaker's rooms at the Palace of Westminster during the reign of William IV. The judges were invited to consider the practical legal consequences of the proposition that the King never dies and is a perpetual legal person and to distinguish between the natural person and the office of the King.[18] The Court acknowledged that the monarch is a legal person with distinct qualities – a corporation sole – but was unwilling to find that Queen Victoria should inherit the liabilities of her predecessor when an 'ordinary' person would not.

There are other ways of viewing this controversy. Distinguishing between the King and Crown posed problems for the early nineteenth-century lawyer similar to those associated with distinguishing between person and office more generally (discussed in Chapter 2). The difficulty in successfully making the King–Crown distinction, however, is not of itself evidence that the monarch was treated in law as an 'ordinary' private person. The actual legal position was rather to the contrary. George III first surrendered the net revenues of the Crown estate (but not ownership of the capital assets) to the Exchequer in return for the civil list in 1760. As a consequence, King George had to ask Parliament for legislation before he was able to hold property as a natural man.[19] In Queen Victoria's time, doubts about her capacity to do things an 'ordinary' private person could do, such as to grant leases over her Duchy of Cornwall Estates, required legislation conferring such 'ordinary powers'.[20] Her right to bring suits on such leases was at the same time

military commissions was dispensed with (Officers' Commissions Act 1862 (25 and 26 Vict c 4)).

15 Slave Trade Act 1837 (7 Gul IV & 1 Vict Cap 63).

16 Adjustments to civil list support for HM Household Civil List Act 1837 (1 Vict c 2). There are many other examples: Acts of Parliament (Mistaken References) Act 1837 (7 Gul IV & 1 Vict c 60); 1 Vict c 1 (commissions of peace continue).

17 (1843) 1 Ph 305; 41 ER 648.

18 For a discussion of this concept, see Chapter one.

19 39 & 40 Geo III c 88.

20 Duchies of Lancaster and Cornwall (Accounts) Act 1838 (1 & 2 Vict c 101), Duchy of Cornwall Management Act 1868 (31 & 32 Vict c 35).

limited.[21] Legislation was enacted to ensure that, upon her marriage, Prince Albert did not acquire interest in her property as a husband normally would have done under the law at that time.[22]

Until the passing of the Sovereign Grant Act 2011, the civil list arrangements have been reign specific. Each successive sovereign has been required voluntarily to consent to surrender the net surplus of the Crown Estate to the Exchequer in exchange for the civil list. Ironically – and confounding popular political notions – the result in legal terms, is that 'the people', by way of the governmental apparatus, act as trustee for the Queen rather than the other way around.[23] Nineteenth-century legislation, then, treated the monarch as a singular office rather than as a private individual. It is, indeed, hard to discern anything by way of legislative recognition of the monarch's 'private capacity' (in the sense of her being treated as an *ordinary* natural person) before the Petition of Right Act 1860, and in any case even that usage is in the context of recognizing her *unique* privileges in litigation.

It is not the monarch's ordinary person status but rather her distinct constitutional status that accounts for some of the case law, including much of the reasoning in the *Viscount Canterbury* case itself. There are other, more important, reasons why the Crown was not found vicariously liable in that case (discussed fully in Chapter 7). One additional set of reasons is worth mentioning at this point. As we have seen, law often views issues of personality through its own peculiar lens and an important measure of corporate legal personality is the existence of some kind of public fisc or fund.[24] In 1843, the monarch's relationship to public funds was problematic on two fronts. While the land and buildings of the Palace of Westminster, where the fire occurred, were vested in trust for the Queen, as they had been for her predecessor, the nature of that trust was ambiguous.[25] This had

[21] Duchy of Cornwall (Limitations of Actions and Suits) Act 1860 (23 & 24 Vict c 53).

[22] Prince Albert Annuity Act 1840 (3 Vict c 3).

[23] Statutes would commonly vest public property in Commissioners in trust for 'Her Majesty' though occasionally explicitly also 'for the public service', e.g., 15 Vict c 28, Section 2.

[24] Anderson suggests that one reason the cases take the turn they do in the 1850s and 1860s is because judges could not find any departmental funds against which to satisfy judgment. See S. Anderson, 'Public Law', in W. Cornish, S. Anderson, R. Cocks and M. Lobban et al. (eds.), *The Oxford History of the Laws of England* (Oxford University Press, 2010), vol. XI, p. 370.

[25] Ownership of land is described in the statute book variously as 'held on behalf of Her Majesty by Commissioners', as belonging to 'the Crown' or 'Her Majesty', as held by 'trustees for the Crown on behalf of the public' and all manner of variants.

apparently been exploited by William IV himself when he and his family moved into the Speaker's rooms in the Palace at Westminster for a period shortly before the fire. The Palace of Westminster was vested in trust in the Commissioners of Woods, Forests and Buildings. The trustees were public officers, holding funds personally, and were not part of any clear bureaucratic hierarchy. The revenues vested in them *as individuals* in order to pay the maintenance of the assets and the fees and expenses of their own office (including the costs of employing the allegedly negligent servants). It was only the net revenues which made their way eventually, though by no means regularly, into the consolidated fund. [26] The proper division between public and private revenue *generally*, then (and not just that between King and Crown), was still very much unsettled at the time of that symbolic case.

The position of the royal finances was even more unsettled. Progress on determining which matters should fall within the civil list had been ongoing during William IV's reign[27] when a Select Committee made the telling (and to us obvious) distinction that 'the Civil List should be applied only to such expenses as affect the dignity and state of the crown, and the proper maintenance of their Majesties' Household'.[28] Nevertheless, the position in 1839, for example, was that the expense of building new stables at Windsor Castle did not fall under the civil list but instead came within the jurisdiction of the Commissioners of Woods, Forests and Buildings.[29] There was certainly no provision in the civil list for a fund against which damages could be imposed. Add to this that the civil list was renegotiated when each new monarch came to power and we begin to see a number of reasons why a court would have been reluctant to find the Queen liable for acts performed during the previous reign. The Palace of Westminster, where the fire occurred, was still so closely associated with the monarch that the Court did not even consider whether the suit could be satisfied out of the consolidated fund. But here matters of high constitutional principle were also at stake. The Bill of Rights 1688 required that the monarch could not spend money without Parliament. Neither the King's two bodies nor the corporation sole idea could do the real work of locating the public fisc or a public fund here.

[26] The properties in question would be vested in the Commissioners of Woods and Forests personally with a duty to account. See, 3 & 4 Vict 1840 c 104, Section 7.

[27] J. Jacob, *The Republican Crown: Lawyers and the Making of the State in Twentieth Century Britain* (Dartmouth: Aldershot, 1996), p. 13. See also Civil List Act 1837 (1 Vict c 2).

[28] Chester, *The English Administrative System*, above n. 11, p. 188.

[29] Windsor Stable Act 1839 (2 & 3 Vict c 20).

The absence of a complete separation of King and Crown was indeed at issue, but in neither guise does the monarch look much like an ordinary private person. The issues were practical ones to do with money.

Indeed, the *Viscount Canterbury* case should be viewed as the catalyst for the greater separation of the financial administration of King and Crown. It is likely no coincidence that in the year in which the petition was brought, legislation was passed appointing new Commissioners (this time by the Treasury) and requiring that the surplus revenues held by them personally be paid forthwith into the Exchequer. By 1857 the Commissioners of Her Majesty's Woods and Forests would be listed as a public department for the purposes of the Crown Suits (Scotland) Act 1857.[30] The distinction between the Queen in her personal capacity and the Crown in its public capacity would be to an important practical extent resolved by the fiscal separation of Her Majesty's Household Treasury from Her Majesty's Treasury. By 1860, the Petition of Right Act makes a clear distinction between procedures brought against 'Her Majesty in her private capacity' paid out of Her Majesty's *Household* Treasury and the remainder paid out of Her Majesty's Treasury. Separation of Queen and Crown was in the process of being effected. By the time the Crown Proceedings Act 1947 is enacted, 'the Crown' is used as a term which applies *solely* to the Crown in its political capacity and no longer to the monarch personally. Unlike the Petition of Right Act 1860, the 1947 Act does not treat the 'Crown' as referring to 'His Majesty in his private capacity' at all.[31]

Separation appears to be complete. But these were largely practical arrangements. There is nothing about this important fiscal institutional division that gives us any broader *normative* resources with which to distinguish the Crown's proprietary rights from its other rights, obligations and privileges. Given the political, administrative and fiscal separation of King and Crown long before 1947, why should the Crown Proceedings Act treat the Crown in its public capacity as analogous to a 'private person of full age and capacity' for responsibility purposes? We obviously need some other, better, explanation for why the private law analogy is being applied to the Crown in its public capacity at that time. We shall attempt to account for this when we return to consider the Crown Proceedings Act in the last section of this chapter.

[30] In fact the Commissioners would retain elements of independence, see Anderson, 'Public Law', above n. 24, fn. 186.

[31] See Section 40(1).

In this section I have argued that we should be cautious about too readily linking the incomplete separation of King and Crown with the incomplete identification of the Crown with the public sphere and public law. The explanations are more complex. In the next section, I return to the middle of the nineteenth century and attempt to find explanations for a formalistic turn by the judges that disassociated the Crown from *normative* principles that might have unified the public realm.

The Crown becomes both bigger and smaller

At the same time as these practical financial changes signalled the development of hierarchy and bureaucracy, changes in legislative style were also occurring. Up until the 1860s, 'His Majesty' or 'Her Majesty' had been the preferred terminology. Only at that point do statutes begin more frequently to refer to the 'Crown'.[32] Statutes granting new powers of improvement, however, did not confer such powers on the Queen or Crown. The 'Crown' was not used to represent the whole of the new and expanding public sphere.

One possible explanation is the association of the Crown with the royal dignity. It was one thing to use 'the Crown' to refer to matters of high prerogative, war and the central Treasury, but quite another to associate the Crown with new and frequently *local* public health activities of drainage, sewage and the removal of dust heaps. These new functions of government were not traditionally associated with the centre or the Treasury. The Treasury reforms too treated central government officers differently from those at the localities. It was only the former who were subject to entrance exams, and only they who were entitled to the new statutory civil service pensions. Consequently, the newly professionalized and centralized civil service rose in status over this period and became more, rather than less, aristocratic. Only *they* might share in the Crown's prerogatives. Again this cannot be a complete explanation. The association between the Crown and the royal dignity was not so pronounced in the colonies where the Crown was often involved with major infrastructural projects. Perhaps that was because the royal person did not visit.

There is, however, another way in which to read this shift in usage from 'Her Majesty' to the Crown. One might have predicted that the

[32] Given that Prince Albert died in 1861, this change in practice was unlikely to be due to his influence.

bureaucratization of the public realm would have created favourable conditions for conceiving of the public sphere as a unified set of norms personified by the Crown. Indeed, up until then, the Crown had shared important characteristics in common with other public officers and bodies. As a result of a series of common law cases in the 1850s and 1860s, however, the 'Crown' became the *sole* marker of immunity.[33] The change in terminology is almost certainly related to these changes in the common law – and was newly used to mark areas which would attract immunity and privilege.

In a revealing new study, Anderson explains that there were a number of indicia of 'publicness' recognized in the common law as applying across the public sphere up until the 1850s.[34] These included ideas of public trust, and the various immunities from rating, vicarious tortious liability and contractual liability of public officers performing public services. Anderson argues that these could have formed unifying principles of public law and public service for which the Crown could have become the legal representative – principles which might at the same time have formed the basis of a 'nascent public law'. These developments were, however, forestalled by a crucial turn in the common law that also occurred in the middle of the nineteenth century. In the 1850s and 1860s these potentially unifying common law principles of 'publicness' came to be more selectively applied and restricted to 'the Crown' formalistically understood.

As Anderson carefully argues, the officials enjoying immunities from rating and vicarious liability became restricted to those associated with central government. Charitable trustees, commissioners, *quasi* corporate statutory bodies and local government would no longer be included in these unifying principles of 'publicness'. The justifications for such immunities would move from functional and normative ones – involving ideas of public benefit, public purpose and public trust, and a concern about the incentives for attracting the best people to public office – to newly formalistic ones.

Formerly, whether public officers would be liable to local rating, for example, had depended on a functional test of whether their occupation was for the public benefit or for private profit. This meant that even servants appointed directly by the Crown could be liable for rating if they were making a profit from such occupation.[35] The new rationale became that the 'Crown was only bound by express statutory provision',

[33] This is an argument made by Anderson, 'Public Law', above n. 24, pp. 366–84.
[34] *Ibid.* [35] *Lord Bute* v. *Grindall* (1 Tr 338; 2H Bl 265).

a highly formalistic test that operated as a gloss on the statute. The leading case removed the immunity from rates earlier enjoyed by municipal docks.[36] This was particularly surprising given that quite recent case law had recognized an exemption from rating for municipal property on the basis that the Municipal Corporations Act 1835 treated municipal property as 'public funds appropriated for purposes of a public nature' and no longer as private property.[37] If long-established avowedly 'public bodies' were no longer immune from rating, newly created bodies would certainly not count as 'public' either for those purposes. The new local health boards, for example, were not considered to confer benefits on the public but only on a 'section of the public'.[38] The result was to strip the immunity from rating of its normative functional justification. The Crown's immunity from rating would become a hollow formalistic concept which would be haphazardly applied without reference to principle.

At about the same time, Anderson tells us, the judges began to restrict the general immunity from vicarious liability, previously enjoyed by *all* public officers, to the Crown and its servants.[39] Vicarious liability could now be successfully claimed against a range of officials, who clearly met the pre-existing criteria of 'publicness', as long as they were not strictly Crown servants. In the leading case of *Mersey Docks and Harbour Board* v. *Gibbs*[40] the officials who were denied public immunity were unpaid, did not make a personal profit and acted as trustees for the public benefit. The rationale for the immunity again shifted from a normative to a formalistic one. 'Public offices' no longer attracted immunity. The *sole* basis of immunity from vicarious liability was now that 'the King could do no wrong' understood in a formalistic sense that did not do any normative work. Bodies such as Mersey Docks Trustees would not be treated as part of the Crown but as separate corporate or *quasi*-corporate bodies.

Another doctrinal change occurred around the same time. Under the old understandings of vicarious liability, public officers lost their immunity if they personally directed their subordinates to do wrong or profited from their wrong-doing. A new doctrine emerged that removed potential liability from senior Crown servants (including Ministers)

[36] *Mersey Docks* v. *Cameron* [1864–1865] XI H L C 471, *cf. Mayor of Liverpool* v. *Overseers of West Derby* (1856) 6 E & B 704.

[37] *R* v. *Mayor and Alderman of Liverpool* (1839) 9 Ad & El 435.

[38] *R* v. *Hull Justices* (1854) 4 E & B 29. See Anderson, 'Public Law', above n. 24, p. 372.

[39] Anderson, 'Public Law', above n. 24, p. 376.

[40] (1865–66) 11 HLC 686.

when giving instructions to their subordinates or profiting from them.[41] They were no longer to be treated as superiors or masters. Whatever their place in the bureaucratic hierarchy, they would be treated in law as merely fellow servants of the Crown. The effect of treating all Crown servants as equals rather than as in a hierarchy was to expand the immunity for those in managerial positions in the central bureaucracy. Only those servants performing the wrong-doing would be liable, even if they were following instructions in doing so. If Dicey denied the existence of an administrative hierarchy, it was the common law judges who did so first! Immunities were at the same time removed for those officials who were outside of the central government bureaucracy.

The common law would no longer generate a single unified set of public norms that could have come to reside in or to be represented by the Crown as the personification of the state. The Crown would not be coextensive with the public sphere. Numerous pre-existing 'public' bodies would cease to enjoy immunities and privileges: most of the new bodies associated with initiatives and improvements would never enjoy them. Instead, such immunities would come to be associated exclusively with the Crown but – and this is the important point – *not* on the basis of any functional or other explicitly normative distinction between the public and private.

Anderson's reading of the formalistic turn is convincing and compelling. How are we to account for this normative fragmentation of notions of the public at the very time the administrative bureaucratic state was emerging and expanding?

The changing nature of the public

One reason why the Crown would not come to represent all of these new functions in the public sphere takes us back once more to Maitland's analysis. The differences between the state and other organizations were differences of degree rather than of kind. 'Publicness' existed across a very broad spectrum of both publicly owned and privately owned bodies. The Crown could not represent such a broad and fluid range of bodies. This was especially so given that it was not central government per se but rather a combination of central government and locally led initiative[42] that was at the forefront of expanding functions and

[41] Anderson, 'Public Law', above n. 24, p. 369. [42] Described in Chapter 2.

controversy. Even as early as 1850, the 'nascent public law' distinction between public benefit and private profit was becoming increasingly difficult to maintain.

The *Mersey Docks* cases hint at some of the range of entities performing similar functions. It had been argued in the *Mersey Docks* cases that Mersey Docks were in the same position as docks elsewhere which *were* subject to rating and vicarious liability. The docks on the River Thames, for example, were all operated for the benefit of shareholders and were certainly liable for rating and other tortious and contractual liabilities. Why should the trustees of Mersey Docks, engaged in the same functions, be legally privileged? The formalistic turn, which Anderson observes, may signal that functional tests were becoming increasingly difficult to apply as public purposes were expanding. But we should not rush to conclude that this was to do with a more fundamental division that was taking place between public and private – that would not come until considerably later.

Remarkably, during this age of 'laissez-faire' politics, the common law and legislation would be replete with references to the 'public' as a central normative idea in many contexts besides immunity. Ideas about the common weal, the common good, public good, *salus populi* and *res publica* had existed for centuries, taking different meanings during different periods.[43] The common law would continue to apply such background norms on their own and as a gloss on the statute law.[44] Statutes would adopt common law concepts such as the 'common carrier' doctrine.[45] They would frequently make references to the 'public' – a concept invariably left undefined.[46]

It is not, however, the case that what was considered 'public' would remain static during this time. It was, in fact, an expanding category.

[43] See, e.g., J. A. W. Gunn, *Politics and the Public Interest in the Seventeenth Century* (London: Routledge, 2010) (first published 1969).

[44] An interesting question which we cannot answer here is whether common law notions of the 'public' would decline in the UK as Novak suggests happened after democratization and constitutionalization in the US. See W. Novak, *The People's Welfare* (Chapel Hill: University of North Carolina Press, 1996), p. 245.

[45] E.g., 8 & 9 Vict c 28 (1845) Section 2: railway companies would not be liable to any greater extent than common carriers for tolls. Canal Company tolls would be charged equally to all persons.

[46] E.g., 10 & 11 Vict c 112 (1847) (power to grant land for public purposes), 15 & 16 Vict c 52 (1852) (power to take 'any heriditaments necessary for the public service')); Railways Act 1844 (8 Vict c 20) (the board can be restrained from using its powers except 'for public advantage').

For example 'undertakings of a public nature', which in the 1840s seemed to include 'core' activities such as roads, pavings and drains,[47] by the 1860s also included recreational parks, seating and playgrounds.[48] Parliament did not make the classification by strict legal definition: what counted as an 'undertaking of a public nature' was never positively defined.[49] What determined 'publicness' was that undertakings of 'public works' had to be authorized by 'Special Acts'.[50] The Bill process itself was treated as a contest that would test whether powers being conferred on corporations would be used for the public good.[51] Different rules of incorporation, of capitalization constraining when a profit could be paid, and about the acquisition of land (making it easier for people under a legal disability to sell and providing special processes for resolving disputes), would apply to such undertakings. Conflict of interest rules would also increasingly apply in identifiably 'public' settings (though apart from this constraint, the 'public' classification would apply independently of *who* performed the undertaking).[52] The statutory process was central in determining the degree to which an activity was sufficiently public to attract special rules.

At that time, the 'publicness' of such enterprises was viewed almost exclusively as an issue of *power* as opposed to ownership. Public undertakings were involved in 'breaking up the streets' and interfering with both public and private rights of individuals. They were viewed as a threat to competition and liberty, and hence as needing to be controlled. Corporations engaging in public undertakings, had, by definition, already fulfilled some kind of substantive 'public interest' test. In

[47] See, e.g., Registration Incorporation and Regulation of Joint Stock Companies Act 1844 (7 & 8 Vict c 110) which defines the activities to which it does *not* extend (Section 2).

[48] 23 & 24 Vict c 30 (1860). [49] 8 Vict c 16 (Eng and Wales) 8 Vict c 17 (Scotland).

[50] Railway Companies obtained a general authorization in 1845.

[51] This process was the functional equivalent of *la concession de service public* in French law.

[52] E.g., Gas Works Supplying Towns Act (1847) (10 Vict c 15) (commissioners would not be allowed property holding or contractual conflicts but would be allowed to hold shares in a joint stock company). Compliance with conflict of interest rules, however, was sometimes made a condition of being involved, and became more common in the statute book as the century progresses, e.g., 5 & 6 Vict c 101 (1842), Section 2 (making it unlawful for a member of a municipal corporation to vote in matters involving a pecuniary interest); Factories Act 1844 (7 & 8 Vict c 15), Section 10 (only allowing certification of the age of children working in factories to be made by a surgeon or a Justice of the Peace, 'not being the occupier of a factory, and not being the father, son, or brother of the occupier of a factory'. 8 & 9 Vict c 41, (1845), Section 4, did not allow those involved in making or repairing highways a pecuniary interest even in the form of shareholding.

addition, legislative measures were beginning to make provision for the acquisition of such ventures by public authorities after a specified period of time. The earliest example of this is the Railways Regulating Act 1844. It gave the Lord Commissioners of the Board of Trade an option to purchase railway companies after twenty-one years.[53] Far from being Socialist in its aims, it was intended as a regulatory initiative, on the part of Gladstone, over natural monopoly. The Local Government Act 1858 (which succeeded the Public Health Act 1848) went still further. It recognized private infrastructural initiatives, allowed them to bear the first expense of construction of canals, bridges, roads and railways, and provided that, on completion, municipal corporations could purchase and maintain them at public expense.[54] Given these arrangements, it is not difficult to see why Crown privileges and immunities should have been strictly applied. Why should a municipal trading enterprise enjoy privileges and immunities not enjoyed by those prepared to take the initial risk?

At around the same time as the formalistic turn about the nature of the Crown and the availability of immunity was taking place, changes of ownership of public undertakings were beginning and were increasingly in prospect. The idea of 'publicness' was shifting. Formerly powers were conferred on public undertakings for public benefit. Now, the nature of 'public purposes' and 'public benefit' would begin to be reconceived.

With expansion of the franchise, a new idea began to emerge: publicly owned monopolies were to be preferred to privately owned monopolies. This idea was to be severely tested, as municipalities, particularly in the north,[55] began to supplement their rating bases by engaging in municipal trading activities. Questions began to emerge about what it meant to be 'not for profit'.[56] Even so, these early ventures in municipal trading

[53] Section 2. See, for a discussion of how this squares with laissez-faire, I. McLean and C. Foster, 'The Political Economy of Regulation: Interests, Ideology, Voters, and the UK Regulation of Railways Act 1844', *Public Administration* 70 (1992), 313–31.

[54] Section 39–41. Some regarded these provisions as also having regulatory purposes. See, e.g., the views of Joseph Chamberlain cited in J. Sheldrake, *Municipal Socialism* (Avebury: Aldershot, 1989), pp. 17–18, 25. See, also, Dirk Hartog's ground-breaking study, H. Hartog, *Public Property and Private Power: The Corporation of the City of New York in American Law, 1730–1870* (New York: Cornell University Press, 1989).

[55] The Metropolis was not the subject of such trading but rather of regulated and competing private companies.

[56] Municipal trading enterprises were most common among those towns affected by rapid population growth and industrial development, and without a strong rating revenue base.

were not at first associated with 'municipal socialism' – that phrase would not be used until later in the century.[57] Rather, they tended to be exercises in municipal capitalism.[58] The purpose was not to subsidize such enterprises but to make money from them. The aim of the first municipal gasworks in Manchester in 1843 was to harness the profits of existing enterprises for the benefit of the town.[59] Wilson shows that the pricing and profits of municipally owned gas companies differed little from those of privately owned enterprises.[60] If anything, municipally owned enterprises tended to be more profitable (allegedly because they were better able to exploit their monopoly and were not dependent on local authorities for renewal of their franchises).[61] Manchester's Police Commissioners 'unashamedly set out to subsidize the rates from gas profits'.[62]

By the last quarter of the century, the question of how the municipal trading enterprise ought to be able to use its profits had become increasingly controversial. The statutory regulation of profits varied according to the activity and sometimes also the municipality. In Manchester, profits could be used to reduce general rates.[63] The city of Glasgow could use the profits of trading enterprises to provide amenities that would not otherwise be provided such as parks, recreation and art galleries. Scottish boroughs, by contrast, were able to take over gas companies after twenty-five years but only on the condition that profits could be used solely for the improvement of the service or the reduction of the price. In some areas, municipalities would be under a statutory

57 An early instance of the pejorative use of the term is by W. C. Crofts, *Municipal Socialism* (London: Liberty, Property Defence League, 1885). He simultaneously decries centralization and 'local despotism'.

58 J. Sheldrake, *Municipal Socialism*, above n. 54, p. 2.

59 Gas was one of the more profitable trading enterprises according to E. W. Burdett, 'Municipal Ownership in Great Britain', *Journal of Political Economy* 14(5) (1906), 257–60. The municipalization of the Macclesfield Gaslight Co is an example. It was unlawful for a local authority to supply gas if there was already a private gas company operating in the territory. When the privately owned Macclesfield Gaslight Co sought Parliamentary permission to reinvest its profits in more capital, the local Board of Health accused the company of taking excessive profits. The local board then successfully obtained the Macclesfield Act 1860 which granted it permission to negotiate purchase of the company.

60 J. E. Wilson, *Lighting The Town: A Study of Management in the North West Gas Industry, 1805–1880* (London: Paul Chapman, 1991), p. 207.

61 *Ibid.*, perhaps because they were in a stronger position to exploit their monopoly.

62 Wilson, *Lighting The Town*. above n. 60, p. 206.

63 Liverpool Tramways Act profits could not be used for the relief of general rates before 1912.

duty to supply water, and later electricity, to surrounding towns and rural districts – and in so doing they were little different from private companies.[64] In significant instances, municipal trading enterprises sought to maximize profit in similar fashion to any other capitalist enterprise. Even as early as 1850, the 'nascent public law' distinction between public benefit and private profit was no longer easy to maintain. Who was the relevant public to be benefited? Does the presence of the profit motive itself change the nature of the activity? As the unifying principles of the nascent public law themselves began to conflict, it is not surprising that there was a retreat to formalism. During the course of the century these concepts would only become more contested.

New privileges

If it was becoming more difficult to distinguish between entities as their relationships to the profit motive were changing in the middle of the nineteenth century, the controversies would only deepen as public services expanded. By the end of the nineteenth century, there would be open conflict between individual shareholder-owned corporations and municipal trading enterprises, leading to a Parliamentary inquiry which reported in 1900.[65] There was opposition to the ways municipal enterprises were using their monopoly, and concern that municipalities, often already engaged in gas supply, were inhibiting the growth of electricity supply.[66] Municipal trading was no longer being used for 'purely governmental'[67] or 'ordinary governmental functions' (listed by one critic as including sewage disposal, allotments, slaughterhouses, public libraries and harbours), but also for wash houses, crematoriums, apparatus for games in parks, the manufacture and supply of electrical fittings, the manufacture and sale of ice, and the provision of nurses for infectious diseases.[68] Most damningly the Parliamentary Committee heard that the individual had been sacrificed without 'guarantying a

[64] P. Ashley, 'Municipal Trading in Great Britain', *The Quarterly Journal of Economics* 15(3) (1901), 458–64, 460–1.

[65] Joint Select Committee, Report on Municipal Trading (London: Wyman and Sons, September 1900).

[66] Burdett, 'Municipal Ownership in Great Britain', above n. 59, 296; H. J. Gibbons, 'The Opposition to Municipal Socialism in England', *Journal of Political Economy* 9 (1901), 243–59, 252. The Electric Lighting Acts 1882 and 1888 which gave local authorities an option to purchase after twenty-one years were also blamed for this.

[67] Gibbons, 'The Opposition to Municipal Socialism in England', above n. 66, 246.

[68] *Ibid.*, 245.

compensating benefit to society'.[69] It was, said another commentator, too late to cry the 'bogey of socialism'.[70] The special Parliamentary Committee reported to the effect that public trading should be restricted to 'universalized users' (the agreed example of which was water) and that profits should only be applied to improving services and reducing charges to customers and not to rate reduction or other activities.

About the same time, a new opportunity arose through which judges might have produced normative principles by which once again to unify the public sphere. The judges were drawn into this, now acute, political controversy, in the context of the interpretation of the Public Authorities Protection Act 1893. Though only the Crown *qua* crown would enjoy substantive immunities, the 1893 Act conferred litigation privileges on 'public authorities' as a whole – a concept left undefined. The Act, which extended special privileges across the whole of the public realm, can be seen as emblematic of a more idealist age.

The 1893 Act provided a six-month limitation period and special rules as to costs for claims brought against a 'person for any act done in pursuance ... of any Act of Parliament, or of any public duty or authority ...'.[71] There are two reasons why the cases under this Act are important to the larger narrative. The first is that, once again, the judges reinforce the view that not every person or body considered to be 'public' necessarily attracts litigation privileges. It is a matter, according to Lord Haldane, of assessing which bodies Parliament did *not* mean to include within the words.[72] This is an open acknowledgment that privileges should not apply across the whole of the public realm. As a number of judges reiterated, the words were on their face wide enough to include every railway company, entities which were, as part of the special Act procedure, required to satisfy a public benefit test.[73] Yet numerous commercial organizations for profit (including railways companies), which were undoubtedly regarded as public in this wider sense, did not qualify for the procedural privilege. Commercial enterprises,

[69] W. H. Allen, 'Municipal Trading in England', *Journal of Political Economy* 9 (1900), 123–5, 124.

[70] B. Taylor, 'Municipal Glasgow', *The North American Review* 184 (1907) 590–603, 600, 611.

[71] Section 1.

[72] *Myers* v. *Bradford Corporation* [1916] AC 242, 250. Characteristically Lord Haldane thought that persons could include private persons, natural persons and common law corporations.

[73] E.g., *Attorney-General* v. *Margate Pier and Harbour Company* [1900] 1 Ch 749, 753.

even those with public purposes, but whose profits were enjoyed by identifiable individuals were *not* considered to be covered by the Act.

More importantly, the cases grapple with a much larger philosophical issue about the nature of public power. Is everything that a public authority does, even those activities which would be regarded as commercial if performed by private enterprise, necessarily to be regarded as public? The judges began by saying 'yes' and later struggled to find ways to say 'no' while at the same time purporting to follow the laws of precedent.

In *Ydun*, Sir F Jeune P found that every act performed by a public authority became clothed with a public character and hence attracted the privilege.[74] This included acts which would be considered commercial if performed by private enterprise (he gave the example of acts performed pursuant to contractual agreements). He suggested the same would be true of the state when it was engaged in running the Post Office. This finding, apparently upheld by the Court of Appeal,[75] was reluctantly followed in later judgments – though judges tended to bridle at the prospect that a public body 'voluntarily' trading in competition with private traders should be protected.[76] In one instance, a judge claimed that Parliament had not intended the 1893 Act to extend to trading activities at all – even in cases where the profits were applied to rates reduction.[77] A clawing back of the scope of the Act came in *Lyles* v. *Southend-on-Sea*.[78] Vaughan Williams LJ restricted the scope of the protection by drawing a distinction between obligations imposed upon public authorities (which attracted protection) and obligations undertaken voluntarily (which did not).[79] Statutory and common law duties tended to be treated as in the former category and contractual undertakings as in the latter.[80] Subsequent cases distinguished between instances where 'the act' complained of was substantially tortious (the special protection would apply) and where it was substantially contractual (the protection would not).[81] This distinction was presumably intended to protect public authorities in their core 'governmental

74 [1899] P 236, 240.

75 In *Myers* v. *Bradford Corporation* [1916] AC 242 this was subsequently determined not to have been so.

76 *Ambler* v. *Bradford Corporation* [1902] 2 Ch 585, 591 per Vaughan Williams LJ.

77 *Parker* v. *London County Council* [1904] 2 KB 501, 505 per Channell J.

78 [1905] 2 KB 1. 79 *Ibid.* at 13. 80 *Ibid.*, at 14.

81 *Myers* v. *Bradford Corporation* [1916] AC 242; *Milford Docks Co* v. *Milford Haven UDC* [1901] 15 JP 483 discussed in C. S. Emden, 'The Scope of the Public Authorities Protection Act 1893', *Law Quarterly Review* 39 (1923), 341–56.

functions' but not their novel initiatives. It protected those activities which municipal bodies were under a duty to perform and not those which they were only *empowered* to perform. But it was also flexible enough to allow protection for those activities, such as the supply of electricity, which might once have been voluntarily undertaken but had subsequently come to be regarded as a core service. And while sometimes the distinction would treat commercial acts differently from governmental acts, it would not do so directly but would rather depend on how much the act performed was of a contractual nature. This was not a functional test properly so-called but was a kind of a source of power test. These kinds of tests would later find echoes in the tests for judicial intervention under the law of judicial review. This second example of a retreat to formalism, only partial this time, is another instance of judge-made law restricting the scope of special privileges.[82]

A non-statist approach to the expanding public sphere

What is striking, in retrospect, is that English law took a completely different approach to the expansion of state services from that of the French. In post-Revolutionary France, the state was conceived as a distinct and unified entity. In the late nineteenth century, French case law developed public law rules of tort and contract to apply to the state. The standards of conduct to which the state was held, however, varied on a sliding scale 'according to the needs of the service and the necessity to reconcile the rights of the state with private rights'.[83] The state was a static category but the rules that applied to it in its different functions and activities varied. In Britain the exact opposite happened. A range of entities qualified, by various, mainly political, processes, to be included within the public realm. That range included railway companies, public undertakings, trustees and commissioners, municipal trading entities, municipal corporations, the Post Office and central government departments. The degree to which their activities were to the public benefit was commonly assessed at the point at which powers were conferred. This sliding scale of 'publicness' reflected the diversity of the English

[82] Section 21 of the Limitation Act 1939 extended the limitation period to one year for public authorities so defined under the Public Authorities Protection Act 1893.

[83] See the judgment of the Tribunal des conflits in Blanco (TC 8 February 1873) discussed in L. N. Brown and J. Bell, *French Administrative Law*, 5th edn (Oxford: Clarendon Press, 1998), pp. 183 ff.

fellowships. But the common law case law that applied to them was essentially binary: either an entity qualified for a special immunity or privilege or it did not. If not, the default position was that the ordinary private law of contract or tort would apply. In the absence of a distinct administrative law, there was no sliding scale of liability that could reconcile 'public rights with private rights'.

British and French law need not have been so far apart. Indeed, some have argued that it was English law that gave the French their system of liability.[84] The Public Authorities Protection Act 1893 did not present the first opportunity to consider the question of whether a public authority should be treated as legally privileged in all of its dealings, and it would not be the last. The general philosophical question of whether sovereigns always act as sovereigns had been raised much earlier by both Hobbes and Bodin. The former thought that sovereign rights should be treated as inseparable,[85] while the latter was prepared to make the distinction between the promises of a sovereign as to laws (promises made in a governmental capacity) that are not binding, and promises of an ordinary civil character which are binding.[86]

Of more immediate currency were Adam Smith's criticisms of the East India Company. His, widely shared, view was that monopolies and exclusions harm the public, and that this is especially so when they are combined with sovereign powers: 'As sovereigns, their interest is exactly the same as the country which they govern. As merchants their interest is directly opposite to that interest'.[87] It was in relation to the East India Company that one of the earliest attempts to make a functional distinction in British law between a sovereign's commercial and trading activities and its truly 'sovereign functions' can be found.[88] In promoting the Regulating Bill 1773 which aimed to increase ministerial control of the Company, Lord North emphasized 'that military and civil commands

[84] Anderson, 'Public Law', above n. 24, pp. 380–1.

[85] T. Hobbes, *Leviathan*, R. Tuck (ed.), (Cambridge University Press, 1996), Part II, Chapters 18 and 30; J. D. B. Mitchell, *The Contracts of Public Authorities: A Comparative Study* (London: Bell and Sons, 1954), p. 5.

[86] J. Bodin, *The Six Books of a Commonweale*, R. Knolles (tr.) (London: Impensis G Bishop, 1606), p. 95 discussed by J. D. B. Mitchell, *The Contracts of Public Authorities*, above n. 85, pp. 4–5.

[87] A. Smith, *The Wealth of Nations* (Edinburgh: Adam & Charles Black, 1850), p. 288.

[88] French companies were described by Grewe as the 'artificial products of a clearly conceived political will of [the] State' and as lacking in the individualistic spirit of enterprise of the English and Dutch: W. G. Grewe, *The Epochs of International Law*, M. Byers (tr.) (Berlin: De Gruyter, 2001), p. 301.

should be separate from the commercial'.[89] We get a sense from the proceedings that there was something new and experimental in Lord North's proposed distinction. Contemporaries on the other side of the debate, such as Laurence Sulivan, argued that no such line could or should be drawn. He refused to make a distinction between 'commands' and 'commercial' activities, arguing that 'executive authority' was indispensable to the Company for the exercise of its commercial activities. The native population, he said, would 'never part with their money but by compulsion'.[90] The passage of the Bill went some way to achieving North's objectives and his approach attracted influential support from key figures such as James Mill.[91]

By the mid-nineteenth century, a functional approach had been accepted both politically and legally in relation to the East India Company. The courts demonstrated an increasing willingness to treat trading and sovereign functions differently – sometimes viewing the actions of the company as the exercise of delegated political powers or acts of state[92] and at others treating the company as a private contractor or owner.[93] Only an 'act of state' attracted immunity. This approach was preserved at the point at which the Crown took over from the Company. Legislation provided that the Secretary of State for India could be sued on the same basis as the East India Company had been.[94] The Secretary of State was immune only in relation to those actions 'only the sovereign'

89 H. V. Bowen, *Revenue and Reform: The Indian Problem in British Politics 1757–1773* (Cambridge University Press, 1991), p 179. Debate of 2 June 1773.

90 *Ibid*

91 This was the first of a series of Acts that foretold the Company's eventual dissolution. It was followed by the India Act 1784, and the Government of India Act 1833 which put an end to the Company's trading. Eventually the Government of India Act 1858 transferred the government of India from the Company to the Crown and the army to the service of Her Majesty. James Mill argued for the separation: R. Harris, *Industrializing English Law: Entrepreneurship and Business Organization 1720–1844* (Cambridge University Press, 2000), pp. 205–6.

92 *Doss* v. *Secretary of State for India in Council* [1875] 19 Eq 509; *Nabob of the Carnatic* v. *East India Co* [1793] 2 Ves Jun 56; *Secretary of State for India* v. *Kamachee Boye Sahaba* [1859] 7 Moore's Indian Appeals 476, 19 ER 388 (PC); [1869] 13 Moore 22 15 ER 9. See also the argument in *Attorney-General* v. *Brodie* [1846] 4 Moore's Indian Appeals 190, 18 ER 671 about whether the Crown or the East India Company could exercise *parens patriae* power in India.

93 *Moodalay* v. *East India Co* [1785] 1 Bro Ch C 469; *Government of Bengal* v. *Mussamat Shurruffutoonissa* [1860] 8 Moore's Indian Appeals 225, 19 ER 516; *Gridhari Lall Roy* v. *Bengal Government* [1868] 12 Moore's Indian Appeals 448, 20 ER 408.

94 Government of India Act 1858 c 106, Section LXV.

could perform. This became, in turn, the model for French government liability[95] (an example of the British lending a model of statehood and public law to the French).

The Public Authorities Protection Act offered an opportunity to develop some of these functional distinctions across the whole range of public bodies including the Crown. But while the tests often had a functional flavour, their strict focus was the source of power. Another opportunity to create a distinct public law presented itself in the middle of the twentieth century at the point at which the Crown Proceedings Act 1947 was enacted and various British industries were nationalized. Again there are various reasons why that did not happen.

Nationalization

The process of nationalization was a gradual one. For the Fabian Socialists, such as Beatrice and Sidney Webb, it seemed almost inevitable that the central government itself should eventually take over municipal trading enterprises as part of the progressive evolution of the business enterprise. Britain did not need a revolution, they said, it had 'gas and water socialism' already. In a move that would not have surprised Maitland or Dicey, the Webbs contended that it was the development of the corporation that made their arguments possible. Businesses were no longer operated by individuals or partnerships, but by corporations. Corporations were usually run by professionalized management and owned by impersonal shareholders. From the ownership–management split it was a short step, they argued, to substitute public shareholding for private shareholding while retaining an impersonal management structure. In other words the similarities between state and corporation, to their eyes at least, made public ownership seem inevitable. Their case appeared to be strengthened by the success of the experiments involving mixed government and enterprise boards during the War and inter-War years. These had been established to ensure better co-ordination of industry and efficient supply of essential services.

Even if the process may have been more gradual than it appeared, at the political 'moment' at which the state nationalized railways, coal,

[95] Anderson, 'Public law', above n. 24, pp. 380–1 citing D. Fairgrieve, *State Liability in Tort: A Comparative Law Study* (Oxford University Press 2004), pp. 12–13, 20–3. The Secretary of State for India was able to sue and be sued as a body corporate and the liabilities were met from the general revenue.

electricity and much else, the Crown could have come to represent the whole of the public realm and a new 'public service state' might have been conceived as a legal concept. Once again that did not happen. Instead, political ideas about what it meant to be 'public' became more amorphous than formerly, and the variegated range of public-ness would be lost to legal memory long before it would be needed again in an era of privatization.[96] Conceptions of the 'public' declined in the UK during this period, as they had in the US after democratization and constitutionalization.[97]

The basic model for nationalized industry adopted by the Labour Party was that a series of 'professional' boards would be established to manage the various industries. These would include trade union and business representation. This effected a kind of corporatism. The board model was essentially that originally proposed by the Webbs and, though there were undoubtedly other reasons to adopt the board structure, the Webbs's rationale is particularly revealing. If everything were directly owned and managed by central government, a strike might look like rebellion – hence they preferred strikes to be brought against a national board rather than against the state itself.[98] Ministers enjoyed extensive powers to give the boards directions in the 'public interest' but were not expected to intervene in day-to-day operational matters. Litigation determined that the boards and their servants would not be considered as part of the Crown, though they would in certain instances qualify as public authorities for reduced limitation periods in litigation.[99]

Tamlin v. *Hannaford*.[100] the case which decided that nationalized boards and their servants should not be considered Crown agents and servants, drew academic criticism from commentators as different as Wade and Griffith at the time.[101] The degree of control exercised by Ministers over boards did not seem to have been sufficiently recognized. Lord Denning's reasoning in the case is, however, in familiar terms. He locates the British Transport Commission within a spectrum of *public*

[96] Novak, *The People's Welfare*, above n. 44. [97] *Ibid.* p. 245.

[98] B. P. and S. Webb, *A Constitution for the Socialist Commonwealth of Great Britain* (London: Longmans Green, 1920).

[99] Section 11 Transport Act 1947 which stated that the Public Authorities Protection Act would not apply but reduced the standard limitation period from six to three years.

[100] [1950] 1 KB 18, 24.

[101] J. A. G. Griffith, 'Public Corporations as Crown Servants', *University of Toronto Law Journal* 9 (1951–2), 169–193, 189. See also H. W. R. Wade, *Administrative Law* (London: Clarendon Press, 1961), pp. 34–5.

bodies. It is a public authority, its purposes are public purposes, but it is not a government department and neither do its powers fall within the province of government. It is made up of entities which in their former lives had included private for profit railway companies. Its property is not Crown property. Once again the actual question for decision had only two possible answers: should it share in immunity or not. The answer was no.

This idea, that there is a range of bodies within the broader public sphere, which includes but is not restricted to the Crown, was, however, at risk of being lost as a result of nationalization itself. The Labour Party had been confident that the difficulties of the past had been the result of allowing municipal trading enterprises a profit motive. Their solution was to eliminate private competition, and to remove the profit-making requirement from the new public enterprises. This reflected a general belief in Socialist circles that the profit motive should give way to what was variously referred to as the 'national interest', 'public service', 'social responsibility' and 'the negative of private interest'.[102] There was, however, no clear sense of which of the different meanings of the 'public interest' or its variants, previously employed in the political process, the newly nationalized industries were to serve. Nationalization led to the withdrawal of law and legal rules from this area of the public sphere.

Formerly there had been a variety of tests of 'publicness' operating simultaneously. Special statutes mandated reinvestment and capitalization requirements, restrictions on profits and the fulfilment of public purpose and public benefit tests. Statutory conflict of interest rules recognized another aspect of publicness. There were different and potentially conflicting sites for political oversight of the range of public undertakings: in the special statute process, municipal politics and franchising processes, and in the Board of Trade's central oversight.

When industry was nationalized, these different versions of publicness which had been applied and regulated by separate, mainly political processes, were collapsed into one amorphous concept. A contemporary economist observed that while the Acts specified that total costs must not exceed total revenue, they did not state the relation that prices must bear to costs. Neither did they prioritize the most important duties.[103] Was, for example, ensuring supply more important than making ends

[102] A. M. De Neuman, 'Some Economic Aspects of Nationalization', *Law and Contemporary Problems* 16 (1951), 702–51, 718.

[103] *Ibid.*, 749.

meet? Those duties that were stated were themselves unclear: one requirement was to 'make ends meet taking one year with another' whatever that might mean.[104] Duties to consumers were assumed rather than mandated. It was considered enough to remove the profit motive, the consumer was not in need of any further protection and enjoyed little by way of representation.[105] Not only were these different tests of publicness merged, but a single Minister as the central organ of control was substituted for previously separate sites of political control: now a Minister could give directions in the 'public interest'.[106] Worse, in practice, Ministers preferred to exercise very real pressure and influence on Boards privately rather than through the formal and transparent means of official directions. Judges rarely had an opportunity to exercise oversight.

Prosser has argued that in pursuing nationalization policies, the Socialists were not sufficiently interested in public law and institutional design and were too quick to trade accountability for pretended efficiency.[107] As a general proposition that is almost certainly true. Some public lawyers on the Left, however, were asking important questions at the time. These public lawyers argued that government ownership by itself was not enough. What was needed was a distinct public law morality to apply to such activities. Reacting to a Labour Party position paper advocating the large-scale acquisition by government of private enterprise,[108] Robson warns his fellow members of the Socialist movement:[109]

> The State should not behave like an avaricious private individual. It should not give way to a mere desire to acquire wealth regardless of the purpose for which it is needed and the source from which it comes. There may on occasion be a genuine public interest to justify a State investment

104 D. N. Chester, *The Nationalisation of British Industry, 1945–51* (London: Stationery Office, 1975), p. 562.

105 *Ibid.*, p. 641.

106 That is not to say that there were no other bureaucratic forms of control. See C. Winter, 'Parliamentary, Ministerial, and Judicial Control of Nationalized Industries in Great Britain', *Law and Contemporary Problems* 16 (1951), 670–701.

107 T. Prosser, 'Markets, Planning and Socialism', *Journal of Law and Society* 15 (1988), 42–57, 44.

108 Labour Party Pamphlet, *Industry and Society: Labour's Policy on Future Public Ownership* (London: Labour Party 1957).

109 W. A. Robson, *Nationalized Industry and Public Ownership*, 2nd edn (London: Allen & Unwin, 1962), p. 483.

> in a particular industry or firm: but where that occurs the State should have some share in its policy.

For Robson, nationalization, like the state, is not an end in itself.[110] The state's role ought not to resemble the 'functionless property owner',[111] nor should the 'functionless private shareholder' be merely replaced with the 'functionless state'.[112] All then, for Robson, must be judged against the state's purposes, or the ends for which the state exists.

The young Mitchell is more judicially oriented in his response to these issues. He looks to French and US law as well as to UK practice to establish that a government has a special position as contractor and litigator and that the law's recognition of this special position is necessary for governmental effectiveness. He argues for a functional approach to regulating public authorities. Different rules should apply depending on whether an entity is acting as employer, commercial actor, proprietor, regulator or public service provider. Hence a nationalized industry may be performing an ordinary commercial function and thus be subject to ordinary rules, or be carrying out a large-scale construction project for some central economic purpose that has been the subject of a Ministerial direction which should attract different rules.[113] He says: [114]

> The search for precise definitions of who is a Crown servant, so that the position of the new boards of nationalized industries may be settled, becomes unnecessary in this connexion. It is unnecessary since the classification as being, or not being, a Crown servant, is not of critical importance ... What matters ... is whether or not it is performing a public service. It is from the necessities of that service that the special rules and privileges are derived.

Mitchell suggests a positive way forward along French administrative law lines. He prefers functional to institutional tests of publicness and suggests the need for more nuanced public law rules rather than binary tests of whether an entity is or is not immune. Public duties need to be imposed in exchange for public privileges, citizens

[110] *Ibid.*, p. 486. Bosanquet, in similar terms, opposed nationalization as 'absentee ownership at its worst' but applauded the extension of ownership to workers. See M. Carter, 'Ball, Bosanquet and the Legacy of T. H. Green', *History of Political Thought* 20 (1999), 674–94, 688.

[111] Robson, *Nationalized Industry*, above n. 109, p. 491.

[112] *Ibid.*, p. 480.

[113] Mitchell, *The Contracts of Public Authorities*, above n. 85, p. 225.

[114] *Ibid.*, pp. 223–4.

should enjoy correlative rights, and we should think in terms of compensation rather than damages.[115]

It is Griffith who indirectly identifies the central problem for achieving Mitchell's programme. Griffith is adamant that nationalized industries should be included as agents of the Crown according to the control test he advocates, but he does not want them to be subject to immunity.[116] How was the common law, by its interstitial case law method, to chart the suggested course from ideas of Crown immunity to ideas of Crown obligation? It could not, or at least not very quickly or easily. This points to another, potentially fatal, reason why what Anderson calls 'nascent public law principles' did not grow into a distinct public law. Except for the public trust tests (which tended to be politically rather than judicially enforced and applied), all of Anderson's 'nascent public law principles' (rating, vicarious liability and contractual agency) relate to judicially applied immunities. These were not principles of public law duty, obligation or constraint. They do not represent 'law' but rather its absence. The judges took a consistently restrictive approach to which bodies or activities should attract immunities and privileges precisely because such judicially applied 'public law principles' made for thin gruel indeed. It was private law which appeared to be the natural candidate to fill the void of controlling power.

That seems to be a more compelling explanation for why the Crown did not come to represent the whole of the public sphere at that time. There were obvious rule of law reasons why judges wanted to limit the scope of privileges and immunities to a core Crown. If the prevailing doctrines of sovereignty treated the sovereign as unlimited by law for much of this period, this was good reason to limit what was treated as part of the sovereign. In doing so, the common law did not *necessarily* mean to restrict the public sphere per se to those actors. There is no reason why immunity and obligation should attach to the same set of actors. It also explains why the Crown could not readily come to be identified with a distinct public law. And, as we shall see in the next section, by the time the Crown Proceedings Act 1947 was enacted, the decision to treat the Crown as if it were a private person of full age and capacity also reflected other historically important political commitments.

[115] His terms are reminiscent of the Scottish approach to the application of the Public Authorities Protection Act discussed by Lord Shaw in *Bradford Corporation* v. *Myers* [1916] AC 242, 264.

[116] Griffith, 'Public Corporations as Crown Servants', above n. 101, 189, 191.

The Crown Proceedings Act moment

The project to reform the law relating to Crown proceedings actually began in 1920.[117] The resulting Crown Proceedings Act 1947 restricted immunities, particularly from tortious liability, formerly enjoyed by the Crown. (These will be discussed at greater length in Chapter 7.) In so doing, it allowed the further spread of private law norms into the public sphere. Mitchell's great disappointment was that the Crown Proceedings Act 1947, which came into force at the same time as nationalization, treated the Crown (understood in its political capacity) as an ordinary private person rather than a distinct set of functions or a separate moral personality subject to special public law norms. That was no accident. Even though the reforms to Crown Proceedings were very much in the realm of lawyers' law and were not the subject of open political debate, they nevertheless reflected a fierce ideological contest that paralleled that taking place in the context of the nationalization reforms.

One handwritten comment on the documents leading up to the reform was to the effect that the Crown Proceedings Act would serve as an important prophylactic measure should the Labour Party ever become the majority government.[118] Of course, we should be careful not to read too much into a single comment. Nevertheless it is pretty clear that extending private law norms to the Crown and its agents was viewed as particularly important at a time when the functions of the state were expanding in an unprecedented manner. The nationalization reforms had the effect of making the state the owner of one fifth of the economy.[119] But it was not only expanding state functions which were regarded as a problem. Many lawyers distrusted the newly emerging administrative law which conceived the state as 'special' and not necessarily subject to the ordinary law in the ordinary courts. For Lord Hewart and Morgan,[120] for example, reform of Crown proceedings was considered a preferable alternative to such developments and their associated ideology. Dicey's arguments about the rule of law were mobilized against attacks by administrative lawyers and bureaucrats.

[117] See J. M. Jacob, 'The Debates Behind an Act: Crown Proceedings Reform 1920–1947', *Public Law* (1992), 452–84.

[118] Jacob, *The Republican Crown*, above n. 27, pp. 235–6.

[119] H. Maddick, 'Book Review', *The Economic Journal* 63 (1953), 148–52.

[120] G. M. Morgan 'Remedies Against the Crown', in G. Robinson, *Public Authorities and Legal Liability* (University of London Press, 1925).

Expanded Crown liability would, Lord Hewart and others hoped, restore the main features of Diceyan constitutionalism to its rightful place in the legal order. I will discuss these developments and the associated debate in more detail in the next chapter. For the moment it is sufficient to suggest that the 'private law conception of the Crown' which was incorporated into the Crown Proceedings Act is likely to have had as much if not more to do with contemporary politics than with the arguments inherent in the nature of the legal personality of the Crown.

Understandings about the nature of the legal personality of the Crown were still relevant to this debate though, to be sure. By the middle of twentieth century – after two world wars – the idea of the Crown as corporation sole attracted renewed currency both in academic writing and also in the approach of government lawyers. Conceiving of the Crown as a corporation sole appeared now to serve a two-fold purpose. First, it was a convenient way of conferring powers on the government without explicit statutory authority: the King *as a corporation sole* has plenty of legal personality to will and to act as any legal person might do. If the King has such power then a Minister exercising that power on his behalf could also do anything he was not precluded by law from doing. In a significant internal memorandum written in 1945, Granville Ram (First Parliamentary Counsel), appeared to invoke the idea of the Crown as corporation sole when asked to clarify the internal approach of government lawyers to the question of who may exercise prerogative and other kinds of power (such as to appoint committees, organize departments, enter contracts or employ staff) within the modern state apparatus. He advised that a Minister of the Crown is unlike a statutory corporation which owes its powers to statute:

> [A] Minister of the Crown, even though there may be a statute authorizing his appointment, is not a creature of statute and may, as an agent of the Crown, exercise any powers which the Crown has power to exercise, except so far as he is precluded from doing so by statute... [A] Minister may do anything he is not precluded from doing.

This approach became known as the 'Ram doctrine' and to be understood by government lawyers as allowing a Minister to exercise the special prerogative powers of the Crown as well as to do anything a 'natural person' can do.[121] The proposition, of course, bears little

[121] The Text of 1945 Memorandum from First Parliamentary Counsel made available in the Library of the House of Lords on 22 January 2003 and of the House of Commons on 23 January 2003.

relation to the nineteenth-century legislative practice of designating the Queen's powers even over her own lands and contracts. At the time it served the needs of a state whose functions were expanding. As we shall see, this idea that the common law powers of Ministers and their departments were derived from the Queen conceived as a corporation sole would be newly asserted in the era after privatization.[122] The private law powers of the Crown as corporation sole would be useful both in expanding and contracting state functions.

These arguments did not need to rely on ideas about the corporation sole. The arguments for such powers could have been made on the basis of governmental effectiveness. Indeed, in Dicey's 1915 article in which he admits the existence of an English administrative law for the first time, he defends the government's need for greater powers as its functions and duties have expanded while attempting (characteristically but unsuccessfully) to avoid any reference to 'the Crown':[123]

> [W]e must remember that when the State undertakes the management of business properly so called, and business which hitherto has been carried on by each individual citizen simply with a view to his own interest, the Government, or in the language of English law, the servants of the Crown, will be found to need that freedom of action necessarily possessed by every private person in the management of his own personal concerns.

Analogizing the Crown to an ordinary person – a corporation sole – is not only a convenient shorthand which empowers the state, it also carries humanizing connotations. The Crown is both empowered and simultaneously brought 'down to size'. It is not 'superhuman', it cannot claim for itself a special morality distinct from that which applies to individuals: it enjoys *only* an ordinary will and not a mystical collective will.[124] The idea of the Crown conceived as a corporation sole coincided with a deep philosophical commitment to the idea of a constrained and humanized state. It also served the pragmatic requirements of a modern and expanding state which needed a range of unenumerated powers.

These arguments too could, of course, have been made without recourse to ideas about the nature of the Crown at all – as indeed the

[122] In modern times Baroness Scotland has invoked this idea. See A. Lester and M. Weait, 'The Use of Ministerial Powers Without Parliamentary Authority: The Ram Doctrine', *Public Lawyer* (2003) 415–28, 416 at fn. 4. HL Deb Vol 645 col WA59 March 24 2003.

[123] A. V. Dicey, 'The Development of Administrative Law in England', *Law Quarterly Review* 31 (1915), 149–53, 150.

[124] *Ibid.*

émigré international lawyer Hersch Lauterpacht did.[125] Lauterpacht called in support of his arguments the work of Dicey and Maitland in order to reject the central tenets of a version of Idealism which elevates the state above all other entities. He emphasized how much the state shared in common with other legal entities. He sought to build international law on private Roman law ideas rather than on public law concepts that varied widely among nations and appealed too readily to absolutist ideas of sovereignty. It was ordinary trade between states on the same basis and laws as individuals that would save international law, and, he hoped, the human race.

The UK law of state liability made a dramatic turn during the same period. From 1880, the English common law had operated an absolute doctrine of state immunity. All activities of government were immune from legal process in foreign courts. Britain successfully resisted pressure for a more restricted form of state immunity until the mid-twentieth century when it accepted a distinction between a state's trading purposes (for which it would not be immune) and its governmental purposes which would continue to attract immunity. These tests followed the form rather than the substance or purpose of the transaction: even if such dealings were in pursuance of public purposes they were treated as having a private character.

Summary

There were several points at which the Crown could have come to personate the state and to represent unified public law norms. That never happened. Instead, the Crown came to represent only a part of the public sphere and became the subject of, and often defined by, formalistically applied immunities and privileges. In this way, private law norms spread into the remainder of the public sphere – at least where economic and commercial activities were concerned.

What happened to Mitchell's project to exchange public duties for public privileges and to develop a distinct set of public law norms? As we shall see in the next chapter, the public law *obligations* that did eventually develop in the twentieth century did not depend on the legal personality of the Crown at all – though the Crown sometimes continued to appear as representative of the public and the common good. Judicial

[125] H. Lauterpacht, *Private Law Sources and Analogies of International Law (with special reference to International Arbitration)* (London: Longmans Green 1927), pp. 72–80.

intervention in the new emerging field of public administrative law would depend, instead, on a test of whether a body had a 'duty to act judicially'. It is not surprising, given this starting point, that judges would be unwilling to extend their judicial review supervision to commercial and highly discretionary activities. A duty to act judicially is a long way from a public benefit test – and it took us down a very different path.

6

Public law without a state: The new administrative justice

'Let no man weakly conceive that just laws, and true policy, have any antipathy, for they are like the spirits and sinews, that one moves with the other.'[1]

'Thus the modern state crept up, in a sense unobserved, upon both politicians and lawyers'[2]

A law of the administrative

If the Crown did not come to represent the whole of the public sphere or to unify public law norms, on what basis did distinctly public law norms eventually emerge? In this chapter we shall trace the genesis of the new twentieth-century version of administrative law, or rather 'the law of the administrative'. Administrative law was originally understood as laws, rules and policies made by the administration itself rather than supervisory principles developed by the courts. One reason for this was that the politics and social order of the new administrative state was initially conceived as antithetical to the common law, its institutions and values. Eventually, however, a new set of administrative law-oriented values came to be enforced by the common law courts in their supervisory jurisdiction. We witness for the first time the conscious, if belated, realization by the judges, politicians and members of the practising profession that there *is* an administrative state in Britain.

I argue that prevailing political thought of the time, especially the values of Idealism, Fabian Socialism and the new Liberalism, greatly influenced the new 'lawyers of the administrative'. Theirs was a view of

[1] Francis Bacon, 'Of Judicature', in *Essays Civil and Moral*, vol. III, part 1 The Harvard classics (New York: P. F. Collier and Son, 1909–14), chapter 56, p. 110, quoted by S. A. De Smith, *Judicial Review of Administrative Action* (London: Stevens, 1959), title page.

[2] J. D. B. Mitchell, 'Administrative Law and Policy Effectiveness', in J. A. G. Griffith (ed.), *From Policy to Administration: Essays in Honour of William A. Robson* (London: Allen & Unwin, 1976), pp. 174–83, 181.

individual rights socially conceived, the product of, and not prior to, social and collective life. Such views conflicted with common law constitutionalism and it was for this reason that an explicit debate was required about whether the values of the common law, particularly those associated with laissez-faire, such as freedom of contract and rights of property, should properly apply in the public sphere. Do such values offer a desirable, sufficient or appropriate set of legal norms by which to guide and control the new 'public service state'? Dicey's late nineteenth-century explanation of the constitution, as having its source in the ordinary law enforced in the ordinary courts, was subjected to sustained challenge for the first time and was vigorously reasserted in response. This contest about what role constitutional common law rights should play never completely goes away.

There were other connections between the new administrative lawyers and the prevailing political thought of the day. Robson is the most interesting administrative lawyer in this respect. He instantiates 'the common will' and 'common mind' in what he calls 'judicial habits of mind'. Judicial habits of mind, the ability to overcome self-interest, he argues, can be inculcated in civil servants and enforced by judges. This, then, represents a legal representation of a particular, organic version of statehood. It gains surprising traction in the common law as the prerogative writs, which were initially used to supervise inferior courts, were adapted for the supervision of the bureaucracy. In the application of the prerogative writs or orders, we begin to see new constraints develop on the *manner* in which public power should be exercised – constraints modelled on those which already applied to judicial actors. A new public law morality begins to emerge out of the new administrative concerns. More conservative and 'mainstream' legal scholars, such as C. T. Carr, and especially De Smith and Wade, begin self-consciously to extract and construct a new set of *general* principles gleaned from the common law and designed for the judicial control of the administration by way of special rules.

This distinctly public law morality has the potential normatively to unify the public sphere once more. However, that project would not by any means be completed. There would be areas in which the state would still be 'allowed a private life' and where, for example, in relation to economic matters, high politics and the prerogative, public law would not enter. Nevertheless, significantly, the question of whether the public sphere should be treated to different legal norms was being asked outside of the narrowing context of whether an entity should attract Crown immunity.

One of the striking things during this period is that, although reform of Crown proceedings and Crown immunity in tort played some part, this debate was no longer framed, in Maitland and Laski's terms, exclusively around issues of legal personality in general or the moral personality of the Crown in particular. The task of fashioning a distinct public law could get along without a legal person of the state per se. There were a number of reasons for this. Not everyone who was attracted to the 'altruism, organicism and ethical rationality of idealism' agreed with its methodology or 'its emphasis on the real corporate identity of society and the state'.[3] This did not matter. It would be possible to conceive of 'the state', not as a single *personne morale*, but rather as a diffuse and variegated complex of entities whose 'unity' is created by the application of shared 'public law'[4] norms. Indeed, such an approach would be much more compatible with common law method and history (including the concept of office discussed in Chapter 2) and the shifting functions of public and voluntarist associations (discussed in Chapters 4 and 5). It would also avoid the Austinian objection (which had not yet been countered by Hart) that the state *qua* state could not be held to law. This struggle to determine the norms that should apply to the disaggregated public sphere is a distinct and alternative approach to the search for 'statehood' from that which focused on the state as a legal person. The extent to which this strategy 'worked' can be explained by the way in which the central–local division of administrative functions was structured. Old common law forms of control and supervision would be developed for new purposes. Once again the law would look backwards and forwards at the same time.

This chapter is not about the history of British administrative law per se. It will not discuss, for example, the nature and controls on delegated legislation or reforms to administrative tribunals or the doctrinal details of jurisdictional error and the law–fact distinction – all issues which would be central for administrative lawyers for decades.[5] It will not take a 'great cases' approach. Its focus will be on the new *normative* standards that were being developed to apply to the British state as it expanded

[3] J. Harris, 'Political Thought and the Welfare State 1870–1940: An Intellectual Framework for British Social Policy', *Past and Present* 135 (1992), 116–41, 124.

[4] This was not a term used in the debates at the time.

[5] See M. B. Taggart, 'From Parliamentary Powers to Privatization: The Chequered History of Delegated Legislation in the Twentieth Century', *University of Toronto Law Journal* 55 (2005), 575–627.

into many areas of life. What was it that was distinct about the state and public authority? And in answering this question, what did the new administrative lawyers owe to prevailing political thought?

A clash of values and cultures

Dicey had famously argued that administrative law was unknown in England. There was only one 'ordinary law' enforced by the ordinary courts that applied to public and private actors alike. The new administrative lawyers rejected these ideas. Who were the protagonists in this debate about whether the state should be held to distinct moral standards? What was at stake?

The clash was cultural, professional and ideological. On one side was the civil service, supported by the social science departments of the universities. The civil service was Oxford-trained and professional. At least until the 1930s, Idealist philosophies and values had an important ideological influence. Both Green (1836–62) and Bradley (1846–1924) had attracted 'large inspiration seeking audiences' at Oxford.[6] Green had been widely accorded prophet status (something his Cambridge contemporary, the Utilitarian Sidgwick, had resented).[7] Bradley too had made a charismatic figure (and had been venerated as the greatest philosopher of his day).[8] Idealism also enjoyed a broader range of academic and more populist adherents beyond philosophers and the philosophically trained. Jose Harris records that, especially after World War I, when its influence is supposed to have faded, it supplanted the dominance of Positivists and Empiricists working in social science.[9] At the London School of Economics (LSE), in particular Edward Urwich, the first head of the Department of Social Science and Administration, was an important exponent of Idealist concepts and methodology.[10] Even the Webbs, J. A. Hobson and L. T. Hobhouse, all theorists who professed to be hostile to Idealist thinking, shared a great deal of common

6 M. Francis and J. Morrow, *English Political Thought in the Nineteenth Century* (London: Duckworth, 1994), p. 283.

7 *Ibid.*, p. 284.

8 See the dedication in J. H. Muirhead, *Contemporary British Philosophy: Personal Statements* (2nd edn) referred to by S. Candlish, 'Francis Herbert Bradley', *Stanford Encyclopaedia of Philosophy* (2006).

9 Harris, 'Political Thought and the Welfare State', above n. 3, 123.

10 *Ibid.*, 125. See further E. J. Urwick, *A Philosophy of Social Progress* (London: Methuen, 1912).

philosophical ground with the Idealists.[11] It was a philosophy that had the capacity for both conservative and radical applications and hence it also attracted adherents of different political hues within parliamentary politics.

Idealism was not, of course, the only or even necessarily a *distinct* influence. There was, at the time, a *general* revival of interest in Platonic thought (in which Idealists like Green and Bosanquet played a part).[12] The idea of society as an 'organic spiritual community'; of an ethical version of citizenship whereby individuals found 'happiness' in 'mind' and 'character' and in service to the larger whole; of a 'higher democracy' based on a corporate moral life;[13] and that the basis of the state was not coercion but justice, all chimed with central tenets of Idealist thought.[14] The third Reform Act was to bring into fruition some version of the 'virtuous republic'. Rousseau and his theories of 'general will' would also gain a certain ascendancy in the Edwardian period: he would become the 'moral godfather of the democratic state'.[15] These trends together can be seen as part of the process of modern democratization: the vision is one of responsible and ethical citizenship rather than of a tyrannous majority, or of an oppressed and resentful ruling class under attack from the clamorous mob. Fabians, such as the Webbs and Ritchie, were at the same time rehabilitating Utilitarian thought. It could be a philosophy for social progress as well as an individualistic creed. From within the Utilitarian tradition, Sidgwick suggested that Utilitarianism could offer a more analytically robust and defensible conception of the 'common good' than that offered by Idealism. This version of Utilitarianism could sometimes justify state intervention.[16] Through

[11] See Harris, 'Political Thought and the Welfare State' above n. 3, 133. They shared the belief that 'private and public virtue were interdependent, that "state-conscious idealism" was the goal of citizenship, and that social-welfare policies could be socially as well as materially constructive'. See further (rejecting accusations of Bosanquet's anti-socialist leanings), M. Carter, 'Ball, Bosanquet and the Legacy of T. H. Green', *History of Political Thought* 20 (1999), 674–94; S Collini, 'Hobhouse, Bosanquet and the State: Philosophical Idealism and Political Argument in England, 1880–1918', *Past and Present* 72 (1976), 86–111.

[12] See, e.g. B. Bosanquet, *A Companion to Plato's Republic, for English Readers*, 2nd edn (London: Macmillan, 1895) referred to in Harris, 'Political Thought and the Welfare State', above n. 3, 128–30. Plato was claimed by many – including the Totalitarians and Communists. See, further, M. S. Lane, *Plato's Progeny: How Plato and Socrates Still Captivate the Modern Mind* (London: Duckworth, 2001), especially Chapter 4.

[13] Harris, 'Political Thought and the Welfare State', above n. 3, 135 at 47.

[14] *Ibid.*, 128–30. [15] *Ibid.*, 126–7.

[16] Francis and Morrow, *English Political Thought in the Nineteenth Century*, above n. 6, p. 284. The examples he gave of when state intervention would be justified more or less reflected the status quo.

Ritchie, Fabians would also embrace an Idealist view of freedom conceived as positive liberty.[17] All of these philosophies shared the view that pursuit of the common good, and the suppression of selfish desires, is the goal of public life. Such a public philosophy, based on an optimistic view of human nature, is the antithesis of public choice theory (which presumes that actors will behave self-interestedly) which would later achieve dominance in public administration in the 1980s as we shall see in Chapter 8.[18]

Our immediate question is where law fits within this cultural and ideological framework, if at all. There were few lawyers openly identified with these ideas. In contrast with the continent, the British civil service itself did not include many lawyers. Apart from Haldane,[19] whose philosophical ideas often elicited bemused amusement from many of his colleagues and whose political career had almost been destroyed by his association with Hegel and German Idealism,[20] practising lawyers and judges did not significantly figure in these intellectual debates. By the late 1920s, however, a small group of self-styled academic 'administrative' lawyers (the description was significant at the time) were beginning to emerge at LSE. They were, to a man, allied on the side of the civil service. While they were influenced by some of these more general British ideological debates, they also drew on distinctly *legal* resources from across the Atlantic and formed important intellectual allegiances with North American scholars engaged with New Deal politics such as J. M. Landis, the leading US scholar of 'the administrative' (as he called it), Ernst Freund, Felix Frankfurter, John Willis (in Canada), and, in the case of Laski, with Holmes in the United States and Duguit in France. Administrative law had already gained general recognition in the United States decades before it was widely recognized in the UK and Commonwealth, and as such it would offer an 'Anglo-American'

[17] M. Stears, *Progressives, Pluralists and Problems of the State: Ideologies of Reform in the United States and Britain, 1909–1926* (Oxford University Press, 2002), p. 41 See also M. Loughlin, 'The Functionalist Style in Public Law', *University of Toronto Law Journal* 55 (2005), 361–403, 384–7.

[18] Discussed in Chapter 8.

[19] Haldane was a scholar of Hegel, translator of Schopenhauer and a close friend of Bosanquet. He also helped to found the LSE and was a member of the Coefficients Dining Club of Social Reformers set up by Sidney and Beatrice Webb in 1902. See further D. Schneiderman, 'Harold Laski, Viscount Haldane, and the Law of the Canadian Constitution in the Early Twentieth Century', *University of Toronto Law Journal* 48 (1998), 521–60.

[20] A. Vincent, 'German Philosophy and British Public Policy: Richard Burdon Haldane in Theory and Practice', *Journal of the History of Ideas* 68(1) (2007), 157–79, 177.

common law-based alternative to continental systems of *droit administratif*.[21] The UK scholars would read the US scholars for their discussions of the design of regulatory systems and of the historical origins of the common law 'public law' writs and for judicial explications of separation of powers and delegation doctrines. Nearly everyone would read and 'blush' at Dicey's denial of the very existence of administrative law in England.[22]

Loughlin has suggested that administrative lawyers such as Robson, Jennings, Laski and Griffith (at LSE), Street (in Manchester), and J. D. B. Mitchell (in Scotland) formed the beginnings of a 'dissenting tradition in public law'[23] that was broadly aligned with these socially progressive ideas. In a rich analysis of the thought of the period, Loughlin suggests that they shared in common a certain 'functionalist' style which brought together elements of pragmatism, Pluralism, Idealism, Utilitarianism and evolutionary theory.[24] He describes that style thus:[25]

> Functionalism in public law views this apparatus of Government as serving to promote a distinct set of purposes. These purposes are most readily associated with the objectives of the modern state which emerged towards the end of the nineteenth century and which are summed up in the idea of the government as an institution which promotes evolutionary change.

While such a 'style' is broadly to be discerned, this is too sweeping. There were important differences within this group as they grappled with the juristic consequences of the prevailing social theories.[26] Moreover, for a time at least, this *dissenting* tradition was pretty much all there was: they dominated the field of self-identifying 'administrative lawyers' and contributed significantly to the 'mainstream' administrative law project. The first 'mainstream' text to draw together general, *common law-based*

21 E.g., F. J. Goodnow, *Comparative Administrative Law; An Analysis of the Administrative Systems, National and Local, of the United States, England, France and Germany* (New York: Putnam's Sons, 1893).

22 W. A. Robson, *Justice and Administrative Law*, 2nd edn (London: Stevens, 1947), p. 369. J. Griffith and H. Street, *Principles of Administrative Law* (London: Pitman, 1952), p. 3 but see H. W. R. Wade, *Administrative Law* (Oxford: Clarendon Press, 1961), p. 35 who describes 'Dicey's purely verbal misunderstanding about the existence of administrative law'.

23 Loughlin, 'The Functionalist Style in Public Law' above n. 17, 398.

24 *Ibid.*

25 M. Loughlin, *Public Law and Political Theory* (Oxford University Press, 1992), p. 134.

26 Loughlin, 'The Functionalist Style in Public Law', above n. 17, 361.

principles of 'judicial review of administrative action' would not appear until 1959 – long after their own initial contributions to the subject.[27] Some of the ideological tensions and contradictions that they brought to the project of administrative law remain today.

The new social theories, which emphasized the collective good and the suppression of selfish desires, met strong resistance among common lawyers, judges and, to a limited extent, constitutional lawyers in the academy. Power seemed to be shifting from this group to a new set of elites. The traditional expertise of lawyers was being supplanted by the new 'experts' in the civil service.[28] Common law methods and values were being superseded by a new and alien set of commitments. Common law conceptions of 'liberty' were being challenged by the new Liberalism, which now defined individual freedom in terms of 'the social'. Legal controls were being supplanted by political controls (which often appeared to be inadequate). In other words, legislative and administrative changes, which had been going on largely unnoticed by lawyers since the 1830s, finally penetrated their consciousness. Despite the fact that Dicey 'a trusted watchman had chanted reassuringly that all was well'[29] (namely that England was safe from *droit administratif*), there now appeared to be an established administrative state in their midst and 'lawyers' law' itself was under threat.[30]

The ideological position of lawyers threatened by these developments is best encapsulated by Lord Hewart's *The New Despotism* which appeared in 1929 while he was Lord Chief Justice of England.[31] The work is pitched at the educated general public – a public readership who would also have been a general audience for Dicey's works on constitutional law. Hewart attributes to civil servants a certain scorn towards Parliamentary sovereignty and the rule of law. These sacred values, he claims, are regarded by civil servants as 'a kind of fetish worship by the ignorant public'. He relies heavily on Dicey and is partly responsible for the continued reception of Diceyan thought, understood as exalting 'ordinary law' while denying the existence of English administrative law. In fact, long before then, in an article appearing in 1915, Dicey

[27] De Smith, *Judicial Review of Administrative Action*, above n. 1.

[28] G. Hewart, *The New Despotism* (London: Ernest Benn, 1929), p. 20 suggests that 'the only persons fit to govern are experts'.

[29] C. T. Carr, *Concerning English Administrative Law* (New York: Columbia University Press, 1941), p. 21.

[30] *Ibid.* [31] Hewart, *The New Despotism*, above n. 28.

had conceded both the existence of English administrative law and the development of 'special rules' of fairness and equity which applied to decisions made by government departments.[32] Dicey's ultimately equivocal stance would scarcely be acknowledged in these debates by either those reasserting or rejecting the common law and its values. It was the earlier Dicey who was alternately venerated or derided.

Lord Hewart at once describes the British civil service as the 'best civil service in the world'[33] *and* as assuming to itself a *despotic* power that places it above the sovereignty of Parliament and beyond the jurisdiction of the courts. It has, he says, 'ingeniously' used Parliamentary sovereignty to destroy the rule of law. The passage of skeletal legislation requires gaps to be filled by executive regulation. Modern legislation delegates power to officials to make final decisions without any evidentiary requirements, treats the fact of decision as proof of legality, prevents appeals to courts of law and includes power to modify statutes by executive act. All these techniques defeat the operation of the ordinary law in the ordinary courts, the separation of powers, the protections wrought by the independence of the judiciary and, ultimately, Parliamentary sovereignty itself. Parliament has been given an 'anaesthetic'.[34] They may be 'scientific and benevolent',[35] but civil servants have become a law unto themselves. They are anonymous, secretive and apparently care nothing for law – theirs is a system of 'administrative lawlessness'. These developments in attitudes and administrative technique are, he surmises, a consequence, in part, of the practices adopted leading up to and during World War I – and his concerns relate in part to the erosions of liberties associated with that period.[36] He even makes the obligatory comparisons between the system of administrative tribunals and the notorious Star Chamber.[37]

Hewart styles himself as reasserting basic constitutional principles. The source of the constitution, he claims, is the ordinary law and the rights it protects: '[the] general principles of our constitution are mainly the result of judicial decisions determining the rights of private persons in particular cases brought before the courts';[38] '[t]he principles of the

[32] A. V. Dicey, 'The Development of Administrative Law in England', *Law Quarterly Review* 31 (1915), 148 citing the *Arlidge* decision discussed below.

[33] Hewart, *The New Despotism*, above n. 28, p. 14. [34] *Ibid.* p. 17. [35] *Ibid.*, p. 14.

[36] See for a discussion of what followed, M. Aronson, 'The Great Depression, This Depression and Administrative Law', *Federal Law Review* 37 (2009) 165–204.

[37] Maitland suggested that the Star Chamber effectively saved the constitution – a view cited in Carr, *Concerning English Administrative Law*, above n. 29, p. 126.

[38] Hewart, *The New Despotism*, above n. 28, p. 24.

Constitution are, in Dicey's phrase, inductions or generalizations based upon decisions pronounced by the courts as to the rights of particular individuals.'[39] If the ordinary courts and the ordinary law are removed, then the constitution is itself at risk.

According to Hewart, the separation of powers is also at stake. Judges who are independent of the executive should decide disputes that concern the rights of individuals or 'decisions of a judicial nature', not bureaucrats who are effectively deciding in their own cause. Judicial processes also have the advantage of openness, publicity and the testing of evidence.

While Hewart claims (the early) Dicey as authority, he does so with this twist. In Diceyan mode he describes the French system of administrative law as 'profoundly repugnant'[40] to English ideas, and suggests that 'Between the "Rule of Law" and what is called "administrative law" (happily there is no English name for it) there is the sharpest possible contrast. One is substantially the opposite of the other'.[41] But he later concludes by comparing the French system of 'administrative law' *favourably* against the English system of 'administrative lawlessness'. The administrative tribunals of the continent were at least real courts, even if they apply different rules and principles. British administrative tribunals, by contrast, lacked both system and principle.

Hewart's contribution is polemical and sometimes contradictory. Despite this, many of his criticisms would eventually become the mainstream concerns of those who would later identify themselves as administrative lawyers, even if they were not so at the time. Lord Hewart would set the terms of the legal debate that would ensue. His 'brilliantly written attack',[42] and the public disquiet it engendered, led directly to the Donoughmore Committee on Ministers' Powers which reported in 1932,[43] and to the Franks Committee which reported in 1957.[44] The Donoughmore terms of reference are provocatively described by Carr as asking 'whether Britain had gone off the Dicey standard and, if so, what was the quickest way back'.[45] Together the Donoughmore and Franks Committees set the agenda for academic administrative lawyers and their defence of the administrative state for decades.[46]

[39] *Ibid.*, p. 26. [40] *Ibid.*, pp. 12–13. [41] *Ibid.*, p. 37.
[42] Carr, *Concerning English Administrative Law*, above n. 29, p. 25.
[43] Cmnd 4060 (1932). [44] Cmnd 218 (1957).
[45] Carr, *Concerning English Administrative Law*, above n. 29, p. 26.
[46] See, e.g., D. G. T. Williams, 'The Donoughmore Report in Retrospect', *Public Administration* 60 (1982), 273–92.

Rejecting the common law?

At first the rejection by the new 'administrative law men' of Hewart's ordinary common law model of the constitution, and of common law values more generally, is self-conscious and extreme. Landis and Robson tend to regard the common law at best as incapable of meeting the needs of modern life and at worst as an enemy of social progress. They regard Diceyan constitutionalism as its handmaiden.[47] And for a time the common law, and what it represents of nineteenth-century laissez-faire values, becomes the enemy of the new values of administrative justice. In this section I will investigate the initial rationales for rejecting common law values and institutions before moving to consider how the common law eventually embraced administrative law and became a source of supervision and control over the bureaucracy.

Dicey's rule of law poses a large and potentially fundamental challenge to the ideas of social progress which had come to dominate the civil service and its administrative practices. That challenge went to the very nature of rights and of the British constitution itself. For Dicey, the rights of individuals (understood as common law rights and liberties) are not the *consequence* of the constitution but are its very source and foundation. Perhaps for this reason, the early administrative lawyers (including Robson, Jennings, and Griffith and Street) felt the necessity to ponder the question of the relationship between constitutional and administrative law. Notably, Robson changes his view between the first edition of *Justice and Administrative Law*, written the year before Lord Hewart's *New Despotism*, and the 1947 second edition (written partly in reaction to the findings of the Donoughmore Committee). Robson describes the first edition as 'primarily a work of constitutional law'.[48] In the second edition he promotes modern administrative law as a subject distinct from, rather than derived from, or worse a perversion of, constitutional law. In their writings, Jennings, and Griffith and Street ask themselves whether constitutional law is distinct from administrative law but are unable to draw such a line. The eventual adoption of the

[47] See, e.g., J. M. Landis, *The Administrative Process*, 7th edn (New Haven, CT: Yale University Press, 1966), p. 37 (on practical effectiveness of the common law) and p. 47 (the idea of there being three separate powers was 'too casual a reading of constitutional history') (first edition 1938); Robson, *Justice and Administrative Law*, 2nd edn, above n. 22, p. 4 (on separation of powers).

[48] W. A. Robson, *Justice and Administrative Law: A Study of the British Constitution* (London: Macmillan, 1928), p. xiv.

neutral term 'public law' would obscure these turf wars but the underlying tensions between those who viewed rights as underpinning public law and those who viewed rights as socially conceived would remain.

What is at stake in these different renderings of the relationship between constitutional and administrative law is not just the superficial issue of proper subject boundaries. The underlying question goes to the heart of the issue of whether rights are pre-social, as suggested by Diceyan constitutionalism, or are founded in the social (as the prevailing civil service ideology – and its Idealist, Utilitarian and Socialist foundations – would suggest). Robson is unequivocal about this. Diceyan common law constitutionalism, which regards the legal relationship between the state and the individual as analogous to the relationship between ordinary individuals, wrongly bases the British constitution on individual rights rather than viewing the constitution as the source of rights.[49] Jennings takes a similar view. The Constitution is not built upon individual rights but 'upon the collective responsibilities of administrative bodies'.[50]

Of all of the LSE school, Robson writes the most frankly about the *moral* project of infusing ideas developed in the social sciences into the law and legal institutions.[51] He is also closest to the ideological currents of the civil service itself, in which he worked during World War II.[52] For him, the new administrative law requires the *very nature of justice* as traditionally understood by lawyers to be re-imagined. He quotes Roscoe Pound:

> Administrative law is to supply the need for a new type of justice less like a 'system of hands off while individuals assert themselves freely,' and more like 'a social institution existing for social ends'.[53]

[49] Robson, *Justice and Administrative Law*, 2nd edn, above n. 22 p. 343.

[50] W. I. Jennings, 'The Right of Assembly in England', *New York University Law Quarterly Review* (1931–2), 217.

[51] Robson, *Justice and Administrative Law*, above n. 48, p. 262.

[52] William Robson (1895–1980) published his first book *Aircraft in War and Peace* in 1916 about the manufacture and maintenance of aircraft. He left school at fifteen and served in the Royal Flying Corp in World War I. Reputedly he piloted George Bernard Shaw who after the flight enquired about his demobilization plans and introduced him to Sidney Webb at the London School of Economics (LSE) where he studied law under Laski and later became a Professor: see B. Crick, 'Robson, William Alexander (1895–1980)', in H. C. G. Matthew and B. H. Harrison (eds.), *Oxford Dictionary of National Biography* (Oxford University Press, 2004). His work in the civil service appears to have radicalized his thought.

[53] Robson, *Justice and Administrative Law*, 2nd edn, above n. 22, p. 31.

This new administrative law, says Robson, is 'very largely due to the creation of new types of offences against the community, the growth of a new conception of social rights, and enhanced solicitude for the common good, and the lessening of that belief in the divinity of extreme individualism'.[54] The most obvious connection here with the dominant social theory is in the way in which he conceives of the individual and its relationship to the state and society. The central tasks of the new administrative law are to further the common good and to subdue the worst excesses of nineteenth-century individualism. Administrative law is not simply about technical expertise but about furthering policies of social improvement and social obligation.[55] He admits that what has not been 'consciously recognized' is that new systems of adjudication are required in order to 'enforce and sanction the inevitable infringement of individual legal rights' that the extension of state functions have made 'necessary'.[56] The 'socialisation of government must be accompanied by the socialisation of law'.[57] The other advantages claimed for 'trial by Whitehall' which include an enhanced capacity to set standards, to decide high volumes of matters and to grant citizens cheaper and faster dispute resolution, are merely subsidiary to these central moral goals.[58]

What is at stake for him, then, is the very basis on which the constitution is founded. His is a rejection of common law constitutionalism. The involvement of courts would inevitably limit the functions of government by reference to 'old individualistic ideas'.[59] In the interests of social progress, the private interest must be subordinated to the common weal.[60] More than that, the very nature of the Diceyan ordinary law model presumes that 'questions of the highest social import' can be treated as 'mere private controversies between John Doe and Richard Roe'.[61] He adds in the second edition:

> To say that the only person capable of being a 'party' to a controversy is a private person or party seeking to enforce individual rights, is to advocate a conception more fitted to the nineteenth century than the twentieth.

[54] *Ibid.* [55] *Ibid.*, p. 261.

[56] Robson, *Justice and Administrative Law*, above n. 48, pp. 253–4, Robson, *Justice and Administrative Law*, 2nd edn, above n. 22, p. 430.

[57] Robson, *Justice and Administrative Law*, above n. 48, p. 254.

[58] Workers Compensation and National Insurance claims, e.g., had generated too numerous claims to be handled by the ordinary courts (see Wade, *Administrative Law*, above n. 22, p. 146).

[59] Robson, *Justice and Administrative Law*, above n. 48, p. 251. [60] *Ibid.*, p. 252.

[61] *Ibid.*

> We must now regard the public as very definitely a 'party' to certain kinds of proceedings which are decided judicially. It was, indeed, the failure of the judicature to endow the general public with an enforceable interest in matters where a regard for the social good is of the first moment that led to the development of the Administrative tribunals . . .[62]

Inducting constitutional principles from ordinary common law litigation will by its nature fail to produce the correct result in terms of the common good.

Robson describes the common good and its relationship to 'rights' in at least three different ways. As we have already seen, he suggests that the individual rights must *inevitably* give way to the common good and indeed that is a reason for redesigning decision-making institutions and rejecting the common law.[63] At another point he describes this not as a matter of *simple* subordination of the individual to the collective, but as a matter of giving different concerns their proper weight (notice his use of the word 'equal' and the emphasis on 'duties'):[64]

> If constitutional law emphasises individual rights, administrative law lays equal stress on public needs: on the duties owed by the citizen to the public, on the subordination of private interest to the common weal.

In a third passage, his objection to the common law is that ordinary law is *incapable* of stopping the government from overreaching. He complains that the ordinary law is 'utterly inadequate to safeguard the rights of the individual in the twentieth century state'.[65]

In certain of his formulations Robson could be taken for a simple Utilitarian: the greater good must prevail over the individual. At other times he uses the more idealist language of duty: an evolved and involved citizen owes duties to the whole.[66] Sometimes he is concerned about coercion and arbitrary actions by the state: administrative law must do

62 Robson, *Justice and Administrative Law*, 2nd edn, above n. 22, pp. 68–9.

63 *Ibid.*, p. 430 (emphasis added). In seventeenth-century thought the sovereign common good was not viewed as detracting from individual liberty. Subjection to the common wealth and common good was the only form of subjection which was not a case of domination or tyranny. See A. S. Brett, 'The Development of the Idea of Citizens' Rights' in Q. Skinner and B. Strath (ed.), *States and Citizens* (Cambridge University Press, 2003), pp. 97–112.

64 Robson, *Justice and Administrative Law*, 2nd edn, above n. 22, p. 429.

65 *Ibid.*, pp. 345–6.

66 This ethic of social duty was a distinctive feature of British, as opposed to Hegelian, Idealism: see Francis and Morrow, *English Political Thought in the Nineteenth Century*, above n. 6, p. 271.

more and not less than the ordinary law to protect the rights of individuals against the state. Is he simply muddled or is it possible to reconcile these approaches?

One way to reconcile these apparently inconsistent statements is by viewing them through the lens of the new Liberalism that dominated the period. Green and his followers were 'new Liberals' but Liberals nonetheless. Given that individuals are located in society, rights themselves take on a particular cast. Green defines rights in this way:[67]

> A right is a power by which the exercise by an individual or some other body of men is recognised by a society either as itself directly essential to a common good or as conferred by an authority of which the maintenance is recognised as essential.

Green focused on the individual and not the social group. The social group and state exists for the individual and not the other way round.[68] But the adherents of new Liberalism thought that individual self-realization was much more than the pursuit of private preferences. It was about realizing full human potential and the ideal self. These ideas were adopted by the Fabian Socialists and used to justify paternalistic interventions – in the form, for example, of education. The same ideas also endowed an individual with positive duties towards others. Viewed through this perspective, state intervention and the enforcement of such duties did not interfere with an individual's liberty but enhanced it. In this way liberty could grow at the same time as the state's powers and functions grew. Such views seek to avoid conflict between the individual and the common good: the ideal state works toward the common good by enhancing the ideal self of individuals.

While Robson does not define what he means when he refers to individual rights, he certainly does adopt the view that individuals should seek to overcome self-interest.[69] This, and his invocation of the idea of the duties owed by citizens to the public, suggests that he accepts

[67] T. H. Green, *Lectures on the Principles of Political Obligation* (London: Longmans Green 1948), p. 103.

[68] Bosanquet, by contrast, tends to give greater priority to the group. He asks: 'Why should the community, an individual in a far deeper sense than the citizen, being the nearest approach to a true individual that exists upon the earth, be expected not to follow its conscience?' in B. Bosanquet, 'The Function of the State in Promoting the Unity of Mankind', in D. Boucher (ed.), *The British Idealists* (Cambridge University Press, 1997), pp. 270–95, 281.

[69] Robson, *Justice and Administrative Law*, 2nd edn, above n. 22, p. 35.

that individuals have a duty to each other to realize their best selves. One way to reconcile Robson's different views is to read him as saying that administrative tribunals should 'inevitably' 'infringe' *common law rights* (as opposed to rights conceived in Idealist terms). Such common law rights attach to the hedonist self, rather than to the ideal self. What administrative law seeks to subdue is the wrong kind of self – both for the common good and for the individual's own good. In that way both the needs of the individual and the needs of the whole can be equally balanced. Robson's claim that administrative law should go further than the ordinary law to stop the state from overreaching can also be reconciled with these views. At the same time as we might contemplate a non-ideal self (that must be subdued), we should also allow for the prospect of a non-ideal state – a state which acts capriciously and arbitrarily. In such cases the individual ought to have more and not fewer rights against the state. This too is consistent with Idealist thought. At the same time as Green suggested that an individual could have no rights as against society and the state as such, he would allow an individual to have rights against an unjust society and state.[70] In other words, the individual has rights against the state (and need not obey) if the state is not acting for its proper ends.

Robson revealingly makes a distinction between the state's service and its regulatory functions.[71] Regulatory functions, he suggests, are those involving coercion or 'police powers' (he deliberately uses the US terminology which refers to public order, morals, health and safety). He suggests that regulatory powers ought to remain within the ambit of the ordinary courts of law and that it is only 'service' functions which are best dealt with by administrative tribunals.[72] Presumably service functions are less likely to involve conflicts between the state and the idealized self, and regulatory functions by definition may be more likely to involve the state acting in a non-idealized way. This is a very large concession to make in relation to his wider administrative law enterprise and one that modern readers have tended to overlook. It qualifies significantly his views about the desirability of tribunals and the desirability of the exclusion of the ordinary courts.

[70] A. Simhony, 'Rights that Bind: T. H. Green on Rights and Community', in M. Dimova-Cookson and W. J. Mander (eds.), *T. H. Green Ethics, Metaphysics and Political Philosophy* (Oxford: Clarendon Press, 2006), pp. 236–61, 247.

[71] There are similarities here with Sydney and Beatrice Webb's, *A Constitution for the Socialist Commonwealth of Great Britain* (London: Longmans Green, 1920) where they propose that there should be two Parliaments – one 'political' the other 'social'.

[72] Robson, *Justice and Administrative Law*, 2nd edn, above n. 22, p. 328.

Robson was not an Idealist but rather a Fabian Socialist (the last of them according to Griffith).[73] He was an active member of the Fabian Society and associated with some of its leading figures.[74] The influences of Idealist-derived 'new Liberalism' can, however, be found in Fabianism generally and Robson's work in particular. Fabians embraced Idealist notions of individual freedom in the late nineteenth century and there is evidence that Robson had read work of the Idealist Ritchie (who joined the Fabians briefly during the same period).[75]

Admittedly, Robson's reasons for rejecting common law morality as the proper basis of justice are in part instrumental.[76] The morality manifested in common law doctrines is not able to meet the needs of modern society. But he also has more fundamental objections that go beyond Utilitarian concerns. The common law falls short of representing the *real* interests at stake. The common law or the 'ordinary action of law' is aligned with the pursuit of self-interest.[77] The broader common good or protection of the public is not usually achieved by the pursuit of individual self-interest (presumably even in the aggregate). In his, the first sustained analysis of administrative law in the United Kingdom in 1928, Robson calls for new moral principles to achieve the new social purposes, reflected in new institutions and decision-making processes.

Robson is closest to the prevailing ideology of the civil service. He would even go so far as to deny a conflict between the (true) interests of the individual and the collective. None of the other early administrative lawyers, however, were so ready to reject the common law, apologize for the administrative state or pretend that conflicts between individual rights and the state could be avoided in these ways. In terms of method, Jennings, and Griffith and Street tended to avoid abstract invocations of the common good and preferred to discuss *particular* legislation and regulatory regimes and the public policy questions they are designed to

[73] J. A. G. Griffith, '"Justice and Administrative law" Revisited', in J. A. G. Griffith (ed.), *From Policy to Administration*: Essays in Honour of William A. Robson (London: Allen & Unwin 1976), pp. 200–16, 201.

[74] He was, for example, a personal friend of the Webbs. See B. Webb, *The Diary of Beatrice Webb*, N. and J. MacKenzie (eds.) (London: Virago, 2000).

[75] Robson cites Ritchie's work on Natural Rights in, W. A. Robson, *Civilisation and the Growth of Law: A Study of the Relations Between Men's Ideas About the Universe and the Institutions of Law and Government* (New York: Macmillan, 1935), pp. 297, 299. On Ritchie's evolutionary thought, see further Loughlin, 'The Functionalist Style in Public Law', above n. 17.

[76] Robson, *Justice and Administrative Law*, 2nd edn, above n. 22, p. 69.

[77] *Ibid.*, p. 90.

resolve. Jennings's study of judicial interpretations of housing legislation is a good case in point. He starts with the legislation rather than the common law – itself a radical departure from common law method.[78]

Jennings does not so much attack the common law per se, but rather the presumptions of statutory interpretation that judges bring to new social legislation such as the slum clearance laws. At one place, Jennings suggests:[79]

> The common law assumes the complete liberty of the landowner to use his land as he wishes, subject only to the laws of nuisance. It assumes, also, the liberty of the individual to make any contract that is not illegal or contrary to public policy. But the fundamental assumption of modern statute law is that the landowner holds his land for the public good. It may be subject to all kinds of control; it may be taken away from him altogether in a host of cases where the public needs it for other purposes. Similarly, freedom of contract has been interfered with in respect of employment, in respect of tenancies, and so on. To assume that there is intention not to interfere with common law rights is to assert a proposition that is in direct contradiction to the truth.

His blunt conclusion is that '[t]he purpose of the Housing Acts is to interfere with common law rights'.[80]

Jennings is critiquing an interpretative turn he discerns after 1928. At the very time that Hewart is mounting his challenge to the '*new despotism*', judges are becoming more assertive in their invocation of common law laissez-faire values to *limit* the application of social legislation.[81] Jennings even goes so far as suggesting that 'the common law itself is biased against administrative law'[82] and that judges have used it to 'impede the administrative machine'.[83] The conflict between civil service and common law values identified first by Lord Hewart is beginning to be manifested in the case law and not just in public debate. But clearly for Jennings, as for Griffith, Street, Wade, De Smith and Laski, not *all* common law values are to be rejected. Property and contractual rights are the focus of their hostility and of their distrust of the common law. The law of tort or delict, and its protections against individual injustice, fare rather better.

Jennings is under no illusions about the conservative and anti-collectivist cast of mind of most judges. However, he is prepared to allow that their

[78] See: W. I. Jennings, W. A. Robson and E. C. S. Wade, 'Administrative Law and the Teaching of Public Law', *Journal of the Society of Public Teachers of Law* (1938), 10–14.

[79] W. I. Jennings, 'Courts and Administrative Law – The Experience of English Housing Legislation', *Harvard Law Review* 49 (1936), 426–54, 435.

[80] *Ibid.*, 437. [81] *Ibid.*, 454. [82] *Ibid.*, 434. [83] *Ibid.*, 435.

careful scrutiny and consideration of the impact on individuals may sometimes be advantageous.[84] He allows for the need to balance individual rights against the purposes of the collective. 'Private interests must give way to the public good', but 'the public good is ultimately injured by acts which, though apparently in its favour, lead to individual injustices'.[85] While, like Robson and Laski,[86] he accepts a degree of official expertise in interpreting legislation, he does not automatically exalt the official over the individual. Far from automatically acting as the guardian of public needs, he suspects that an official 'is almost as likely to stretch the law against an individual as is a private person concerned with his own welfare'.[87]

For this reason, he treats the common law of tort as having a place *alongside* the new administrative law. Jennings explicitly allows that delictual remedies *are a part* of administrative law, if only a small part: 'the application of the ordinary law [meaning delictual causes of action], when it applies, is an interesting characteristic of English administrative law'.[88] This was a widely shared view. Most of the early administrative law texts routinely discuss tortious remedies alongside the prerogative remedies.[89] This is revealing given that Dicey's primary examples of ordinary law constitutional protections of the individual involve the intentional torts.

Laski is the strongest promoter of tortious remedies against public authorities and, indeed, against the state itself. He argues that tortious remedies are a means of effecting state responsibility. He is accordingly also the strongest critic of the Crown's immunity which he regards as a licence to state irresponsibility and as treating the state above the law. Influenced by the French system, he argues that there is an 'obvious justice that if the public seek benefit, due care must be taken in the process not to harm the lesser interests therein encountered.'[90] Enforcement of liability is a means to this end. Public funds should normally

84 *Ibid.*, 434. 85 *Ibid.*, 454.

86 H. J. Laski, 'The Responsibility of the State in England', *Harvard Law Review* 32 (1918–19), 447–72, 462.

87 Jennings, 'Courts and Administrative Law', above n. 79, 454.

88 W. I. Jennings, *The Law and the Constitution*, 2nd edn (University of London Press, 1938) pp. 206, 207.

89 H. Street, *Government Liability: A Comparative Study* (Cambridge University Press, 1953); Griffith and Street, *Principles of Administrative Law* above n. 22; Wade, *Administrative Law* above n. 22; De Smith, *Judicial Review of Administrative Action*, above n. 1.

90 Laski, 'The Responsibility of the State in England', above n. 86, 451

compensate for the damage suffered or burden placed on an individual in pursuit of collective ends: the 'exchequer [ought to] lie open for relief'.[91] What is more, he regards the demand for state responsibility in tort as *newly* necessitated by the state's shift from negative to positive functions. Services that used to be supplied by the private sector should not be protected from 'the normal consequences of law' because they are now supplied by that 'great public service corporation'.[92] Ultimately the state is no more than the 'greatest of public service utilities . . . and like a public utility in private hands, it shall act at its peril'.[93]

Aspects of Laski's thought significantly distinguish him from most of his colleagues. He agrees with the later Dicey[94] that the state requires the freedom of action enjoyed by a private person to perform its new functions and argues that the state should accordingly accept the same standard of justice as would be expected of a private person.[95] Accordingly it is necessary to remove the state's special privileges and the 'cloak of sovereignty'. Influenced by Duguit[96] (who was in turn influenced by Comte), Laski rejects the metaphysical and organic terms in which the state is often described. The state is simply a 'public utility' acting like a human being through its officials. Look behind the Crown and you will find 'fallible men'.[97] This approach also means that he rejects any 'special rules' developed for the public authorities, including the iconic decision in the *Arlidge* case discussed below.[98] Given these commitments, it should not have been such a surprise that the report of the Donoughmore Committee, to which he contributed, was as Diceyan as it turned out to be.

Laski is alone in wanting a single set of legal standards to apply to the state and other groups. (He also wanted to democratize all forms of association.) While nearly everyone, even Robson, applauded the passing of the Crown Proceedings Act 1947, there was general disquiet about whether a *private* law basis of tortious liability was appropriate to the Crown and public authorities. Rights (including rights protected by the

[91] *Ibid.*, 452, 468. [92] *Ibid.*, 452, 469. [93] *Ibid.*, 470.

[94] Dicey, 'The Development of Administrative Law in England', above n. 32, 150.

[95] Laski, 'The Responsibility of the State', above n. 86, 469.

[96] See, e.g., L. Duguit, 'The Concept of Public Service', *Yale Law Journal* 32 (1922–3), 425–35, 427.

[97] Laski, 'The Responsibility of the State', above n. 86, 451. Elements here anticipate Kelsen.

[98] *Ibid.*, 463. He considers administrative law to involve recognition of official expertise in the interpretation of legislation, special administrative courts and a 'new system of rights', but none of these ideas are developed.

common law of tort) needed to be tailored to accommodate social needs. This was an important consequence of the social nature of rights.

There were a number of important senses in which most of the new administrative lawyers thought that the ordinary common law did not go far enough in protecting individual rights. Jennings suggests that the nature of the *powers* given to public authorities:[99]

> [P]ut them in a position to injure a private citizen far more seriously than a private citizen can do. The individual therefore needs *larger rights and different remedies* against the administration than against his fellow citizens.

A general problem identified by Jennings, Mitchell and even Wade (the *most* Diceyan of this group)[100] was that the private tortious remedies did not themselves go far enough.[101] There was no compensation available in the common law at the time in the nature of 'enterprise liability'. Jennings goes as far as suggesting that the administration should be treated as a '*personne morale*' for such responsibility purposes.[102] Continental systems of administrative law, such as those operating in France and Belgium, gave greater protections to individuals by compensating for administrative *risk creation* as well as fault.[103] The shared view that rights are socially constructed, led to a concern that the common law was deficient in only recognizing classical liberal rights. There was no 'ordinary' tort law compensation for loss of livelihood or a licence. At one point Jennings suggests that the '"right" to public support' might be at least as important as 'rights' of freedom of discussion. How far one 'right' is more fundamental than another depends, he argues, on 'social, political, and economic conditions which a formal discussion of the constitution must ignore'.[104]

These concerns would be reflected in the way in which administrative law would later develop. What would count as a right, or more accurately an 'interest' giving rise to an administrative law challenge, would gradually expand from classical liberal property rights to the 'new property',[105] including, for example, rights created by government largesse such as in welfare benefits, licences, jobs and immigration status.

[99] Jennings, *The Law and the Constitution*, above n. 88, p. 208 (emphasis added).
[100] Wade for example thinks that rights and remedies are never separate *contra* Jennings.
[101] Wade, *Administrative Law*, above n. 22, p. 83; Mitchell, 'Administrative Law and Policy Effectiveness', above n. 3, p. 178.
[102] Jennings, *Law and the Constitution*, above n. 88, p. 233. [103] *Ibid.* p. 209.
[104] Jennings, 'The Right of Assembly in England', above n. 50, 220.
[105] C. A. Reich, 'The New Property', *Yale Law Journal* 73 (1963–4), 733–87.

There was another important respect in which Jennings considered that individuals were in need of 'larger rights' against the administration. The common law had never actually been that effective in protecting liberty rights. Jennings writes that some of the most basic liberties (with which Dicey was also concerned) such as freedom of speech and assembly were never, in fact, protected by the common law in any remediable or actionable sense. Such freedoms only exist to the extent that under the common law everything is legal that is not illegal. Liberty depends on the *powers* of government rather than on an individual's remedies against it. While Jennings appreciates that the collective interest may sometimes override and damage individual interests and that there may, therefore, still be a role for the common law, he seeks to marginalize these issues from the central focus of administrative law. Dicey's emphasis on remedies, he argues, misses the point. Individual liberty is not so much about legal remedies as about the extent of governmental powers.[106]

This is an important moment for administrative lawyers. As Jennings formulates it, the central enterprise of administrative law is to determine the architecture of public power, and *not* the interests of *particular* individuals. This would have significance for the place of the individual in how administrative law was framed and for what would be considered an effective remedy (as we shall see in the next chapter).

Rapprochement between the common lawyers and their views of individual rights and administrative lawyers and their concerns about power would soon be possible. The antagonism and ambivalence to the common law by administrative law specialists would gradually ease. After World War II, moderating contributions such as those of Sir Cecil Carr began to acknowledge the validity of some aspects of Lord Hewart's attack, and sought to reassure the public that civil servants were not despots, and nor did they wish to be.[107] Sympathetic to both sides of the debate, Carr and others began to offer a middle way. In the first text to attempt to extract from the case law and various legislative schemes *general* principles of judicially applied constraints on the administration, which did not appear until 1959, De Smith places ordinary courts at the very centre of balancing individual rights against the public interest.[108]

[106] Jennings, *The Law and the Constitution*, above n. 88, preface to the 2nd edn, p. xxviii.

[107] Carr, *Concerning English Administrative Law*, above n. 29, p. 27.

[108] De Smith, *Judicial Review of Administrative Action*, above n. 1, p. 3. The first Scottish text (which is more similar to Robson than De Smith in organizing the work around the regulation of various sectors rather than by judicial principles) is J. Bennett Miller,

In doing so he argues that the ordinary courts are uniquely and best placed to fulfil this important role. In admitting that the 'absence of judicial review of the constitutionality of legislation had indirectly conduced to a lack of informed interest among practicing lawyers in the juridical problems of government' he overtly concedes the *constitutionality* of the courts' role.[109] Wade, writing in 1962, does not pretend that we can avoid conflicts between the individual and the collective: 'For the citizen it is vital that all power should be used in a way conformable to his ideas of liberty, fair dealing and good administration. This is a matter of some difficulty, for social needs and ancient liberties are frequently hard to reconcile.'[110] Significantly, given the earlier debate about the differences between constitutional and administrative law, both Wade and Willis would go on to explain to US audiences that administrative law in Britain and Canada often performs the work of constitutional law in the US.[111] They place the constitutional role of ordinary courts at the centre of the enterprise once more.

The new scholars of 'the administrative' viewed the common law as privileging certain rights in a way that was antithetical to the common good. While Robson was alone in denying that the collective good and individual rights and interests could actually conflict – relying as he did on the concept of the ideal self – all of these scholars considered rights to be socially conceived and subordinate to the interests of the collective, and viewed the common law as falling short of recognizing the full range of rights. A deep strain of suspicion towards the common law and common law rights would remain within British administrative law scholarship,[112] and that would later flow into discussions of human

An Outline of Administrative and Local Government Law in Scotland (Edinburgh: Green, 1961). He begins (p. 3)

'The student of administrative law is faced with the initial difficulty of ascertaining the precise contours of the subject. There is no systematised code of administrative law to which he can appeal, and this fact has led some writers to deny entirely the existence of administrative law in Great Britain.' He also asks Lord Hewart's question whether administrative law is an oxymoron (*ibid.*).

109 De Smith, *Judicial Review of Administrative Action*, above n. 1, p. 9.

110 Wade, *Administrative Law*, above n. 22, p. 3.

111 J. Willis, 'Administrative Law and the British North America Act', 53 *Harvard Law Review* 53 (1939–40), 251–81; H. W. R. Wade, *Towards Administrative Justice* (Ann Arbor, MI: Michigan University Press, 1963), pp. 63 ff. (natural justice as due process).

112 See, e.g., the work of Harry Arthurs, Patrick McAuslan, Carol Harlow, D. J. Galligan and Richard Rawlings.

rights.[113] We shall explore these ideas further in Chapters 7 and 9. But in the meantime, the common law gradually embraced the administration and began to exercise a supervisory role in relation to it. The common law principles designed to supervise the bureaucracy and its 'laws' became synonymous with administrative law itself.

I turn now to that part of the story.

What would a new administrative justice look like?

The new UK administrative lawyers, particularly Jennings, Robson, Willis (who began his career in England) and Mitchell, were at the outset attempting a decisive break with the past. They were seeking to remake ideas about the basis of constitutionalism, of justice and of the rule of law in order to meet the demands of the public service state. But if administrative law was not to become *in fact* a version of Lord Hewart's 'administrative lawlessness', they would have to address the question of what values should replace the old laissez-faire common law values. What values would serve 'a theory of administrative law in sympathy with modern tendencies' of administration?[114] One important approach has already been mentioned. Administrative lawyers should focus their best efforts at addressing the nature of *power* – including how legislation and delegated legislation is constructed. Indeed, this is the call that Griffith and Street take up in their text *Principles of Administrative Law* in 1952. Their principal questions are: 'what sort of powers does the administration exercise; what are the limits of those powers, how is the administration kept within those limits?'[115] Wade later adjusts the question, though once again the focus is power. He is not only interested in the extent of administrative power but in the *manner* in which it is and should be exercised. Griffith and Wade would disagree about many things but there is a clear connection between their questions, if not their approach to their resolution. The distinction between their two approaches would be collapsed in the 1969 decision of *Anisminic Ltd* v. *Foreign Compensation*

[113] Galligan's hostile reaction to a proposal for a Bill of Rights in 1982 is in this vein: 'Such suggestions are less concerned with regulating the Welfare State than getting rid of it', D. J. Galligan, 'Judicial Review and the Textbook Writers', *Oxford Journal of Legal Studies* 2 (1982), 257–76, 273.

[114] Carr, *Concerning English Administrative Law*, above n. 29, p. 19.

[115] Griffith and Street, *Principles of Administrative Law*, above n. 22, p. 4.

Commission[116] which held that a decision may be made so badly that it becomes *ultra vires* or outside of the body's jurisdiction.

Making administrative justice completely anew could not, or at least did not, happen. *Judicial* controls on the exercise of bureaucratic power were engrafted onto *procedures* already existing in the common law. That may have been inevitable given the reluctance of some of the judges to relinquish their traditional supervisory powers. What made it more likely was the position that the Committee on Ministers' Powers took on the threshold definition of when courts should intervene in administration. They affirmed the approach of the existing case law that intervention should be triggered by a test of whether the decision-maker had a 'duty to act judicially'. As we shall see, Robson's conception of the 'judicial mind' was at least partly responsible for the Committee's affirmation of this approach and thus for the direction in which administrative law was headed. Both the old legal forms and procedures and the new socialized justice would have a contribution to make.

One of Lord Hewart's concerns about 'the new despotism' was that it should be judges, independent of the executive, who should decide disputes that concern decisions of a judicial nature and not bureaucrats effectively deciding in their own cause. According to Lord Hewart, the separation of powers was at stake. A 'new version of administrative law', a 'socialised law to meet the needs of the new socialised state', could not escape the constraints and overhangs of history.

The early administrative lawyers had debunked what they saw as the mythology surrounding the separation of powers, suggesting that these were the moribund shackles of constitutional law, which have never described the legal position as it really operated and which have been used to inhibit social progress.[117] As Maitland had earlier pointed out, the separation of powers had never existed in any pure form in England. English government had long relied on 'the amphibious old justice who did administrative work under judicial forms'.[118] De Lolme had been misled by viewing 'only the surface of things'.[119] Given the precedent of

[116] [1969] 2 AC 147 [HL].

[117] See, e.g., W. I. Jennings, *Law and the Constitution*, above n. 88, p. 16: 'The doctrine is so remote from the facts that it is better disregarded altogether'.

[118] See, also F. W. Maitland, *The Constitutional History of England: A Course of Lectures* (Cambridge University Press, 1885), pp. 385–501.

[119] See also F. W. Maitland, 'The Shallows and Silences of Real Life', in H. A. L. Fisher (ed.), *The Collected Papers of Frederic William Maitland* 3 vols. (Cambridge University Press, 1911) vol. 1, p. 478, reminding us of the need to look beyond the surface of things.

the local justice who had always combined executive and judicial functions, the combination of administrative and judicial functions in the bureaucracy could be regarded as simply the inevitable consequence of centralization.[120] According to one view, it was not as if the bureaucracy were encroaching on judicial functions, but rather that judges were sometimes engaged in a specialized form of administration.[121] Jennings suggests that it is impossible to divide up functions into categories: better instead to focus on 'what works' and to look at the thing afresh.[122] For two reasons, however, these separation of powers questions never went completely away.

First, a struggle for control was at stake. Justices of the Peace had indeed enjoyed many administrative functions, such as the upkeep of roads and bridges and the licensing of ale-houses. While the Justices had been almost completely free from *political* control, their decisions had been subject to the supervisory jurisdiction of the courts through the prerogative writs of *mandamus*, *prohibition* and *certiorari*. Who or what system of control ought to be put in place at the point when combined functions came to be centralized? Was political control (patchy as it was) enough? Why would or should courts voluntarily abdicate the control they had achieved in the eighteenth century?[123]

Second, a struggle about the proper norms and procedures was at stake. Justices had discharged their administrative functions 'in the most judicial style possible'.[124] Judicial administration had been open and public and, until the middle of the nineteenth century, commonly accompanied by 'a record' of written reasons.[125] None of these conditions attached, as a matter of course, to bureaucratic or Ministerial decision-making. And indeed how could they apply to the sheer bulk and complexity of tasks undertaken by the new social administration? What kinds of procedures, decision-makers and norms would best befit these tasks?

[120] Griffith and Street, *Principles of Administrative Law*, above n. 22, p. 195.
[121] Robson, *Justice and Administrative Law* above n. 48, p. 11 (quoting Sir Josiah Stamp).
[122] Jennings, *Law and the Constitution*, above n. 88, p. 16.
[123] Wade, *Administrative Law*, above n. 22, p. 99. [124] *Ibid.*
[125] *Ibid.*, p. 74. Wade notes that Justices of the Peace had been required to furnish elaborate written statements of evidence and reasoning which were all part of the record and there were ample opportunities for correction. In 1848 the Summary Jurisdiction Act introduced a short form of conviction: 'The effect was not to make that which had been an error, error no longer, but to remove nearly all opportunity for its detection', *King* v. *Nat Bell Liquors Ltd* [1922] 2 AC 128, 159 (Lord Sumner).

What joins these two sets of questions is that, in their supervisory jurisdiction, ordinary courts had traditionally enjoyed powers to review decisions made by those with 'a duty to act judicially' and thus to impose on such decision-making, procedural and normative constraints which had been designed for judicial decision-making. Jealously guarding their oversight function, judges would manipulate the test of what constituted a 'judicial' decision until it was stretched to breaking-point. The case law was contradictory and it became impossible to predict when courts were likely to intervene.[126] The common law, then, modelled administrative decision-making on judicial decision-making, and the ordinary courts based their intervention for certain purposes on a test of whether the decision-maker was exercising a 'judicial' power.

A decisive point came in the *Arlidge* case,[127] in which the House of Lords recognized that strict judicial standards of decision-making should not be applied to administrative decision-making.[128] Viscount Haldane (Idealist and now the Lord Chancellor) determined that when hearing an appeal the Local Government Board had a duty to act judicially.[129] In the same judgment, however, he allows for a nuanced approach to such a standard, adjusting the rules of natural justice to the needs of administration (in the context of taking property). The Minister, for example, unlike the judge, does not need to gather evidence himself or to decide everything personally.[130] He may properly rely on the assistance of his staff. Neither is he bound to hear the respondent orally, provided that the work is done 'judicially and fairly', he acts in good faith and he listens to both sides fairly.[131] Lord Shaw agreed in strong terms: 'But that the judiciary should presume to impose its own methods on administrative or executive officers is a usurpation'.[132] He went further to say that the board was under no duty to disclose the views of the inspector that guided those dealing with the case.[133] For both better and worse,[134] in essence this version of the 'duty to act

126 See, e.g., Griffith and Street, *Principles of Administrative Law*, above n. 22.

127 *Local Government Board* v. *Arlidge* [1915] AC 120. Landis mentions this judgment, suggesting that it changed Dicey's mind about the existence of administrative law, in *The Administrative Process*, above n. 47, p. 3.

128 Laski alone out of the administrative lawyers viewed this case as a licence to tyranny, see Laski, 'The Responsibility of the State', above n. 86, 461, 463

129 [1915] AC 120, 132. 130 *Ibid.*, 133. 131 *Ibid.*, 132–3. 132 *Ibid.*, 138.

133 *Ibid.*, 137 per Lord Shaw.

134 The Freedom of Information Act UK 2000 requiring open decision-making came much later to England and Wales than most other commonwealth countries.

judicially' would come to serve as the foundation for the creation of an idealized version of the character of the official.

It was essentially the *Arlidge* analysis out of which Robson later elaborated his normative ideals of the 'public realm' – which included not only administrative officials and tribunals, but all kinds of domestic tribunals. Robson, like the other administrative lawyers, denied the notion that there was ever a strict separation of powers. He, like Haldane, accepted some sort of functional division but thought that functions could move between the different branches. He forthrightly acknowledged that 'judges often administer and administrators often judge'.[135] When he referred to administrative law in this context he meant 'the jurisdiction of a *judicial nature* exercised by law-administering agencies over the rights and property of citizens and corporate bodies'.[136] And one of his central questions was whether with the rise of administrative law 'there has been a spreading of the judicial outlook to those administrative bodies'.[137] So while he wanted to make administrative justice 'anew' he seems, at least superficially, to have accepted functional distinctions. His theory shared with the procedural common law the notion of 'the judge' as the model administrator.

This may seem surprising from a 'dissenting' left-wing administrative lawyer who disavows the common law (and a central role for the ordinary courts). His idea of the administrator–judge, with the habits and characteristics of the 'judicial mind', is, however, very much a normative construction. These are the characteristics of mind he thinks best able to achieve the common good. Here is a normatively imagined public law which is distinct from private law. And while he reads Frankfurter and Landis for other purposes, this is where Robson (and later Willis) explicitly departs from them. Robson is an advocate for administrative tribunals, not because he thinks they will be cheaper, more efficient, handle large numbers of cases better or attract expertise. It is rather because it is among administrative tribunals he hopes to foster better the 'proper cast of judicial mind'. Like Willis in Canada, for Robson 'internal normativity' is of primary importance.[138] Culture and character matter.

135 Robson, *Justice and Administrative Law*, above n. 48, p. 5.
136 *Ibid.*, p. 31 (emphasis added). 137 *Ibid.*, p. 36.
138 G. Blaine Baker, 'Willis on "Cultured Public Authorities"', *University of Toronto Law Journal* 55 (2005), 335–60, 357.

The 'judicial mind'

While it is true, as later scholars of the LSE have tended to emphasize, that Robson thought that courts should be limited in their powers to intervene in administrative decision-making, and that the new (non-court) procedures better reflected the true nature of the interests concerned, it is not as though he desired that officials (or indeed anyone else) should be legally or morally unconstrained. The exercise by administrative tribunals of broad delegated powers is justified in terms of the (idealized) 'character' of the officials who decide these questions. For Robson, the way to ensure that bureaucrats act for the common good is to encourage in them particular 'habits of mind'. This also suggests a connection between Robson's work and the prevailing political thought of the period.

The importance of 'character' and the idea of the judge as model has a particular resonance in Idealist thought. In his preface to the second edition of the *Philosophical Theory of the State* (1910), Bosanquet cautions against the idea of 'routine bureaucracy' and 'mechanical collectivism'.[139] At the same time, he emphasizes that the idea of the 'general will' needs to be expressed in the working of the system of institutions as a whole, not just in ad hoc elective bodies. He gives the example of the British judges who are capable of expressing the 'general will' while nevertheless maintaining their independence from the 'electoral will' of the people.[140] Bosanquet does not view officials as simple agents of the state. This is because, while officials can have power delegated to them, they cannot have the 'general will' delegated to them.[141] Bosanquet, instead, emphasizes the role and importance of *character* as part of the pursuit of the general will.[142]

Robson was attracted to an organic and evolutionary view of society connected through a common mind. In his revealingly titled *Civilisation and the Growth of Law: A Study of the Relations Between Men's Ideas about the Universe and the Institutions of Law and Government* (1935), Robson identifies both jural law and the scientific laws of nature as

139 B. Bosanquet, *The Philosophical Theory of the State*, 2nd edn (London: Macmillan, 1910), p. xii. (He acknowledges his great debt to the US Scholar Miss Follett's *The New State* (London: Longmans Green, 1918).)

140 Bosanquet, *The Philosophical Theory of the State*, above n. 139, pp. xxx–xxxi.

141 Bosanquet, 'The Function of the State in Promoting the Unity of Mankind', above n. 68, p. 285.

142 Carter, 'Ball, Bosanquet and the Legacy of T. H. Green', above n. 11.

originating in the collective human mind. What distinguishes these is that the former involves the element of will and voluntary activity. He asserts that: 'The discovery of the power to aim at ideal ends freely chosen by his own will and intelligence is the supreme achievement of man'.[143] In *Justice and Administrative Law* he talks of the 'judicial mind' as a kind of collective consciousness from which we derive our aesthetic and moral judgments, and also, among other things, our scientific theories.[144] It is on this idea of the 'judicial mind' that he builds the essentially normative elements of the new administrative justice.

Robson's prescription for the new administrative justice embraces the role of character as part of the pursuit of the general will. This aspect of Robson's thinking too tends to be overlooked by modern readers.[145] In order to achieve his new justice, officials (like 'mankind' as a whole) needed to be imbued with a 'judicial frame of mind'.[146] Such a mind is free from individual caprice, self-interest and the desire for personal favour.[147] In the case of officials, they must achieve a delicate balance – they ought to be free from both personal and 'official' interest in the results of their decisions.[148] They should declare publicly in advance the principles they intend to follow and give reasons for their decisions.[149] They should aspire to be consistent.[150] So while he casts off the courts for the ideological contents of their legal doctrines and their inappropriate procedures, and he takes pains to distinguish the ways in which administrators are, and should be, unlike judges – he by no means rejects the idea of 'the judge'. Indeed, the 'judicial character' becomes the model for the state official (and even at times for a new kind of citizen). Not only is the whole of Chapter 5 of both the first and second editions of *Justice and Administrative Law* devoted to 'the judicial mind', but Chapters 2 and 3 emphasize how much of the work of administrative

[143] Robson, *Civilisation and the Growth of Law*, above n. 75, p. 342.

[144] Robson, *Justice and Administrative Law*, above n. 48. Griffith later confesses himself to be 'unhappy' that Robson got so carried away with these ideas and attributes them to the influence of H. G. Wells (another Fabian). See Griffith, '"Justice and Administrative law" Revisited', above n. 73, 201. See also P. Clarke, *Liberals and Social Democrats* (Cambridge University Press, 1978), p. 149.

[145] See, e.g., the discussion of Robson's work in C. Glasser and C. Harlow, 'Legal Services and the Alternatives', in R. Rawlings (ed.), *Law Society and Economy: Centenary Essays for the London School of Economics and Political Science, 1895–1995* (Oxford: Clarendon Press, 1996), pp. 323–38, 331–2.

[146] Robson, *Justice and Administrative Law*, (2nd edn), above n. 22, p. 35.

[147] *Ibid.*, p. 36. [148] *Ibid.*, p. 62. [149] *Ibid.*, pp. 274–5. [150] *Ibid.*, p. 261.

tribunals resembles the work of the judges. Administrators, he says, should be under a duty to act 'judicially'.

This judicial cast of mind is not merely a moral framework to which to aspire. Robson suggests that the judges of the ordinary courts may properly become the *enforcers* of this new morality.[151] In many ways Viscount Haldane L C in *Arlidge* exemplifies Robson's characterization of the ideal judge. Robson may distrust the ordinary courts but he does not reject them altogether. He suggests, for example, that judges should be 'biased in certain directions'[152] and possess 'a sense of what is socially desirable'.[153] The Lord Chancellor, for example, is forward looking and progressive.[154] In *Arlidge*, Haldane suggests, in terms that blend positivism with socially progressive ideas:

> There is no doubt that the question is one involving property and the liberty of a man to do what he chooses with what is his own. Such rights are not to be affected unless Parliament has said so. But Parliament, in what it considers higher interests than those of the individual, has so often interfered with such rights on other occasions, that it is dangerous for judges to lay much stress on what one hundred years ago would have been a presumption considerably stronger than what it is today.

To such judges Robson would entrust the task of supervising and enforcing 'the judicial habit of mind' in the administrator or tribunal. This is important, because critics of Idealism (such as Laski) regarded as an 'incurable defect of the idealist hypothesis that it makes abstractions of the real persons by whom our destiny is controlled'.[155] It is the judicial enforcement of these moral traits of the idealized official that puts juridical flesh on these Idealist bones. This is Robson's 1947 description of the proper grounds for judicial intervention or review of administrative action. He states:[156]

> [a]dministrative tribunals should be compelled to use their discretion judicially; that where it can be proved by an interested party that the members of such a tribunal did not hear the controversy with an open mind, or had virtually prejudged the issue; where they have misused their power to further unauthorised purposes, however well-intentioned; where they are influenced by sinister motives or extraneous considerations: then in those circumstances the proceedings should be subject to review in the courts of law and the decisions set aside. But apart from that

[151] *Ibid.*, p. 487. [152] *Ibid.*, p. 304. [153] *Ibid.*, 307. [154] [1915] AC 120, 130–1.

[155] Quoted in Stears, *Progressives, Pluralists and Problems of the State*, above n. 17, p. 103.

[156] Robson, *Justice and Administrative Law*, 2nd edn, above n. 22, p. 487.

> special type of exception, the work of administrative tribunals must remain independent of the courts of law, and their decisions to be free from liability to be investigated or quashed.

We begin to see the substantive contours of his 'new justice' and how much it differs from justice as it had been instantiated in common law values. Officials should not be free to enjoy the liberty interests that the common law confers on the contractor or property holder. Contractors and property holders, who are subject only to the ordinary law, are free to pursue their preferences unconstrained by proper motives or proper purposes. They may exercise their discretionary powers with bias and bad faith. Bureaucrats have a duty to uphold a distinct morality enforceable at law. They are the representatives of the common will. We are a long way, indeed, from the archetype of the 'rent seeking official'. Under this model too, the public interest is to be represented by the disinterested official and not by a system of interest representation.[157]

Robson's general framework, however, does not represent a dissenting or marginal view. Disconnected from his deeper ideological and metaphysical commitments, the *mainstream* approach to judicial review of administrative action would also involve building a normative legal framework around the concept of a judicial act. Indeed, Griffith later holds Robson to some degree responsible for the 'judicial' orientation of the mainstream approach that emerged out of the Committee on Ministers' Powers (an orientation later regarded as conservative by left-wing administrative lawyers). Robson himself recognized such a thing as 'pure judicial functions' and his evidence to the Committee seems to advance a system of categorization along these lines. This led to the Committee's 'notorious conceptual analysis',[158] that advanced rigid classifications of judicial, *quasi*-judicial and administrative decisions, to which different decision-making standards attached. Its analysis would contribute to what would become for a time a doctrinal strait-jacket surrounding what constituted a judicial decision triggering judicial intervention and supervision. To be fair to Robson, however, the Committee on Ministers' Powers and later the Franks Committee, rejected Robson's proposals for

[157] The Donoughmore Committee did, however, recommend consultation of interests specially affected by delegated legislation. According to Carr, *Concerning English Administrative Law*, above n. 29, p. 53 over forty advisory councils and committees were created for this purpose and the Ministry of Transport was required by statute to consult up to forty bodies before making regulations.

[158] Griffith, '"Justice and Administrative Law" Revisited', above n. 73, p. 201.

an appeal from administrative tribunals to a higher administrative tribunal. In a memorandum to the Franks Committee (1956), he complains that the courts 'have been unable to provide an efficient and acceptable system of judicial review of public administration in the context of this expanding universe of executive power'.[159] It seems that his confidence in the possibility of *judicial* enforcement by the ordinary courts of the norms associated with the 'judicial mind' (even for exceptional cases) soon began to wane.

Making administration subject to common law supervision

The general textbook writers, however, such as De Smith (at London) and Wade (at Cambridge) placed much more confidence in the abilities of the ordinary courts to perform these tasks. Wade acknowledges the cleavage between the legal and administrative worlds, and that lawyers are rare in administration. But even as he admits that this sometimes creates problems, he also thinks it has the advantage of keeping the principles of administrative law in an 'undefiled form'.[160] Judges, he asserts, are not biased – their neutral task is to subject government to the rule of law.[161] If public law principles do not 'stand out as clearly as they should from the general mêlée', it is Wade and De Smith who do their best to extract and record them.[162] De Smith at least suggests, like Robson, that this work of enforcement will be sporadic, peripheral and exceptional. It was the beginning of a new judicially conceived public law. Of course, there are a number of reasons why common lawyers may have embraced these ideas – not least of which may have been because some of the judges shared Lord Hewart's fears about bureaucratic excess. Some common lawyers would use this idealized notion of the official in order to thwart and constrain bureaucratic power. They would not necessarily be as sensitive as Haldane LC to the bureaucratic setting in which such powers would be exercised.

Though no one would take up Robson's 'judicial mind' terminology, administrative lawyers would turn to the task of constructing the 'ideal administrator'. The normative construction of the values to which public decision-makers should aspire would be distinct from and contrasted

[159] *Ibid.*, p. 214 (Minutes of Evidence, days 13–14, para. 20). [160] *Ibid.*, p. 8

[161] *Ibid.*, pp. 6–7.

[162] Wade, *Administrative Law*, above n. 22; De Smith, *Judicial Review of Administrative Action*, above n. 1.

with private law norms. Wade supplies the classic late twentieth-century view (which appears in successive versions of his text):[163]

> The powers of public authorities are . . . essentially different from those of private persons. A man making his will may, subject to any rights of his dependents, dispose of his property just as he may wish. He may act out of malice or a spirit of revenge, but in law this does not affect his exercise of his power. In the same way, a private person has absolute power to allow whom he likes to use his land, release a debtor, or, where the law permits, to evict a tenant, regardless of his motives. This is an unfettered discretion. But a public authority may do none of these things unless it acts reasonably and in good faith and upon lawful and relevant grounds of public interest . . . [U]nfettered discretion is inappropriate to a public authority, which possesses powers solely in order that it may use them for the public good.

These characteristics bear a remarkable similarity to Robson's version of the judicial mind. Wade is also making large claims about the character of public authorities. These claims were not, however, completely borne out by the case law. As the law developed, these norms would not apply across all bodies or areas of state activity, as the organicist Robson had intended. Indeed, Robson initially meant the concept of a duty to act judicially to apply to a wide range of decisions and decision-makers including the domestic tribunals of voluntary associations.[164] He thought there was something distinctive about public law morality, whatever the activity in which the 'judicial mind' was engaged.

The common law did not proceed in these terms. While the 'duty to act judicially' remained part of the common law test to determine the proper reach of judicial review remedies for a number of decades, it was soon narrowed by Lord Hewart's interpretation[165] of Lord Atkin's

[163] H. W. R. Wade and C. F. Forsyth, *Administrative Law*, 9th edn (Oxford: Clarendon Press, 2004), p. 355 and, for judicial approval, see *R* v. *Tower Hamlets LBC, ex parte Chetnik Developments Ltd* [1988] 1 AC 858, 872 (HL) per Lord Bridge of Harwich. Of course even these seemingly core concepts took a while to establish themselves. In the famous case of *Smith* v. *East Elloe Rural District Council* [1956] AC 736 for example, an ouster clause would be held to prevent courts interfering even where the exercise of public power was fraudulent. Compare this to the discussion of the relevance of motive in public and tort law in the judgment of Rand J in *Roncarelli* v. *Duplessis* [1959] SCR 121 (Que).

[164] See the discussion in the previous chapter.

[165] *R* v. *Church Assembly Legislative Committee, ex parte Haynes-Smith* [1928] 1 KB 411. (See further D. J. Mullan, *Administrative Law*, 5th edn (Toronto: Emond Montgomery, 2003), p. 1095).

dictum in *R* v. *Electricity Commissioners, ex parte London Electricity Joint Committee Co* which confined the availability of judicial review to *statutory* bodies.[166] This had a number of consequences. It ruled out the judicial review of the exercise of the prerogative powers. It denied a general 'public law' basis for the review of the decisions of domestic tribunals of voluntary associations. It also ruled out the review of the government's contractual or commercial functions.

The test would begin to be broadened again to include bodies created by the prerogative in *R* v. *Criminal Injuries Board ex parte Lain.*[167] Domestic tribunals, however, would no longer be regarded as part of the mainstream of administrative law (despite the fact that, as we saw in Chapter 4, some judicial review doctrines originated in domestic tribunal cases), but rather as at the 'margins'.[168] Contractual and commercial functions would remain a separate category of activity. The state would be allowed a certain sphere of 'private life' into which public law norms would not enter. That was also a way of keeping contract law 'pure'. This is significant. How public authorities were normatively conceived was made to depend in large part on what legal instruments they were using to achieve their desired ends. The normative work of making the public law realm subject to distinct norms was not, by any means, complete.[169]

Public law without a state?

The revival and extension of the old prerogative writs as the means to construct a normative public realm had another important aspect and consequence. The writs were not available against the state or the Crown. Indeed, in form, the writ of *certiorari* was conceived as a way in which the Crown kept its courts within jurisdiction – the Crown is not the object of the writ but rather brings the supervisory action on behalf of the subject and general public. In other words, the common law *form* of action still did not recognize a politically directed bureaucratic machine but continued to be based on a diffuse eighteenth-century version of governance under which administrative functions are exercised by dispersed officials and bodies. It would be the intricacies of the legal

[166] [1924] 1 KB 171 (CA) at 205. [167] [1967] 2 QB 864.

[168] See, e.g., D. J. Mullan, 'Administrative Law at the Margins', in M. B. Taggart, *The Province of Administrative Law* (Oxford: Hart, 1997), pp. 134–59, resurrecting the earlier cases involving the review of domestic tribunals for breaches of natural justice.

[169] See Chapter 9.

doctrines, or more accurately opaque tropes to which the doctrines occasionally referred such as deference to 'policy', 'high politics' and 'political questions', on which the recognition of the actual 'power in the machine' would depend. Prerogative writs had formerly been more useful to the Crown than the subject: now that position was reversed, even if the form of the writ did not acknowledge this.

This perhaps made the control of the administration more readily acceptable to common law judges familiar with Diceyan constitutionalism. The Diceyan tradition founded the rule of law in the control of individual officials rather than of the Crown or the state itself (viewed as a collective whole). Remedies would not be available against the sovereign or state as a unified whole but against an official or body of officials.[170]

This did not, however, render the prerogative writs necessarily ineffective. Why they worked is that, at least in the first half of the twentieth century, many of the judicial review challenges concerned the *respective powers* of central and local authorities. Jennings notices, in 1938, for example, that the functions of the Ministry of Transport, Ministry of Health and Board of Education consisted almost entirely of the regulation of the affairs of local authorities. The disputes are about internal power distributions.[171] Many judicial review cases at the time involved disputes between the District Auditors and local authorities, or statutory boards and Ministers about their relative powers, including the power to spend money. Though 'rights' (such as milk for schools) might be indirectly engaged, on the whole disputes were not between individuals and public authorities let alone between individuals and a *unitary* state. The state does not usually appear in these cases as a monolith but rather as a complex series of jurisdictional orbits of power – with varying relationships to each other. The courts' role often involves explaining and delineating the track of those orbits.

170 J. Austin, *The Province of Jurisprudence Determined and the Uses of the Study of Jurisprudence* (London: Weidenfeld & Nicolson, 1954), p. 218: 'Considered collectively, or considered in its corporate character, a sovereign number is sovereign and independent: but, considered severally, the individuals and smaller aggregates composing that sovereign number are subject to the supreme body of which they are component parts. Consequently, though the body is inevitably independent of legal or political duty, any of the individuals or aggregates whereof the body is composed may be legally bound by laws of which the body is author.'

171 Jennings, *The Law and the Constitution*, above n. 88, preface to the 2nd edn, pp. xxviii.

Of the LSE administrative lawyers, it was Jennings who supplied the rationale for this approach: the focus should be on the extent of power. He sees this approach as representing a new twentieth-century conception of the rule of law.[172] It is a response directly to Dicey, who viewed the rule of law too narrowly, and to Austin, who thought that the state could not be the subject of coercive order and therefore could not be held to law. A legal remedy against the Crown or Minister is useful says Jennings 'not because it could be enforced but because it would be obeyed'.[173] Jennings particularly extols the virtues and effectiveness of the declaratory judgment in relation to public authorities.[174] The procedure he says – in terms echoed by Lord Bingham almost eighty years later in *Greenfield*[175] – is 'peculiarly appropriate to public law, because specific relief is generally unnecessary against a great public authority, which is extremely unlikely to break the law deliberately'. Jennings adds that claiming consequential relief against a great authority is often futile because 'many public authorities are under the control of some higher public authority'.[176] This reflects both the way the state is organized and the case law.

The focus on power would be framed around statutes. This emphasis would be attractive and effectual for two reasons. First, legislation (primary and delegated) had by now become the primary mechanism of government. Prerogative powers were becoming residual.[177] Second, everyone in this debate, whether of the Left or Right, agreed that Parliament was sovereign. Ideological differences would be manifested in discussions of which interpretative presumptions should be brought to the reading of such statutes. This political contestation would later be captured by Harlow's and Rawlings' 'green light' or 'red light' metaphor which characterizes judges as either helping government to fulfil its stated purposes or standing in its way.[178] Parliament, says Jennings, is no longer the permanent and personal sovereign contemplated by

[172] W. I. Jennings, 'Declaratory Judgments Against Public Authorities in England', *Yale Law Journal* 41 (1931–2), 407–24, 412.

[173] Jennings, *The Law and the Constitution*, above n. 88, p. 127.

[174] Jennings, 'Declaratory Judgments', above n. 172, 407.

[175] *R (Greenfield)* v. *Secretary of State for the Home Department* [2005] 1 WLR 14.

[176] Jennings, *The Law and the Constitution*, above n. 88, p. 415.

[177] *Attorney-General* v. *De Keysers Hotel* [1920] AC 75.

[178] The metaphor was coined by C. Harlow and R. Rawlings, *Law and Administration*, 2nd edn (London: Butterworths, 1997).

Bodin.[179] The state is taken seriously as a legal entity but not as a monolith. If there is a vision of the state here at all, it is located in Robson's 'common will' enforced by the 'judicial mind'.

Summary

After 1928 the scales drop from the eyes of British lawyers: they are able to 'see' the bureaucratic state for the first time. The conflict that ensues involves a reassertion of Diceyan common law constitutionalism. The countervailing attack treats rights as the product and not the basis of constitutional and social life: common law values must be subdued and transformed by the new administrative justice. The early self-styled administrative lawyers centred at the LSE seek to replace Diceyan understandings with a new more social version of rights, a newly conceived version of the rule of law, reimagined state responsibility and a focus on power.

While they have been characterized as sharing a general functionalist style and as founding a dissenting tradition, this does not do justice to the important differences between them about the nature of the state or to their contributions to mainstream administrative law. Robson's work, in particular, represents a system of thought that was closest to that of the civil service at the time and was also highly susceptible to adoption and adaption by common law forms of procedure. His model of the ideal administrator, endowed with judicial habits of mind (part of a collective consciousness of the ideal self) which were enforceable by the ordinary courts, is adapted (without the metaphysical overtones) by the common law. This becomes the basis of a distinct 'public law' morality – albeit a morality that does not apply to all public decision-making. (As we shall see, according to British practice, for example, decisions about the economy would tend to take place through a more corporatist framework wholly removed from law.)

Many, if not most, administrative lawyers considered that the proper functioning of the bureaucracy was more dependent on a positive culture of public service based on an optimistic view of the selflessness of public officials, than on the courts. They assumed that public law morality was distinct from private law morality and commonly identified that morality as underpinned by ideas about the positive liberty of

[179] Jennings, *Law and the Constitution*, above n. 88, p. 139.

individuals. Together such views support and justify state expansion into new areas of social life. Thus they did not need to construct the state as a *personne morale.* Here is a distinct public law without a state. The closest thing to the state here is the collective judicial mind of objective and unselfish reason.

The reaction to the judicial reception of this progressive age of politics was not yet over. What happened to the idea of state responsibility 'newly conceived'? Could an individual ever assert rights directly against the state under the common law? And how would these benign assumptions about the social nature of the individual and the belief in the collective good fare towards the end of the twentieth century when confronted by the newly prevailing theories that sparked privatization and deregulation? These are the questions I shall attempt to answer in the next two chapters.

7

No rights against the state: government wrong-doing and the common law

Kings who can neither do nor think wrong.[1]

No rights against the state

In the previous chapter we saw how the new administrative lawyers of the twentieth century reconceived the relationship between the individual and the collective in order to reflect the prevailing ideology of the progressive age. They also wanted to reshape ideas of state responsibility. In this chapter I will look more closely at the doctrinal and structural commitments of the common law and the approach it has taken to state or government wrong-doing and responsibility. Political theorists (and perhaps some lawyers) may be surprised to learn that, according to the common law, the state cannot commit a wrong and an individual cannot hold rights directly against the state. It is this area of legal liability and wrong-doing, in particular, in which lawyers have put most of their effort into conceiving – or not conceiving – of the state as a legal person. These doctrinal discussions may at first appear to be technical – even excessively so – but they also represent and reveal important political and philosophical commitments. Understanding the common law starting point, that individuals cannot claim rights directly against the state itself, is also important for understanding the various ways in which the state's relationship to its citizens is currently being reshaped by a reconfiguration of the public–private distinction, and by European Union law and the Human Rights Act 1998. The pressures brought to bear on ideas of the state by these phenomena will be discussed in Chapters 8 and 9.

[1] A paraphrase of Maitland paraphrasing Blackstone.

Put simply, tort law recognizes individual rights (such as to be free from trespass to the person and false imprisonment) but only as against individual officials rather than directly against the state *qua* state. The common law doctrine has been reluctant to allow direct liability or to acknowledge public institutional wrong-doing by government as a whole, even by way of vicarious liability. The Crown Proceedings Act 1947 (the current law) still does not recognize state direct liability in tort law. Rather, the Crown Proceedings Act reformed the law to allow vicarious liability as the modern basis on which the state provides compensation for the acts of individual officials. The state makes good the wrong of its officials without any legal attribution of wrong-doing or fault to the state itself. Real persons and their real powers remain the starting point for findings of tortious liability – as was the case before the advent of the bureaucratic state. There is no direct acknowledgement of institutional wrong-doing or of a *collective* will to do wrong.

Unlike tort law, judicial review is all about *public wrong-doing*. However, as we saw in the previous chapter, judicial review has been ambivalent about rights, and, like tort law, has not recognized the state *qua* state as wrong-doer. In this chapter I will explore further how this ambivalence has been reflected in the detail of judicial review doctrine: it tends to treat public law duties as imperfect duties owed to the public at large rather than to individual citizens; views remedies as discretionary; and does not allow individual monetary remedies for administrative wrong-doing.

Why then this common law reluctance to allow individuals successfully to claim that the state has done them wrong? Why the concomitant reluctance to recognize that the state has a legal as well as a moral obligation to do right by individuals? What does this tell us about how the common law has conceived of the state and what does that reveal of its underlying political commitments about the nature of statehood and citizenship?

The sovereignty problem

One explanation for the reluctance of the common law to hold the state *qua* state responsible for wrongs against individuals is rooted in the problem of sovereignty: how can a truly sovereign state be held to and limited by law? The common law, in advance of certain neighbouring legal systems, apparently avoided this problem. In this section I consider the sovereignty problem, the common law's purported solution and the problems that remained.

How the sovereign state, the source of all law, could be held responsible in law, was a problem that engaged legal theorists throughout Europe. The British produced their own solution – the problem could be avoided by denying the legal personality of the state for responsibility purposes. It should be the individual official and not the state which is held to law. Where does the British approach sit in relation to other European attempts to wrestle with this problem and what issues have attended the British 'solution'? Could British lawyers really get on without a personification of the state? We shall see that the rationales profferred for Crown immunity varied significantly over time. These rationales would have to be considered afresh in light of the privatization policies of the 1980s and the influence of international law – particularly human rights law.

There are a number of ways in which the problem of sovereignty has been expressed in relation to the state's legal liability. Common lawyers have tended to attribute such difficulties to the idea that the 'King can do no wrong' or, the more theoretically inclined, to Austin's sovereign unlimited by law to whom the people have a duty of obedience. Of course the problem was common to all legal systems and one that could be stated without reference to Kingship. Duguit, writing before World War I, summarizes the ways in which the French and Germans framed the issues.[2] For the French there were two ways of conceiving of the state. Either the state expresses the Rousseauian general will – a superior will, which represents the common consciousness of the people and which cannot be limited by law; or the state only exists to protect individuals whose rights are anterior and superior to the state itself. One view is a recipe for absolutism, the other for individualism and perhaps anarchism. Either the state has subjective right or the individual's rights are inviolable – there appears to be no principled way to chart a course between these poles. The Germans, influenced by Hegel, also personified the state's collective will. The state exists in and of itself and makes all of the varieties of social life and civic society possible. It is the source of all liberty. How could such a state be subjected to law? Eminent nineteenth-century German scholars such as Jhering and Jellinek subscribed to a theory of state self-limitation, but conceded that the state's subjective right could and should ultimately prevail. As Jellinek put it: 'International law exists for the states and not the states for international

[2] L. Duguit, 'The Law and the State', *Harvard Law Review* 31 (1917–18), 1–185, 8.

law'.[3] The same could be said for law generally. Schmitt, the Nazi jurist famous for the proposition that 'he is sovereign who determines the state of the exception',[4] sits within this well-established tradition of German thought.

Duguit objected to all of these views and proposed instead a state empowered for the performance of and therefore limited by 'duty' (which he called the duty of 'public service'). We shall return to Duguit's own view and its influence on British writers such as Laski shortly. The important point for now is that he suggested that the key to the juridical limitation of the state was to *deny* its personality and thus the idea of the state's subjective right (its sovereignty).

Unlike their continental counterparts, the British have never acquired the habit of discussing these matters quite so abstractly or directly. The common law is much less abstract and more result oriented and notions of the Crown so often dominate and obscure the discussion. It is striking, however, how much the 'British solution' instituted by the common law judges in cases such as *Entick* v. *Carrington*,[5] and made famous by Dicey, in fact had long achieved at least part of the solution for which Duguit advocated. British law denied the personality of the state for *responsibility* purposes. It is not the state but the ordinary official – from the highest officer (the Prime Minister) to the lowliest constable – who is limited by law. There is no state here conceived in *legal* terms, only real individual human beings. And while no British scholar or lawyer of the time would have described Dicey's 'ordinary law doctrine' in terms of the 'collective will' (with the possible exception of Maitland), the common law doctrine performs a neat trick – simultaneously acknowledging the existence and superiority of the collective will while allowing redress for the individual. This is how Duguit describes the British and US common law 'solution':[6]

> [The state] cannot be responsible by means of the law, which is the mere expression of its sovereignty. Nor can it be responsible on account of any executive, jurisdictional or administrative acts. If these acts are in conformity with law, the question of responsibility does not arise, either with respect to the state, or with respect to the public official. If they are

[3] Paraphrased by L. Duguit, 'The Concept of the Public Service', *Yale Law Journal* 32 (1922–3), 425–768, 429.

[4] C. Schmitt, *The Concept of the Political*, G. Schwab (tr.) (University of Chicago Press, 2007).

[5] (1765) 19 St Tr 1030.

[6] *Ibid.*, 434.

> opposed to law, it does not arise with respect to the state, since it has made the law and created the right, and has willed that this law be enforced. If it is not executed, or if it is violated, the official has substituted his own will for that of the sovereign state. There is therefore only one will that can be responsible – that of the public official.

Though this formulation may at first appear foreign to the common lawyer, the quotation quite neatly captures the *ultra vires* doctrine of the common law. If a public officer is acting within the power conferred on him, he will not be liable in the ordinary law. But if he acts outside of the power conferred (that is, unlawfully), he will be liable for tortious wrongs in the same way as an ordinary person would.[7] He is, then, no longer acting as an official but rather as an individual. He cannot, therefore, claim he is acting on behalf of the state (even if a superior commanded the wrong-doing). The will to do wrong will be treated as his *personal* will and not the *collective* will. As Bosanquet reminded us in the last chapter, only power, and not the 'collective will', is able to be delegated to the official. Much of the nineteenth-century tort law case law reflects this reasoning.

Dicey was justifiably proud of this as an instantiation of the rule of law. Even Maitland, who urged that the law should recognize the Crown's collective wrongdoing, acknowledges this:[8]

> We can hardly lay too much stress on the principle that though the King cannot be prosecuted or sued, his Ministers can be both prosecuted and sued, even for what they do by the King's express command. Law, especially modern statute law, has endowed [Ministers] with a great many powers, but the question whether they have overstepped those powers can be brought before a court of law, and the plea 'this is an official act, an act of state', will not serve them. A great deal of what we mean when we talk of English liberty lies in this.

The state only does right and therefore cannot be responsible for wrong-doing, but individual officials can still be held to law. This approach avoids some of the problems of sovereignty – for even Austin's scheme would allow the component parts of the sovereign to be limited by law. And while the avoidance of metaphysical constructions and the focus on real persons and real power is in sympathy with

[7] There were, of course, numerous exceptions that extended the immunity for particular officers.

[8] F. W. Maitland, *The Constitutional History of England: A Course of Lectures delivered by F. W. Maitland* (Cambridge University Press, 1908), p. 484.

Bentham's eighteenth-century views, the English solution was also in many ways ahead of its time. The state is not vested with superhuman powers, it merely acts through real individual ordinary humans. In the first half of the twentieth century, Kelsen, Duguit and Lauterpacht would feel the need to belabour the point that persons in authority are only individuals like the rest of us. One has the sense that they had French and German audiences particularly in mind.

But is it true that British legal thought has been able to get along without a person of the state completely for responsibility purposes? Are individual legal rights against individual officials (acting outside of their official roles) sufficient? Maitland in the nineteenth century and Skinner in the twenty-first have suggested that we cannot do without a person of the state.[9] In order to evaluate this we must once more return to the nature of the Crown and its legal personality and the gaps which have been left by the British 'solution' to the problem of state wrong-doing.

The Crown and the public

If *ultra vires* doctrine avoids any suggestion that unlawful acts are the product of the collective will, the benign qualities of the 'common will' have also been reinforced in other strands of common law thinking. The common law has often located the collective will in the Crown conceived as a moral exemplar. Long before democratic reform, the Crown has been frequently manifested in the common law as the representative of the collective public and of the common good. This is one important instantiation of the idea that the King can do no wrong. The question of whom and what was represented by the Crown has always depended very much on the legal context. So, for example, the Crown was quite capable of appearing as both a private and an abstract person when the Attorney-General brought an action to enjoin encroachments and obstructions on public ways.[10] The fiction that operated in such cases (to some good effect) was that an obstruction on a public highway was both against the private rights of the King as property holder, and also against the public rights of travel and passage. Both private and public rights could be protected by the Attorney General in the name of the Crown. In other words, by fiction, the common law made the Crown the ultimate protector of public rights and public ways.

[9] See Chapter one. [10] *Attorney General* v. *Richards* 2 Anstr 603 (Eng) 1795.

The Crown's role as place-holder for the public is also evident in much of the criminal law. In relation to particular offences, the Crown displaces the victim as the object of harm. The Crown, as representative of the public, is also considered to have been harmed, for example, when an official acts fraudulently or in abuse of office – regardless of whether that official was appointed by the Crown.[11] Given that the Crown represents the public as victim in this context, it is difficult to conceive of the Crown as one who could commit a crime. Judicial review also understands the Crown in this way. Wade suggests that the Crown 'lends its prerogative' to the citizen to enable him to bring a judicial review action against a named body or official. Formally (at least in England) the Queen (*Regina*) is always named as part of the action.

Understood in these ways, the concept that the 'King can do no wrong' is not a simple licence for executive fiat. The Crown instead is conceived as a moral exemplar ensuring that right be done by its subjects. In these cases, the Crown represents the 'public' and even something close to the 'law' or the collective will.

The problem for common lawyers, then, was the same as that for the French and German jurists. How could this abstract representation of the public and the law be simultaneously held to law? How could this legal paragon 'will' to do wrong? The idea that the Crown represents the law and the public seems to be incompatible with the idea that the Crown could also represent the state apparatus for responsibility purposes. It is not strictly the case that the state has not been personified by the common law. The Crown personifies 'the state' here in the sense of the 'commonwealth' or 'common weal' rather than the government apparatus. What has not been 'personified' is a legal person who can be held limited by law.

This apparently benign idea of the Crown as personification and representative of 'the public' also had more inconvenient and even malign applications – particularly in the context of Empire. It was the sovereign as a whole that was the representative of the public – and in practice that often meant the *UK* government's institutions and interests rather than the interests of the colonies or the different peoples of the Empire. This is the example Maitland had foremost in his mind when he argued for the moral and legal personality of the state or commonwealth. The different peoples of the Empire should enjoy distinct personalities.

[11] *R* v. *Bembridge*. See, also, *Henly* v. *Mayor of Lyme* (1828) 5 Bing 92; 130 ER 995, 107–9.

The different 'publics' of the British Empire

British colonial law created particular obstacles which made it difficult to identify a state to sue or to hold responsible. The doctrine that the Crown is one and indivisible had the effect that the distinct 'publics' of the self-governing colonies could not be given separate legal recognition. Maitland and Laski considered that legal recognition of the group was necessary in order to protect the individual. This example highlights the differences between Maitland's and Gierke's practical political motivations (which we encountered in Chapter 3). Gierke was worried about the continuing identity of the different parts of a Germany that had not yet been unified. Maitland was concerned that the law should recognize the separate collective identities and interests of different parts of the British Empire – albeit unified under a single Crown.

A number of anomalous legal controversies had arisen toward the end of the nineteenth century relating to the legal status of the self-governing colonies.[12] The dilemma was caused by a gap between the 'real' and the situation as it was recognized as a matter of law. The 'real' situation in this case was signified by the, by now well-established, principle of responsible government – the idea that different Ministers advised the monarch in the different self-governing colonies, administered their own funds, incurred their own debts and entered into their own contracts. The legal position, however, was that 'the King or Crown represents not merely the Empire as a whole but each of its parts' as the sole legal representative.[13] More than that, it was difficult to locate someone to sue even when a contract had been made in the monarch's name on behalf of a colony. One case, for example, involved an unsuccessful attempt to sue the Governor or government of New Zealand for non-performance of a contract for assisted passage and settlement of immigrants.[14] The contract was made by Her Majesty the Queen for and on behalf of the Colony of New Zealand. In the English Court of Appeal, James LJ said:[15]

> there is no body politic residing in England, or having a place of business in England called the Governor or government of New Zealand...

[12] E.g., *Attorney General* v. *The Collector of Customs* 20 W N 52 (NSW); *Sloman v New Zealand* (1875–6) LR 1 CPD 563; *In re Holmes* (1861) 2 J & H 527; 70 ER 1167.

[13] J. Salmond, *Jurisprudence*, 7th edn (London: Stevens and Son, 1924), pp. 353–4.

[14] *Sloman* v. *New Zealand* (1875–6) LR 1 CPD 563. See G. McLay, 'The Problem With Suing Sovereigns', *Victoria University of Wellington Law Review* 41 (2010), 403–25, in which he investigates the archival and other contextual material surrounding the *Sloman* case.

[15] Ibid, 555–6.

> There is an individual who, for the time being, is the Governor of New Zealand; there are certain persons carrying on the Government; there are probably a Secretary, a Treasurer, an Attorney-General and others; and there are members of the representative Assembly and Council who constitute the Legislature; but to call them a corporation seems to be an abuse of language. We must take notice that there is no such corporation as the Governor or Government of New Zealand.

Neither could the Governor be treated as a corporation sole for this purpose. There was no person to sue.

Australian federalism raised different problems given that each of the states enjoyed separate representative and responsible government and separate governors, and yet all the properties and liabilities of each of the states were vested in the King or Queen. There was no legal person who could represent these distinct interests in disputes between states and between states and the federal government.[16] Even those who subscribed to the fiction theory of corporations, such as Salmond, came to consider the legal position of the self-governing colonies as unprincipled and unsatisfactory.[17]

In the 1920s there were flirtations with the idea of imperial federation and associated charters of rights.[18] As it transpired, however, the struggle for separate identity for parts of the Empire would not be resolved so much by *legal* ideas of federation or corporation, but rather gradually through mainly political means in the first half of the twentieth century as the settler colonies acquired Dominion status, equality[19] and more formal independence through the adoption of the Statute of Westminster 1931.[20] The monarch would come to represent separate legal entities in right of the different Dominion territories such as the Queen in right of Canada, New Zealand and Australia.[21] Notably there is

[16] *Williams* v. *Howarth* [1905] AC 551, 553; *Attorney General* v. *The Collector of Customs* 20 W N 52 (NSW). See further P. Cobbett, '"The Crown" as Representing "The State"', *Commonwealth Law Review* 1 (1903–4), 23–30; W. Harrison Moore, 'The Crown as Corporation', *Law Quarterly Review* 23(1)(1907), 12–27.

[17] J. Salmond, *Jurisprudence*, (London: Sweet & Maxwell, 1902), pp. 364–5.

[18] For the contributions of H. G. Wells and R. W. G. MacKay, see A. W. B. Simpson, *Human Rights and the End of Empire: Britain and the Genesis of the European Convention* (Oxford University Press, 2004), pp. 161–9.

[19] 1926 Imperial Conference, Balfour Declaration.

[20] L. Zines, 'Commentary' in H. V. Evatt (ed.), *The Royal Prerogative* (North Ryde, New South Wales: Law Book Co, 1987), Chapter 2 and 3.

[21] The practice began to change earlier and in an incremental fashion. See, e.g., *Municipal Council of Sydney* v. *The Commonwealth* 1 Commonwealth LR, 231 per Griffith CJ cited

a 'plural' version of the corporation sole at work here. It is the sovereignty of the reigning monarch that becomes the constitutional link between the various parts of the Commonwealth.[22]

Once again Maitland would be an important figure in identifying the problem and attempting to provide a legal solution. Once again his diagnosis would be acute but his proposed solution would not be adopted. The legal and the political would not be brought together here as Maitland had hoped by way of the idea of the Crown as corporation. Powers over the self-governing Dominions were still technically retained by the UK Parliament but by convention were no longer exercised. Instead the widespread embrace of a distinction between the legal position and the position according to constitutional convention (propagated in the nineteenth-century work of Freeman, Bagehot and Dicey[23]) would be used both to *explain* and (consciously or unconsciously) sometimes to *maintain* the disjunction between the legal and the 'real' as far as constitutional law was concerned. Political practice would ultimately determine the matter. Only politics would be capable of reflecting 'the reality' of the situation. This was a way of ensuring that disputes would have to be resolved as a matter of politics rather than of law.

These are not merely issues of historical interest. The position in relation to non-self-governing dependant colonies remains controversial. For example, the UK imperial power had it both ways in *R (Bancoult)* v. *Secretary of State.*[24] The case involved the claims by the inhabitants of the British Indian Ocean Territory (Chagos islanders) to a right of abode in the islands. They had been compulsorily removed by colonial orders in the interests of British foreign policy (the islands were made available to the United States for the purpose of maintaining a military presence there). The Judicial Committee considered the British

in J. Salmond, *Jurisprudence*, 2nd edn (London: Stevens and Haynes, 1907), p. 301. In 1914 Asquith entered the war against Germany on behalf of the Dominions. However, Canada, Australia, New Zealand and South Africa were separate signatories to the Treaty of Versailles and enjoyed separate representation at the League of Nations.

[22] In relation to the relationship between the UK and Scotland post-devolution, the issue has been resolved in the Scotland Act 1998 thus: the Crown in right of the Scottish administration is a separate entity from the Crown in right of the UK for particular purposes. See section 99 Scotland Act 1998.

[23] E. Freeman, *The Growth of the English Constitution From the Earliest Times* (Leipzig: Tauchnitz, 1872); W. Bagehot, *The English Constitution*, 2nd edn (London: Chapman & Hall, 1873); A. V. Dicey, *Introduction to the Study of the Law of the Constitution* (London: Macmillan, 1886).

[24] [2008] UKHL 61.

Indian Ocean Territory to be a distinct legal entity for the purposes of the non-application of both the European Convention on Human Rights and the Human Rights Act 1998.[25] But the majority held that Her Majesty (acting on the advice of UK Ministers) was able to legislate for a non-self-governing territory in the interests of her *undivided* realm, effectively preferring the interests of the United Kingdom over those of the inhabitants of the dependant colony.[26]

A related set of controversies has arisen in New Zealand and Canada, when indigenous peoples have raised claims against the Crown with whom they entered treaties at the point of colonization. It is unclear whether they are asserting rights against the Crown in right of the UK (with whom they originally treated) or against the post-colonial version of the Crown in right of New Zealand or Canada.[27] In these contexts, determining which 'public' the Crown represents is at the heart of the legal issues – and sometimes has consequences for whether legal rights claims can even be raised, let alone have a chance of success.

British colonial law's treatment of the Crown's will as unified and indivisible across the whole Empire frustrated rights claims and did not recognize the legal personification of particular peoples and publics. A common will located in the colonial Crown effectively obliterated the distinct political wills of the different publics that made up the Empire. That has not, however, been the only problem for asserting rights against the state which has been framed by reference to conceptions of the Crown.

A common will to do wrong?

The most prominent question in the domestic common law has not been 'which is the relevant public represented by the Crown', but rather how to locate a legal person to sue and what is meant by the idea that the

[25] See Lord Hoffmann at paras. 64–5. On the issues of the application of the European Convention to the colonies belonging to the European member states and the impact of the Convention on decolonization, see A. W. B. Simpson's extensive treatment in *Human Rights and the End of Empire*, above n. 18.

[26] [2008] UKHL 61, 47–9 per Lord Hoffmann with whom Lords Rodger and Carswell agreed (Lords Bingham and Mance dissenting). *Cf. R (Quark Fishing)* v. *Secretary of State* [2005] UKHL 51, paras. 9 and 10, in which Lord Bingham suggests that the Crown is no longer one and indivisible and that in the given case the Secretary of State was acting on behalf of the Crown in right of government of SGSSI. See, for commentary, A. Twomey, 'Responsible Government and the Divisibility of the Crown', *Public Law* (2008), 742–67.

[27] See, e.g., *R* v. *Secretary of State for Foreign and Commonwealth Affairs* [1982] QB 892.

'King can do no wrong'. The idea that the King could do no wrong has been around for centuries. But the doctrine took on a new complexion and meaning with the advent of a centralized and expanding bureaucracy. Could the new 'state machine' be legally liable? Could there be a common will to do wrong originating in collective decision-making?

As I discussed in Chapter 5, the position of the Crown needs to be understood in the general context of the treatment of the wider public sphere. The ability of the new public commissioners, boards and trustees of the expanding nineteenth-century public sphere to sue or be sued as collective bodies depended on statutes giving them corporate status or representative liability.[28] Statutory incorporation was a relatively straightforward device for locating a body to sue, but it was not able to be readily adapted for application to the Crown itself. This was because of the various common law complications surrounding the nature of the Crown including the fact that the Crown was already commonly regarded as a corporation sole.[29] Another approach was to identity a person who could sue and be sued on behalf of a government entity. Representative liability, as it is known, was adopted in the Crown Suits (Scotland) Act 1857 (which identified Her Majesty's Advocate as the representative who could sue or be sued on behalf of Her Majesty and in respect of specific named government departments). The UK Petition of Rights Act 1860 also set out procedures by which a citizen could bring an action in the name of the Attorney General, and identified the funds (Her Majesty's Household and the Exchequer) against which to enforce judgment depending on whether the suit was against the Queen in her public or private capacity.

These statutes were, however, procedural. They did not affect the substantive law about which rights could be claimed against the state. As we saw in Chapter 5, in the early nineteenth century *all* public officials (regardless of whether they were servants of the Crown) enjoyed substantive immunity from the wrongs committed by their agents and servants (vicarious liability), except for actions under their personal direction and control. This had everything to do with Victorian notions of individual responsibility and was not a consequence of any special status attaching to the Crown. It also reflected the older ideas of

[28] Statutes typically allowed suit in the name of the Secretary who could sue and be sued but who was immunized against personal liability on contracts and the like, and against whom there was no abatement.

[29] I am grateful to Stuart Anderson for these points.

authority that I investigated in Chapter 2. It was not only the Crown and its servants but a range of public actors who could be regarded as exercising the common will. However, by mid-century, the common law judges took a formalistic turn and restricted this immunity to the Crown: the rationale for the immunity changed from the protection of individuals called to public office, to the formalistic application of the idea that the King or Crown could do no wrong. Other public bodies with corporate status began to attract vicarious liability for the actions of their servants irrespective of whether those actions were within their direction and control. The effect was that the Crown's relationship to the law became increasingly distinct from that of other public bodies as the century wore on. One might be tempted to attribute the cause to an exaggerated nineteenth-century version of sovereignty, though that was not an explanation articulated at the time. The following cases illustrate this formalistic turn.

The Crown becomes increasingly distinct

The King, like any other feudal lord, could not be sued in his own courts, unless he voluntarily consented to such litigation. A practice developed by which the King routinely consented to such petitions which gradually became formalized in the Petition of Right procedures. The Crown would still enjoy a number of special procedural privileges in relation to discovery, *laches* and costs, but whether an action could be brought within these special procedures in the first place depended on the cause of action and whether it involved a finding of a 'legal wrong' from which the King enjoyed a substantive immunity. The first case we consider concerned the extent of the substantive immunity. This case is commonly read as authority for the proposition that the Crown is not liable for the actions of its servants. A closer contextual reading suggests that the result had more to do with the absence of the preconditions for responsibility – political, financial and administrative control. As I discussed in Chapter 2, power, duty and responsibility was reposed in the concept of office in the early nineteenth century. The state machine was still under construction.

The case of *Viscount Canterbury* v. *AG*[30] (decided in 1842 and relating to events in 1834) first raised the issue of whether a petition of right could be maintained for the vicarious liability of the Crown in

[30] [1843] 1 PH 305; 41 ER 648.

negligence. In the peculiar way in which legal authority is asserted and law time runs, the case would later be used to stand as authority for the proposition that the Crown is not vicariously liable for the actions of its servants for negligence – a proposition firmly linked in those later discussions with the proposition that the King can do no wrong. In fact, despite the Attorney General's attempts to press this argument on the Court, the Court's reasoning did not rely on the doctrine that 'the King can do no wrong' at all, but rather rested on notions of responsibility and control that were prominent in Victorian morality and which were affected by the way that administration was organized at the time the case was heard. The Crown's 'will' was simply not engaged.

The petition alleged that servants of the Commissioners of Woods, Forests and Buildings had negligently caused a fire that damaged or destroyed the Speaker's possessions in his lodgings in the Palace of Westminster (Parliament buildings). It asked that the Crown accept vicarious liability for the damage. Lyndhurst LC found that there were a number of impediments to such an action in these circumstances, but the idea that the King can do no wrong was not one of them.[31]

Viscount Canterbury illustrates the way in which the still emerging state apparatus engaged with legal issues of responsibility. The case did not, in fact, involve the Crown's servants per se but rather the servants of the Commissioners of Woods, Forests and Buildings. While the Commissioners themselves were appointed by order in council, (nominally by the Crown) and made up a small office which was nominally part of the Board of Trade, there was no *direct* administrative or financial link between the Commissioners' servants and the Crown, Ministers or Parliament at the time. Commissioners were paid out of the revenues of the lands which were vested in them. The Commissioners' servants were appointed and supervised by the Commissioners and paid out of those same funds rather than out of appropriations voted by Parliament. At the time of the alleged negligence, Commissioners were not required to report to Parliament, individual Commissioners were prohibited by law from sitting in the Commons and there appeared to be no regular mechanism by which to pay into the Exchequer the surplus revenues they received. While the Court did not go into all of these ways in which the Crown, Ministers and Parliament had no direct control over these

[31] Some of these issues are discussed in Chapter 6.

servants, the general absence of control weighed heavily on its reasoning. Lord Lyndhurst LC said:[32]

> Now, assuming that the fire had been caused by the personal negligence of the commissioners, would the Crown, in such case, have been liable to make good the loss? They are, indeed, styled servants of the Crown; but they are, in truth, public officers appointed to perform certain duties assigned to them by the Legislature, and for any negligence in the discharge of such duty, and any injury that may be thereby sustained they alone are, I conceive, liable. Is it supposed that the Crown is responsible for the conduct of all persons holding public offices and appointments, and bound to make good any loss or injury which may be occasioned by their negligence or delinquency? At least some authority should be cited in support of such a doctrine. But then, it is said, these officers are appointed by the Crown, and are removable at the pleasure of the Crown. That circumstance alone will not, I conceive, create any such liability. The Keeper of the Great Seal and other persons holding high situations in the State have authority to appoint to many offices, and also to remove the persons so appointed at their pleasure. But they are not, on that account, subject to make compensation for injury occasioned by the neglect or misconduct of the persons so appointed. The mere selection of the officers does not create a liability. But if the Crown would not be responsible for the act done, had it been done by the superiors, it follows that it cannot be held liable for the negligence of their subordinate agents whom they appoint and remove, and with the selection or control of whom the Crown has no concern.

At the time it would have been astonishing even to contemplate that the Queen or Crown should be held responsible for her public officers merely on the basis that she nominally appointed them. As the Lord Chancellor hints in the above quotation, public officers were, moreover, subject to their own liability regime. According to the common law at the time, the Commissioners, having the legal status of public officers, were not *themselves* vicariously liable for the acts of their servants except for matters *directly* within their direction and control.[33] An important indicator of 'public office' was that the superior should not be vicariously liable for the acts of his servants. The Victorian emphasis on

[32] [1843] 1 PH 305, 323–324; 41 ER 648, 655.

[33] *Whitfield* v. *Lord Le Despencer* [1778] Cowp. 754, 766: 'Whoever holds an office which renders him responsible for any act done in it, ought to have the entire management and control of it. If responsible for the acts of his servants he alone ought to have the privilege of appointing them, upon his own terms and at his own discretion, and with absolute power over them in every respect, as he has over the servants of his own house.'

personal and individual responsibility was combined with a concern that good people should not be deterred from public office by the risk of liability. Practice required subordinates to pay a surety in the event of administrative failures for which they were personally responsible. So if Commissioners, being public officers, were not liable for matters which were not within their direction and control how could 'the Crown', at one step removed, be liable? Equally, if the Commissioners enjoyed their own corporate fund from which to satisfy judgment, why should the Crown and not the Commissioners be liable?[34] The Court could not find a 'collective will' to do wrong here at all.

Control mechanisms did significantly evolve over the next decade. By 1844 the Commissioners would themselves be incorporated and be required to report annually to Parliament. As their functions and powers significantly increased, they would be required to obtain prior Parliamentary approval for certain purposes.[35] By 1851 the salaries of their subordinates would be paid out of appropriation and the Commissioner for the Treasury would assign distinct duties to each Commissioner. The financial reporting of the Commissioners would be tightened. By 1857 the Commissioners of Her Majesty's Woods would be listed as a public department for the purposes of the Crown Suits (Scotland) Act 1857.[36] In other words, a corporate Crown capable of exercising control and therefore also responsibility was beginning to emerge. It was not yet in place at the time *Viscount Canterbury* was decided. It was these issues of control (and hence responsibility) that weighed on the Court, rather than issues of immunity.[37] There was no controlling mind.

In the way that the common law sometimes works, however, the decision in *Viscount Canterbury* became decontextualized from its facts and institutional setting. It became authority for the principle that the

[34] Note that often their 'corporate funds' were limited by statutes for particular projects. See *R* v. *Commissioners of Her Majesty's Woods (ex parte Budge)* 117 ER 646 (1850). See S. Anderson 'Public Law', in W. Cornish, S. Anderson, R. Cocks and M. Lobban (eds.), *The Oxford History of the Laws of England* vol. XI 1820–1914: English Legal System (Oxford University Press, 2010), pp. 299–52, on the question of why UK law did not develop a system of departmental liability.

[35] They went from building new stables at Windsor to performing important central scrutinizing functions.

[36] In fact the Commissioners would retain elements of independence, see Anderson, 'Public Law', above n. 34, p. 343, n. 186.

[37] Compare for example *Winterbottom* v. *Wright* 152 ER 402, which was decided in the same year, where the judges demonstrated an unwillingness to find responsibility on the basis of privity of contract. I am grateful to Michael Moreland for this reference.

Crown is not vicariously liable for the actions of its servants – a scenario that the Court was never actually asked to consider. Despite significant developments in central government control, the reluctance to recognize collective as opposed to individual control and responsibility continued. The maxim that the King can do no wrong would now be successfully invoked – even in cases where there *was* central control.

In the leading case of *Tobin* v. *Queen*,[38] the Commander of a Queen's ship employed in the suppression of the slave trade on the coast of Africa mistakenly seized and destroyed a schooner. By this time, private law would have held the master responsible for the acts of his servant acting in the course of his employment. Should it apply here? *Viscount Canterbury* offered an easy answer. The servant was not appointed by the Queen personally but under her authority by one of her servants. He was purporting to act in performance of a duty imposed by Parliament, rather than in obedience to the Queen's command or will. In such cases the employer was not responsible for her agent. Moreover, as the Court noted, the Slave Trade Act 1824[39] made the captor personally liable for restitution in these circumstances (presumably to be made good out of prize and bounty monies). There could be no proper analogy with the ordinary master–servant relationship.

Given this easy way of disposing of the matter, what is puzzling about *Tobin* is that the decision went much further than was needed. Instead of resting on these responsibility principles, the Court invoked 'the King can do no wrong' to the effect that the King cannot even *command* a wrong (a point which was never at issue in the case):[40]

> The maxim that the King can do no wrong is true in the sense that he is not liable to be sued civilly or criminally for a supposed wrong. That which the sovereign does personally, the law presumes will not be wrong: that which the sovereign does by command to his servants, cannot be a wrong in the sovereign, because, if the command is unlawful, it is in law no command, and the servant is responsible for the unlawful act, the same as if there had been no command.

Clearly the reasoning was not for this case but for a future case. If the logic of the plaintiff had been accepted then the Crown (and not the captain) could be held responsible for the negligence of errant seaman as well. The fact that the state's foreign-affairs interests and strategic naval

[38] (1864) 16 *Common Bench Reports (New Series)* 310; 143 ER 1148.

[39] 5 Geo IV c 113, Section 35.

[40] (1864) 16 *Common Bench Reports (New Series)* 310, 353–4; 143 ER 1148, 1166.

dominance were at stake was likely a significant factor, even if the case was not argued in those terms. Neither was the 'state interest' or 'act of state' directly invoked. If 'sovereign right' was at play here, it was disguised.

Feather v. *R*, decided around the same time,[41] is even more striking for the Court's novel and formalistic invocation of the idea that the 'King can do no wrong' and was the first of the line of cases in which responsibility and control appeared not to be in any doubt. The case involved the use of a patent by the Admiralty without any payment to the patentee. Until that time there had been an established practice of remunerating patentees for inventions used by government departments, and the terms of the actual grants of patents sometimes explicitly excluded the Crown (appearing to indicate that in the absence of such a term the Crown was otherwise bound by them). The case signals an important turn in the practice of the Crown. The Attorney General urged as a matter of 'public convenience', that *whatever the terms of grant of the patent rights*, Crown immunity relieved the Crown of any obligation to pay the patentee. The Court agreed:[42]

> For the maxim that the King can do no wrong applies to personal as well as to political wrongs; and not only to wrongs done personally by the Sovereign, if such a thing can be supposed to be possible, but to injuries done by a subject by the authority of the Sovereign.

Feather v. *R* is significant. Crown immunity now trumps responsibility principles (which had not been sufficiently engaged in the earlier cases). It goes some way to recognizing the corporate existence of the administration (in this case the Admiralty) by extending Crown immunity to certain officials in their official capacities. What it refuses to recognize, however, is a corporate will to do wrong. Both *Tobin* and *Feather* explicitly leave open the possibility that officials could be sued personally for the wrong-doing. In that way (says the Court in *Feather*), the dignity of the Crown can be upheld alongside the rights and liberties of British subjects.

Also around the same time, the court in *Mersey Docks* made it impossible to hold one crown servant vicariously liable for the acts of a subordinate.[43] The senior Crown servant was to be treated in law

[41] *R* v. *Feather* 122 ER 1191 (1865). [42] *Ibid.* at 1206.

[43] *Mersey Docks and Harbour Board* v. *Gibbs and Penhallow* (1865–6) 11 HLC 686.

as merely a manager and not an employer. Both manager and subordinate are Her Majesty's servants.

Together the *Tobin, Feather* and *Mersey Docks* cases deny the existence of an administrative hierarchy for responsibility purposes. There cannot be a collective will to do wrong. And yet what these cases are beginning to reveal is a state in which officials operate under the control and direction of a central hierarchy. Is it fair for liability to fall on the official personally in such circumstances? Is not the effect of these cases to allow the sovereign an element of subjective right?

The idea that 'the King can do no wrong' gained new life in English case law in the 1860s. We can only speculate about the reasons for this turn. Two of the most significant cases involved the Admiralty and foreign policy (functions traditionally associated with the prerogatives of the Crown). The franchise was expanding. There was undoubtedly an apprehension that an increasing number of petitions would be brought under the new Petitions of Right Act 1860.[44]

The decisions were to the effect that where 'legal wrongs' were concerned (breach of patent rights and tortious wrongs), Petition of Right procedures were not available. For claims of legal wrong-doing there was effectively no state to sue. A subject could not claim rights against the state, or even against a departmental manager, but only against another subject *qua* subject – the servant who had personally done wrong. The state is submerged – rights can only be enforced as between citizens, or (as discussed in Chapter 5) as against local government and other statutory offices. There is no centralized state to sue, only 'fellow citizens in uniform'.[45]

That is not the complete story, however. The 'state' was differently manifest in different areas of law.[46] As discussed in Chapter 3, H. L. A. Hart reminds us that how a legal person is conceived depends on the rights and liabilities that attach to it. A Petition of Right *could* be entertained in relation to claims in restitution and contract.[47] Such claims, according to the Court in *R* v. *Feather*, did not involve legal wrong-doing *properly understood.* In such cases there *was* a state to be held liable (even if satisfaction of a successful claim would be left to Parliament). Moreover,

[44] The Court in *Tobin* v. *R* treats *Irwin* v. *Sir George Grey* as a troubling case at 368.

[45] G. Samuel, 'Public and Private Law: A Private Lawyer's Response', *Modern Law Review* 146 (1983), 558–83.

[46] See the discussion of H. L. A. Hart in Chapter 3.

[47] *R* v. *Feather* 122 ER 1191 (1865), 294.

in such cases the Crown's servant or agent could *not* be sued – there could be no personal liability for officers entering contracts on behalf of the public.[48] The law was prepared to construct a unified 'collective will' for property and contractual purposes. Dicey's ordinary law story did not apply to *all* the legal forms used by government. It was only wrongdoing which was singled out for special treatment.

This is an important point and it has been the subject of a great deal of confusion. As we shall see in more detail in Chapter 8, the common law has been remarkably adroit at constructing a unified will which *empowers* government to act. So, for example, decisions made by civil servants could be treated as the decisions of Ministers. Contracts made by Ministers could be treated as contracts made by the Crown.[49] Civil servants would be empowered by common law doctrines to become the *means by which the Crown acts.* The Crown has been imagined as a 'corporation of the many' for these purposes. Despite this, the common law has been consistently reluctant to conceive of a corporate will to do wrong. While it would be important for politicians and administrators to design a state apparatus that unified political will for *control* purposes, common lawyers would be much more reluctant to conceive of a 'unified will' to do wrong or to act unlawfully. How could the personification of the collective will will wrongdoing?

Maitland supplies a theory too late

It would have been possible to construct the corporate Crown's will or intent to do a legal wrong in these cases. But there was no theoretical framework in English law from which to work through these questions. What was missing at the time *Viscount Canterbury* was decided, and for much of the nineteenth century, was any modern *theory* of the corporation, corporate will and action or corporate personality generally. Dicey laments that Bentham and his followers never addressed the key tensions between corporate power (whether public or private) and personal responsibility.[50] He suggests that '[c]ollectivism, in so far as it may be

48 *Macbeath* v. *Haldimand* (1786) 1 TR 172; *Dunn* v. *MacDonald* [1897] 1 QB 555; *Thomas* v. *The Queen* LR 10 QB 43.

49 *Town Investments* v. *Department of Environment* [1978] 1 AC 359.

50 Dicey himself recognizes this in *Lectures on the Relationship Between Law and Opinion in England in the Nineteenth Century*, 2nd edn (London: Macmillan, 1914), p. 158. It may be that this points to deeper ambiguities in Bentham's thought as a whole – whether it is primarily a system of public morality as opposed to a system of private morality and how

considered a doctrine, has never, in England at least, been formulated by any thinker with anything like the commanding ability or authority of Bentham'.[51] Neither would it be considered deliberately or consciously in relation to law.[52] Bentham's emphasis on real people and real power would no longer always work as power itself began to be exercised collectively. It would be Maitland who, through his translation of the work of Gierke, would introduce such a theory into English legal thought, but not until the very end of the nineteenth century. Maitland's suggestion that the Crown was capable of representing the state as a legal person would come too late to influence these legal developments.

As we know from previous chapters, Maitland's project was to align the law with the 'real'. For the state and other corporations to have the capacity corporately to will wrong-doing, their 'real personality' must be recognized. An artificial person, created by law, by contrast, has no will of its own and hence no will to act wrongly.[53] Given that law can only be used for the furtherance of the good, those who subscribed to the artificial person theory argued that the will imputed by law to a corporation could only effect lawful ends.[54] Consequently an artificial person could not be charged with a crime or be held responsible for a delict. Such arguments assumed even greater force when applied to the Crown. Maitland responded to such arguments with the claim that recognizing the state's 'real will' could free us from Blackstonian 'talk' of Kings who can neither 'do' nor 'think' wrong. He observed that many people will

the two aspects relate to each other. From the late 1790s Bentham had begun to be interested in the benefits of collective *private* as opposed to collective public enterprise. Although at times he advocated for departments conceived along functional lines, on the whole he disliked public bureaucracy: he preferred private contractors and used the East India Company as a joint stock model for his 'National Charity Company'. All the while he also emphasized personal responsibility (as did almost all Victorian moralists).

51 Dicey, *Law and Opinion*, above n. 50, p. 67.

52 This view is adopted by O. MacDonagh, *Early Victorian Government 1830–1870* (London: Wiedenfeld and Nicolson, 1977), p. 11.

53 Fiction theorists, by contrast, would assume that the capacity of the corporation was the same as an individual unless the contrary clearly appears. See further G. Sawer, 'Government as Personalized Legal Entity', in L. C. Webb (ed.), *Legal Personality and Political Pluralism* (Melbourne University Press, 1958), p. 160.

54 See, e.g., *Ashbury Ry Carriage and Iron Co* v. *Riche* (1875) L & H 653, 693 describing a railway company as 'a mere abstraction of law. All that it does, all the law imputes to it as its act, must be that which can be legally done within the powers vested in it by law' quoted by M. Loughlin, 'Why the History of Administrative Law is Not Written', in D. Dyzenhaus, M. Hunt and G. Huscroft (eds.), *A Simple Common Lawyer: Essays in Honour of Michael Taggart* (Oxford: Hart, 2009), pp. 151–77, 171.

refuse to admit that a corporation or state is a thoroughly real person with a real will and able to alter its purposes until they are convinced that corporations and states can 'sin':[55] 'It is a wholesome sight to see "the Crown" sued and answering for its torts'.[56] This aspect of Maitland's thought is significant. He may have accepted the idea of collective will but he did not place it above the law.

It is worth noting here that conceiving of the Crown as a corporation aggregate rather than a corporation sole could not, of itself, resolve the question of whether the Crown or state could commit a delictual wrong, as some have been too quick to suggest. Merely recognising the Crown as a corporation aggregate does not *necessarily* lead to corporate liability.[57] For Maitland, the correct *metaphysical* theory also has to be applied. The law must recognize that such a corporation is capable of exercising a will that is distinct from but related to the will of its individual members – including a malign will.

These controversial theories about the basis of the corporation would come too late to provide any assistance to the common law judges, who, in the middle of the nineteenth century, were struggling to work out whether the Crown as either a corporation sole or aggregate should be held vicariously or even directly liable. But they did potentially offer a framework through which to reconsider that approach in the twentieth century. As we shall see, however, the resistance to finding a will to do wrong persisted.

Almost all the early twentieth-century constitutional law writers, including members of the Donoughmore Committee,[58] took up the cause for the Crown to be made liable in some way. Justifications for reform varied widely. Some saw the extension of the ordinary law of tort to the Crown as a means to forestall the development of a distinct administrative law.[59] Others, such as Jennings and Mitchell, saw it as an opportunity to conceive of a distinct form of state liability along

55 F. W. Maitland, 'Introduction', in O. Gierke, *Political Theories of the Middle Age* (Cambridge University Press, 1968), p. xl.

56 F. W. Maitland, 'The Crown as Corporation', in H. A. L. Fisher (ed.), *Collected Papers of Frederic William Maitland*, 3 vols. (Cambridge University Press, 1911), vol. III, pp. 244–70, 263.

57 See for example the cases of *Feather* v. *R* 122 ER 1191 (1865) 6 B & S 257; *Dixon* v. *London Small Arms* (1875–76) LR 1 App Cas 632.

58 Report of the Committee of Ministers' Powers, Cmnd 4060/1932.

59 G. H. Morgan, 'Remedies Against the Crown', in G. Robinson, *Public Authorities and Legal Liability* (University of London Press, 1925), p. xxx.

French administrative law lines. The critical difference between them was whether or not the Crown should be placed on an equal footing with private persons for liability purposes. The legislation that eventually introduced a right to sue the Crown in tort took a very long time coming. When it was finally enacted, it treated the Crown as a 'private person of full age and capacity' and it still did not take the final step of recognizing the Crown as fully capable of willing a wrong. The Crown Proceedings Act 1947 (which is still the law today) had a piecemeal, common law quality that focused on particular actions and remedies. I turn now to that story.

The Crown Proceedings Act 1947 as partial reform

The cloak of *Crown* immunity (as opposed to public officer immunity) in the UK never extended to local government and other statutory bodies.[60] The British Crown's activities were a subset of the functions and actions that would be attributed to the 'state' in continental Europe and even to the Crown in other parts of the Empire. Nevertheless these central functions were growing. During World War I they substantially increased. It was during this time that Laski took up Maitland's call that the 'English state' should be held morally and legally responsible for its expanded activities.[61] Once again the struggle was framed in terms of the need for the law to support and recognize the 'real'. While acknowledging that holding civil servants personally liable in tort creates an incentive for officials to be more careful, Laski urged that the principal ought to be held directly responsible for the acts of its agents. Adopting Duguit, he at once rejected any personification of the state but sought to hold that 'great public service association' tortiously liable. He described his argument as 'no more than a plea that realism be substituted in the place of fiction'.[62]

In fact the early twentieth-century practice was far more fictional than even Laski realized. Typically, to take an actual example, the negligent

[60] The Public Authorities Protection Act 1893, however, introduced procedural protections when suing public authorities, such as notice requirements and a six-month limitation period (which did not apply to contractual proceedings or workers' compensation claims). The Act was partially reformed by the Limitation Act 1949, and more thoroughly by the Law Reform (Limitation of Actions Act) 1954.

[61] H. J. Laski, 'The Responsibility of the State in England', *Harvard Law Review* 32 (1918–19), 447–72, 451.

[62] *Ibid.*, 452.

driver of a Post Office van could be sued personally in negligence for injuries he caused in the course of his employment, but not the Post Office itself.[63] Nevertheless the government bureaucracy loomed as a shadow. The government routinely stood behind its servants and indemnified officials (according to its own assessment of fault). The practice was for the government and claimant to identify a nominal defendant who could stand in the government's place. Not only did this device obscure the reality of the situation and subvert the very responsibility principles the common law had previously treated as determinative, but also it did not always work. The House of Lords eventually unmasked the full extent of the fiction in the case of *Adams* v. *Naylor*.[64] It involved the death and injury of children playing on a beach which was known to contain land mines and from which the public was inadequately protected. The Lords warned that even if the case had not been out of time, the Crown servant who was the named defendant could not have been held liable in tort because the duty was one owed by the *occupier*, and on ordinary legal principles could not be owed by a servant. This was but one example of a more general problem of attempting to hold the state responsible through individual officials. In a range of situations, including those involving breaches of statutory duties, Crown servants were not considered by law to owe statutory duties directly to the public but rather only to the Crown (unless a statute explicitly suggested otherwise). A remedy was not always available even through a servant of the crown. The common law 'solution' was not working.

Legislative reform, when it came, was partial. Jacob has documented in detail the stuttering progress of the reform commencing in 1920 under a committee convened by Lord Hewart.[65] He records how insulated those debates were from external academic and political critique. One aspect of this insularity which Jacob does not mention is the absence of any reference to Commonwealth precedent. In some parts of the Empire where there was a shortage of private capital, and public improvements were almost entirely publicly funded, the state as a whole was able to be sued for vicarious or even direct institutional liability. The Secretary of State for India, for example, could by legislation be sued on matters for which private commercial actors would also be liable

[63] *Bainbridge* v. *Postmaster-General* [1906] 1 KB 178.

[64] [1946] AC 543.

[65] J. M. Jacob, 'The Debates Behind an Act: Crown Proceedings Reform, 1920–1947', *Public Law* (1992), 452–84.

(though not for those actions 'only the sovereign' could perform). The legislation reflected the common law as it had previously been applied to the East India Company – a creature of Charter. It would become, in turn, the model for French government liability (an example of the British leading the French).[66] The Australian states and the New Zealand colony had, on the whole, enacted more straightforward and effective legislation as early as 1853 which could also have provided a model for the UK.[67] In those colonies the construction of railways, canals and other infrastructure was almost entirely undertaken by government and not by private enterprise. In these circumstances, the argument that government should be treated in the same way as a private enterprise would have had far greater traction. Associating the Crown with the building of roads and sewers would not have been considered a potential slur on the royal dignity in the colonies where the Crown had always been more abstract than real.

The Crown Proceedings Act 1947[68] did not draw benefit from these comparative approaches. It retains a narrow and piecemeal quality.[69] It holds the Crown vicariously liable for the actions of *individuals* who commit wrongs in its service. It allows direct liability only in very limited named instances: in relation to duties owed to employees; flowing from the occupation of property (the *Adams* v. *Naylor* situation); and for breach of patent rights.[70] Liability of the Crown under a statutory duty is limited to those cases where ordinary persons would be liable under the same statute.[71] In other words the statute does not concede as a *general proposition* that the Crown is capable of 'willing to do wrong'.[72] The

[66] Anderson, 'Public Law', above n. 34, pp. 380–1 citing D. Fairgrieve, *State Liability in Tort: A Comparative Law Study* (Oxford University Press, 2004), pp. 12–13, 20–3. The Secretary of State for India was able to sue and be sued as a body corporate and the liabilities were met from the general revenue.

[67] Claimants Relief Act 1853 (SA); Claims Against the Government Act 1857 (NSW); Claims against the Crown Act 1858 (Vic); Claims Against the Government Act 1866 (Qld); Crown Suits Act 1881 (NZ); Crown Redress Act 1891 (Tas); Crown Suits Act 1898 (WA); Claims Against the Commonwealth Act 1902 (Cth). The Victorian and Tasmanian statutes were more complex.

[68] Scotland and New Zealand became 're-colonized' in different ways via the UK Crown Proceedings Act 1947 and its New Zealand copy, the Crown Proceedings Act 1950. In both jurisdictions, the extent of Crown immunity was broadened by the 'reform'.

[69] The closest in coverage is the Victorian legislation. See P. W. Hogg, 'Victoria's Crown Proceedings Act', *Melbourne University Law Review* 7 (1969–70) 342–52.

[70] Section 2(1)(b) and (c). [71] Section 2(2).

[72] The provisions concerning liability for intellectual property infringements observe a similar form – the breaches of Crown servants are attributed to the Crown.

statute leaves a residue of common law *immunity* for other actions not identified (as has been recognized in a recent case).[73]

The structure of the Act is worthy of closer examination. It excludes direct liability of the Crown in tort. According to section 2, the Crown is subject:

> to all those liabilities in tort to which, if it were a private person of full age and capacity it would be subject:-
>
> (a) *In respect of torts committed by its servants* and agents...
>
> Provided that *no proceedings shall lie against the Crown* by virtue of paragraph (a) of this subsection in respect of any act or omission of a servant or agent of the Crown *unless the act or omission would* apart from the provisions of this Act *have given rise to a cause of action in tort against that servant or agent or his estate.* (emphasis added)

This section does not recognize any originating fault in the Crown such as an unlawful direction. The actions and omissions of individuals (but not their mental states) are instead *attributed* to the Crown which can be held liable for them. The understanding of vicarious liability on which this section relies has developed to treat the employer, or in this case the Crown, as liable in the sense of making good the wrong but without any implication of blame or fault. It has become a modern means of recognizing the social desirability of loss-spreading. This allows liability to be typically based on the attribution of conduct to another person or body regardless of that other person's or body's mental state[74] so long as those actions are 'sufficiently connected' to the employer's business and purposes. Importantly, the individual remains personally and primarily responsible and is the *source* of the employer's responsibility. Vicarious liability, so conceived, is a means by which to give the victim an alternative avenue of redress but, conceptually at least, does not carry the same level of moral opprobrium as direct liability,[75] and neither does

[73] Hogg, 'Victoria's Crown Proceedings Act', above n. 69, 347. See also G. Sawer, 'Crown Liability in Tort and the Exercise of Discretions', *Res Judicatae* 5 (1951), 14–20. See for a recent example, *Morgan* v. *Ministry of Justice* [2010] EWHC 2248 (HC) in which the Crown could not be held directly liable for the treatment of prisoners at risk of self-harm.

[74] P. Cane, *Responsibility in Law and Morality* (Oxford: Hart, 2002), p. 162.

[75] Even so, there remains a marked reluctance to hold employers even vicariously liable in the modern sense for the most egregious and self-gratifying conduct of their employees. It was not until *Lister* v. *Wesley Hall* [2002] 1 AC 215 that the House of Lords was prepared to hold an employer (a private school) vicariously liable for acts of sexual abuse committed by an employee who was a warden of a boarding house.) The test was whether there was sufficient connection between the acts of abuse and the work that the warden was employed to do.

it concede an agent-independent corporate will to do wrong. Indeed, the Crown Proceedings Act 1947 does not concede that the Crown can command a wrong.

As was the case with the nominal defendant procedure, the actions, deeds and thoughts of individual servants must constitute the tort. That also means, at least in theory, that complex institutional wrong-doing may be difficult to attach to the Crown.[76] So, for example, if an individual servant is inexperienced or inadequately trained or supervised for the job, it may not be that she is herself individually liable, or, indeed, that any other individual may be found personally to have committed a tort, and hence the Crown cannot be vicariously liable. The proviso to section 2(1)(a) allows that an official's personal defences are also available to the Crown (which is not the usual case for vicarious liability).[77] This also reinforces the idea that liability derives from the acts of a real person. The effect of section 2(1) and 2(4) is that the Crown shares in whatever legislative immunity or privilege attaches to the particular Crown servant. Vicarious liability through an individual official rather than direct liability may in certain cases prove an obstacle to establishing systemic failure.[78] The strict wording of the Act seems to preclude a successful action for that kind of institutional wrong-doing unless it can be located in a particular person or persons who can be held jointly or severally liable. At least as it is framed, the Crown Proceedings Act 1947 is a repudiation of 'real will' theories. The state as an enterprise does not itself commit the wrong but may be held liable for the wrongs of its servants.

One may be forgiven for not recognizing these technical points in the case law itself. These arguments have not been raised by the Crown in the iconic cases extending the duties of care owed by officials. The limitation in section 2(2) of the Crown Proceedings Act 1947 on when the Crown

[76] See *Couch* v. *Attorney General* [2008] 3 NZLR 725 (in relation to a provision to the same effect in the Crown Proceedings Act 1950 (NZ)) and the illuminating discussion in S. Anderson, '"Grave Injustice", "Despotic Privilege": the Insecure Foundations of Crown Liability for Torts in New Zealand', *Otago Law Review* 12(1) (2009), 1–21.

[77] H. W. R. Wade, *Administrative Law* (Oxford: Clarendon Press, 1961), p. 215.

[78] This question was raised as a matter of law under equivalent provisions in the New Zealand Act discussed in *Couch* v. *Attorney General* [2008] NZSC 45 and *Couch* v. *Attorney General (No. 2)* [2010] 3 NZLR 149. The point is elegantly made by Anderson, '"Grave Injustice"', above n. 76, 1 and 2. Tipping J raises but fails to address or decide Anderson's point in *Couch No. 2* at para. 173.

can be held liable for a breach of statutory duty has been circumvented by the development of a duty of care to the public in administering the statute. In *Home Office* v. *Dorset Yacht*,[79] for example, the finding of the House of Lords was that the three borstal officers who were variously alleged to have disobeyed lawful instructions, fallen asleep and generally failed to prevent the escape of the borstal detainees, owed a duty of care in the performance of their (statutory) functions to third parties whose property was subsequently damaged. It was conceded that the Home Office was *vicariously liable* if such a duty were established. Where the allegations of fact tended to support a case that the Home Office (for the Crown) was itself negligent (e.g., in allowing a system of open detention in the first place), Lords Morris and Diplock, in particular, were much more cautious.[80] But rather than relying on the direct/vicarious liability distinction, they introduced instead the policy/discretionary dichotomy. This was aimed at protecting 'policy' decisions from negligence claims but not 'operational' ones.

These creative evasions of the restrictions on holding the Crown directly as opposed to vicariously responsible, have had a number of important consequences. In many ways they have helped realize the ambitions of the new administrative lawyers that tort law should compensate for risk creation rather than fault. Vicarious liability recognizes the desirability of loss spreading and is not focused on systemic wrongdoing. It represents the state bearing the losses on behalf of individual citizens without the need for, or often even the possibility of, a finding of collective fault.

The expansion of negligence law has resulted in government authorities owing duties of care and protection well beyond those protected by the traditional 'police' or 'trespass' torts such as trespass to person and property, battery, wrongful arrest and detention, false imprisonment and the seizure and destruction of goods. These traditional torts protect both common law rights and something approximating to civil rights. The idea of duties of care in negligence law significantly expands the range of protectable interests. Is it necessarily surprising that this loss-sharing version of Crown liability flourished alongside the expansion of the welfare state, and various other loss-spreading schemes such as the Criminal Injuries Compensation Scheme? This is a socialized system of liability for a socialized state.

[79] [1970] AC 1004. [80] Lord Morris, 1036, Lord Diplock 1068.

An important element of coherence has remained. The reluctance to hold the state directly liable, while holding it vicariously liable on a loss-spreading basis, preserves the benign nature of the collective will. Underlying all of these technical subtleties are two fundamental common law commitments: the state/Crown does not deliberately will wrong-doing and the law serves the general will. In the twentieth century we should not be surprised that the law should also be used to reinforce social solidarity and 'social rights'. The judges still resist findings that the state itself was at fault or directly committed a wrong.

Judicial review of administrative action

If tort law doctrines, which on one version of the British constitutional story form the basis of constitutional rights, have not traditionally recognized the state as wrong-doer, what of the area of law that claims to control public power and public wrong-doing – judicial review of administrative action? As the previous chapter sketched, the state as a unified whole is absent here too. There is no 'collective will' to do wrong. Judicial review tends to focus on particular decision-makers and statutory bodies: it proceeds on the basis that the state is disaggregated and that the judges are themselves part of the mechanism for bureaucratic control. While it investigates fault and intent, such intent is located in particular decision-makers.

The presence of the Crown presents formidable problems for locating a person of the state who can be held responsible. In form, at least in England, the Crown is always the nominal plaintiff in relation to the prerogative remedies. Wade describes the situation thus: 'the Crown will lend its legal prerogatives to the subject so that they may collaborate to ensure good and lawful government'.[81] As a consequence, such prerogative orders are not available against the Crown per se. Traditionally, the prerogative writs of prohibition treated the Crown as representing the state and the public in ensuring that the courts were kept within the bounds of their jurisdiction. This was considered as a matter 'within the care of the Crown' (exercised on behalf of the Crown by the Queen's judges of the superior courts).[82] The form of this and other of the prerogative orders can be viewed as yet another iteration of the idea that

[81] H. W. R. Wade, *Administrative Law*, 2nd edn (Oxford University Press, 1967), p. 116.

[82] J Shortt, *Informations (Criminal and Quo Warranto) Mandamus and Prohibition* (London: William Clowes, 1887), p. 426.

the 'King can do no wrong'. In order to preserve this central idea, complex distinctions have been required to be made between whether an official is acting in discharge of the Crown's duty or is discharging duties which are personal to the official and thus susceptible to the writ.[83] Writs of *mandamus* were not available against the Crown, though in certain cases they were available against Crown servants.[84]

All of the prerogative remedies attach to real persons, officers and bodies. As such, they also reflect the disaggregated and dispersed state administered by judges and officials as it existed at the very beginning of our period, discussed in Chapter 2.[85] While judicial review actions directly confront public wrong-doing, the most difficult questions today arise when the source of the public wrong-doing appears to be located at the apex of the collective government hierarchy. As with tort law, the courts have been incremental and creative in attempting to circumvent the logical difficulties which would appear to preclude judicial review at the highest levels. So, for example, the prerogative orders have been used successfully to review the exercise of the prerogative itself. The prohibition on the grant of injunction or specific performance against the Crown in section 21(1) of the Crown Proceedings Act 1947 has been avoided on the basis that a judicial review action is not itself a 'civil proceeding'.[86] Though judges have come close to identifying the Crown itself as the potential subject of an order, they have never quite been prepared to take that final step.[87]

Importantly, the remedies that are available under the prerogative writs are not remedies to which an individual is entitled as of right: they are rather a matter for judicial discretion. This reflects the fact that an individual cannot assert her rights in judicial review – or at least not in a strict Hohfeldian sense. It is an area of law that has tended traditionally to be ambivalent about rights understood in an individualized sense.

83 *The Queen* v. *Lords Commissioners of the Treasury* [1872] L R 7 QB 387; *cf The Queen* v. *Special Commissioners of Income Tax* [1888] 21 QBD 313.

84 *R* v. *The Lords Commissioners of the Treasury* (1835) 4 A & E 286. See also Anderson, 'Public Law', above n. 34, p. 346.

85 A recent and rare example of the Crown being treated as a unity in judicial review is the case of *BAPIO Action Ltd* v. *Secretary of State for Home Department* [2008] UKHL 27 where the majority of the House of Lords treated the representation of one government department as fettering the statutory discretion of another.

86 *R* v. *Licensing Authority, ex parte Smith Klein and French* [1990] 1 QB 574; *M* v. *Home Office* [1994] 1 AC 377 (HL).

87 See M. Loughlin, 'The State, the Crown and the Law', in M. Sunkin and S. Payne (eds.), *The Nature of the Crown* (Oxford University Press, 1999).

This ought not to be a surprise given the controversial twentieth-century evolution of judicial review discussed in Chapter 7. The early twentieth-century arguments revolved around the very question of whether rights instantiated in the 'ordinary law constitution' should be displaced by a new system of justice and 'larger' rights socially conceived.

Scholarly disputes about the place of rights in the administrative law project have taken a number of different forms. They arise, for example, in relation to the question of the very purpose of judicial review and the wider administrative law project. Is its purpose to improve the administrative process, ensure power is exercised by officials for the public good, to enhance citizen participation and interest representation in administration and to regulate risk? If so, it is concerned primarily with the government's duties to the public at large – imperfect rather than correlative duties. Or is its primary purpose to protect individuals against abuses of power?[88] Is it some fluid mixture of both – upholding the public interest which of itself includes the minimum protection of individual rights (as Jennings seemed to suggest).[89] And even if, as some scholars have claimed, the individual *is* central to the enterprise, opponents question whether it is likely that courts could effectively serve as the primary vehicle for mass citizen redress by way of judicial review. Administrative procedures for redress, such as ombudsmen and tribunals and compensation schemes, are likely to be much more important to individuals than courts exercising only supervisory power.

Sometimes these different perspectives take the form of differences in emphasis. Wade, for example, who is the most Diceyan of the textbook writers, emphasizes the usefulness of the judicial review challenge as a means by which to establish that an official has acted *ultra vires* or outside the powers conferred on him by law. Once that has been established, a collateral ordinary law challenge, for example, in trespass or nuisance, can be framed to give the individual redress. Jennings, by contrast, is primarily concerned with the architecture of power rather than with individualized remedies. His account does not make the place of individual rights within judicial review necessarily central. He contends that in any event the dispute will often not involve individuals at all, but more likely involve jurisdictional disputes between different agencies of government. Hence the remedies in judicial review are highly discretionary, forward-looking, oriented towards stopping the public

[88] Wade is most commonly identified as representing this strand of scholarship.
[89] See discussion in Chapter 6.

wrong from occurring and relatively independent of the claimant's relationship to the public wrong.

Some of these larger controversies are reflected in the detail of the doctrinal debates. The question of what a claimant needs by way of an interest before she has standing to bring a judicial review action, for example, remains controversial. All citizens presumably have some interest in ensuring that governments act within their powers and all citizens benefit from judicial orders which have the effect of stopping the excessive use of power. And yet, in order to bring a judicial review action, claimants often have to show they have been specially affected by the impugned decision or action. If the remedies are oriented towards getting the 'architecture' of public power right, why should the individual have to establish a special interest in order to bring an action?

Even where the individual obviously *does* have an interest in the matter in judicial review actions, the rights at stake do not necessarily have a direct connection with the remedy. The presence of 'right-like' interests, however, has often operated as an overt (or even covert) trigger for the sometimes apparently random interventions by the courts. Certainly before the advent of modern human rights consciousness, a decision that a body was operating outside its power would not in itself necessarily have had the effect of upholding an individual's rights or interest. The example Griffith and Street give in an early text is of a tribunal finding a person not guilty.[90] The tribunal is subsequently reviewed for committing a procedural error within its jurisdiction. The consequence of a finding that the tribunal's decision was technically a nullity is that the unlucky accused could again be tried without the opportunity to plead *autrefois acquit.* As Griffith and Street are at pains to point out, the focus on holding public authorities within the boundaries of the power conferred does not, in this example, directly protect the accused's interests. When the case law does protect individual interests, it often does so *indirectly* or even by happenstance. The role of the law here is to supervise and deter public wrong-doing rather than to vindicate individual rights. Unravelling the consequences of a finding of nullity or invalidity remains a doctrinal minefield even today. Not every illegality constitutes fault or wrong-doing per se.

What follows from this is that remedies are only discretionary and they do not include monetary remedies for administrative wrongs.

[90] J. A. G. Griffith and H. Street, *Principles of Administrative Law* (London: Pitman, 1952), p. 207.

Monetary compensation has never been directly available to an individual by way of judicial review but only by way of a collateral ordinary common law action. Indeed, until the most recent edition, one of the leading texts, De Smith's *Judicial Review of Administrative Action*, described the non-availability of monetary remedies in judicial review as one of judicial review's basic commitments:[91]

> A fundamental tenet of English law is that the failure of a public body to act in accordance with public law principles *of itself* gives no entitlement at common law to compensation for any loss suffered. ... To recover damages, a recognized cause of action in tort must be pleaded and proved.

All these doctrinal niceties and controversies reflect the fact that, although judicial review is focused on public wrong-doing, it views the state's duties as imperfect – owed to the public at large rather than to any particular individual.

There is still a strong tradition within administrative law scholarship of positive hostility to human rights claims – or at least rights claims of a certain kind. This hostility seems to be based on a fear that individual rights claims will be enforced to the detriment of the collective good. Galligan, writing in 1982, disparages the suggestion that a Bill of Rights would give judges a substantive set of standards against which any grant of power could be read saying: 'such suggestions are less concerned with regulating the welfare state than getting rid of it'.[92] Such an attitude, in which Galligan is by no means alone, draws on a tradition of left-wing politics among administrative lawyers that goes directly back to Robson (as discussed in Chapter 6). It continues in the work of scholars such as McAuslan, Arthurs and Harlow.[93]

[91] S. De Smith, J. L. Jowell and H. Woolf, *Judicial Review of Administrative Law*, (London: Sweet & Maxwell, 5 edn, 1995) (chapter 19 'Pecuniary Remedies in Administrative Law' 19–003 (italics original). I am grateful to Edrick Child of the New Zealand Crown Law Office for drawing this to my attention and pointing me to the 6th edition of the work (2007) where the reference to fundamental tenet is omitted. Both editions, however, contain the comment that 'the major question is whether a system of remedies in administrative law can be complete without the provision of rights to compensation and restitution to people harmed by *ultra vires* acts or omissions of public authorities', 5th edn, 19–006; 6th edn, 19–027.

[92] D. J. Galligan, 'Judicial Review and the Textbook Writers', *Oxford Journal of Legal Studies* 2 (1982), 257–76, 273.

[93] E.g., P. McAuslan, 'Administrative Law, Collective Consumption and Judicial Policy', *Modern Law Review* 46 (1983), 1–20; B. Arnold and H. Arthurs, 'Does the Charter

On the other hand, one of the much overlooked contributions that judicial review has made to human rights considered more broadly has been the procedural recognition of social and economic rights which Reich called the 'New Property'[94] in 1963. 'Rights' or 'interests' previously regarded as mere privileges by the common law would be recognized for the first time as sufficiently significant and relied on to trigger primarily procedural obligations and safeguards. These have included rights in respect of welfare benefits, licences, jobs and immigration status.

Finally, and perhaps most importantly, in terms of the emphasis on power rather than individual rights, judicial review actions have traditionally stopped short of reviewing on the merits of a decision and have concentrated instead on questions of legality. This has inhibited the development of a focus on individual rights generally and human rights in particular. Because courts are never able to act as the final decision-maker for all administrative decisions, and also to maintain the distinction between appeal and review, courts would not put themselves in the place of the primary decision-maker or second guess their policy choices. In the past few years, almost certainly influenced by a new human rights consciousness, the distinction between review on legality and review on the merits has become increasingly blurred. The effect of a focus more on the substance rather than process has made it more difficult to treat the remedies as discretionary or unrelated to the interests of the individual.

It remains very much the case that these matters remain controversial in judicial review. Some writers, for example, have suggested that only in cases where there are human rights (rather than other interests) at stake should judicial review involve intensive consideration of the merits.[95] The matter of how much judicial review is concerned with rights and in particular human rights is very much a live controversy.[96] Over the last

Matter?', *Review of Constitutional Studies* 11(1) (2006), 37–110; C. Harlow, 'Damages and Human Rights', *New Zealand Law Review* (2004), 429–50.

94 C. A. Reich, 'The New Property', *Yale Law Journal.* 73 (1963–4), 733–87.

95 M. B. Taggart, 'Proportionality, Deference, Wednesbury', *New Zealand Law Review* (2008), 423–82 advocating a bifurcated approach whereby cases where fundamental or human rights are involve attract proportionality review and other cases only the less intensive rationality review.

96 See the special issue 'Proportionality, Deference, Wednesbury: Taking Up Michael Taggart's Challenge', *New Zealand Law Review* (2010) Part 2. See also T. Poole, 'Between the Devil and the Deep Blue Sea: Administrative Law in the Age of Rights,' in C. Harlow,

ten years there has been a turn in the scholarship which has attempted to rehabilitate rights as a traditional – if covert – concern of judicial review. Rights, once eschewed as individualistic, have come to be seen as a way of pursuing collectivist rather than individualistic ends for *classes* of the weak and dispossessed (refugees, prisoners, minorities). But the fact is that rights have *required* such rehabilitation within judicial review and administrative law generally. At the beginning of the twentieth century, at least, rights concepts were viewed as a threat to the very existence of administrative law as a separate subject. The main point for now is that although judicial review has had public wrongs as its focus, it has not conceived of such wrongs in terms of individual rights claims against the state.

Summary

There are a number of obstacles to asserting individual rights (including human rights) against the state in the common law. Traditionally, tort law recognized rights but allowed them to be asserted against officials and not the state *qua* state. The Crown Proceedings Act 1947 reformed the law to make the state or Crown vicariously liable for the acts of its servants but still does not recognize that the Crown can be directly liable for institutional wrong-doing (except in very limited cases such as occupier's liability). Judicial review actions, on the other hand, have as their focus public wrong-doing but neither recognize the state as a unified person as the wrong-doer, nor make individual rights central to the cause of actions or remedies. Neither the doctrines of tort law nor judicial review recognize that an individual can claim rights directly against the state *qua* state as wrong-doer or that the state can will wrong-doing. Both areas of law are underpinned by concepts of the benign common or collective will (ideas that have come from an earlier age). How can the Crown, conceived as the government apparatus, be responsible for wrong-doing, when the Crown also represents the 'state as society in a moral guise'?[97]

Nevertheless, creative means have been used to remedy public wrongs. The state has been held vicariously liable for acts of its agents without

L. Pearson and M. B. Taggart (eds.), *Administrative Law in a Changing State: Essays in Honour of Mark Aronson* (Oxford: Hart, 2008) pp. 15–44.

97 K. H. F. Dyson, *The State Tradition in Western Europe: A Study of an Idea and Institution* (Oxford: Martin Robinson, 1980), p. 187 (quoting Burke).

itself being found to be at fault. Public wrong-doing has been found against parts of the state apparatus if not the whole. Has the problem of responsibility been solved then for almost all practical purposes?

There are reasons both philosophical and practical to think not. Skinner, for example, asks who is responsible for the national debt?[98] In times of environmental uncertainty we might also ask who is responsible for the well-being of future generations? Contemporary philosophers have returned to the questions asked by Maitland about whether a collective entity can be held morally responsible and if so on what basis. Such arguments no longer necessarily depend on Maitland's borrowed and controversial metaphysics discussed in Chapter 3. Of the contemporary theorists though, Finnis is possibly the closest to Maitland's approach. According to Finnis, the reality of the group 'is the reality of an order of human, truly personal acts, an order brought into being and maintained by the choices . . . of persons'.[99] It is these *human* qualities of the group from which their rights and liabilities derive. Pettit argues that the group *qua* group is capable of attracting moral responsibility when it has sufficient autonomy from its individual members in its collective decision-making processes, exercises control and makes value judgments. In such circumstances, the group is more than a mere aggregation of individuals.[100] Cane uses insights from Hart to reach a similar conclusion and to extend the moral analysis into a legal setting. He argues that both moral and legal personality are human artifacts and thus the capacity for all legal responsibility, including group responsibility, is the product of legal rules (rather than something inherent in the nature of moral personality (human or otherwise)).[101]

Despite moves in English law to recognize that corporations are capable of criminal wrong doing, English tort and judicial review law are yet to recognize collective state wrong-doing.

But international law *does* conceive of the state as an entity, as a legal person, and now views the state as capable of doing wrong. Human rights and European Union law hold the state responsible for its actions including at times for those taken at the highest policy levels, by the

[98] Q. Skinner, 'A Genealogy of the Modern State', *Proceedings of the British Academy*, 162 (2009), 325–70.

[99] J. Finnis, 'The Priority of Persons', in J. Horder (ed.), *Oxford Essays in Jurisprudence* (Oxford University Press, 2000), pp. 1–15, 11.

[100] P. Pettit, 'Responsibility Incorporated', *Ethics* (2007) 117 (2), 171–201, 175.

[101] Cane, *Responsibility in Law and Morality*, above n. 74, esp. pp. 39–43.

legislature and the judges. The exact basis of such responsibility is opaque. It is unclear, for example, whether responsibility depends on control and what constitutes 'fault'. It is ironic, given that traditionally it was thought that international law existed for states and not the other way around, that it has been changing conceptions of statehood and sovereignty in international law that has brought pressure to bear on the domestic common law.

In the next two chapters, we shall see how there is a new and greater willingness to conceive of the state as the source of problems rather than of the common good, and to regard the proper role of the law as constraining the state rather than as its servant. Lawyers and judges have also become increasingly impatient about doctrinal distinctions in the way that tort law and judicial review have conceived individual rights. One proposed solution is that the law should decide which cause of action takes precedence – public law or private law. Another is that there should be greater convergence between the different approaches to public wrong-doing. That is, the state's moral and legal personality should not depend on which area of law defines it (as Hart described the position) but should flow from our notions of the state itself as reflected in a separate and distinctive public law. Surprisingly, as I shall argue, a major trigger for these challenges and tensions has been the privatization policies of the 1980s and the way in which those policies imagined the state's relationships with its citizens. We turn now to consider the philosophical and doctrinal challenges wrought by that phenomenon. Readers who are particularly interested in the legal doctrine may wish to turn directly to Chapter 9.

8

Privatization, deregulation and reconceiving the state

a world of greed and chaos, of private self-interest and public incoherence[1]

No society

In the last chapter I examined the Crown's different faces in the common law. Whether it is representing the public (society in a moral guise) or the state apparatus, it is conceived of as benign. In this chapter we encounter a major political challenge to these ideas about the nature of the British state – and assess the law's response.

In 1987, Margaret Thatcher famously declared that 'there is no such thing as society'. Taken in context, she was suggesting that what we call 'society' consists only of individuals acting, making decisions and taking or failing to take responsibility for themselves and one another.[2] The statement, and the commitments which lay behind it, became emblematic of an era in which British government was radically rethought. It is not, however, the absence of 'society', but, rather, the 'absence of a developed concept of 'State' in British political and legal theory' that has been credited with the apparent ease with which changes were made to state functions, state organization and the state's relationship with its citizens, during that time.[3] In this

[1] J. L. Mashaw, *Greed Chaos and Governance: Using Public Choice to Improve Public Law* (New Haven, CT: Yale University Press, 1997), p. 4.

[2] Interview for *Woman's Own* 1987. The quotation appeared in several slightly different versions. One of these is: 'There is no such thing as society. There is living tapestry of men and women and people and the beauty of that tapestry and the quality of our lives will depend upon how much each of us is prepared to take responsibility for ourselves and each of us is prepared to turn round and help by our own efforts those who are unfortunate.' (See Thatcher Foundation website www.margaretthatcher.org/document/106689.)

[3] M. B. Taggart, 'The Nature and Functions of the State', in P. Cane and M. Tushnet (eds.), *Oxford Handbook of Legal Studies* (Oxford University Press, 2003), pp. 101, 108; T. Daintith and M. Sah, 'Privatisation and the Economic Neutrality of the Constitution',

chapter I will test this hypothesis. I will argue that it was not exactly an *absence* of state conceptions but particular ways in which the state has been conceived in British legal thought that helped effectuate privatization and its associated policies. Other rival state traditions, also present in British legal thought, or lately entering British thought from outside sources, have proved resistant to some of these policies and have aided in the re-conceptualization of the state. Indeed, as I will argue in this and the chapter that follows, far from the state disappearing, there has emerged a more juridified state and a newly self-conscious legal inquiry into the nature of statehood.

Hayek: law and liberalism

The British experience has to be seen as part of a broader Western global phenomenon. To a certain extent, Hayek was its philosopher and public choice was its theory. But the way these ideas were incorporated into, and sometimes resisted by, legal and political institutions differed even among those nations with a shared common law heritage. How British institutions and law received (and withstood) these ideas is the subject of this chapter. We begin by setting out the broad commitments which served as the ideological underpinnings of deregulation, liberalization and privatization policies at a more global theoretical level, and then move to the British incorporation, resistance and, at times, even anticipation of these ideas.

Hayek is an important figure in this global story. He has influenced leading public choice theorists such as James Buchanan; the conception of 'economic man' that populates his, and later, theories provides a stark contrast to the concept of the individual associated with the new Liberalism of the earlier twentieth century; and his political philosophy explicitly engages with questions about the proper relationship between law, liberty and the state. Although he was initially sympathetic to Fabian Socialism, – Socialism, Totalitarianism and all forms of central planning became his primary targets.

For Hayek, the state does not have any particular purpose. It 'achieves its human purposes only to the extent that it is itself

(1993) Public Law, 465–87; C. Graham and T. Prosser, *Privatizing Public Enterprises: Constitutions, the State and Regulation in Comparative Perspective* (Oxford: Clarendon Press, 1991); C. Laborde, 'The Concept of the State in British and French Political Thought', *Political Studies* 48 (2000), 540–57.

purposeless'.[4] There is not, and neither should there be, a unified state 'will'. Indeed the state does not exercise a 'will' at all. His theory privileges 'spontaneous' over 'designed' social orders – and he counts among such spontaneous orders the state itself, the market, the cultural evolution of moral norms and the common law.

His conception of spontaneous legal order seems to recall an earlier, if romanticized, Diceyan view of the common law legal order. For Hayek, in contrast to Hobbes and Austin, law is not the creation of the state or the command of the sovereign but antedates the state.[5] It is this common law 'unencumbered judicial process'which is the 'true' and 'spontaneous' representation of such law.[6] Its role is to create and limit both individual liberty and governmental authority. The same law or *nomos* governs the state and private person alike. It is decentralized and relies on fragmented knowledge. For Hayek the evolutionary character of the common law is essential for the realization of the economic goals of the market system. He regards modern legislation, by contrast, as usurping many of the functions of 'true law'.[7] Together the market and this 'true law' constitute:

> a social organisation which is not deliberately brought about and has no specific purpose, but which enables individuals (including judges) to make decisions about courses of action within an environment of limited information and uncertainty.[8]

If Hayek's view of the law bears characteristics in common with a version of common law constitutionalism, his view of the individual is close to that of classical liberalism. His is a form of preference Utilitarianism.[9] The individual does not exist for wider purposes or the greater good. The proper question is whether, under a given system, an autonomous individual has a chance of achieving his unknown purposes.[10]

Public choice theory, which emerged in the 1970s and gained prominence in the 1980s, shares Hayek's central commitments. Nothing is inherently public: private spontaneous ordering and decentralized decision-making are to be preferred to central planning. An individual's

[4] F. Hayek, *The Road to Serfdom*, B. Caldwell (ed.) (University of Chicago Press, 2007); F. Hayek, *Law, Legislation and Liberty* (London: Routledge, 1976).
[5] J. Gray, *Hayek on Liberty*, 3rd edn (London: Routledge, 1998), p. 69. [6] *Ibid.*
[7] *Ibid.*
[8] Quoted in A. Ogus, *Regulation: Legal Form and Economic Theory* (Oxford: Hart, 2004), p. 27.
[9] Gray, *Hayek on Liberty*, above n.5, p. 58.
[10] F. Hayek, 'Use of Knowledge in Society', *American Economic Review* 35(4) (1945) 519–30.

preference ordering is superior to the social or collective ordering of preferences. There is no such thing as a 'group mind'or purpose.[11] Voters, politicians and bureaucrats are not Kantians, Idealists or Benthamite Utilitarians who rank their own interests equally with the interests of others: they are, instead, motivated by self-interest. Public choice theory adds a new element: democratic-representative government creates rent-seeking behaviour whereby individuals and groups actually profit at the public expense rather than promote the public interest. Public choice then, produces a diagnostic of government failure. Mashaw suggests that it describes 'a world of greed and chaos, of private self-interest and public incoherence'.[12] Governments must be constitutionally constrained and restrained.

It is striking to encounter public choice theory at this point in our narrative because it shares important similarities with a number of already established ideas in British political and legal thought, while decisively rejecting others. It bears elements in common with the anti-centralization debate in the middle of the nineteenth century in its distrust of unified and centralized authority. It contains elements of common law constitutionalism (and, presumably, would not regard judicial review as common law properly so called). It provides new reasons to suspect and contain democratic institutions and impulses and, like classical Liberalism, views democracy as a potential threat to freedom. Like political Pluralism it recognizes the sociological aspects of society and gives a place to private ordering without privileging the state. It is concerned about the conferral of discretion and its consistency with the rule of law. It bears a striking contrast to an administrative law which was originally born out of a hostility to the common law and its ideological pre-commitments, and whose adherents have seen themselves (often uncritically) as working to promote the public good and distinctly public law values. Indeed, it seems to reignite the debate between the early administrative lawyers and Lord Hewart which we discussed in Chapter 6. It thoroughly rejects the account (associated with Robson and Willis) that would suggest that bureaucrats could be

[11] K. Arrow, *Social Choice and Individual Values*, 2nd edn (New York: Wiley, 1963) discussed in J. M. Buchanan, 'Politics Without Romance: A Sketch of Positive Public Choice Theory and its Normative Implications', in J. M. Buchanan and R. D. Tollison (eds.), *The Theory of Public Choice II* (Ann Arbor, MI: University of Michigan Press, 1984), p. 15.

[12] Mashaw, *Greed Chaos and Governance*, above n. 1, p. 4.

trained in the 'proper characteristics and habits of mind' to serve the public good. It rejects the view that there are distinctive public law values. And, at least in its more rudimentary forms, it is unable to entertain the idea that individual interests are socially constituted.[13] Instead it privileges individual preferences within plural systems of social ordering – including market systems. The citizen's relationship to the state is that of a consumer, whose choices should be maximized. The contractual and property concepts that describe the relationships between citizen and state within this system of thought are in many respects closer to the political thought of the eighteenth than that of the nineteenth or twentieth centuries.[14]

Public choice theory comes in many and sophisticated guises and I am painting only its broad early commitments. It was not the only theory in town. Institutional economics and related theories of the firm were also influential at the time and introduced some potentially contradictory commitments. Institutional economics was concerned to model the state on a firm and to introduce private sector disciplines into the public sector. Such theories share with public choice the presumption that the public and private spheres are essentially alike and should be treated in the same way. Institutional economics, however, differs in important respects. It diagnoses one of the problems with bureaucracy as the problem of agency. Bureaucrats are unreliable agents: what is needed is a range of better disciplines to ensure that bureaucrats more faithfully pursue the interests of their principals (politicians). What is expected of the public service, then, needs to be better specified in advance in agreements, contracts and legislation. Having received a set of clear goals, however, public agencies need to be protected from political interference and to be held accountable as far as possible by private law disciplines. In Osborne and Gaebler's famous metaphor, the 'state steers, it does not row'.[15]

These theories depart from central commitments of public choice theory in important ways. Notwithstanding Arrow's scepticism about

[13] More recent social theory does investigate the collective nature of individual choice. See, e.g., J. Elster, *Examining Social Behaviour* (Cambridge University Press, 2007); C. Bicchieri, *The Grammar of Society: The Nature and Dynamics of Social Norms* (Cambridge University Press, 2006) but earlier public choice theory was unapologetic about its methodological individualism and its central actor 'economic man' or '*homo economicus*'. See, e.g., Buchanan, 'Politics Without Romance', above n. 11, p. 13.

[14] Buchanan, 'Politics Without Romance', above n. 11, p. 15.

[15] D. Osborne and T. Gaebler, *Reinventing Government* (Reading, MA: Addison Wesley, 1992), p. 59.

the coherence or authenticity of collective decision-making, institutional economics reintroduces the notion of state purposes and of a politically instituted 'will' delegated from the centre. Perhaps that is inevitable if Maitland is correct that all forms of collectivity are capable of exercising a will of their own – but it does once again raise the possibility that the firm and the state are alike in ways that are more public than private. Unlike public choice theory, these theories tend to privilege fidelity to *political* will over, for example, the will of an agent – there is a hierarchy of purpose here. Nothing is particularly spontaneous or decentralizing about this legal order – its object is greater control from, and accountability to, the political centre. This requirement of greater transparency assumes some particular forms of intervention and regulation. It also recognizes that public agency heads are managers and not simply servants (something which the common law has never done). From the start, then, there were contradictions in the theories underpinning privatization and deregulation – particularly in relation to their centralizing and decentralizing tendencies. These will only become more obvious when we consider their reception into the UK political system.

The 'reception' of 'theory'

The UK became one of the world leaders in implementing policies of privatization and deregulation, and in reorganizing the bureaucratic sphere to take account of the insights of institutional economics about agency capture. Between 1984 and 1991, one third of the total assets privatized in the world had formerly been under UK public ownership.[16] Britain took the lead in innovative regulatory techniques, including the contracting out of former governmental functions and services, and in the reorganization of the public sector (which came to be known as the New Public Management). What was law's role in accommodating and resisting those changes?

As far as the privatization (or re-privatization as it was sometimes called) of former public assets was concerned, it seems pretty clear that any 'programmatic' rationale was mostly supplied after the fact.[17]

[16] V. Wright, 'Industrial Privatization in Western Europe: Pressures, Problems and Paradoxes', in V. Wright (ed.), *Privatization in Western Europe: Pressures, Problems and Paradoxes* (New York: St Martin's Press, 1994), p. 10.

[17] V. Wright (ed.), *Privatization in Western Europe: Pressures, Problems and Paradoxes* (New York: St Martin's Press, 1994) especially the essays of Jeremy Richardson, 'The Politics

A desire for short-term gains in showing debt reduction figured significantly at the time. Reasons that *were* given included that the public sector was not subject to the same market disciplines as the private sector and was therefore not as efficient, that people ought to be given more choice, that private initiative should be fostered, that sales of shares would broaden the property-owning democracy and that the private sector would be in a better position than government to constrain trade union power. For our purposes, the most important stated objective, was that of redrawing the public–private boundary. And what was striking about that was that it was not considered a matter of constitutional moment but was presented primarily as a question of efficient instrument choice (just as redrawing that same boundary at nationalization had largely been treated as an empirical matter of achieving efficiency).[18] The political actors of both the 1940s and 1980s viewed law's role as purely instrumental.

A critical factor in the reception of these ideas into the UK was that these were theories framed for the far more legalistic US setting. Public choice and associated literature was diagnostic of what seemed to be wrong with US administrative and political practice – a system characterized by heavily rule-bound and formalized economic regulation, and by constitutional rights protection.[19] The UK system could not have been more different. It was characterized instead by an absence of formal legal rules. Executive power was highly centralized in order that the state should enjoy as much capacity as possible to serve 'the people' and the public interest. If there were constraints on such power, the traditional story was that these were already to be found in common law constitutionalism. Public choice ideology was not only able to take advantage of the existing highly centralized state and its powers, but, at the same time, to embrace anti-statist common law constitutionalism rhetorically as its own. The common law constitution did not impose much by way of real constraint in any event. This combination of factors meant that policies of privatization and deregulation met with relatively little by way of legal resistance.

and Practice of Privatization in Britain', pp. 57 ff and Ray Rees, 'Economic Aspects of Privatization in Britain', pp. 44 ff.

18 Bold claims were made for the greater efficiency of government owned industries at the time of nationalization. See, e.g., D. Chester, *The Nationalisation of British Industry, 1945–51* (London: Stationery Office, 1975), p. 20.

19 M. Moran, *The British Regulatory State* (Oxford University Press, 1992).

What had characterized British economic government between the late 1940s and late 1970s had been a version of corporatism which had its intellectual origins in G. D. H. Cole's Guild Socialism. Much of Britain's social and economic life was regulated by powerful quangos such as, for example, the National Economic Development Council. The participation of business and unions in such bodies had also been intended as a check on bureaucratic power and a supplement to political oversight.[20] At the time when corporatist practices were most in evidence in the UK, corporatism was associated in the public mind with the Fascist Totalitarian regimes of Italy and Germany. It was understandable, therefore, that there had been a public disavowal of corporatism as a deliberate policy.[21] Thatcher would target quangos rather than corporatism explicitly for criticism in the mid-1970s. After the fact, the regulatory practices of the time would be misleadingly described in 'economist-speak' as 'command and control'. Control there may have been, but it was certainly not by 'command'.

Corporatism, as it was practised in Britain, had these important features. Unlike Idealism it acknowledged distinct class and functional interests. Unlike Socialism it did not embrace pluralistic bargaining but rather co-operation. The state's role was not to regulate competition but to organize agreement for collective ends. Persuasion was much preferred to coercion. Corporatism did not view the state as neutral, above or apart from the people, but rather it regarded the state *as* the people. A number of things followed from this: the law was not capable of being used against the state; the emphasis was not on civil liberties but on 'civil duties, the individual's obligations to the collective which it is the state's task to see are fulfilled'.[22] Law was viewed solely as an instrument for attaining collective ends. It was not the *preferred* instrument, however, because law by its nature is too inflexible: corporatism resisted codification and embraced discretion. Intermediaries, in the form of quangos, advisory committees and self-regulated professions were co-opted to help fulfil state purposes.[23]

[20] This had been one of the recommendations of the Donoughmore Committee.

[21] J. Winkler, 'Law State and the Economy: The Industry Act 1975 in Context', *British Journal of Law and Society*, 2(2) (1975), 103–28, 104. N. Harris, *Competition and the Corporate Society: British Conservatives, the State and Industry, 1945–1964* (London: Methuen, 1972).

[22] Winkler, 'Law State and the Economy', above n. 21, 117.

[23] *Ibid.*, 119.

In practice so-called 'advisory' committees made up of industry players, such as the Import Duties Advisory Committee, exercised real powers of decision over the economy.[24] Governments negotiated with economic actors, including trade unions, in attempting to establish acceptable policies, for example, by way of voluntary wage control.[25] Corporatism also embraced a form of self-regulation on the basis that: 'the State organises society but the constituent elements regulate themselves'.[26] The professions were crucial players in government decision-making – none more so than those associated with the National Health Service.[27] The nature and extent of state and other control was never made explicit in law.

While the period between the late 1940s and 1970s might now be regarded in economic terms as one where government exercised 'command and control' over the economy, the reality was quite different. Scholars such as Marquand, Moran and Page characterize this time as a period of 'club government'.[28] This describes both the public and private spheres as well as the interactions between them. According to Moran:[29]

> The British system was unique in the extent to which it was run by private institutions beyond the reach of the state or the law . . . displaying cultures and institutional patterns that originated in the nineteenth century.

It seems, then, that, despite appearances, some of the English fellowships were still very much alive and well, especially in the economic realm, after the establishment of the welfare state and nationalized industries – they had merely gone underground and their roles had become virtually unknown to law. Interest group politics, however, took a very different form from the transparent approach mandated by the US Administrative Procedure Acts (which had taken up recommendation of the Donoughmore Committee that regulations should be published in advance and subject to public notice and comment). Interest groups politics in the UK would, by contrast, fall under the legal radar. Of course many of the consequent agreements did take

[24] A. Page, 'Public Law and Economic Policy: The United Kingdom Experience', *Journal of Law and Society* 9 (1982), 225–52, 230.

[25] *Ibid.*, 228. [26] Winkler, 'Law State and the Economy', above n. 21, 119.

[27] Moran, *The British Regulatory State*, above n. 19, pp. 82–3.

[28] D. Marquand, *The Unprincipled Society: New Demands and Old Politics* (London: Jonathan Cape, 1988); Moran, *The British Regulatory State* above n. 19; A. Page, 'Public Law and Economic Policy', above n. 24, 230.

[29] Moran, *The British Regulatory State*, above n. 19, p. 3.

legal form – usually by way of secondary or even tertiary legislation, or collective agreements. Broad conferrals of discretion and the over-use of delegated powers were matters about which public lawyers raised concerns.[30] One of the biggest questions among judicial review lawyers at the time was how properly to control *discretion* or, as Dworkin describes it, 'the hole in the donut'.[31]

There were, of course, other more obvious ways in which the UK government was not limited by legal rules. It was not just that there were no explicit guarantees of a publicly owned 'service public', or 'of social property' as appear in the Constitutions of France and the former Yugoslavia, there were no constitutionally mandated *procedural* requirements for the divestment of such assets.[32] There was no equivalent of the US non-delegation doctrine – which, though today all but operationally defunct, at the time created a legal forum in which to determine whether there were such things as 'public functions' that could not be delegated or contracted away. Neither was there a federal–state division which would have allowed pluralism of policy choice and could have become a matter of states' rights (such as the New Jersey constitutional requirement that the state provide 'a thorough and efficient system of free public schools').[33] Local authorities in the UK were simply compelled by ordinary legislation to open their operations to compulsory competitive tendering.[34]

Selling state assets merely required ordinary legislation and, in some cases, not even that.[35] Some transfers of shares and sales of subsidiaries, for example, were implemented by Ministerial decision alone (not even requiring collective cabinet decision) – relying on the Ram doctrine discussed in Chapter 5 – but this time for the purpose of *contracting*

[30] See, e.g., G. Ganz, *Quasi-legislation: Recent Developments in Secondary Legislation* (London: Sweet and Maxwell, 1987).

[31] R. Dworkin, *Taking Rights Seriously* (London: Duckworth, 1978), p. 31.

[32] Daintith and Sah, 'Privatisation and the Economic Neutrality of the Constitution', above n. 3, 471, 476. Even New Zealand, which was another world leader in implementing liberalization and privatization practices, encountered constitutional procedural impediments to divesting state assets because of Crown undertakings to Maori at its founding incorporated as the principles of the Treaty of Waitangi in Section 9 State Owned Enterprises Act 1986 (NZ).

[33] Daintith and Sah, 'Privatisation and the Economic Neutrality of the Constitution', above n. 3, 477.

[34] *Ibid.*, 483.

[35] For the varieties of privatization techniques, see *ibid.*, 468, and C. Graham and T. Prosser, 'Privatising Nationalised Industries: Constitutional Issues and New Legal Techniques', *Modern Law Review* 50 (1987), 16–51.

rather than *expanding* state functions.[36] Just as the Crown enjoyed all the powers of a natural person, so too could an individual Minister exercise those powers and thus bind the government as a whole.[37] Personifying and bodifying the Crown in this way was an important means of effecting the divestment of state assets. The idea of the Crown as a corporation sole gained new life and significance.[38] It was instrumentally important for a government seeking to divest itself of assets and functions. Daintith and Sah describe various of these phenomena as indicators of Britain's 'constitutional neutrality' around economic questions – though one might quibble about what they mean by 'neutrality'.[39] If there is law here it is entirely empowering rather than normatively limiting.

The relative absence of formal legal rules did not end there. Although public undertakings had been designated politically and subjected to different legal regimes in the nineteenth century, by the time privatization was effected there was no active body of public service law, nor any broader domestic common law concepts to apply to monopoly service providers – these too had been all but lost to legal memory. Unlike in North America, seventeenth-century common law doctrines which had imposed special obligations on 'common carriers' and 'businesses affected with a public interest' had never been developed to apply to British public utilities.[40] Judicially enforced public law control of nationalized industries was notable for its absence. Indeed, in relation to economic matters, the common law courts had simply been irrelevant. Wade said in 1961 that in Britain the protection against arbitrary power would not be formal legal rules but judicial power.[41] Wade was indeed heralding an important decade in which the courts significantly expanded the supervisory jurisdiction of judicial review – in iconic cases such as *Ridge* v. *Baldwin*,[42] *Anisminic Ltd* v. *Foreign Compensation Commission*,[43] and *Padfield* v.

[36] See p. 161 above.

[37] *Town Investments* v. *Department of the Environment* [1978] AC 359 (Lord Morris dissenting).

[38] The recent release by Baroness Scotland of the Ram memorandum reflects the ongoing and newly efficacious relevance of the doctrine.

[39] Daintith and Sah, 'Privatisation and the Economic Neutrality of the Constitution', above n. 3, 466.

[40] M. B. Taggart, 'The Province of Administrative Law Determined?' in M. B. Taggart (ed.) *The Province of Administrative Law* (Oxford: Hart, 1997), p. 7. There are, however, occasional statutory references to these concepts in the nineteenth-century statute book.

[41] H. W. R. Wade, *Administrative Law*, 1st edn (Oxford: Clarendon Press 1961), p. 1.

[42] [1964] AC 40 HL. [43] [1969] 2 AC 147.

Minister of Agriculture.[44] But while these cases have properly been regarded as important symbols of a reawakening of administrative law after a long sleep,[45] judicial review was a 'paper tiger' in so far as commercial and economic matters were concerned. The law simply did not reach these issues.[46] And, finally, in terms of the absence of law, there were no independent regulatory agencies – nor any tradition of such.

Less obviously, most of the forms and practices through which the civil service was organized and controlled from the centre were regulated by the prerogative, which was not yet susceptible to the supervisory jurisdiction of the courts.[47] This area too was the subject of informal unwritten rules, executive policy and constitutional convention.[48]

The legal system, then, into which privatization and deregulatory policies were introduced was *relatively* free from formal legal constraints. This is important to understanding the nature of the encounter between the new deregulatory ideology and the UK state. The legal framework into which these policies were introduced was highly permissive and minimally rule bound, and informed by the idea that the state represented the public interest of the people as a whole. This helped make reception possible and eased the way for the implementation of privatization and deregulation policies.

Paradoxes abound – a legal framework designed for a 'public interest' state was used to bring into being a state which could no longer be trusted to pursue the public interest. What actually emerged looked much more like the very US administrative state that is critiqued in the public choice literature, than anything which had existed before. Taggart describes the process that followed privatization as 'raiding the American public law larder'.[49] After privatization, control by ownership quickly turned into control by regulation. Independent administrative

[44] [1968] AC 997.

[45] Harlow and Rawlings describe these cases as giving judicial review 'a new lease of life' in C. Harlow and R. Rawlings (eds.) *Law and Administration*, 3rd edn (Cambridge University Press, 2009), p. 100.

[46] See, e.g., A. McHarg, Ph. D. Thesis 'Accountability and the Public/Private Distinction: Privatisation of the United Kingdom Electricity Supply Industry', University of Edinburgh, 1997.

[47] *Council for Civil Service Unions* v. *Minister for the Civil Service* [1985] AC 374 first signalled the potential reviewability of the prerogative in the context of an industrial dispute.

[48] T. Daintith and A. Page, *The Executive in the Constitution* (Oxford University Press, 1999).

[49] Taggart, 'The Nature and Functions of the State', above n. 3, 103.

agencies were almost immediately established to regulate the newly privatized natural monopolies and to encourage competition (in contrast with New Zealand's liberalization practices which explicitly contemplated Hayekian rule by the ordinary common law).[50] Administration became much more rule bound and legalistic, and this included increasingly explicit regulatory control of the (expanding) private sector. The civil service was disaggregated into separate units of policy and delivery and subjected to much more by way of centralized audit and performance measurement and management.

A 'hollowed out' state?

In a well-known article in 1994, Rhodes described these and other phenomena, including the loss of state functions to the EU, as the 'hollowing out of the state'. He described fragmentation, diminished accountability and the erosion of central capacity and discretion. State functions were being depleted, moving sideways or being transferred to the private sector. Rhodes foresaw the potential for catastrophe.[51] Less than ten years later, however, Moran would present a different picture – rejecting 'images of state withdrawal and dissolution of hierarchy' and suggesting instead increased centralization and the colonization of once independent spheres of civil society. The new network governance, he claimed, is dependent on the state, even if the state itself has shifted from command, to surveillance and control. The picture is a complicated one and subject to a variety of interpretations.

Though successive governments of different political hues have brought changes in emphasis and new regulatory experiments, there have not been any *fundamental* changes to the new mixed system of public–private 'governance' since its inception. Everyone seems to agree that regulation has not disappeared but has taken new forms. The re-regulation and risk regulation literature has burgeoned, and so much so that leading public lawyers such as Harlow and Rawlings suggest that regulation and regulatory theory are now at the centre of the

[50] New Zealand's deregulation policies were more thorough-going and longer lasting. The Treasury documents which provided their rationale were much more ideological. A very important difference too was that New Zealand was (and arguably still is) recovering from the trauma of the Muldoon administration and its operation of a truly 'command and control' style economic policy.

[51] R. Rhodes, 'The Hollowing Out of the State: the Changing Nature of the Public Service in Britain', *Political Quarterly* 65 (1994), 138–51.

administrative law discipline.[52] There remains disagreement about whether in fact there is more or less discretion, more or less accountability, more or less 'decentred governance' and more or less club government. Clearly, however, the rumours about the death of the state turn out to be exaggerated. No one responded to terrorism, immigration pressures, global financial crises and the collapse of the banking system with the expectation that these problems could be solved by spontaneous social and legal orders alone.

What is plain is that privatization and liberalization brought two new things: a new state apparatus and more legalistic or, in Teubner's terms, more 'juridified' government.[53] Both factors are significant for our central narrative. Skinner is right to suggest that treating the state as merely the 'apparatus of government' in a Weberian way tends to be normatively 'impoverished'.[54] But those very changes in the government apparatus prompted a new and explicitly *normative* reconsideration of the nature of the state, its authority, its values and its relationship to the citizen. In the remainder of this chapter, I will suggest that, as the state became increasingly juridically defined, what followed was the most serious and relatively self-conscious examination of the state and its nature that British lawyers have undertaken in at least 150 years.

Harlow and Rawlings begin their ground-breaking 1983 work, *Law and Administration*, with the revelation that: 'Behind every theory of administrative law there lies a theory of the state'.[55] This was revelatory for the very reason that lawyers had long ceased to draw connections between law and political science. Of course, given lawyers' general dislike of theory, and the particular contexts in which law is articulated, the resurrection of the inquiry has not been particularly systematic, or coherent, but lawyers have once again begun to ask, as Maitland did, 'who or what is the state?'. Perhaps the most well-known aspect of this has been the debate about the nature of 'public functions'. But the debate has gone much wider than functions, to the nature of authority and

[52] Harlow and Rawlings, *Law and Administration*, 3rd edn, above n. 45, p. 93. See, e.g., E. Fisher, *Risk Regulation and Administrative Constitutionalism* (Oxford: Hart, 2010); M. Power, *The Risk Management of Everything: Rethinking the Politics of Uncertainty* (London: Demos, 2004)

[53] G. Teubner, 'Juridification: Concepts, Aspects, Limits and Solutions', in G. Teubner (ed.), *Juridification of Social Spheres* (New York: Walter de Gruyter, 1987).

[54] Q. Skinner, 'A Genealogy of the Modern State,' *Proceedings of the British Academy* 162 (2009), 325–70, 326.

[55] C. Harlow and R. Rawlings, *Law and Administration*, (London: Butterworths, 1983), p. 1.

hierarchy, the content of public values and the relationship between the citizen and the state.[56] Law and legalistic notions have played a much more central role in these debates than during most of our period. UK devolution and greater integration of the European Union also occurred during this time, reinforcing the need for reconsideration.

Authority and hierarchy

We shall begin with the 'hollowing out' critique and assess whether state capacity has been affected. The most significant development which Rhodes regarded as potentially 'hollowing out of the British state' was the UK's increasing loss of power, discretion and accountability to Europe. This is the hardest aspect of 'hollowing out' to assess and it merits a much fuller treatment than I am able to give it here. The European Union has the characteristics of both a supranational institution and an intergovernmental one and there is a vast literature on whether it is closer to one or the other model. On balance, I argue that while the scope of the UK's sovereignty and functions has undoubtedly been affected, its membership of the EU's institutions has in many respects actually reinforced a centralized and controlling domestic UK state. At the same time, membership of the EU has raised questions that go to the very fundamentals of what it means to be a state and has created a site for self-conscious consideration of what statehood means 'after sovereignty'.

It is hard to imagine what Hayek would have made of the European Union and its institutions. In many ways it is the antithesis of a purposeless, spontaneous, social and legal order. Its aim was to enable European economic integration so that another European war would be inconceivable. It was artificially conceived through an explicit social contract which has been articulated in successive treaties. The UK's very capacity to accede to the Treaty of Rome and to consent to later treaties was fundamentally dependent on the UK's status as a legal person at international law. Treaty making and accession are exercises

[56] See, e.g., M. Loughlin, *The Idea of Public Law* (Oxford University Press, 2003), M. Loughlin, *Foundations of Public Law* (Oxford University Press, 2010); N. W. Barber, *The Constitutional State* (Oxford University Press, 2011), M. Sunkin and S. Payne, *The Nature of the Crown*, (Oxford University Press, 1999); J. A. W. Allison, *The English Historical Constitution: Continuity, Change and European Effects* (Cambridge University Press, 2007).

of statehood according to a traditional hierarchical view of state authority. States still matter in European Union politics.[57] Indeed, Keohane and Hoffman have argued that, without the reversal of French economic policy in 1983 and the British decision to accept the Treaty amendments to institutionalize deregulation, progress on a single internal market would have been impossible.[58]

Other scholars tell the story of European integration and the incremental removal of barriers and deregulation as a much more logical and natural process. European integration has been forged, in part, they suggest, by Jean Monnet's neo-functionalist vision.[59] Integration of particular areas of economic activity has tended to spill over to other areas creating supranational institutions (rather in the way in which the local government and later the state's acquisition of functions in the late nineteenth and early twentieth centuries led to a proliferation of state functions). These scholars tend to describe the process as a natural, spontaneous one, driven from below by interest groups and policy communities with the help of the European Commission.[60] The European Commission, chosen for its technocratic expertise and relatively insulated from politics, has undoubtedly been an important initiator and driver of these EU policies, particularly in relation to the development of a single internal market. Moran suggests that by encouraging numerous sites of subject-specific expertise and different policy communities, the EU Commission may have helped break down the UK's system of club government and reconstituted it in other more contingent and specialist forms.[61]

Emphasizing the importance of technical expertise and policy networks, as many commentators have done, however, tends to underestimate how much the EU continues to operate as an international rather than a supranational organization. While it is true that the UK can and

[57] See, especially, A. Moravcsik, 'Negotiating the Single European Act: National Interests and Conventional Statecraft in the European Community', *International Organization* 45 (1991), 19–55.

[58] R. Keohane and S. Hoffman, 'Conclusions: Community Politics and Institutional Choice', in W. Wallace (ed.), *The Dynamics of European Integration* (London: RIIA, 1990), pp. 276–300, 287.

[59] See M. Holland, *European Community Integration* (London: Pinter, 1993), pp. 7, 8.

[60] See, e.g., C. Barnard, *The Substantive Law of the EU: The Four Freedoms*, 3rd edn, (Oxford University Press, 2010), p. 14 citing E. Haas, *The Uniting of Europe: Political Social and Economic Forces* (Stanford University Press, 1958).

[61] Moran, *The British Regulatory State*, above n. 19, pp. 164–8.

does blame Europe for unpopular policies, the UK is represented 'as the UK' in the Council of the European Union and the European Council. In certain areas, such as tax, external foreign affairs and external immigration, the requirement of unanimity in the Council of the European Union effectively allows the UK a power of veto over EU policies – though admittedly those areas have decreased in number after the Lisbon Treaty. Even then, the UK retains some degree of control through qualified majority voting which is weighted in favour of the more populous member states of the UK, Germany, France and Italy.[62]

Neither of these models, intergovernmental or neo-functionalist, however, fully captures the unique nature of the Union.[63] EU institutions exercise authority through law created centrally through technocratic, directly democratic and indirectly democratic processes.They are implemented and enforced primarily at the Member State level. In many respects this is an archetypal Kelsenian 'law state' – integration has been primarily forged and sustained by law and legal doctrine. It is the EU's judicial body, the European Court of Justice, which has created the legal framework through which to drive European integration.[64] It declared European law to be supreme over national law and national constitutions and to have direct effect, enforceable by individuals in national courts. These rulings long predate any explicit agreement about supremacy in the Treaties themselves (though at accession Member States are taken to have agreed to all the laws of the Community including the rulings of the European Court of Justice (the *acquis communautaire*)).

How much the UK merely implements laws 'made elsewhere' depends on the subject matter, where the policy has originated and the legal form used for its implementation. The UK retains a significant role in steering (if sometimes sharing the rudder) and it also enjoys an important role in rowing (to strain Osborne and Gaebler's overused metaphor). In recent years, the EU institutions have themselves embraced many of the techniques of the 'new governance' in their commitment to the 'open policy of co-ordination' and principles of proportionality and subsidiarity. The principle of subsidiarity, for example, adopted in 1992, requires

62 In numerous areas the Council shares a power of co-decision with the European Parliament.

63 See, e.g., J. Shaw, 'The European Union: Discipline Building Meets Polity Building', in P. Cane and M. Tushnet (eds.), *Oxford Handbook of Legal Studies* (Oxford University Press, 2003), pp. 325–52.

64 E. Stein, 'Lawyers, Judges and the Making of the Transnational Constitution', *American Journal of International Law* 75 (1981), 1–27.

decisions to be taken at the most appropriate level of government.[65] An EU regulation is binding on and directly applicable to the UK. Directives, however, leave room for discretion and flexibility in the form and method of their implementation.[66] A directive might, for example, state a policy objective such as pollution target, but leave scope for the UK (and hence Northern Ireland, Scotland or Wales) to work out the detail of its implementation. Those implementation obligations create incentives on the UK domestically to maintain centralized capacity and control – particularly over devolved and local governments.

Importantly, member states also have the *primary* role in enforcing EU law. Part of the genius of the EU legal system is the way in which the ECJ has effectively co-opted the coercive powers of the national courts – including the UK courts – in order to enforce EU law and its supremacy throughout the Union. Member States may owe compensation to citizens for non-compliance with EU law, including for the actions of their courts.[67] The monopoly on coercive force of the nation state is co-opted in the cause of the supranational one. Relying on the Member State as the primary means of enforcement also creates incentives for the EU to maintain, and sometimes enhance, Member State *capacity.*

The area is so complex, the sites where political will is exercised so numerous and the political temptation to 'blame it on the EU' so great, there is an understandable *perception* of lost capacity. In certain areas the autonomy of the UK has undoubtedly been reduced. Institutional and legal complexity has itself hindered accountability and transparency. Yet, ultimately, the capacity of the EU depends on maintaining and even enhancing the capacity of the Member States. Hence there is a fundamental and dynamic tension between integration, democracy and enforcement.

More than that, the existence of the EU as a phenomenon, has triggered an important debate and reflection about the very nature of sovereignty and statehood and how these concepts relate to law. What makes a state and what are its characteristics?[68] In discussing the prospects for the constitutional unity of the European Union, Lindahl, for example, imagines the problem of unity not simply in relation to those political units that already exist but also in relation to those which may

[65] Article 1 TEU. [66] Art 288 TFEU.

[67] Case C-241/01 *Köbler* v. *Osterreich* [2003] ECR I-10239.

[68] See, e.g., N. Walker (ed.), *Sovereignty in Transition* (Oxford: Hart, 2003); N. Walker and M. Loughlin, *The Paradox of Constitutionalism* (Oxford University Press, 2007), N. MacCormick, *Questioning Sovereignty* (Oxford University Press, 1999).

yet come into being: 'unity cannot be derived from plurality without already presupposing unity'. He suggests:[69]

> [A]ll representations of political unity lead back to a representational act that is not mandated, yet without which no genesis of a polity is possible. Not only does this suggest . . . that there is a core of irreducible groundlessness at the heart of every political community, but also that *no polity is contemporaneous with its own genesis.*

Increasing integration has also brought a renewed inquiry into national identity and the 'essence of statehood'. The German Constitutional Court has been the most forthright in this regard, suggesting that a national constitution forms the basis of a state's identity[70] and that there may be '[e]ssential areas of democratic formative action' in which the EU should not intrude.[71] These kinds of arguments are much harder to turn into a legal question in Britain given the absence of a written constitution and its pronounced constitutional neutrality about the nature of state functions. Laws LJ in *Thoburn* v. *Sunderland City Council*,[72] however, has attempted to create a British constitutional identity against which to judge and possibly resist EU law through the notion of 'constitutional statutes'.

The deepest questions about how the law and the state relate to each other, whether states are spontaneous or artificial or some peculiar mixture of both, are never far away. These are the very same issues which the Idealists, Pluralists and Positivists pondered in relation to the nation state at the beginning of the twentieth century (the subject of Chapter 4). The EU experiment in post-sovereign statehood, and law-led rather than political unity, will likely be seriously tested as the Eurozone continues to be engulfed in a severe economic crisis.

Domestic authority

I move now, somewhat artificially given that the boundaries between domestic and international have become increasingly fluid, to the prophesied 'hollowing out' of state authority in the domestic sphere. What we shall see is that constitutional law has helped *maintain* state capacity against the increasing disaggregation of the public sphere and

[69] H. Lindahl, 'Sovereignty and Representation in the European Union', in N. Walker (ed.), *Sovereignty in Transition* (Oxford: Hart, 2003), pp. 87–114 (italics original).

[70] *Internationale Handelsgesellschaft mbH* v. *Einfuhr – und Vorratstelle für Getreide und Futtermittel* [1974] 2 CMLR 540.

[71] 2 BvE, 2/08, 30 June 2009, paras. 249, 252.

[72] [2003] QB 151.

increasing resort to contract as a means of governance. Power remains reposed in the personified and bodified state. Dyson refers to this as 'constitutional anthropomorphism' and 'the extreme personification of authority at the heart of British government'.[73] Moran suggests that this habit of personification – the tendency for individual ministerial reputation to sit at the centre of British politics – has been a source of resistance to the disaggregation of the state.[74] I shall suggest that the state has been even more personified than he, or Dyson, have, perhaps, fully recognized.

As we have seen, part of the reorganization of central government administration had two potentially contradictory aims – to design incentives to ensure that bureaucrats are more faithful agents of their principals and to maintain a division between policy making and delivery so as to preserve operational matters from political interference. There were a number of techniques used to achieve these objects. Policy was split from operational functions, explicit goal and standard-setting was undertaken, and functions and services were contracted out.

The theories of the firm on which these techniques were based, treated the Minister as the principal and the chief executive as her contractual agent. Fundamental understandings of British constitutional law, however, have proved resistant to these ideas. First the relationship between Ministers and civil servants has never been regarded in law as contractual. Ministers and civil servants are both, technically, servants of the Crown and their relationships with the Crown are governed by the prerogative and are matters of grace and favour. In order to maintain the neutrality and merit-based ethos of the civil service, Ministers are not directly involved in appointment decisions – even for those officials appointed at the highest levels. This might, of course, be a reason to think that the principal–agency problem is likely to be even more acute in British constitutional life than contemplated by the US theorists. Admittedly, the practice of Ministers personally appointing 'special advisors' has become more frequent in recent years and short-term appointments and performance pay has been introduced.[75]

[73] K. H. F. Dyson, *The State Tradition in Western Europe: A Study of the Idea and Institution* (Oxford: Martin Robertson, 1980), p. 210.

[74] Moran, *The British Regulatory State*, above n. 19, p. 181.

[75] New legislation has restricted the powers of special advisors and provided for the creation of a special code of conduct. Constitutional Reform and Governance Act 2010, Section 8.

The constitutional neutrality of the vast majority of these relationships has, however, more or less remained unchanged. In any case, even if the law *had* treated these relationships as contractual, contract law would not have been capable of *empowering* public servants to exercise the powers of government against all the world. The way the common law resolved the issue of empowerment represents another source of resistance to the New Public Management.

The common law constitution had to devise ways in which to confer power on Crown servants. As the bureaucratic hierarchy emerged, it became the legislative practice to vest functions, powers and duties in Ministers or Secretaries of State. Legal fictions operated to ensure flexibility by allowing such functions, powers and duties to be transferred between and shared among the various Secretaries.[76] That, of itself, does not solve the problem of capacity, because Ministers cannot do everything personally. How did British constitutional law adjust to the existence of bureaucracy in so far as *power* was concerned? The *powers* of civil servants to act on behalf of Ministers are also the product of common law constitutional doctrine. The so-called *Carltona* doctrine created a constitutional presumption that the powers of a Minister could be exercised by civil servants unless the statute indicated otherwise.[77] The doctrine served to prevent legal challenges in the numerous cases in which the legislation conferred decision-making powers on the office of the Minister but the Minister personally did not undertake any independent inquiry, have the relevant knowledge or expertise, or even put his mind to the task. There have been various formulations of this doctrine: that it is an exception to a rule against delegation of power; that civil servants are the Minister's *alter ego*;[78] that power is not delegated to civil servants but rather devolved upon them; and that they exercise powers collectively on the Minister's behalf.[79] The effect of the

[76] Ministers of the Crown Act 1975.

[77] See the statements of Lord Greene in *Carltona Ltd* v. *Commissioners of Works* [1943] 2 All ER 560 (CA) at 563

[78] *R* v. *Secretary of State for the Home Department, ex parte Oladehinde* [1991] 1 AC 254, 284 per Lord Donaldson. *Cf.* Lord Rodger asking whether the Prison Governor was acting as the *alter ego* of the Minister or was answerable for his own conduct in *Beggs* v. *Scottish Ministers* [2007] 1 WLR 455, para. 46.

[79] Sedley LJ has attempted to update this by suggesting that it is not necessary to accept the *alter ego* principle. He says that the Minister's 'implied power to delegate functions depended, therefore, on two things: the conferment of a power in terms which explicitly permitted their delegation and the existence of persons to whom he could delegate them

doctrine is that government departments become the *means by which the Crown acts* rather than actors which are separate from the Crown (contractually or otherwise). This is the bureaucratic state personified in order to act.

Powers, then, continue to be, to an important degree, conferred on persons in a hierarchy – and these 'persons' can be comprised of many bodies and minds. Whatever the exact formulation, the agreed *quid pro quo* is that the Minister remains politically responsible to Parliament. As Lord Hope said, in a Scottish case heard by the House of Lords: 'Ministerial responsibility for acts and failures of civil servants cannot be delegated'.[80] If the Minister remains responsible, she has an ongoing incentive to maintain both capacity and control.

These doctrines have had remarkable resilience notwithstanding changes in the organization of the public service, attempts to separate policy from operational responsibilities and the advent of next step agencies.[81] Even though agency heads are now more frequently called publicly to account in Parliament or the media, Ministers remain subject to Parliamentary and media questioning. Of course, in accounting for the conduct of a department or agency, a Minister may attempt to defend her own conduct by suggesting that a matter was operational and outside of her responsibility or direct control, but whether that explanation is viewed as credible or acceptable depends ultimately on public opinion. There are several reasons for this resilience. The 'new governance' did not bring a substantial rethink of the constitution. The statute book has not been rewritten. Formally, legislation still reposes functions, duties and powers primarily on Secretaries of State. 'Next step agencies' are creatures unknown to statute and lack any autonomous legal existence. Most of the techniques of the new public management which seek to disaggregate the state and remove hierarchy continue to rely on internal mechanisms unknown to law.[82] More than that, the courts have supported a 'whole of government'

without parting with ultimate responsibility.' *R (Chief Constable of the West Midlands Police)* v. *Birmingham Justices* [2002] EWHC 1087 (Admin), paras. 9 and 10.

80 *Beggs* v. *Scottish Ministers* [2007] 1 WLR 455, para. 9.

81 Recent political controversies about continuing Ministerial Responsibility for the NHS demonstrate the strength of this Convention.

82 One might have thought that the Constitutional Reform and Governance Act 2010 is an exception. However, it effectively reasserts the constitutional neutrality of the civil service, recognizes the civil service code and restricts the powers of 'special advisors' who *can* be appointed *personally* by Ministers.

approach.[83] In a recent case, Lords Rodger and Mance treated the Secretary of State for the Home Department as creating legitimate expectations which the Secretary of State for Health was also required by law to respect and uphold. Different 'emanations of the Crown' are expected to act consistently with each other – and do not operate in 'separate boxes' but formulate and implement the policies of a single entity.[84]

British constitutional law 'bodifies' the state apparatus for the important purposes of conferring and maintaining its capacity. In doing so, it maintains a hierarchy and creates incentives for the maintenance of political control.[85]

Contract as authority

Of course the Deregulation and Contracting Out Act 1994 set out a procedure by which Ministers and office holders could contract out their statutory functions. Moreover, there has been a general move away from legislation to more contractual forms of governance. This was intended to reflect a more flexible, strategic and enabling state. The shift to contract has allegedly destabilized some of the conventional legal and political ideas about authority and hierarchy. Nevertheless, contractual governance itself turns out to be a highly centralizing form of authority.

Public choice analysis tends to treat contractual relationships as representing individualistic values, choice and formal equality between citizen and state. Contracts are not considered to be coercive, or, at the very least, they do not involve the kind of coercion on which the state has a monopoly. On the other hand, contracts have long held a special place in public law and political theory – often connoting a kind of sovereignty. Treaties were, after all, originally contracts between Princes. Contracts also, as Maitland reminds us, have resonance with the political language and concepts associated with the social contract.[86] And, in H. L. A. Hart's analysis, contracts effectively operate as primary rules constituting 'legislation as between the parties'.[87]

[83] *R (BAPIO Action)* v. *Secretary of State for Home Department* [2008] UKHL 27.
[84] *Ibid.*, per Lord Rodger, paras. 34, 35–6; per Lord Mance, paras. 34–5.
[85] M. Bevir and R. A. W. Rhodes, *The State as Cultural Practice* (Oxford University Press, 2010) supports this analysis at pp. 103 ff.
[86] F. W. Maitland, 'Introduction', in O. Gierke, *Political Theories of the Middle Age* (Cambridge University Press, 1968), p. xxiii (Maitland citing Gierke) (First edition published in 1900).
[87] See pp. 86 ff. above.

Once again, at least where central government is concerned, UK constitutional doctrine constructs a personification of the state that is empowered to enter into contractual arrangements. Ministers have a common law power to enter a contract and in doing so they are able to bind the Crown.[88] When a Minister exercises a common law power to enter a contract, his act will be treated by law as performed by the Crown. The *Town Investments* case on which this doctrine is based is controversial. Lord Morris wrote a spirited dissent objecting to the idea that a 'Minister is or becomes "the Crown"' in relation to all executive acts of government.[89] Lord Morris is understandably worried that such a doctrine could automatically endow a Minister with Crown immunity. It is less concerning when considered as a doctrine which is a consequence of the operation of contract law and of how contract law constructs the person of the state.[90] Every Crown servant, however high or low, escapes *personal* liability in relation to contracts entered into on behalf of the Crown. This is the result of the operation of *contract* law and how it constructs the person of the state, and is not a general proposition which applies to all executive acts. There are other executive acts for which the Minister *could* be held personally liable – as *M* v. *Home Office*[91] later showed – but this does not affect the finding in *Town Investments*. The important point for our immediate purposes is that – whether or not moving to contract has been empowering of citizens – in relation to the central government, contracting reinforces hierarchy and has a centralizing tendency.

Contracting, however, is an exercise of authority and capacity centred in the executive rather than Parliament. Parliament and other mechanisms of democratic accountability tend to be marginalized. When legislation is the source of government duties and obligations, such duties and obligations tend to be generally stated, known to all the world and democratically mandated. By contrast when central government enters a contract, Parliamentary legislation is not always necessary, the agreement only operates between the specified parties,[92]

[88] *Town Investments Ltd* v. *Department of the Environment* [1978] AC 359 (HL).

[89] *Ibid.*, 393.

[90] See, further, J. McLean, 'The Crown in Contract and Administrative Law', *Oxford Journal of Legal Studies* 24 (2004), 129–54.

[91] [1994] 1 AC 377.

[92] This is subject only to the limited exceptions allowed in the Contracts (Rights of Third) Parties Act 1999.

like cases may be treated under different terms, commercial confidentiality may attach and transparency may be lost.

Government by contract attracts some but not all of the indicators of 'hollowing out'. The question of whether the content or substance of contracts actually fetter government and reduce its capacity depends on the nature and content of the contracts themselves and the specifics of the contractual practices. Seddon's studies of the contractual practices of the Australian Federal Government show that standard clauses may be used to protect government capacity.[93] Arguably such terms only make explicit the common law doctrines which would allow governments to invoke executive necessity when they are unable to perform their undertakings for reasons of state. Flexibility can be bargained and paid for.

On the other hand, the long-term nature and consequences of specific agreements relating to some private financing initiatives and public–private partnerships have attracted criticism – effects that are only now being observed. Certainly there is a widely held view that such contracts are not necessarily cheaper or more efficient. Any 'hollowing out' in these instances, however, is not *necessarily* the consequence of the nature of contractual governance itself.

Contracting does, however, decentre the state in more fundamental ways. When the state apparatus uses the private law mechanism of contract is it, in the nature of things, necessarily exercising coercive power? Is it only when the state is exercising coercive power that we seek to hold it to different (and sometimes *higher*) legal standards? Might all instances of contracting when there are inequalities of power be viewed as coercive? Resort to contractual mechanisms provokes a reconsideration of the nature of state power, and the public law values that ought to *constrain* such power. These questions shift us from considering contract as a regulatory technique to more normative issues.

The problem of instrument choice

One important aspect which corporatism and the New Public Management share in common is that they both view law and its relationship to the state as merely an issue of instrument choice. Though their versions of government effectiveness are normatively distinct, both corporatism and public choice are concerned about which legal instruments would be

[93] N. Seddon, *Government Contracts: Federal State and Local*, 3 edn, (Annadale, New South Wales: Federation Press, 2004), p. 36.

the most efficient and effective. It was the administrative lawyers who first reacted to privatization and deregulation policies,[94] and it was they who were first to view the problem as not merely one of instrument choice but rather as one of competing legal and political values.[95] As the state apparatus seemed to have become increasingly fragmented and diffuse, and as the boundary between the public and private spheres was being redrawn, their reaction was to respond with a set of 'public law values' enumerated in forthright terms. The list included:[96]

> openness, fairness, rationality, accountability, participation, independence, transparency, legitimacy, equity and equality.

This was much more in the nature of a normative rather than a descriptive or historical exercise. Many, if not most, of the stated norms had scarcely been articulated in the courts or instantiated in public institutions prior to privatization. For example there were no statutory freedom of information regimes operating in Britain until after 2005,[97] accountability was a word brought into the vocabulary in the context of the New Public Management reforms[98] and open participation was seldom legislatively mandated until after the institution of new governance (unless one considers the Special Act procedures of the nineteenth century as an example). None of this mattered. These and other statements of 'traditional public law values' were, in truth, a deliberate re-articulation of the concept of the public interest in the face of its rejection by public choice ideologues and narrowing by economists. Market freedom and competition, administrative law scholars argued, was never the beginning and end of the public interest.[99]

[94] Taggart, 'The Nature and Functions of the State', above n. 3, p. 106. [95] *Ibid.*, p. 103.

[96] *Ibid.*, drawing on the work of P. McAuslan, 'Public Law and Public Choice', *Modern Law Review* 51 (1988), 681–705; Harlow and Rawlings, *Law and Administration*, 3 edn above n. 45. See also, especially P. Cane, 'Theory and Values in Public Law', in P. Craig and R. Rawlings (eds.), *Law and Administration in Europe* (Oxford University Press, 2003), pp. 3–21.

[97] There had been a code of conduct but this was not given statutory form until the Freedom of Information Act 2000 (UK) and the Freedom of Information (Scotland) Act 2002.

[98] R. Mulgan, *Holding Power to Account* (New York: Palgrave Macmillan, 2003), p. 6 suggests that the term 'accountability' only achieved its current meaning and popularity from the 1980s onwards (having formerly referred to financial oversight) and that it is a term without an obvious equivalent in many other European languages.

[99] M. Aronson, 'A Public Lawyer's Responses to Privatization and Outsourcing', in M. B. Taggart, *The Province of Administrative Law* (Oxford: Hart, 1997), pp. 40–70, 43.

These 'public law norms' would be put to distinct and various uses. For some, there was an urgent sense that public law values and controls were being lost: that bodies formerly held up to public law standards would become self-interested, profit motivated and would no longer serve the common good.[100] For these scholars there seemed to be a shared sense that in the absence of an administratively unified set of state actors, a different kind of unity could be achieved with a set of unifying public values. This was a striking, but understandable, reversal of what had occurred in the middle of the nineteenth century, as bureaucratic hierarchy replaced personal office holding and public law values had fragmented.[101]

A unified and unifying set of public law values might not only substitute for administrative hierarchy but actually be preferred to it. For some public lawyers this was a chance to go even further and for public law values to colonize the private sector bringing new rigour, public spiritedness and accountability than there had been before.[102] For still others, this was an opportunity to identify the values that public and private law shared in common.[103] Some scholars, with perhaps more realistic views of the state of public law *prior* to privatization, suggested that the *new* mechanisms of accountability in a mixed system of instrument choice might add substantially to existing controls and values. In one of its incarnations, this later developed into a re-conception of the social contract in the welfare setting.[104]

The problem for all but the last of these approaches was that at the time of privatization and deregulation whether public or private values applied, at least as far as the courts had been concerned, depended very much on instrument choice. That is, tests of whether the courts should intervene to judicially review particular exercises of power depended on the sources of that power. Though it was not articulated at the time in

[100] See, e.g., P. Craig, 'Public Law and Control Over Private Power', in M. B. Taggart, *The Province of Administrative Law* (Oxford: Hart, 1997) pp. 196–216.

[101] See the discussion in Chapter 2.

[102] J. Freeman, 'The Private Role in Public Governance', *New York University Law Review* 75 (2000), 543–675; J. Freeman, 'The Contracting State', *Florida State University Law Review* 28 (2000), 155–214.

[103] See, e.g., D. Oliver, *Common Values and the Public Private Divide* (London: Butterworths, 1999); H. Collins, *Regulating Contracts* (Oxford University Press, 1999).

[104] See, e.g., Aronson, 'A Public Lawyer's Responses', above n. 99. See further the discussion in P. Vincent-Jones, *The New Public Contracting* (Oxford University Press, 2006), especially at Chapter 9 where he discusses the use of contracts in the welfare context.

these terms, this was a practical consequence of Hart's insight that there was no such thing as the person of the state conceived as a unified *personne morale* but that the state and its emanations were defined by particular areas of law in distinct ways. To put it crudely, at the time of privatization it was only if an authority were exercising a statutory power of decision, as opposed to, for example, a contractual power, that public law norms would apply to its conduct. Values followed instrument choice. Or to put it another way, the state took on different moral properties depending on the legal instrument it chose to pursue its policies. So, for example, administrative law held public authorities to an objective test of rationality (called *Wednesbury* unreasonableness),[105] whereas one of the central assumptions of the classical common law of contract is that a contractual agreement is the product of subjectively rational choices, which courts are loathe to look into or to unravel. Instrument choice effectively defines the legal and moral character of the state and other legal persons.

Of course, as we have seen in Chapter 5, this need not have been the case. Mitchell had attempted to extract from the common law case law a distinct 'public law of contract' conceived along French or even US lines. He viewed the state as 'state in all of its dealings' and saw the possibility that even in its most apparently 'commercial' activities, the state may be pursuing important public policies. Mitchell was particularly worried about maintaining the state's capacity: contractual obligations should not be allowed to fetter state discretion or limit its ability to be effective.[106] But as we have seen, despite Mitchell's efforts, the 'ordinary law conception of the state' was too resilient. The state would be differently defined by different areas of law and private law analogies would be applied as far as possible.

When the common law judges responded directly to the issues of instrument choice arising out of deregulation and privatization, for the first time, they did so in a somewhat faltering way. While it would be wrong and misleading to exaggerate the impact of their responses, at the same time we should not too readily ignore the normative aspirations that are to be found in this common law reaction and what it may tell us about changing common law conceptions of statehood.

105 *Associated Provincial Picture Houses Ltd* v. *Wednesbury Corporation* [1948] 1 KB 223.
106 *Rederiaktiebolaget Amphitrite* [1921] All ER 542.

Procedural exclusivity

The first response was technical and procedural – as is so much of the common law. This was the so-called concept of 'procedural exclusivity' articulated by Lord Diplock in *O'Reilly* v. *Mackman*.[107] The decision in the case was almost certainly *not* explicitly motivated by concerns about the political redrawing of the line between public and private but rather about preserving the procedural protections against legal challenge enjoyed by public authorities (specifically special leave requirements and shorter time limits). It required that a person 'seeking to establish that a decision of a public authority infringed rights to which he was entitled' bring a judicial review claim to the administrative courts first before proceeding by way of an 'ordinary' (private law) action. This had the effect that any potential (and sometimes quite speculative) 'public law' aspects of the cases were identified early and aired fully. In other words, the courts gave themselves the explicit task of determining their own public–private law boundary, and in doing so explicitly prioritized public law analysis over private law analysis. Hence, in the late 1980s and early 1990s, a plethora of cases can be found which seek to determine whether persons and bodies including the Chief Rabbi, the Disciplinary Committee of the Jockey Club, the Football Association, the Advertising Standards Authority, the British Pharmaceutical Industry Association and the Panel of Mergers and Takeovers were sufficiently public in their nature, powers and functions for the claim to proceed by way of judicial review and public law procedures and norms.[108]

These cases raise the questions of 'who' or 'what' is public at a time when many politicians and policy makers were rejecting the very idea of 'inherently public' functions. They sparked a sustained set of arguments from scholars and lawyers that the public nature of a body or activity should not, as had previously been the case, depend on a source of power test.[109] In other words, these lawyers took the view that the legal values that should apply in relation to public bodies and activities should not depend on instrument choice and that *public law* values

[107] [1983] 2 AC 237 (HL).

[108] See M. Hunt, 'Constitutionalism and the Contractualisation of Government', in M. B. Taggart, *The Province of Administrative Law* (Oxford: Hart, 1997), p. 21 and the references therein.

[109] *Ibid.*, p. 36.

should be given priority over other legal values. This looks very close to asking 'what is the state and what are its inherent characteristics?' – the very question which H. L. A. Hart suggested was not susceptible to a legal solution.

The defining decision of this period was the case of *R* v. *Panel on Take-Overs and Mergers, ex parte Datafin plc.*[110] It concerned a challenge to a decision by the Panel which controlled the city markets in a deregulated environment. Members of the Panel were appointed from government and industry. The body was constituted 'without visible means of legal support' being without charter, warrant, Act or statutory instrument. It implemented, but was not bound by, its own rules and there were no formal processes for their amendment. The consequences of its decisions, however, were recognized by statute. The Court of Appeal found it to be subject to judicial review. In 'extending' judicial review in this way,[111] the judges did not outrightly reject source of power tests. Lloyd LJ said: if the source of a body's power were statutory then it would be subject to judicial review; if it were contractual it would not; only if it were somewhere between these two extremes should the judges look at the *nature* of the power that the body exercises. Then the test would consider whether the body were exercising public functions, or if such functions were likely to have public law consequences.[112] All the judges agreed that judicial review should be available in this case, but they also signalled that the level of scrutiny would be minimal.

Reactions to the case were various. For some it represented an important shift away from source of power tests to more functional assessments of state functions.[113] In contrast, Aronson said:[114]

> *Datafin* has failed to dent the common law's refusal to treat contractual power as public power, with the result that contractual power is usually not amenable to the common law of judicial review.

[110] [1987] 1 QB 815 Court of Appeal.

[111] See the discussion of judicial review of the friendly societies discussed in Chapter 5.

[112] In the same case, Lord Donaldson MR, by contrast, was only concerned to exclude from judicial review those bodies whose power was 'solely based on consensual submission' p. 838.

[113] See, e.g., Craig, 'Public Law and Control Over Private Power', above n. 100, p. 196, and Hunt, 'Constitutionalism and the Contractualisation of Government', above n. 108, p. 21.

[114] Aronson, 'A Public Lawyer's Responses to Privatisation and Outsourcing', above n. 99, pp. 40, 46.

With hindsight we can see that Aronson had the better argument on the specifics. While it is certainly now the case that exercises of the prerogative power can be the subject of judicial review, contractual sources of power still largely remain outside its scope. In the commercial cases that have followed *Datafin*, source of power tests have continued to be applied and it is only when these do not provide clear answers that functional tests have even been entertained.[115] A series of cases, for example, decided that Lloyds of London was not amenable to review. Despite the fact that its corporate arrangements were the product of private Acts of Parliament, its decisions have been treated as the working out of private contractual arrangements.[116] These cases and their results demonstrate another set of paradoxes in relation to what 'deregulation and liberalization' actually effected. None of the judicial review cases during this era got even close to challenging central government's own decisions or activities in contracting out former governmental services or duties. Instead they raised questions about the extent to which different kinds of government sponsored self-regulation should be supervised by the courts. This would seem to support Moran's contention that government has extended its surveillance into previously insulated areas of civil society. If that is so then, rather than controlling central government, the judicial review courts have added their own mechanisms of surveillance over 'club government' to those of central government. It is also true, at least in the case of the courts, that surveillance has largely been minimal and ineffective – and merely lent constitutional legitimacy to such government sponsored self-regulation. It has been the auditors (financial and otherwise) not the courts, who have been the primary agents of 'external' control.[117] After the collapse of many financial institutions it is hard to be as comfortable as Moran was in 2002 about the degree to which central government control by way of auditing mechanisms has broken down club government either.

115 E.g., *R (Beer)* v. *Hampshire Farmers' Market* [2004] 1 WLR 233, para. 16; *Re Wylie's Application for Judicial Review* [2005] NI 359. The Judicial Committee of the Privy Council (in an appeal from New Zealand) was prepared to treat a commercial contract as per se reviewable but restricted the substantive basis of review so dramatically that the decision effectively quelled further challenges (see *Mercury Energy* v. *Electricity Corporation* [1994] 1 WLR, 521).

116 *R (on the application of West)* v. *Lloyds of London* [2004] EWCA 506 (civ).

117 Harlow and Rawlings, *Law and Administration*, 3rd edn above n. 45, p. 59.

From source of power to function?

Looking beyond the judicial review case law, however, we are able to discern a more significant trend after the *Datafin* decision towards more functional tests of public-ness across a range of public law and regulatory instruments. 'Public function' type tests, in their various case law and statutory incarnations, have achieved wide currency in the United Kingdom where they now inform (at least in part) freedom of information jurisdiction,[118] aspects of European Union law[119] and the scope of the application of the Human Rights Act 1998.[120] This reliance on the notion of 'public function' is striking given that the widespread restructuring of public sector seemed to signify the victory of an ideology that denied the very existence of 'inherently' public functions and viewed all human activity as the exercise of private preferences.

The idea that certain, even commercial, activities are inherently public and should be treated according to public law norms has a variety of sources. One source is EU law and the concept of 'services of general economic interest'. While EU law is formally neutral as between publicly and privately owned undertakings, and seeks to enforce competitive equality between them, it also recognizes that Member States may properly impose public service obligations on certain undertakings which provide 'services of general economic interest'[121] and (more recently) on non-market services of a general interest. The provisions were originally part of a compromise between the Benelux countries (whose industries were mainly privately owned) and France and Italy whose public sectors were large and likely to enjoy a competitive advantage.[122] The concept of services of 'general economic interest' was deliberately chosen to be wider than that of the French administrative law idea of 'service

118 Under Section 5(2)(a) Freedom of Information (Scotland) 2002, e.g., Scottish Ministers can make a designation order for organizations that appear to exercise functions of a public nature or provide under contract made with a Scottish public authority, any service whose provision is a function of that authority.

119 E.g., rules about state aid and environmental information reporting, and the scope of horizontal direct effect of directives.

120 Section 6 Human Rights Act (UK).

121 The Commission has more recently recognized non-market services of a general interest. See P. Craig and G. De Búrca, *EU Law: Text, Cases and Materials*, 5th edn (Oxford University Press, 2011), p. 1073.

122 For the earlier history, see A. Page, 'Member States, Public Undertakings and Article 90', *European Law Review* 7 (1982), 19–35, 20.

public'[123] and it was originally left to Member States to define the concept for themselves.[124] Such obligations have included territorial coverage, universal access especially for those with special needs, security of service and quality of supply, and environmental protection. If Member States comply with certain conditions when granting subsidies to off-set the cost of these obligations, such payments are not treated as state aid.[125] What is striking about these rules is that they attained a new importance and complexion only *after* many public services had been privatized. Then, as one Commission document suggested, 'in spite of the positive effects of liberalization' they became a mechanism for 'meeting concerns about the quality of services'. Some version of these ideas can be found in the UK domestic idea of the Citizens' Charter.[126] The responsiveness of such undertakings to social values has come to be regarded (by the Commission at least) as an essential element of European citizenship.[127] This is still the citizen understood as consumer but substantially remade from the 'economic man' of public choice theory. These concepts also have the potential to serve as conduits for the creation of public services law in the British common law. Transparent subsidization decisions and decisions about which services should be contracted *for* offer opportunities for more self-conscious appraisals of what government ought to be doing.[128]

The idea of inherently public functions has its most prominent incarnation in the Human Rights Act 1998. In that case it has been possible to argue that the statutory public function test was deliberately chosen as a potential counterweight to privatization policies and a judicial means to regulate 'government' as constituted in its new post-privatization forms. The clearest evidence can be found in the UK White Paper that preceded the Human Rights Act 1998. The White Paper explains that the

[123] *Ibid.*, 28.

[124] See Official Journal of the European Communities 2001 C 17/13, 1996 communication

[125] Craig and de Búrca, *EU Law*, above n. 121, p. 1074.

[126] White Paper, The Citizens' Charter: Raising the Standard, Cm 1599 (1991).

[127] Communication from Commission, White Paper on Services of General Interest, COM (2004) 374 and see T. Prosser, *The Limits of Competition Law, Markets and Public Services* (Oxford University Press, 2005), p. 172, and M. Freedland and S. Sciarra (eds.), *Public Services and Citizenship in European Law: Public and Labour Law Perspectives* (Oxford: Clarendon Press, 1998), discussed in Harlow and Rawlings, *Law and Administration*, 3 edn, above n. 45, p. 59.

[128] It is European law too that is the source of the environmental information regulations, which also refer to public function tests.

definition of what constitutes a public authority is in deliberately wide terms and includes within its scope:[129]

> to the extent that they are exercising public functions, companies responsible for areas of activity which were previously within the public sector, such as privatized utilities.

There is a sense here, so it has been argued,[130] that despite radical institutional changes, the political decisions of an earlier era about what should be regarded as 'public' should somehow prevail.

An earlier text on which much of the UK Human Rights Act 1998 was modelled (including its application provisions)[131] is the New Zealand Bill of Rights Act 1990. The 1985 background paper to the New Zealand Act also supports the idea that there was an intention that human rights norms should sometimes extend into the private sphere (though that document predated privatization in New Zealand).[132] It references a number of well-known US state action doctrine cases and suggests that what these examples have in common is that 'the action can be seen as having a public character in some substantive sense even though the actor is not a public body'.[133] Is there an intention then that public law norms should apply to 'private' bodies?

In terms of this narrow exposition of the legislative history then, it is possible to mount an argument that public function tests were 'intended' to fill a regulatory gap left by privatization policies (at least where human rights were concerned). Given the timing, the case is stronger in relation to the United Kingdom than New Zealand. Of course, that cannot be the end of the matter. Parliament speaks with a forked tongue. It is also possible to argue that the liberal and state-limiting values contained in Bill of Rights and the values that spawned economic liberalization shared a great deal in

[129] Rights Brought Home: The Human Rights Bill, cm 3782 24 October 1997, para. 2.2. See also the speeches by the Home Secretary, HC Deb, 16 February 1998, col 773; 17 June 1998, cols 409–410.

[130] See Lord Bingham (dissenting) in *YL* v. *Birmingham City Council* [2007] UKHL 27, para. 20.

[131] The proposed Section 2 (eventually enacted as Section 3) stated: 'This Bill of Rights guarantees the rights and freedoms contained in it against acts done by the legislative, executive, or judicial branches of the government of New Zealand; or in the performance of any *public function*, power or duty conferred or imposed on any person or body by or pursuant to law' (my emphasis).

[132] A Bill of Rights For New Zealand: a White Paper 1985 A6.

[133] *Ibid.*, 70.

common.[134] At the same time as it was enacting the Human Rights Act 1998, Parliament was passing legislation (and executive government was taking executive action) restructuring, privatizing and contracting out various matters.

Unsurprisingly given this provenance, the application of the 'public function' tests here too has been highly problematic.[135] The Human Rights Act 1998 is a subject that will be given extended treatment in the next chapter. For now it is sufficient to say that one important challenge to the idea that the state can be defined by instrument choice alone is the idea of inherently public functions and that this idea only proliferated *after* the privatization and liberalization policies of the 1980s.

Convergence of legal persons – a unified public law?

Alongside attempts to enforce procedural exclusivity (making public law norms prior to private law norms) and the development of 'functional' rather than 'source of power tests' (privileging normative standards over instrument choice), there is another new and emerging approach to publicness, though one still very much in its infancy. In Chapter 7, we saw that tort law and judicial review law treat government wrong-doing and liability differently. As we shall see in the next chapter, human rights law treats government wrong-doing differently again, as does European Union law. This is simply a consequence of the fact that the state does not exist as a single moral and legal person, but that its rights and liabilities are separately defined by different areas of law. In recent years, however, there has been a new impatience about these apparently arbitrary differences, and a newly expressed desire for a distinct public law to apply to the government as a distinct legal and moral person. Davies, for example, has raised the prospect of a separate 'public law of contract' emerging out of the particular circumstances of government contracting.[136] The Law Commission of England and Wales has recommended that a distinct scheme for public law redress should be created for cases involving activities and bodies which it defines as 'truly public' or

[134] R. Hirschl, 'The Political Origins of the New Constitutionalism', *Indiana Journal of Global Legal Studies* 11 (2004), 71–108, 105.

[135] The designation provisions under the Freedom of Information Acts have also proved problematic and reliance on case law has hampered their operation as a political tool.

[136] Harlow and Rawlings, *Law and Administration*, 3rd edn above n. 45, p. 210 and A. C. L. Davies, *Accountability: A Public Law Analysis of Government by Contract* (Oxford University Press, 2001), p. 185.

'governmental'.[137] Such a scheme would allow monetary damages for public law wrongs for the first time and combine elements of judicial review and the ordinary law of tort. It would also align these remedies with public law remedies available under European Union Law and the European Convention on Human Rights. There has been some judicial support for the Law Commission's suggestions, and doubts expressed about the capacity of the common law to reconcile and consolidate these different elements of administrative redress in the absence of direct legislative reform.[138] And notwithstanding that the UK government effectively halted any further Law Commission work on the issue, the pressures to create a more coherent schema for government redress are unlikely to go away. The legal qualities of the state as a person are squarely the subject of legal consideration in an unprecedented way.

Summary

Hayek's vision of statehood rejected the central assumptions and commitments of the public interest politics of the first half of the twentieth century. Public choice theory and the institutional economics that informed privatization, government restructuring and economic liberalization shared many of Hayek's central commitments. The main reason that these policies were so easy to effect in the UK was not that the UK had no conception of the state, but that the legal framework designed for the 'public interest' state presented few barriers to the introduction of the new state apparatus. Ironically, that new apparatus was no longer to be trusted to pursue the public interest (as public choice theory asserted).

What has resulted is a much more juridified state and many more legal rules that attempt to define 'publicness' in normative terms. The common law has been the source of ideological, if often practically ineffectual, resistance to many of the challenges wrought by privatization and liberalization.

Ironically, and almost certainly unintentionally, what emerges in the UK after privatization is a legal system which much more closely resembles the US system which was the subject of the public choice critique in

[137] Law Commission for England and Wales, Administrative Redress: Public Bodies and the Citizen (Consultation Paper 187) (London: Stationery Office, 2008); Law Commission for England and Wales, Administrative Redress: Public Bodies and the Citizen, Law Com 322 (London: Stationery Office, 2010).

[138] *Home Office* v. *Mohammed* [2011] EWCA Civ 351, per Sedley LJ.

the first place. The remaining element of the US legal structure (and Hayek's account of the limited state) missing from the UK, is full-scale constitutional rights protection. The earlier UK corporatist model of the state did not admit of the law being used against the state: the state after all *was* the people. It was not a competitive but a co-operative model of governance. But the process of bringing law more centre stage and the new distrust of state as a reliable protector of individual liberty and choice makes constitutional rights protection against the state much more politically possible and important. The state, no longer 'us', is now 'the problem'. In the next chapter we investigate the new state 'that can do wrong'.

9

Rights against the state

> The explanation for why the UK promoted and ratified the [European] Convention [on Human Rights] must not be sought in the history of English Constitutional thought, but in the general political history of the period.[1]

> [The] state did not exist except for foreigners.[2]

Rights against the state

The earlier UK corporatist model of the state did not admit of the law being used against the state: the state after all *was* the people. As we saw in the previous chapter, however, privatization brought with it a much more juridified version of the state and a new distrust of the state's reliability as a protector of rights and individual choice. I turn in this chapter to another element of Hayek's prospectus for a limited state – constitutional rights protection. In the UK this took the form of the Human Rights Act 1998. It *appears* to reorient the relationship between the British state and citizens. This newly limited constitutionalized state can now 'do wrong' to individuals. It is no longer benign and representative of the 'public': the state is now the 'problem'. The state *qua* state in all its activities owes duties to individuals *qua* individuals. The Human Rights Act is undoubtedly significant. Despite appearances, however, the legal and political controversies surrounding the Human Rights Act and its operation reflect and replicate many of competing versions of the state and its relationship to law that we have already encountered. The Human Rights Act has been interpreted not only as limiting the state's

1 A. W. B. Simpson, *Human Rights and the End of Empire: Britain and the Genesis of the European Convention* (Oxford University Press, 2004), p. 10.

2 W. R. Sorley, *The International Crisis: The Theory of the State* (Oxford University Press, 1916), quoted by M. Francis, 'Nineteenth Century Theories of Sovereignty and Thomas Hobbes', *History of Political Thought* I (1980), 517–40, 519.

powers over individuals, but as having *positive* obligations to the people to protect their rights. Many of these duties are treated as imperfect – owed to the public at large rather than to individuals. The state, then, is conceived both as a potential threat to the individual and as the means of protecting rights at large. It is not wholly diminished.

In this chapter, I consider the extent to which the Human Rights Act represents continuity and change. In the second part of the chapter, I turn to the question of how the Human Rights Act requires the legal identification of the state itself for the purposes of applying its protections and constraints. This raises issues we have encountered earlier about the relationship between the state and other forms of civil society, the extent to which the question of whether something is or is not a part of the state is susceptible to a binary decision, how we view authority and whether common law constitutionalism still has a place in the new human rights framework.

Origins and traditions

Whether and how citizens are able to hold rights against the state has been the subject of various distinct strands of British legal thought. The most resilient has been the British constitutional narrative of rights and liberties protected by the common law against individual officials. As a 1946 colonial office document suggested, in Burkean tones, other countries might rely on theoretical guarantees of citizens' rights against the state, but the British way is to prefer their 'actual embodiment in a system of law by the provision of practical and effective remedies'.[3] In the Victorian era, one of the most important practical consequences of this idea was that legislative power was needed in order to do anything that would otherwise be unlawful. Not only was that the rationale for a great proportion of Parliament's legislative activity, the limits of statutorily conferred power would be judicially enforced by way of the *ultra vires* doctrine and the operation of the ordinary law against officials who had acted outside of the powers conferred on them.[4] Such strategies for holding power to account could even survive the onslaught of Austin's

[3] Paper to Commission of Human Rights 1946, discussed in Simpson, *Human Rights*, above n. 1, pp. 49–50.

[4] In modern times, a version of this approach takes the form of the 'principle of legality' which is used to control broad conferrals of power: if Parliament intends to limit rights, it must do so explicitly and not by implication.

version of a sovereign undefined or limited by law. If the sovereign as a determinate body is considered to be above the law, component parts of the sovereign body are able to be so defined and limited. According to this narrative, rights are typically held against officials as individuals rather than against the state *qua* state.[5] There is no state here, only 'the citizen in uniform' either acting inside or outside his official role.[6] As we saw in Chapter 7, the common law had long been engaged in developing strategies by which to hold governments to law without having to confront the sovereignty problem directly. None of these common law strategies, however, openly conceded that individuals are able to assert legal rights directly against the state in respect of its 'wrongs'.

This was undoubtedly the dominant narrative about rights leading up to World War II. There were, however, other significant debates about rights in the late nineteenth and early twentieth centuries. Maine, writing about the 1867 extension of the franchise, flirted with the idea that some kind of formal Bill of Rights protection might just about make democracy 'tolerable'.[7] Dicey also appeared to have some degree of sympathy for this view.[8] For the most part, however, the idea of formal declarations of rights was antithetical to public lawyers of all political persuasions. That was not because they were necessarily sanguine about possible threats to rights. Dicey, in the late nineteenth century, identified collectivities (and not just the state per se) as posing a threat to the individual. Laski, by contrast, would argue that groups should enjoy rights against the state and by that means the individual would be protected.[9] The early administrative lawyers, such as Robson and Jennings, shared with Laski the view that rights are socially conceived and rejected Diceyan constitutionalism and its associated individualism. They tended to be sceptical about individual rights which they associated with common law, laissez-faire values. For them, individual rights had to

[5] The exception is contract law where an official could not be sued for the contract.

[6] The expression 'citizen in uniform' is from G. Samuel, '"Public and Private Law": A Private Lawyer's Response', *Modern Law Review* 46 (1983), 558–83.

[7] H. S. Maine, *Popular Government* (New York: Henry Holt, 1886), p. 110 complimenting the American system, and cautioning Englishmen to consider what kind of constitution they trust to limit powers.

[8] See discussion in Chapter 2.

[9] Interestingly, S. A. De Smith notes in 'Fundamental Rights in the New Commonwealth (1)', *International and Comparative Law Quarterly* 10 (1961), 83–102, 93 that the reservation of seats in representative assemblies for members of a particular community in, e.g., New Zealand, Fiji, Kenya, Uganda and Nyasaland, was the most characteristic safeguard of rights in British dependent territories.

be for the common good or be suppressed. But they also wanted 'larger rights' than the common law appeared to offer. By providing such 'larger rights', Robson and Jennings believed the state could become an instrument of progress that would ultimately enhance the individual as well as the common good. This project was partially achieved as the law of negligence expanded and judicial review recognized a wider range of interests than the common law had previously.

In hindsight, Laski's and Robson's view that rights should be suppressed for the common good would seem reckless. Laski's interest in protecting individuals from the state – which motivated his early work on Pluralism – appeared to wane as the decades passed. By 1941, Laski is rather too complacently defending the British government's record of protecting civil liberties during a time of 'Total War' and despite the widespread British practice of detention without trial. He congratulates Parliament and the government for their restraint, simultaneously extolling the virtues of a planned economy. In so doing he defines freedom 'as a social freedom in which the individual is end as well as means'.[10] Robson's trust in the 'judicial character' of civil servants also looks naïve from this historical distance. He had earlier described Sir John Anderson as one of the members of the Committee on Ministers Powers 'from whom progressive ideals might reasonably be expected'.[11] As a result of Simpson's investigation of the archives,[12] we now know the extent to which the administration in general, and Sir John Anderson in particular, exhibited a cavalier attitude towards law, legal process and the liberty of individuals during World War II.

The horrors of World War II would change everything – if not in relation to the British domestic legal position at least in relation to the notion of sovereign right. After World War II, the concept of 'human rights' entered the mainstream legal and political vocabulary for the first time.[13] With the idea of human rights came a rejection of the traditional view in international law that states are absolutely sovereign in the treatment of their subjects within their own territories. The new 'human

[10] H. J. Laski, 'Civil Liberties in Great Britain in Wartime', *Bill of Rights Review* 2 (1941–2), 243–51, 250.

[11] See W. A. Robson, 'The Report of the Committee on Ministers' Powers', *The Political Quarterly* 3 (1932), 346–64, 350.

[12] A. W. B. Simpson, *In the Highest Degree Odious: Detention Without Trial in Wartime Britain* (Oxford University Press, 1992).

[13] See Simpson, *Human Rights*, above n. 1, p. 10. The history of the idea of human rights itself within political thought is beyond the scope of this chapter.

rights' rhetoric conceived of sovereign states as having the capacity to 'do wrong': states are 'the problem'. The Universal Declaration of Human Rights and associated covenants, and the European Convention on Human Rights (ECHR) (all initiatives in which the UK took a major lead) would affirm basic human rights that an individual (theoretically at least) enjoys against the state *qua* state.

Of these instruments it would be the ECHR which was the most legally robust: it took the form of a multilateral treaty, imposed obligations on state parties, and included permanent institutional arrangements to give it teeth. But, as Simpson has explained, the ECHR (which came into force in 1953) 'was a product of British foreign policy, not of the British legal tradition, much less of British domestic policy ... The explanation for why the UK promoted and ratified the Convention must not be sought in the history of English constitutional thought, but in the general political history of the period'.[14]

If, at its inception, the ECHR was foreign to British legal thought, how has the British legal tradition adjusted to its ratification and later incorporation? How does the ECHR system, which starts with the premise that the state is the 'problem', sit alongside a common law system which has as its starting premise that the 'King can do no wrong'? Equally, how can the individual rights-centric approach of the ECHR sit alongside English public law (which has been focused on public wrongdoing and the common good and not so much on individuals)? Given that the ECHR was never the product of the British legal tradition, how would it be 'incorporated' and how would it affect how 'rights' and 'the state' are perceived in UK domestic law? How much does the ECHR system introduce a new conception of the relation between citizen (and often non-citizen) and the state?

A state for foreigners

We need to start, then, with international law and the international thought out of which the Human Rights Act 1998 eventually emerged. It might be tempting to tell this as a straightforward story of law's struggles to adjust from absolutist to more limited conceptions of sovereignty. The sovereignty debate does have a role to play here but it

[14] *Ibid.* p. 18.

is not a straightforward one. The international and domestic legal debates need to be considered separately.

The story of how sovereignty was reconsidered in international law in the nineteenth and twentieth centuries is a complex and rich one about which I can offer only the briefest sketch. The conflicting strands of Positivism and Idealism played an important role in the international law debates, as they had domestically.[15] Austinian Positivism defined sovereignty in terms of state effectiveness: a state's sovereignty was evidenced by the fact that its people were in habitual obedience and that other states recognized it as sovereign. This is not statehood defined by limiting legal rules, but rather by political fact. This view was adopted by influential British international lawyers such as John Westlake.[16] The other important school of thought in the nineteenth century was the Idealist historical school. It considered the state to be the product of the history, culture and ideology of a people – all of which constituted an expression of its sovereign will. Standards of lawful conduct could not, therefore, be imposed from outside the state but could only be generated from within the state itself as part of its national culture.[17] International law (and particularly customary law) was, accordingly, a projection of national will. While both schools allowed the possibility of sovereign self-restraint, neither of these schools of thought allowed much prospect for a notion of sovereignty defined and limited by legal rules – let alone a sovereignty limited in respect of the human rights of individuals.

It was Kelsen, and his student Lauterpacht, who provided the most robust reaction to both schools of thought in the first half the twentieth century. For them sovereignty was only a bundle of rights and powers accorded to the state by the legal order. Both resisted any suggestion that the state ought to occupy a higher moral sphere than other forms of human organization – a dangerous idea particularly associated with German Idealism at the time. It was this particular strand of Positivism that would allow sovereignty to be limited and, ultimately, remake international law. Lauterpacht emphasized the treaty-making powers of

[15] See Chapter 3 for their role in relation to domestic debates.

[16] Austin was, surprisingly, adopted by international lawyers despite what he had to say directly about international law itself. Westlake describes it thus: 'we are fortunately able to retain most of the fruits of [Austin's] labour, unaffected by the doubt that has arisen about [Austin's definition of law]', J. Westlake, *The Collected Papers of John Westlake an International Law* L. Oppenheim (ed.) (Cambridge University Press, 1910), p. xxi.

[17] A. Carty, *The Decay of International Law?: A Reappraisal of the Limit of Legal Imagination in International Affairs* (Manchester University Press, 1986), p. 28.

states and analogized these to the ordinary contractual and self-binding powers of individuals. He also argued that individuals should be recognized as potential subjects in international law. After 1945, a pragmatic and functionalist mood took hold and international lawyers got on with the project of limiting states by treaties without protracted navel gazing about the nature of sovereignty. It was during this period, and the urgent circumstances post World War II, that the human rights treaties, including the ECHR, were agreed. The ECHR was ground-breaking in that it purported directly to limit the state and gave individuals the right to enforce rights directly against the state. This, as we have seen in previous chapters, was long before that was the case in the domestic common law of the UK.

Kelsen and Lauterpacht were attempting to escape some of the worst consequences of personifying the state, such as the idea that the state enjoys subjective right unlimited by external legal constraints. They were, however, unable to avoid personifications of the state altogether: the state was and remains the fundamental legal subject of international law.[18] International law treats the state as a single, unified legal personality. This has had a number of consequences for domestic law generally and for the domestic application of the ECHR in particular.

Both Kelsen and the earlier Idealist school of international law scholars had created sophisticated theories to address the question of the proper role domestic legal orders should play in the international legal order, as had much earlier international law scholars such as Vattel.[19] Kelsen, for example, rejected Anzilolli's view that the state enjoys different legal personalities in domestic as opposed to international law and offered instead a hierarchy of legal norms unified by the *grundnorm*.[20] The general doctrinal approach of international law in a new age of treaty making was, however, that domestic law,

[18] The issue of the role that legal personality plays in international law remains controversial today. Responding to a more pragmatic and functional approach to issues of legal personality, Colin Warbrick, for example, suggests that it is the general qualities of legal personality of states at international law which gives the concept of legal personality its meaning and value. States should have rights that derive from their status. See M. Evans (ed.), *International Law* (Oxford University Press, 2003), p. 219.

[19] E. Vattel, *The Law of Nations, or, Principles of the Law of Nature Applied to the Conduct and Affairs of Nations and Sovereigns* J. Chitty (tr.) (London: Sweet, 1834), pp. 8, 14 emphasizes the representative nature of the monarch and its connection through the constitution to the body politic.

[20] See, generally, H. Kelsen, *General Theory of Law and State*, A. Wedberg (tr.) (Cambridge, MA: Harvard University Press, 1949), p. 377.

especially constitutional law, scarcely had a role to play in the international legal order. International law should be binding on the state *qua* state whatever its domestic constitutional arrangements. The broader institutional concerns motivating this approach are obvious. A state should not be able to escape its international commitments by reference to its federal arrangements, the separation of powers or its internal constitutional restrictions on state powers to enter such international agreements. The variability of domestic public law should not be allowed to undermine the universalist project of international law. Westlake puts it starkly in nineteenth-century language: it is 'irrelevant to international law, as to where in any political body the Austinian sovereignty lies'.[21]

Precisely where the domestic constitution located sovereignty, however, did create problems for the domestic applicability of international obligations. The sovereignty questions for Britain can be stated in this way: how is domestic constitutional law, which locates sovereignty in the Queen in Parliament, to be reconciled with international law which recognizes the UK as a sovereign state with the capacity to enter treaties through its accredited diplomatic representatives (effectively the Queen's representatives exercising pre-Act of Settlement prerogative powers to enter treaties without Parliamentary authorization). British law solved this through the doctrine of dualism. This was to the effect that while treaty law is binding at international law, it must be incorporated into domestic legislation before it is able to affect domestic law. This was a nineteenth-century response to the problem of reconciling domestic and international sovereignty concepts.

Thus the British ratified the ECHR in 1953 and in 1966 acceded to the optional protocol giving individuals a right to petition the Strasbourg Court, but did not incorporate these commitments into domestic law. They confidently did so in the belief that they were giving rights to the rest of Europe and that everything would proceed as usual at home. These undertakings were binding in international law, but did not alter the UK's domestic constitutional law. Much to Britain's surprise and chagrin, however, soon after its accession to the optional protocol, successful petitions were brought against it to the Strasbourg Court.[22] Britain was found wanting. On these occasions there was no prior

[21] Westlake, *Collected Papers*, above n. 16, p. xxiii.

[22] E.g., *Golder* v. *UK* [1975] 1 EHRR 524 involving prison discipline.

opportunity for the British courts to consider whether the government had breached rights under the Convention.

The ECHR was not incorporated into domestic UK law until the Human Rights Act 1998 and the statutes giving effect to the devolution settlements for Wales, Northern Ireland and Scotland, made in the same year. In a very important sense, incorporation at that time should be seen as an *exercise* of domestic sovereignty. Bringing Rights Back Home, as the White Paper introducing the Human Rights Act was entitled, meant that the domestic British judges would now be the first to consider whether there had been a breach of the Convention rights by the British government rather than have an international court make the first pronouncement. This was a kind of repatriation and the expression of a 'sovereigntist impulse'. British judges, it was thought, would be more likely to understand the British political context and legal tradition, and, if necessary, be in a position to explain this to the Strasbourg Court. At the same time, the devolution arrangements denied the newly devolved legislatures and governments the *capacity* to make law inconsistent with the ECHR or the EU Treaties. This was the logical consequence of the fact that it is the UK as a whole which is bound by those commitments at international law. Such constraints maintain an important element of UK control over the devolved governments and parliaments.

The enactment of a constitutional Bill of Rights in the UK, then, does not fit squarely with Hirschl's theory that the widespread adoption of Bills of Rights in the 1990s was prompted by a neo-Liberal agenda informed by a Hayekian analysis. 'Economic elites', he suggests, were concerned to confine the 'boundaries of the state through constitutionalization'.[23] While it is it is still conceivable that some of the support for the measure came from sectors sympathetic to such ideas, that was not the principal motivation and neither, as we shall see, is that necessarily how the Human Rights Act has operated in practice.

Domesticating the ECHR: continuity and change

Continuity

According to its preamble, the Human Rights Act 1998 is an Act 'to give *further* effect to rights and freedoms guaranteed under the European

[23] R. Hirchl, *Towards Juristocracy: The Origins and Consequences of the New Constitutionalism* (Cambridge, MA: Harvard University Press, 2004), p. 212.

Convention on Human Rights' (emphasis added). In what ways is it continuous with the British public law tradition that we investigated in Chapter 7 and how much does it alter earlier understandings?

The obvious way in which the UK Human Rights Act 1998 has been made a part of the British constitutional tradition is that it preserves Parliamentary sovereignty. The judge's role is to interpret legislation consistently with the Human Rights Act and not to invalidate it. The UK Parliament ultimately is *able* to enact valid laws which are incompatible with the ECHR.

The way that these rules operate in practice also reflects older constitutional traditions. At the introduction of the Act, Lord Irving predicted that the primary remedy for the individual would be by way of Section 3 which requires a court to interpret legislation consistently with the Convention to give effect to rights for the individual claimant (effectively determining the scope of government power consistently with a rights respecting approach). This interpretative approach to limiting power is part of a recognizable British constitutional tradition, even if the proper bounds of interpretation have been dramatically extended by the application of the Human Rights Act. If such an interpretation is not possible without doing violence to the impugned Act (now a much higher threshold than formerly) the court, in its discretion, may make a declaration of incompatibility.[24] A declaration does not have the effect of invalidating the statute but triggers a procedure by which Ministers may at their discretion fast track amendments to redraw the statute to remove the incompatibility.[25]

Once a declaration has been granted, the focus is on the architecture of power, as much as on the individual.[26] At the Bill's introduction, it was not contemplated that the declaration procedure would be frequently used. An interpretative approach was to be preferred given that it allows an individual a more individualized remedy. A declaration is remedial in the sense that it explicates and thereby vindicates rights for all the world, but it does not change the effect of the law on the aggrieved individual. As it has transpired, however, judges have granted declarations more frequently than was originally predicted. They have even allowed claimants to bring free-standing declaration of incompatibility challenges, and do not require an action for a declaration to be attached

[24] Section 4 Human Rights Act 1998. [25] Section 10 Human Rights Act 1998.

[26] I owe the architecture metaphor to Kim Scheppele.

to a claim for a more individualized remedy.[27] In these respects the operation of the Human Rights Act, like judicial review, does not *necessarily* place the individual at the centre of the cause of action.[28] In these cases, the focus, as in judicial review, is on the proper extent of government power rather than on the individual.

Some have objected that declarations of incompatibility are not sufficiently focused on the rights of the individual and do not necessarily reward an individual for bringing an action with an individualized remedy.[29] The Strasbourg court appears to support this view: it does not consider the declaration even to constitute a remedy (at least for the purpose of requiring that a claimant exhaust her domestic remedies before bringing a claim to the European Court at Strasbourg). Old habits die hard. The UK domesticated version of the ECHR seems to have been at least, if not more, concerned with the architecture of power as with granting individuals rights against the state – especially where the terrorism cases have been concerned.

Not only have there been more declarations than was originally contemplated but when declarations have been granted, in all but one controversial case (the consequences of which are still ongoing),[30] the government has *voluntarily* taken action to change the law to make it more rights compliant. The remedy is effective not because the government or Parliament is coerced but because it voluntarily obeys – Jennings's 'new' version of the rule of law.[31] We can see new conventional understandings developing about the nature of constitutional propriety. As with their earlier manifestations, the operation of such proprieties does not depend on where the legal power ultimately resides. Parliamentary sovereignty, by itself, does not explain the operation of the British constitution. Once again, the operation of the Act draws on older constitutional traditions.

[27] *R (Animal Defenders International)* v. *Secretary of State* [2008] UKHL 15; *R (on the application of L)* v. *Commissioner of Police of the Metropolis* [2009] UK SC 3; and in Scotland *SM as Guardian of JM* v. *Advocate General for Scotland* [2009] CSOH 91.

[28] Ewing laments that despite the dramatic and important human rights cases successfully challenging the detention without trial of foreigners suspected of being a security threat (e.g., *A* v. *Secretary of State for the Home Department* [2005] 2 AC 68), the individual detainees remain in some kind of detention (K. Ewing, *The Bonfire of the Liberties: New Labour, Human Rights and the Rule of Law* (Oxford University Press, 2010)).

[29] See, e.g., A. Kavanagh, *Constitutional Review Under the UK Human Rights Act* (Cambridge University Press, 2009) and Ewing, *The Bonfire of the Liberties*, above n. 28, p. 262.

[30] This is the prisoners' voting rights case *Hirst* v. *UK (No. 2)* [2005] All ER 59.

[31] Page 201 above.

And change?

The Human Rights Act also, however, introduces challenges to traditional understandings. First, and most importantly, the Human Rights Act has been read as applying to the state in *all* its dealings: *everything* done by *core* government is now subject to (legislatively protected) human rights constraints.[32] This represents an important break with public law as it stood at the time the Human Rights Act was adopted. At that time, source of power type tests still determined whether public law norms applied to particular activities of core government. The 1998 Act heralds a significant change in approach: it has been interpreted to the effect that the core parts of government are no longer entitled to a 'private life' (at least where human rights are concerned). It does not matter whether they are contracting or engaged in commercial dealings. The application of public law no longer depends on the legal instrument government chooses to affect its policies. That is a significant development in relation to a question about which the common law has historically waxed and waned for more than 150 years and one on which administrative law remains uncertain.[33] The public law of human rights and its conception of the moral contours of statehood is prior to all other ways of conceiving of the state as a juristic person.

To get a sense of the extent to which this signals a sea change, recall the statement of Lloyd LJ in the judicial review case of *Datafin* where he suggests that if a source of power is statutory it is subject to public law norms, but not if it is contractual and without any public element.[34] Contrast this with the approach of La Forest J, in a 1997 Canadian case responding to the argument that the Canadian Charter should not apply to government when it engages in activities that are 'private, commercial, contractual or non-public in nature':[35]

> We no longer expect the government to be simply a lawmaker in the traditional sense; we expect government to stimulate and preserve the community's economic and social welfare. In such circumstances, government activities which are in form 'commercial' or 'private' transactions are in reality expressions of government policy, be it in the support of a particular region or industry or the enhancement of Canada's overall

[32] Their Lordships in *Aston Cantlow & Wilmote & Billesley Parochial Church Council* [2003] UKHL 37 use the expression 'core public authorities'. See the discussion below.

[33] See Chapter 5.

[34] *R* v. *Panel on Mergers and Takeovers ex parte Datafin plc* [1981] 1 QB 815.

[35] *Eldridge* v. *British Columbia* (1997) 3 SCR 624, para. 40, per La Forest J.

> international competitiveness. In this context, one has to ask: why should our concern that government conform to the principles set out in the Charter not extend to these aspects of its contemporary mandate? To say that the Charter is only concerned with government as law maker is to interpret our Constitution in light of an understanding of government that was long outdated even before the Charter was enacted.

I ought to pause here. This represents an important moment for public law in the common law tradition. A government cannot choose to be treated in law as a private person by the choice of contract as its preferred legal instrument (at least where human rights are concerned). In another Canadian case, La Forest J puts the point even more directly: 'To permit government to pursue policies violating Charter rights by means of contracts or agreements with other persons or bodies cannot be tolerated.'[36] Public law norms administered by judges, and not the executive state itself, should determine how the government is legally manifested in any particular transaction. It is law that defines the state, rather than the other way around. We are a long way from an Austinian conception of the state as merely coercive power.

While the UK judges have not yet had to rule on this issue directly, the approach taken so far in *Aston Cantlow*[37] is consistent with the Canadian view. These changes logically follow from the language, structure and treaty origins of the Act. We shall consider how the activities of 'non-core' parts of the state should be treated presently.

If human right norms apply to the state in *all* of its dealings and not simply to those of a 'public nature', it also follows that human rights apply to all state entities including its highest political organs. As a matter of logic this would appear to circumvent Crown and other public law immunities, and other common law doctrines which have preserved a realm of 'high politics' and certain other types of decision-making free from legal constraint and oversight. These matters too are still very much in the process of being tested. An early example helps to illustrate these points.

The controversial Scottish case of *Napier* v. *Scottish Ministers*[38] (the 'slopping out' decision) concerned prison conditions and over-crowding. Lord Bonomy found the Scottish Ministers to have acted *ultra vires* the ECHR and Section 57 of the Scotland Act 1998. He made a

[36] La Forest J in *Douglas/Kwantlen Faculty Assn* v. *Douglas College* [1990] 3 SCR 570, 585.
[37] *Aston Cantlow & Wilmote & Billesley Parochial Church Council* [2003] UKHL 37.
[38] 2004 SLT 555.

finding of 'fault' or negligence, and gave damages to the complainant. In other words he found systemic failure and conflated delictual (tortious) and ECHR remedies.

It was not possible to identify an individual through whom to channel liability – even the prison governor would not do in relation to this case. In any event, the Scottish Prison Service is not a legal person with a corporate fund separate from that of the Scottish government. The positive breach of the Convention was found to be a resource allocation decision by the Scottish Ministers collectively. At least one of the government's reasons for failing to improve prison conditions earlier was that £13 million that had been in the Scottish Prison Service budget for this purpose had been reallocated for drug enforcement, preventing domestic violence and witness support. Lord Bonomy described this as a 'positive decision deliberately made not to improve conditions for remand prisoners' such as Mr Napier. This is not the sort of resource allocation decision in which a judicial review court would have readily intervened.[39] Given its policy content such a decision would also likely have survived a tortious negligence action. The potential implications of this new approach are far-reaching. This is about institutional wrong-doing – even at the highest levels of policy-making and polycentric decision-making. The Court uses the language of collective wrong-doing and fault. Admittedly, the precedent effect of this decision may be limited: the actual finding of fault was contestible given that the other allocation decisions also had implications for the protection of individual rights; and the case involved the Scottish Ministers and not the UK collective cabinet, or anything approximating 'the Crown'. Nevertheless, the logic of the state's acceptance of obligations under the ECHR is that those legal protections should operate to constrain even the highest levels of government.

The Convention itself identifies the circumstances in which rights constraints will not operate on government and these are much more limited than those allowed under domestic law. This is another important consequence of the influence of international law on rights against the state. On the other hand, the personification of the state in the ECHR sometimes brings with it the idea that the state itself has interests and 'rights' including the obligation to defend itself. Thus in the iconic terrorism case of *A* v. *Secretary of State* (the *Belmarsh* case involving the

[39] *Friends of the Earth* v. *Secretary of State for Energy and Climate Change* [2009] EWCA Civ 810.

detention without trial of non-citizens considered to be a terrorist threat)[40] one of the questions the House of Lords had to address was the extent to which there existed a threat to 'the life of the nation' sufficient to allow the state to derogate from certain rights guaranteed to individuals under the ECHR. The majority of the House of Lords declined to press on the issue of what constituted such a threat. Lord Hoffmann alone was willing to venture that no such threat existed. He was obviously concerned that the exercise of powers to derogate from Article 5 of the ECHR in limited circumstances should not be able to be used in ways that could become the equivalent of claims to subjective right. For him, a high threshold needed to be overcome before the 'common good' could be held to be genuinely engaged. This sense of the state as 'the people or nation' (in the UK surely 'nations') and their 'way of life' has achieved greater legal prominence in recent years. This is not only a by-product of the debates about terrorism but also of the new statism and (ironically) of its individual rights guarantees.

In addition to the expansion of the kinds of decision that the law may now reach, the Human Rights Act introduces the idea of bringing damages claims for human rights breaches. This also poses a challenge to traditional common law ideas contained in the law of tort and judicial review. Commonwealth case law, including a decision of Lord Diplock in the Judicial Committee of the Privy Council,[41] has squarely raised the question of whether what is newly contemplated by constitutional Bills of Rights is *state* liability for breach of human rights obligations. As Lord Cooke argued in *Simpson* v. *Attorney General*,[42] '[t]hese are public law claims against the state, not based on vicarious liability and not within the purview of any statutory exemption for liability'. Apparently freed from the presumption that the King can do no wrong, and from the 'ordinary law' basis of tortious liability, there appears to be a new blank canvas on which a distinct public law version of liability may be drawn – with implications for the relationship between citizen and state.

A recent New Zealand controversy explores these issues. It involved a claim for compensation for the actions of the judges which involved a breach of protected rights. Under the common law, judicial immunity would have applied against a claim for monetary damages. The Crown

[40] [2005] 2 AC 68.

[41] See the judgment of Lord Diplock in *Maharaj* v. *Attorney General of Trinidad and Tobago (No.* 2) [1979] AC 385, 399 (PC).

[42] *Simpson* v. *Attorney General* (also known as *Baigent's* care) [1994] 3 NZLR 667, 742.

would have shared in that immunity under provisions identical to those in the Crown Proceedings Act 1947 (UK). The New Zealand Court of Appeal reiterated the views of Lords Diplock and Cooke that old ideas of immunity no longer apply: 'We would characterize Bill of Rights compensation as a separate remedy directly against the state independent of the Crown Proceedings Act'.[43] Such liability does not depend on any analogy to private law claims, and does not necessarily derive from the actions of individual officials. It may also be used to challenge more systemic failures for which the state, and not the individual official, is responsible. Jennings's and Mitchell's arguments for a distinct public law liability now have a new reason to be revived.[44]

The Chief Justice in the Supreme Court drew on this line of reasoning. She treated international human rights law as providing a new blank canvas against which to assess public law damages against the state *qua* state. Judges' personal immunities remain, but, unlike in a vicarious liability action under the Crown Proceedings Act, the Crown does not get to share in those immunities.[45] This, she argued, is the natural consequence of the state's international human rights treaty commitments. (Elias CJ explicitly treated the Crown and State as equivalent concepts throughout the decision.[46]) Three of the other judges accepted that this was a public law course of action rather than a private law one and should not be decided by analogy to private law. Two of these judges, however, in considering the issue of public law damages 'afresh', as it were, decided that 'the public policy reasons which support judicial immunity also justify confining the scope of Crown liability for governmental breaches of Bill of Rights actions to the executive branch'.[47] Only one judge rejected the 'new' public law approach to damages, viewing it as an illegitimate circumvention of the Crown Proceedings Act.[48] In the result, the Court was split 3:2 with the consequence that damages are not available against the state for judicial acts in New Zealand.

The UK Human Rights Act is also a potential vehicle for the development of a new conception of state liability. The UK too could be

[43] *Attorney General* v. *Chapman* [2009] NZCA 552, para. 95 per Glazebrook J in the judgment of the Court.

[44] See Chapter 5. [45] *Attorney General* v. *Chapman* [2011] NZSC 110, para. 56.

[46] See, e.g., para. 79.

[47] Per McGrath and William Young JJ, para. 204. In the UK, Section 9(3) of the Human Rights Act disposes of the matter. It restricts remedies of damages for judicial acts done in good faith to those damages required by Article 5(5) of the ECHR.

[48] Per Gault J, para. 211 ff.

considered as owing *distinct* obligations under its international commitments in the ECHR. Though the Human Rights Act 1998 itself does not refer to the Crown or state explicitly but rather to 'public authorities', some kind of institutional direct obligation and therefore responsibility is implied. The Strasbourg Court has been developing the concept of 'just satisfaction' under Article 41 to include damages awards from the state to the individual whose rights have been violated. These are in the nature of 'public law' rather than tort law damages. They are discretionary, relatively modest and only necessary when remedies such as a declaration, apology, restitution and prevention are not considered effective. Their focus is not necessarily on the individual but on 'vindicating the right' owed to the public at large. The UK courts are required to take account of this international jurisprudence.

So far, however, the UK courts have been cautious in their reception of these ideas. When considering damages claims for human rights violations for the first time, the House of Lords in *R (Greenfield)* v. *Secretary of State for Home Department*[49] seemed to recognize that they were in new, public law, territory. It emphasized the residuary nature of the damages remedy and that the primary objective of the ECHR is to ensure that states act promptly to prevent a repetition of the rights violation. It said that the finding of a violation in itself should be considered an important part of the remedy and vindication of the right. Lord Bingham emphasized that the Human Rights Act 1998 was not a tort statute and attempted to reduce expectations of generous damages awards. But in other respects the Court's response was reflexively similar to traditional approaches to tortious liability. Lord Bingham demonstrated a resistance to even conceiving of institutional liability for human rights breaches. He suggested that the Court would be more willing to give a damages remedy when an official has 'run amok' than for systemic failure, saying:[50]

> Damages need not ordinarily be awarded to encourage high standards of compliance by member states, since they are already bound in international law to perform their duties under the Convention in good faith, although it may be different if there is a felt to be a need to encourage compliance by individual officials or classes of official.

This analysis seems to take us back into familiar common law territory: individual officials may be blameworthy but the state wishes the best for

[49] [2005] 1 WLR 14. [50] *Ibid.* Para. 9.

its citizens.[51] The King can do no wrong but his officials may need checking. But this ignores the logic of international law ideas of responsibility. An individual official 'run amok' is not an 'ordinary private person' acting outside of his official capacity: at international law he is the human agent by which the state acts and for whom the state is liable.

Common law structures of thought, which tend to view illegal acts of Crown servants as necessarily *ultra vires* – and therefore as actions *not* undertaken on behalf of the state – are difficult to shift. So, for example, in domestic cases involving the application of the international Torture Convention, the judges have had to engage in mental gymnastics.[52] Torture is only an international crime when the state engages in it; immunity attaches to certain officials but only in relation to state and not personal acts. For claimants to bring a successful claim in a domestic court against official acts of torture in international law, Lord Bingham suggested that they have to overcome the difficulty that:[53]

> [T]o bring themselves within the Torture Convention they must show that the torture was (to paraphrase the definition) official; yet they [also have to successfully] argue that the conduct was not official in order to defeat the claim to immunity.

The international law idea that criminal and illegal acts can be official acts of state is foreign to the common lawyer and requires a significant shift in methodology. The increasing penetration of international legal notions in domestic law is likely to press further on such common law structures of thought.

It seems unlikely that the UK courts will be able to avoid the challenges wrought by ideas of state liability for long. The additional conundrum for the common law is how human rights damages, which are said to be nominal, residuary and discretionary, should fit with tortious damages which are primary remedies, available as of right and usually much more generous in quantum. These difficulties are made more

[51] The Scottish courts, by contrast, have so far have been much more willing to conflate delictual and human rights liability – though the results were controversial in *Napier* v. *Scottish Ministers* [2005] SC 229, 2004 SLT 555 (the slopping out case) discussed above.

[52] *R* v. *Bow Street Metropolitan Stipendiary Magistrate, ex parte Pinochet Ugarte (No. 3)* [2000] 1 AC 147;

[53] *Jones* v. *Ministry of Interior* [2007] 1 AC 270, para. 19. Lords Saville and Brown-Wilkinson were prepared to treat these as two separate inquiries in the earlier *Pinochet* decision in order to deny the immunity. In *Jones* the conclusion that the acts of torture were official had the effect of also conferring immunity on the officials and denying the civil claim to damages.

acute, given that certain violations of rights, such as false imprisonment, trespass, assault and battery, will be actionable in ordinary tort law as well as under the Human Rights Act. Judges do not have a principled way of ordering these different causes of action, especially given that the effect of preferring a human rights action to a tort law one is likely, in many cases, to be the reduction or elimination of the damages award to the individual. This issue represents a direct challenge to the traditional British constitutional narrative of rights and liberties protected by the common law. It exposes the problem of whether and how these two systems of thought can be reconciled by interstitial common law method and of whether and how the law should give priority to public law conceptions of the state over private law constructions.

The idea of a distinct direct public liability has also been developing through the EU law jurisprudence of the European Court of Justice. Institutionally and substantively, like the ECHR, it too is a product of international law which treats the state as a unified legal person.[54] The ECJ jurisprudence is potentially even more confronting of traditional British constitutional understandings. Member States of the EU have, for example, been held liable, at the instigation of their own citizens, for failing to carry European directives into effect.[55] The logic of these cases has been carried even further in *Köbler* v. *Austria*[56] in which the ECJ extended this rule of state liability to allow an individual to bring a suit for damages against his Member State on the basis that its judiciary wrongly applied European law.

The *Köbler* case exposes in stark fashion the differences in how the state is conceived in public international law as compared with British constitutional law (and with the approach of the New Zealand Supreme Court in *Chapman*). In international law, it is uncontroversial that the state includes its judiciary, whereas in the British tradition there is a constitutional imperative that the judiciary should be independent of governmental direction and control and, indeed in these terms, it is often viewed as standing between the citizen and state. In *Köbler*, the ECJ emphasized the logic of the international law position: in international law the state is viewed as a unified entity – and includes the judiciary.

[54] International Law Commission, Draft Articles on Responsibility of States for Internationally Wrongful Acts with Commentaries 2001 *Yearbook of the International Law Commission* 2(2) (2001) [6].

[55] *Francovich* v. *Italy* C-6/90 and C-9/90 1991 ECR I-5357 [1993] 2 CMLR.

[56] Case C-224/01 (30 September 2003).

Rejecting the argument that such a ruling could undermine judicial independence, the ECJ argued that entity liability runs against the state and does not involve the personal liability of an individual judge – the very opposite of the common law approach in tort.

State liability, however, must mean something different from state responsibility in this context. In all the versions of direct responsibility I have considered, an element of control appears to be a prerequisite. In this case, not only is the element of control absent but it is normatively prohibited. The political branch of government not only *cannot* but *should not* control the judicial branch. State liability is serving particular institutional purposes in *Köbler*. It is being used as an unusual kind of vicarious liability. Effectively it is a means of further integrating the domestic courts of the Member States into a European Court hierarchy.[57] State liability, as was used in *Köbler*, had the effect of enforcing the law made in international institutions in domestic courts.

The combined effect of the decisions from the international courts in both Strasbourg and Luxembourg is that public law damages are available against the UK state *qua* state under the ECHR and in EU law. Damages are also available in relation to domestic tortious claims (some of which protect civil rights and some of which protect against risk), but not for most other public law wrongs. Recall that De Smith's leading judicial review textbook has described the non-availability of monetary remedies as one of judicial review's basic tenets.[58] There is no uniform approach to the basis of the remedy or to how the state is conceived in these different areas of the law. This often appears to be anomalous and unjust. For these reasons, and because of concerns about the unpredictable and unprincipled expansion of tort liability over recent years,[59] the English Law Commission began a project on remedies against public authorities in March 2005.[60] It recommended that a distinct scheme for public law redress should be created for cases involving certain activities and bodies which it defined as 'truly public'.

[57] See further J. E. Pfander, 'Köbler v Austria: Expositional Supremacy and Member State Liability', *European Business Law Review* 17 (2006), 275–97.

[58] See discussion in Chapter 7.

[59] Law Commission for England and Wales, *Administrative Redress: Public Bodies and the Citizen*, Law Com 322 (London: Stationery Office, 2010), paras. 1.17, 1.18.

[60] Law Commission for England and Wales, *Administrative Redress: Public Bodies and the Citizen* (Consultation Paper 187) (London: Stationery Office, 2008); Law Commission for England and Wales, *Administrative Redress: Public Bodies and the Citizen*, above n. 59.

The ordinary law of tort should not apply in such cases and there should be a requirement of serious fault (and not mere negligence) before a public authority can be found liable for monetary payment. By 2010, however, the UK government forestalled any further work on the project – an intervention which has drawn sharp criticism from Sedley LJ in the Court of Appeal who had reservations about the capacity of the common law to reconcile these different approaches in the absence of legislative intervention.[61] This can be seen as yet another example of the normative turn after privatization. While the work of reform has been forestalled, these issues about the distinctiveness of public law are unlikely to go away.

The Human Rights Act represents both continuity with and a significant challenge to British constitutional thought. The emphasis on the scope and architecture of power, and on constitutional practice rather than strict legality, is continuous with earlier habits. Personification of the state as a unified legal person poses significant challenges to traditional structures of British legal thought, and particularly in relation to responsibility questions. Is the so-called direct liability of the state at international law really another version of vicarious liability (which circumvents an individual officer's immunity)? What constitutes fault? Is the existence of illegality of itself sufficient? How do these new monetary remedies fit alongside state compensation schemes and common law tortious remedies? Do we have the necessary intellectual resources from which to construct a distinct public law out of a legal system characterized by a mixed public/private law system?

Who is the state for human rights purposes?

If the international law origin of the Human Rights Act 1998 is the source of challenges to the structures of British legal thought and its traditional views of the state, another significant challenge posed by the Human Rights Act 1998 is that it requires the judges to determine the contours of the state as a legal entity. It turns the definition of the state into a legal question. This is not, of course, the first time the law has asked the question: 'who or what is the state?' What makes it novel is that the question is being asked this time in order to impose human rights obligations (to extend the law) rather than to determine immunity

[61] *Home Office* v. *Mohammed* [2011] EWCA Civ 351.

or privilege (to determine a sphere into which law does not extend). The new focus is on the proper extent of public power. Some of the confusions here too spring from the international law origins of human rights obligations under the ECHR.

Modern international law treats the state as unified and indivisible: it is not concerned with how the state organizes its functions and powers internally. How is international law, which holds the state responsible for human rights breaches, to apply in internal domestic law? The answer which the Human Rights Act gives is through a test of 'public function'. This is another example of the 'functional turn' of public law, after privatization. The test not only asks which bodies are 'truly public' but which may constitute in law a 'public–private' hybrid.

Section 6(1) makes it unlawful for a 'public authority' to act incompatibly with human rights and defines a public authority in Section 6(3)(b) as 'any person certain of whose functions are functions of a public nature'. Judges have read this as defining 'core public authorities' 'all of whose functions are of a public nature'.[62] But Section 6(5) also applies the same prohibition to 'any body which is not a public authority but certain of whose functions are of a public nature, save in respect of a particular act if the nature of that act is private'.[63] These formulations are hardly straightforward and have been the subject of controversial attempts at elaboration in the case law. Effectively they: (1) oblige all of the 'core' parts of government to comply with human rights in all their activities; and (2) subject some bodies which are not otherwise public authorities to observe rights when they are exercising public functions which are also public acts.[64] There is some imagined public–private line here: finding it has, however, proved elusive.

The object of this part of the chapter is not to embark on a detailed evaluation of the case law or operation of these tests, but rather to draw

[62] Lord Hobhouse, *Aston Cantlow*, para. 85, Lord Rodger, para. 144.

[63] I am borrowing from Lord Bingham's formulation in *YL*, para. 3.

[64] See *Aston Cantlow* v. *Wallbank* [2004] 1 AC 546 where a distinction was made between core public authorities which must always act compatibly with the Human Rights Convention and hybrid public authorities to which a functional test applies (see Lord Nicholls at paras. 7–12 and Lord Hope at paras. 35–8 and especially at 38 where he decides that the functional test does not apply to core public authorities); Baroness Hale in *YL* v. *Birmingham City Council* [2007] UKHL 27 para. 37. See further, D. Oliver, 'The Frontiers of the State: Public Authorities and Public Functions Under the Human Rights Act' *Public Law* (2000) 476–93 and D. Oliver, 'Functions of a Public Nature under the Human Rights Act', Public Law (2004) 329–52; P. Cane, 'Church, State, and Human Rights: Are Parish Councils Public Authorities', *Law Quarterly Review* 120 (2004), 41–8.

connections between these tests and our general themes.[65] As I discussed in Chapter 8, the legislative history of the Human Rights Act 1998 indicates that the reference to public function was intended to create a flexible *normative* test that would accommodate the shifting *institutional* character of the public sphere at a time of privatization and contracting out. Part of that legal test requires an assessment of the relationship between the state and civil society – something which, as we have seen, has been particularly fluid in the UK legal tradition. It is partly due to this factor that judicially applied functional tests do not have a very firm provenance in public law. The test also raises issues about the relationship between Human Rights Act guarantees and the common law constitution – or to paraphrase Jennings 'the peculiar public private character of English public law'.[66] First, however, we need to consider how the courts approach these issues at international law. As we shall see, one can achieve a wide coverage of human rights norms without necessarily having to rely on public function tests.

At international law

The Strasbourg Court of Human Rights has treated the question of 'who is the state' as a kind of non-delegation test. This may surprise those who may have thought that the constitutionalization of rights would necessarily *limit* state powers. Instead, the Court has focused on the question of what are the state's *positive* obligations under Article 1 to secure rights and freedoms in its domestic law to everyone within its jurisdiction. States cannot absolve themselves of responsibility by delegating their obligations to private bodies or individuals. The corporal punishment of a seven-year-old boy by the private headmaster of an independent school, for example, may engage the responsibility of the state, as was

[65] [2007] UKHL 27. For more detailed analysis of the case law and references to the abundant secondary literature, see P. Rishworth and J. McLean, 'Human Rights Obligations in the Private Sector: Reflections on *YL* v. *Birmingham City Council* and the Meaning of Public Function' in C. F. Forsyth, M. Elliott, S. Jhaveri, M. Ramsden and A. Scully Hill (eds.), *Effective Judicial Review: A Cornerstone of Good Government* (Oxford University Press, 2010), pp. 101–19. For particularly helpful analyses see S. Gardbaum, 'The Horizontal Effect of Constitutional Rights', *Michigan Law Review* 102 (2003), 387–459, and P. Rishworth, 'New Zealand Taking Human Rights into The Private Sphere', in D. Oliver and J. Fedtke (eds.), *Human Rights in the Private Sphere: A Comparative Study* (London: Routledge-Cavendish, 2007), pp. 312–350.

[66] W. I. Jennings, *The Law and the Constitution*, 2nd edn (University of London Press, 1938), pp. 206–7.

found in *Costello-Roberts* v. *United Kingdom*.[67] States are under an obligation to secure a right to education under Article 2 Protocol No. 1, and a school's disciplinary system fits within the ambit of that guarantee. The question for the Court, in that case, was whether the state had done enough in prohibiting the use of immoderate or unreasonable corporal punishment. It focused on the state's legal controls and protections – including the civil common law of trespass. The state was not allowed, at international law, to permit a system of private schools to be operated in a way that disregarded ECHR guarantees – but the partially dissenting judges did make clear that the ECHR would not apply 'as such' between private parties. The focus at international law is on the state's positive obligations under treaties and whether there is a legal regime in place to uphold and protect such obligations.

The approach to how state responsibility is engaged at international law, then, has a number of noteworthy features. The private school was not itself the defendant in the Strasbourg Court – it was the UK which defended the action. The private headmaster's method of punishment could be impugned without any decision to the effect that he was himself 'a part of the state' or providing a public function. The question at issue was not whether the *act* of punishment was excessive and rights-infringing but whether the law would have allowed excessive, rights-infringing punishment to go unregulated. At international law the state cannot escape its obligations by divesting services or contracting out functions. Moreover, the European Social Charter and Charter of Rights and Freedoms explicitly enumerate many of the obligations implied by the ECHR, such as the right to education. In structure, these arguments came close to protecting the republican conception of liberty associated with Skinner and Pettit.[68]

The domestic 'incorporation' of the ECHR through which bodies owe duties under the Human Rights Act takes a very different approach. Unsurprisingly, it does not mention the state at all, only public authorities. In addition to subjecting core public authorities to human rights obligations, it seeks directly to limit the lawful acts or omissions of private entities when those entities are performing public acts in relation to public functions (the example given by the Joint Committee on

[67] (1995) 19 EHRR 112. The Court found no violation under Articles 3, 8 or 13.

[68] See, e.g., Q. Skinner, *Liberty Before Liberalism* (Cambridge University Press, 1997) and P. Pettit, *Republicanism: Theory of Freedom and Government* (Oxford University Press, 1999).

Human Rights is that a 'private security firm would be required to comply with Convention rights in its running of a prison, but not in its provision of security to a supermarket').[69]

Examining the question of who is subject to the ECHR rights in domestic law from an international law perspective may help clarify some of the current problems relating to the operation of Section 6. *Distinct* inquiries are presumably contemplated into the obligations of the core public authorities and the obligations of Section 6(5) 'hybrid entities', respectively. The duties and the breaches of each are likely to differ markedly. Indeed, only the core state can be held responsible for statutes which offend ECHR rights or for the absence of a system of law which is rights-protecting, and the existence of Section 6(5) certainly does not *exclude* consideration of those issues in a domestic court. The commonly cited rationale of the need for Section 6(5), that if private entities were not included, the state would otherwise escape its commitments, is simply not correct. So, to take a recent example, if a private for profit care home, acting under a contract with a public authority to provide rest home care to elderly patients with dementia, sought to terminate the contract for an individual patient's care (the facts in *YL* v. *Birmingham City Council*)[70] the public authority would be answerable at the very least for the terms of its contract with the rest home.[71] That inquiry could go further into areas such as contractual monitoring, other contractual terms, the general law, care home standards and licensing frameworks. Indeed, the Supreme Court of Israel has recently gone so far as to find that the *transfer* of authority for managing a prison from the state to a private contractor whose aim is to make a monetary profit is unconstitutional because that in itself would severely limit rights to dignity and freedom.[72]

The approach of international law demonstrates that many of the rights arguments can be reached through a challenge to the core public authority even in cases in which services have been contracted out.

[69] Joint Committee on Human Rights, The Meaning of Public Authority under the Human Rights Act, Seventh Report of the Session 2003–2004 HL Paper 39, HC 382 para. 6.

[70] [2008] 1 AC 95.

[71] In that particular case the contract required the rest home to comply with the Human Rights Act and that termination should only take place for good reason. Note that the European Social Charter guarantees social protection to elderly persons whether they are cared for in public or private institutions (CETS 128 Art 4).

[72] *Academic Center of Law and Business* v. *Minister of Finance* HCJ 2605/05 (in an 8:1 decision).

To return to the care home example, a direct claim against the Section 6(5) entity would presumably canvas the *different* issue of whether the particular 'act' of termination of the contract was indeed 'for cause' and justifiable in rights terms. Seen in that light, Section 6(5) may *itself* be regarded as a *means* by which the core state complies with its Human Rights Act obligations. From this perspective the state is not diminished but strengthened by constitutional rights restraints.

Public function

If we can achieve a great deal of coverage of Human Rights Act obligations without necessarily resorting to the public function test in Section 6(5), how should it be applied?

One judicial approach has been to treat the idea of 'public function' as an historical test. Thus in the rest home case of *YL* v. *Birmingham City Council*,[73] Lord Bingham (in the minority) suggested that acceptance by the British state of a welfare responsibility for the elderly under Sections 21 and 26 of the National Assistance Act 1948, and continuing funding support for those who cannot pay, indicated that in relation to publicly assisted residents, provision of care was a public function.[74] Lord Bingham, with whom Baroness Hale agreed, read into the legislative history of the Human Rights Act an intention that what had been delivered by government before privatization and contracting out should be considered a public function after the enactment of the Human Rights Act.[75] They regarded Section 6 as providing a means by which public law could continue to be applied despite privatization and contracting out, and as a regulatory counterweight and additional safeguard, against such policies. Public law norms should trump the private law form of the transaction. Leaving the result to one side, some of the associated reasoning is problematic.

An overly historical approach to the question of function does not yield much certainty. What is the proper time frame? If the focus is on the political practice immediately preceding privatization and contracting out, that approach is likely to be increasingly difficult to operate the further we are from the point of contracting out. Moreover, if one takes a

73 [2007] UKHL 27; [2008] 1 AC 95. 74 *Ibid.*, para. 20.

75 Rights Brought Home: The Human Rights Bill, cm 3782, 24 October 1997, para. 2.2. See also the speeches by the Home Secretary, HC Deb, 16 February 1998, col 773; 17 June 1998, cols 409–410.

longer time frame, as I did in Chapters 5 and 6, we can see that the concept of 'public function' is highly historically contingent, and the minority's approach may be too narrow. 'Public functions' typically developed *outside* of state institutions in the nineteenth century and were only subsequently 'taken over' by the government apparatus. The state and the English fellowships were never so very far apart. That did not matter for most purposes because the same (private) law applied to them both at the time. Often too what had been considered 'public' was politically, rather than legally, designated. Even the existence, or not, of a profit motive proved an unreliable predictor of 'publicness' in the past – especially in the nineteenth-century age of 'municipal capitalism'.

The minority's related focus on public funding may also lead to arbitrary and historically contingent results. In modern practice, the government usually *partially* funds both public and private institutions, and, through subsidies, individual people. Individuals attracting subsidies are often amongst the most vulnerable. In the care home case of *YL*, a distinction was made by the minority judges between those residents who were wholly self-funding (who would *not* attract human rights protections) and those who were partially self-funding or entirely publicly funded (who *would* attract human right protections). The logic of this argument would mean that a government decision to change from a universalized to a means-tested benefit of any kind would be an indication that human rights should no longer apply to those with means. This approach becomes even more arbitrary when one considers that self-funding and subsidized patients are not fixed categories – one is likely to become a subsidized patient as one's personal funds run out. Focusing on funding arrangements leaves human rights too much in thrall to institutional fashion (something which Section 6 was presumably intended to avoid). A more positive way to view these funding rules is to regard the presence of any public funding of a service as a decision that everyone should be able to access such services *even if* (rather than *only if*) they do not have the personal means by which to do so.

If the approach of the minority judges has its problems, the approach of the majority judges in *YL* also raises difficulties which also by now should be familiar. The majority retreat to a kind of formalism, reminiscent of the judges' reaction to the question of 'what is a public authority', when considering the Public Authorities Protection Act 1893.[76]

[76] Discussed in Chapter 5.

The majority of the House of Lords found that a private care home operating as a commercial entity for profit, without direct public funding[77] or special statutory powers, is not a private body exercising a public function for the purposes of Section 6. These judges resort to traditional forms of common law and judicial review analysis.[78] They each place emphasis on the contractual source of the home's obligation to deliver care.[79] Lord Scott's analysis is particularly striking. In answer to the question of how it could be that the functions of a local authority in operating its own care homes could unquestionably be of a public nature while the operation of the same functions by a privately owned care home could not, he resorts to a source of power test. The local authority carries out its tasks pursuant to statutory powers and duties (that are, therefore, imposed by public law) and the private care home carries out its tasks pursuant to powers and duties imposed by tort and contract law (making the same activities private).[80] This approach not only elevates instrument choice over normative principles but it also denies the mixed public–private character of the common law constitution. Liberty is narrowly understood as freedom from coercion.

Maitland and Laski could possibly help us here. As we have seen, the idea that public functions are *necessarily* delegated from the state is a relatively new one: the issue was highly controversial at the turn of the nineteenth and twentieth centuries. How much associations have been governed by statute and treated as exercising delegated rather than self-governing authority has changed drastically since the nineteenth century and may well be in the process of shifting once more. Indeed, that may be one of the ideas behind the 'Big Society'. Maitland thought that the law had a role in recognizing the moral personality of groups and in holding them responsible. His view did not depend on the presence of delegated authority.

Instead the majority find that there is already a sufficient regulatory scheme in place – both provided by the state in its general regulation of care homes and by contract law. Indeed, for Lord Mance, the extensive

[77] Some of the patients, including the claimant, received funding as an individual subsidy – a matter which the dissenting judges, Lord Bingham and Baroness Hale, emphasized.

[78] Lord Neuberger regarded it as relevant that a private care home would not be susceptible to judicial review, para. 160.

[79] Lord Neuberger, para. 133.

[80] *YL*, para. 29. For Lord Neuberger the existence of a statutory power is not necessarily determinative of whether the function is public but is a very powerful factor, para. 167.

general regulatory system already in place is indicative of the private nature of the enterprise.[81] The contracts, between the local authority and the care home and between the care home and the resident, each impose an obligation on the care home to observe ECHR rights. But that is to focus on whether the *government* has done enough to ensure it has met its human rights obligations. They could have interpreted Section 6(5) of the Human Rights Act as Parliament's creation of a distinct mechanism for the enforcement of human rights obligations *directly* against a private body requiring judges to assess acts taken under the contract against human rights standards. The majority would not entertain that approach – they thought contracts should be governed solely by contractual causes of action. There should be no mixing of public and private law. They should be kept procedurally distinct, even when they both address the issue of human rights. This takes us back to where we were before the so-called functional turn and robs Section 6(5) of its purpose.

The problem with all of these approaches is that what is contemplated by the Section 6 functional test is neither historical and institutional or formalistic. It is a normative test about the proper reach of human rights norms and what is contemplated by particular rights and freedoms. Common lawyers have never squarely faced the question of what is a public function, or, indeed, of what is the state, as a purely abstract matter, and have scant evidential or other intellectual resources with which to do so. Hart reminded us of this in his inaugural lecture.[82] All of the judges struggle with the methodology here which seems to force a determination of the status of the function *a priori* without reference directly to the rights at stake. This leads to 'all or nothing' determinations of whether a function is public or private.

The majority in *YL*, for example, is concerned that if a care home is found to be performing a public function in this case, then its managers and nurses would be considered a public authority for all other purposes.[83] Conversely, Baroness Hale, in dissent, is concerned that if a care home is found not to be exercising a public function here then it will not be considered to be doing so when it is detaining particularly vulnerable patients receiving treatment for psychiatric orders, or (an example she

[81] *YL*, para. 116. See also Lord Scott, para. 32.

[82] H. L. A. Hart, 'Definition and Theory in Jurisprudence', reproduced in H. L. A. Hart, *Essays in Jurisprudence and Philosophy* (Oxford: Clarendon Press, 1953).

[83] *YL*, para. 30 per Lord Scott.

gives) feeding and toileting patients at the same time.[84] In the earlier case of *Aston Cantlow*, the judges introduced another binary test. They raised the concern that if a body owes rights under the ECHR, it cannot simultaneously enjoy such ECHR rights against the government. Hence, they argued, the category of bodies subject to the Human Rights Act should be narrowly construed.

We saw earlier that binary approaches to the questions of whether or not an entity is public or private for the purpose of enjoying immunities or privileges had the effect that many of the nuances attaching to the public sphere were lost. An all or nothing approach to the public function threshold test is at risk of having the same effect.

The section itself provides part of an answer. It requires the focus of the inquiry to be on the 'acts' of a body performing a public function. For some acts, a body or person will be able itself to enjoy rights and freedoms against the state, but not for others. The domestic public law and common law routinely allows reciprocal duties and rights – indeed, that is the very basis of the common law constitution and a central aspect of the British state tradition After all, many of the rights which protect the security of the person, as against, for example, false imprisonment and trespass to the person, are already protected in the common law. In other words, some existing rights obligations are not only owed by the state, but are owed by everyone to everyone. Section 6(5) suggests the need for a consideration of whether particular rights obligations should be *extended* to private bodies in relation to certain functions and activities. Starting with the rights themselves may lead to a much more fruitful analysis.

Such an approach, however, has so far enjoyed little support among academic public lawyers. Those who favour the 'procedural exclusivity' of forcing the priority of public over private law tend to be loath to legitimate any of the claims of the common law constitution. Their suspicions are justified because the common law constitution itself inherently denies the priority of the public law cause of action. We are back then to the debate between Lord Hewart and the new administrative lawyers discussed in Chapter 6. Those who favour formalism do not like the suggested approach because it threatens to 'pollute' private law with public law norms (forgetting that public and private norms

[84] *Ibid.* para. 69.

were never such distinct categories). It may be that political designations of public functions are the best way forward as they proved in the past.[85]

The Human Rights Act 1998 raises the question of what is the state's relationship with civil society directly in a contemporary context. Understanding the distinctive British tradition gives us resources with which to approach these questions at a time when civil society is being expected to take a more central role once again. Jaffe criticized Maitland's historical method on the basis that it considers all law as validated from its past but: 'at the moment of its present it can evolve nothing new'.[86] This part of the chapter has attempted to demonstrate that old controversies about the nature of statehood and of the public–private divide have tended to repeat themselves, and to clarify what is historically contingent and what is new about the contemporary challenges.

Summary

In this chapter we have considered the impact of international human rights law on traditional British notions of statehood. In many respects the Human Rights Act 1998 is consistent with earlier tradition: while preserving parliamentary sovereignty it relies on what Austin called positive morality and Jennings described as the new rule of law, for its effective operation. Government is not coerced but it obeys. It does not necessarily diminish the state but also imposes positive obligations on the state to protect rights through the law – an approach also consistent with common law constitutionalism. The Human Rights Act, however, significantly challenges traditional conceptions in that it subjects *all* that core government does to human rights norms – giving priority to public law norms. It introduces a new notion of state liability that challenges common law approaches to government responsibility and circumvents concepts associated with the Crown. By extending the scope of human rights obligations to bodies engaged in 'public functions', it provides a new legal forum in which to determine the relationship between the state and civil society.

[85] Section 145(1) of the Health and Social Care Act 2008 designated the provision of accommodation alongside nursing and personal care as a 'public function' in response to the *YL* decision. The difficulties presented by the case law have also created problems for those being asked to make 'political designations' of what is a public function (as allowed, for example, by the UK and Scottish Freedom of Information legislation). If determinations of 'publicness' become too judge-centred there is a risk they will become ineffective.

[86] L. Jaffe, 'Law Making by Private Groups', *Harvard Law Review* 51 (1937–8), 201–53, 208.

Epilogue

Skinner has eloquently urged that we need *a personne morale* to represent the state.[1] In this telling of the state tradition in British legal thought we have encountered a number of personifications of statehood. The Crown has sometimes represented the state, meaning the public. The Crown has also sometimes represented a part of the government apparatus, though never the whole of the public sphere. The state has been represented by the judges and the protections of the common law, and in the 'judicial mind' which suppresses individual interests for the common good.

We have also encountered a number of theorists who have been distrustful of personifications of statehood. Hart thought personifications of the collective will were dangerous and preferred to think of legal systems as systems of rules. He did not think it helpful to conceive of a person standing behind the law. For similar reasons, others thought that if the state apparatus was to be personified at all, it should be treated as an ordinary private person.

When distinctly public law norms of obligation and duty did emerge in the twentieth century, they did not attach to a personification of the state but were rather in the nature of a system of rules applied to public authorities on behalf of the public.

Contemporary phenomena have posed new challenges to these traditional understandings about statehood. The philosophies underpinning privatization rejected ideas of the collective will and any suggestion that the state could be a benign influence. At the same time personifications of the state deriving from international law entered into the common law via human rights and European Union law doctrines. At times these new conceptions of statehood have challenged traditional British notions such as ideas about state responsibility. At others they have forced the

1 Skinner, 'A Genealogy of the Modern State' *Proceedings of the British Academy* 162 (2009), 325–70.

more explicit consideration of the indicia of statehood such as what constitutes state functions, what is the state's relationship to civil society, what is constitutional identity?

There is a state tradition in British legal thought. It is contested, adaptable and complex. These features have given it the flexibility to adjust to changes in state institutions and functions. At times, though, we have been at risk of losing useful intellectual resources which could help us face contemporary challenges.

Yet we may still need some way better to represent the state, as Skinner urges. Maitland's question about who owes the national debt is even more pressing today than it was during his time. Will the new focus on individual rights, which regards the state as the problem and as needing to be restrained, but also as owing positive obligations to individuals, allow the state to comprehend future persons who are quite possibly facing worse economic and environmental conditions than our own? Is there a way for the structures of legal and constitutional thought to more effectively remind us that sovereigns come and go but the state endures?

We need all the resources we can in order to face these questions. The search for the state will continue.

SELECT BIBLIOGRAPHY

Alborn, T.L., *Conceiving Companies: Joint Stock Politics in Victorian England* (London: Routledge, 1998)

Regulated Lives: Life Insurance and British Society, 1800–1914 (University of Toronto Press, 2009)

Allen, W.H., 'Municipal Trading in England', *Journal of Political Economy* 9 (1900), 123–5

Allison, J.A.W., *The English Historical Constitution: Continuity, Change and European Effects* (Cambridge University Press, 2007)

Anderson, S., '"Grave Injustice", "Despotic Privilege": The Insecure Foundations of Crown Liability for Torts in New Zealand', *Otago Law Review* 12 (2009), 1–21

'Public Law', in W. Cornish, S. Anderson, R. Cocks, M. Lobban, P. Polden and K. Smith (eds.), *The Oxford History of the Laws of England, Volume XI, 1820–1914: English Legal System* (Oxford University Press, 2010), pp. 299–523

Anghie, A., *Imperialism, Sovereignty and the Making of International Law* (Cambridge University Press, 2005)

Aronson, M., 'A Public Lawyer's Responses to Privatisation and Outsourcing', in M. B. Taggart, *The Province of Administrative Law* (Oxford: Hart Publishing, 1997), pp. 40–70

'The Great Depression, This Depression and Administrative Law', *Federal Law Review* 37 (2009), 165–204

Arrow, K., *Social Choice and Individual Values*, 2nd edn (New York: Wiley, 1963)

Ashley, P., 'Municipal Trading in Great Britain', *The Quarterly Journal of Economics* 15 (1901), 458–64

Austin, J., *A Plea for the Constitution*, 2nd edn (London: Clowes, 1859)

'Centralization', *The Edinburgh Review* 85 (1847), 221–58

Lectures on Jurisprudence, R. Campbell (ed.), Student Edition (London: John Murray, 1875)

Lectures on Jurisprudence, or the Philosophy of Positive Law, R. Campbell (ed.), 2 vols., 3rd edn (London: John Murray, 1869)

The Province of Jurisprudence Determined and the Uses of the Study of Jurisprudence, H. L. A. Hart (ed.) (London: Weidenfeld & Nicolson, 1954)

The Province of Jurisprudence Determined, W. Rumble (ed.) (Cambridge University Press, 1995)

Avineri, S., *Hegel's Theory of the Modern State* (London: Cambridge University Press, 1972)

Bagehot, W., *The English Constitution*, 2nd edn (London: Chapman and Hall, 1873)

Barker, E., 'Introduction', in O. Gierke, *Natural Law and Theory of Society*, E. Barker (tr.) (Cambridge University Press, 1950)

Political Thought in England from Herbert Spencer to Present Day (New York: Holt, 1915)

Barnard, C., *The Substantive Law of the EU: The Four Freedoms*, 3rd edn (Oxford University Press, 2010)

Bayles, M.D., *Hart's Legal Philosophy: An Examination* (Dordrecht: Kluwer, 1992)

Bennett Miller, J., *An Outline of Administrative and Local Government Law in Scotland* (Edinburgh: Green, 1961)

Bentham, J., *A Fragment on Government*, W. Harrison (ed.) (London: Basil Blackwell, 1948)

Beveridge, W., *Social Insurance and Allied Services* (New York: Macmillan, 1942)

Voluntary Action: A Report on Methods of Social Advance (New York: Macmillan, 1948)

Bevir, M., and R.A.W. Rhodes, *The State as Cultural Practice* (Oxford University Press, 2010)

Blackstone, W., *Commentaries on the Laws of England*, 4 vols. (Oxford: Clarendon Press, 1765–9)

Blaine Baker, G., 'Willis on "Cultured" Public Authorities', *University of Toronto Law Journal* 55 (2005), 335–60

Bosanquet, B., *A Companion to Plato's Republic, for English Readers*, 2nd edn (London: Macmillan, 1895)

The Philosophical Theory of the State (London: Macmillan, 1899)

The Philosophical Theory of the State, 2nd edn (London: Macmillan, 1910)

The Philosophical Theory of the State, 4th edn (London: Macmillan, 1958)

'The Function of the State in Promoting the Unity of Mankind' in D. Boucher (ed.), *The British Idealists* (Cambridge University Press, 1997), pp. 270–95

Bosanquet, H., *The Poor Law Report of 1909: A Summary Explaining the Defects of the Present System and the Principal Recommendations of the Commission, so far as Relates to England* (London: Macmillan, 1909)

Boucher D., 'British Idealism, the State, and International Relations', *Journal of the History of Ideas* 55 (1994), 671–94

(ed.), *The British Idealists* (Cambridge University Press, 1997)

Bowen, H.V., *Revenue and Reform: The Indian Problem in British Politics 1757–1773* (Cambridge University Press, 1991)

Brebner, J.B., 'Laissez-Faire and State Intervention in Nineteenth-Century Britain', *The Journal of Economic History* 8, Supplement: The Tasks of Economic History (1948), 59–73

Brett, A.S., 'The Development of the Idea of Citizens' Rights' in Q. Skinner and B. Strath (eds.), *States and Citizens: History, Theory, Prospects* (Cambridge University Press, 2003), pp. 97–112

Brewer, J., *The Sinews of Power: War, Money, and the English State, 1688–1783* (Cambridge, MA: Harvard University Press, 1990)

'Servants of the Public – Servants of the Crown: Officialdom of Eighteenth Century Government', in J. Brewer and E. Hellmuth (eds.), *Rethinking Leviathan* (New York: Oxford University Press, 1999), pp. 127–48

Brown, L.N. and Bell, J., *French Administrative Law*, 5th edn (Oxford: Clarendon Press, 1998)

Brown, W., 'The Personality of the Corporation and the State,' *Law Quarterly Review* 21 (1905), 365–79

Buchanan, J.M., 'Politics Without Romance: A Sketch of Positive Public Choice Theory and its Normative Implications', in J.M. Buchanan and R.D. Tollison (eds.), *The Theory of Public Choice II* (Ann Arbor, MI: University of Michigan Press, 1984), pp. 11–22

Buchanan, J.M. and Tollison, R.D. (eds.), *The Theory of Public Choice II* (Ann Arbor, MI: University of Michigan Press, 1984)

Burdett, E.W., 'Municipal Ownership in Great Britain', *Journal of Political Economy* 14 (1906), 257–314

Cane, P., 'Church, State, and Human Rights: Are Parish Councils Public Authorities', *Law Quarterly Review*, 120 (2004), (41–8)

Responsibility in Law and Morality (Oxford: Hart, 2002)

'Theory and Values in Public Law', in P. Craig and R. Rawlings (eds.), *Law and Administration in Europe* (Oxford University Press, 2003), pp. 3–21

Cannadine, D., 'The Context, Performance, and Meaning of Ritual: The British Monarchy and the "Invention of Tradition",' in E. Hobsbawn and T. Ranger (eds.), *The Invention of Tradition* (Cambridge University Press, 1983), pp. 101–64

Carr, C.T., *Concerning English Administrative Law* (New York: Columbia University Press, 1941)

The General Principles of the Law of Corporations (Cambridge University Press, 1905)

Carter, M., 'Ball, Bosanquet and the Legacy of T.H. Green', *History of Political Thought* 20 (1999), 674–94

Carty, A., *The Decay of International Law?: A Reappraisal of the Limits of Legal Imagination in International Affairs* (Manchester University Press, 1986)

Chafee, Z., 'The Internal Affairs of Associations Not for Profit', 43 *Harvard Law Review.* (1929–30), 993–1029

Chester, D.N., *The English Administrative System, 1780–1870* (Oxford: Clarendon Press, 1981)

The Nationalisation of British Industry, 1945–51 (London: Stationery Office, 1975)

Clark, E.C., *Practical Jurisprudence: A Comment on Austin* (Cambridge University Press, 1883)

Clarke, P.F., *Liberals and Social Democrats* (Cambridge University Press, 1978)

Cobbett, P., '"The Crown" as Representing "The State"', *Commonwealth Law Review* 1 (1903–1904), 23–30

Cocks, R.,'Statutes, Social Reform and Control', in W. Cornish, S. Anderson, R. Cocks, M. Lobban, P. Polden and K. Smith (eds.), *The Oxford History of the Laws of England, Volume XIII, 1820–1914: Fields of Development* (New York: Oxford University Press, 2010), pp. 465–720

Cole, G.D.H., 'Conflicting Social Obligations', *Proceedings of the Aristotelian Society NS* 15 (1914–15), 140–159

Collini, S., 'Hobhouse, Bosanquet and the State: Philosophical Idealism and Political Argument in England 1880–1918', *Past and Present* 72 (1976), 86–111

Public Moralists: Political Thought and Intellectual Life in Britain, 1850–1930 (Oxford: Clarendon Press, 1991)

Cotterrell, R., *The Politics of Jurisprudence: A Critical Introduction to Legal Philosophy* (London: Lexis Nexis, 2003)

Craig, P.P., 'Public Law and Control Over Private Power', in M.B. Taggart (ed.), *The Province of Administrative Law* (Oxford: Hart, 1997) pp. 196–216

Craig, P.P., and G. De Búrca, *EU Law: Text, Cases and Materials*, 5th edn (Oxford University Press, 2011)

Crofts, W.C., *Municipal Socialism* (London: Liberty & Property Defence League, 1885)

Daintith, T., and A. Page, *The Executive in the Constitution* (Oxford University Press, 1999)

Daintith, T. and M. Sah, 'Privatisation and the Economic Neutrality of the Constitution', *Public Law* (1993), 465–87

Daunton, M.J., 'Payment and Participation: Welfare and State-Formation in Britain 1900–1951', *Past and Present* 150 (1996), 169–216

Davies, A.C.L., *Accountability: A Public Law Analysis of Government by Contract* (Oxford University Press, 2001)

De Lolme, J.L., *The Constitution of England* (London: Robinson, 1788)

De Neuman, A.M., 'Some Economic Aspects of Nationalization', *Law and Contemporary Problems* 16 (1951), 702–751

De Smith, S.A., 'Fundamental Rights in the New Commonwealth (I)', *International and Comparative Law Quarterly* 10 (1961), 83–102

Judicial Review of Administrative Action (London: Stevens, 1959)

De Smith, S.A., J.L. Jowell, and H. Woolf, *Judicial Review of Administrative Action*, 5th edn (London: Sweet & Maxwell, 1995)

Deiser, G., 'The Juristic Person, III', *University of Pennsylvania Law Review* 57 (1909), 300–14

Dewey, J.,'The Historic Background of Corporate Legal Personality', *Yale Law Journal* 35 (1926), 655–73

Dicey, A.V., *Lectures Introductory to the Study of the Law of the Constitution* (London: Macmillan, 1886)

Introduction to the Study of the Law of the Constitution, 3rd edn (London: Macmillan, 1889)

Introduction to the Study of the Law of the Constitution, 7th edn (London: Macmillan, 1908)

Introduction to the Study of the Law of the Constitution, 10th edn (London: Macmillan, 1959)

Lectures on the Relation Between Law and Public Opinion in England During the Nineteenth Century (London: Macmillan, 1905)

Lectures on the Relation Between Law and Public Opinion in England During the Nineteenth Century, 2nd edn (London: Macmillan, 1914)

'The Combination Laws as Illustrating the Relation between Law and Opinion during the Nineteenth Century', *Harvard Law Review* 17 (1903–4), 511–32

'The Development of Administrative Law in England', *Law Quarterly Review* 31 (1915), 148–53

Digby A. and N. Bosanquet, 'Doctors and Patients in an Era of National Health Insurance and Private Practice, 1913–1938', *Economic History Review* 41 (1988), 74–94

Duguit, L., 'The Concept of Public Service', *Yale Law Journal* 32 (1922–3), 425–35

'The Law and the State', *Harvard Law Review* 31 (1917–18), 1–185

Duxbury, N., *Frederick Pollock and the English Juristic Tradition*, (Oxford University Press, 2004)

Dworkin, R., 'Hart's Postscript and the Character of Political Philosophy', *Oxford Journal of Legal Studies* 24 (2004), 1–37

Taking Rights Seriously (London: Duckworth, 1978)

Dyson, K.H.F., *The State Tradition in Western Europe: A Study of an Idea and Institution* (Oxford: Martin Robertson, 1980)

Emden, C.S., 'The Scope of the Public Authorities Protection Act, 1893', *Law Quarterly Review* 39 (1923), 341–56

Evans, M. (ed.), *International Law* (Oxford University Press, 2003)

Ewing, K.D., *The Bonfire of the Liberties: New Labour, Human Rights and the Rule of Law* (Oxford University Press, 2010)

Fairgrieve, D., *State Liability in Tort: A Comparative Law Study* (Oxford University Press, 2003)

Fifoot, C.H.S. (ed.), *The Letters of Frederic William Maitland* (London: Selden Society 1965)

Figgis, J.N., *Churches in the Modern State* (Bristol: Thoemmes Press, 1997)

Finer, S.E., *The Life and Times of Sir Edwin Chadwick* (London: Methuen, 1952)

Finn, P.D., 'Official Misconduct', *Criminal Law Journal* 2 (1978), 307–24

'Public Officers: Some Personal Liabilities', *Australian Law Journal* 51 (1977), 313–18

Finnis, J., 'The Priority of Persons', in J. Horder (ed.), *Oxford Essays in Jurisprudence* (Oxford University Press, 2000), pp. 1–15

Fisher, E., *Risk Regulation and Administrative Constitutionalism* (Oxford: Hart, 2010)

Forbes, R., 'Judicial Review of the Private Decision Maker: The Domestic Tribunal', *University of Western Ontario Law Review* 15 (1976), 123–50

Francis, M., 'Nineteenth Century Theories of Sovereignty and Thomas Hobbes', *History of Political Thought* (1980), 517–40

Francis, M. and J. Morrow, *A History of English Political Thought in the Nineteenth Century* (London: Duckworth, 1994).

Fraser, D. (ed.), *Municipal Reform and the Industrial City* (Leicester University Press, 1982)

Freeman, E.A., *The Growth of the English Constitution from the Earliest Times*, (London: Macmillan, 1872)

Freeman, J., 'The Contracting State', *Florida State University Law Review.* 28 (2000–1), 155–214

'The Private Role in Public Governance', *New York University Law Review.* 75 (2000), 543–675

Galligan, D.J., 'Judicial Review and the Textbook Writers', *Oxford Journal of Legal Studies* 2 (1982), 257–76

Ganz, G., *Quasi-Legislation: Recent Developments in Secondary Legislation* (London: Sweet & Maxwell, 1987)

Gardbaum, S., 'The "Horizontal Effect" of Constitutional Rights', *Michigan Law Review* 102 (2003), 387–459

Geldart, W., 'Legal Personality', *Law Quarterly Review* 27 (1911), 90–108

Gibbons, H.J., 'The Opposition to Municipal Socialism in England', *Journal of Political Economy.* 9 (1901), 243–59

Glasser, C. and C. Harlow, 'Legal Services and the Alternatives', in R. Rawlings (ed.), *Law Society and Economy: Centenary Essays for the London School of Economics and Political Science, 1895–1995* (Oxford: Clarendon Press, 1996), pp. 323–38

Goodnow, F.J., *Comparative Administrative Law; An Analysis of the Administrative Systems, National and Local, of the United States, England, France and Germany* (New York: Putnam's Sons, 1893)

Graham, C. and T. Prosser, 'Privatising Nationalised Industries: Constitutional Issues and New Legal Techniques' *Modern Law Review* 50 (1987), 16–51

Privatizing Public Enterprises: Constitutions, the State and Regulation in Comparative Perspective (Oxford: Clarendon Press, 1991)

Gray, J., *Hayek on Liberty*, 3rd edn (London: Routledge, 1998)

Green, L., 'General Jurisprudence: A 25th Anniversary Essay,' *Oxford Journal of Legal Studies* 25 (2005), 565–80

Green, T.H., *Lectures on the Principles of Political Obligation* (London: Longmans Green, 1948)

Grewe, W.G., *The Epochs of International Law*, M. Byers (tr.) (Berlin: De Gruyter, 2001)

Griffith, J.A.G., 'Justice and Administrative Law Revisited', in J.A.G. Griffith (ed.), *From Policy to Administration: Essays in Honour of William A. Robson* (London: Allen & Unwin, 1976), pp. 200–16

'Public Corporations as Crown Servants', *University of Toronto Law Journal* 9 (1951–2), 169–93

'The Political Constitution', *Modern Law Review* 42 (1979), 1

Griffith, J.A.G., and H. Street, *Principles of Administrative Law* (London: Pitman, 1952)

Gunn, J.A.W., *Politics and the Public Interest in the Seventeenth Century* (London: Routledge, 2010)

Hager, M.H., 'Bodies Politic: The Progressive History of Organizational 'Real Entity' Theory', *University of Pittsburgh Law Review* 50 (1989), 575–654

Harling, P., *The Waning of 'Old Corruption': The Politics of Economic Reform in Britain, 1779–1846* (Oxford: Clarendon Press, 1996)

Harlow, C., 'A Punitive Role for Torts?', in C. Harlow, L. Pearson and M. B. Taggart (eds.), *Administrative Law in a Changing State* (Oxford: Hart, 2008), p. 247–72.

'Damages and Human Rights', *New Zealand Law Review* (2004), 429–50

Harlow, C. and R. Rawlings, *Law and Administration* (London: Butterworths, 1983)

Law and Administration, 2nd edn (London: Butterworths, 1997)

Law and Administration, 3rd edn (Cambridge University Press, 2009)

Harris, J., *Civil Society in British History* (Oxford University Press, 2003)

'Enterprise and Welfare States: A Comparative Perspective', *Transactions of the Royal Historical Society* 40 (1990), 175–95

'Political Thought and the Welfare State 1870–1940: An Intellectual Framework for British Social Policy', *Past and Present* 135 (1992), 116–41

'The Webbs, The Charity Organisation Society and the Ratan Tata Foundation: Social Policy From the Perspective of 1912', in M. Bulmer, J. Lewis and D. Piachaud (eds.), *The Goals of Social Policy* (London: Unwin Hyman, 1989), pp. 27–63

'War and Social History: Britain and the Home Front during the Second World War', *Contemporary European History* 1 (1992), 17–35

Harris, J.W., *Legal Philosophies*, 2nd edn (London: Butterworths, 1997)

Harris, N., *Competition and the Corporate Society: British Conservatives, the State and Industry, 1945–1964* (London: Methuen, 1972)

Harris, R., *Industrializing English Law: Entrepreneurship and Business Organization, 1720–1844* (Cambridge University Press, 2000)

'The Transplantation of the Legal Discourse on Corporate Personality Theories: From German Codification to British Political Pluralism and American Big Business', *Washington and Lee Law Review* 63 (2006), 1421–78

Harrison Moore, W., 'The Crown as Corporation', *Law Quarterly Review* 20 (1904), 351–62

Hart, H.L.A., 'Introduction' in J. Austin, *The Province of Jurisprudence Determined* (London: Weidenfeld Nicolson, 1954), pp. vii–xviii

'Definition and Theory in Jurisprudence', reproduced in H.L.A. Hart, *Essays in Jurisprudence and Philosophy* (Oxford: Clarendon Press, 1983), pp. 21–48

The Concept of Law (Oxford: Clarendon Press, 1961)

Hart, J., 'Sir Charles Trevelyan at the Treasury', *English Historical Review* 75 (1960), 92–110

Hartog, H., *Public Property and Private Power: The Corporation of the City of New York in American Law, 1730–1870* (New York: Cornell University Press, 1989)

Hayek, F., *Law, Legislation and Liberty* (London: Routledge, 1976)

The Road to Serfdom, B. Caldwell (ed.) (University of Chicago Press, 2007)

'Use of Knowledge in Society', *American Economic Review* 35 (1945), 519–30

Hearn, W.E., *The Government of England: Its Structure and its Development*, 2nd edn (Melbourne: George Robertson, 1886)

Hewart, G., *The New Despotism* (London: Ernest Benn, 1929)

Hirschl, R., 'The Political Origins of the New Constitutionalism', *Indiana Journal of Global Legal Studies* 11 (2004), 71–108

Towards Juristocracy: The Origins and Consequences of the New Constitutionalism (Cambridge, MA: Harvard University Press, 2004)

Hobbes, T., *Leviathan*, R. Tuck (ed.) (Cambridge University Press, 1996)

Hogg, P.W., 'Victoria's Crown Proceedings Act', *Melborne University Law Review* 7 (1969–70), 342–52

Holdsworth, W.S., *Essays in Law and History*, A.L. Goodhart and H.G. Hanbury (eds.) (London: Oxford University Press, 1946)

Holland, M., *European Community Integration* (London: Pinter, 1993)

Holland, T.E., *The Elements of Jurisprudence* (Oxford: Clarendon Press, 1880)

Hood Phillips, O., 'Constitutional Conventions: Dicey's Predecessors', *Modern Law Review* 29 (1966), 137–48

Hoppen, K.T., *The Mid-Victorian Generation 1846–1886* (Oxford University Press, 1998)

Hughes, E. and H. O'Brien, 'Sir George Trevelyan and Civil Service Reform, 1853–5', *English Historical Review* 64 (1949), 53–88

'Sir George Trevelyan and Civil Service Reform, 1853–5: Part II', *English Historical Review* 64 (1949), 206–34

Hume, L.J., *Bentham and Bureaucracy* (Cambridge University Press, 1981)

Hunt, M., 'Constitutionalism and the Contractualisation of Government', in M. B. Taggart (ed.), *The Province of Administrative Law* (Oxford: Hart Publishing, 1997), pp. 21–39

Jacob, J.M., 'The Debates Behind an Act: Crown Proceedings Reform, 1920–1947', *Public Law.* (1992), 452–84

The Republican Crown: Lawyers and the Making of the State in the Twentieth Century Britain (Dartmouth: Aldershot, 1996)

Jacobsen, A.J., 'The Private Use of Public Authority: Sovereignty and Associations in the Common Law,' *Buffalo Law Review* 29 (1980), 599–666

Jaffe, L.L., 'Law Making by Private Groups', *Harvard Law Review* 51 (1937–8), 201–53

Jennings, W.I. 'Central Control,' in H.J. Laski, W.I Jennings and W.A. Robson (eds.), *A Century of Municipal Progress* (London: Allen & Unwin, 1935), pp. 417–54

'Declaratory Judgments Against Public Authorities in England', *Yale Law Journal* 41 (1931–2), 407–24

The Law and the Constitution, 2nd edn (University of London Press, 1938)

'The Municipal Revolution', in H.J. Laski, W.I. Jennings and W.A. Robson (eds.), *A Century of Municipal Progress* (London: Allen & Unwin, 1935), pp. 55–65

'The Right of Assembly in England', *New York University Law Quarterly Review* 9 (1931–2), 217–21

'Courts and Administrative Law – The Experience of English Housing Legislation', *Harvard Law Review* 49 (1936), 426–54

Jennings, W.I., W.A. Robson and E.C.S. Wade, 'Administrative Law and the Teaching of Public Law', *Journal of the Society of Public Teachers of Law* 10 (1938), 10–14

Jowett, B. and C.E. Trevelyan, *Papers Relating to the Re-organisation of the Civil Service* (London: Eyre and Spottiswoode, 1955)

Kantorowicz, E., *The King's Two Bodies: A Study in Mediaevel Political Theology* (Princeton University Press, 1957)

Kavanagh, A., *Constitutional Review under the UK Human Rights Act* (Cambridge University Press, 2009)

Kelsen, H., *General Theory of Law and State*, A. Wedberg (tr.) (Cambridge, MA: Harvard University Press, 1949)

Introduction to the Problems of Legal Theory, B.L. Paulson and S.L. Paulson (tr.) (Oxford University Press, 1992)

Keohane, R. and Hoffman, S., 'Conclusions: Community Politics and Institutional Choice', in W. Wallace (ed.), *The Dynamics of European Integration* (London: Pinter, 1990), pp. 276–300

Laborde, C., 'The Concept of the State in British and French Political Thought', *Political Studies* 48 (2000), 540–57

Lacey, N., *A Life of H.L.A. Hart: The Nightmare and the Noble Dream* (Oxford University Press, 2004)

Landauer, C., 'Ernst Kantorowicz and the Sacralization of the Past', *Central European History* 27(1) (1994), 1–25

Landis, J.M., *The Administrative Process*, 7th edn (New Haven, CT: Yale University Press, 1966)

Lane, M.S., *Plato's Progeny: How Plato and Socrates Still Captivate the Modern Mind* (London: Duckworth, 2001)

Laski, H.J., *Authority in the Modern State* (New Haven, CT: Yale University Press, 1919)

'Civil Liberties in Great Britain in Wartime', *Bill of Rights Review* 2 (1941–2), 243–51

'Early History of the Corporation in England', *Harvard Law Review.* 30 (1916–17), 561–88

'Judicial Review of Social Policy in England: A Study of Roberts v. Hopwood et al.', *Harvard Law Review* 39 (1925–26) 832–48

Studies in Law and Politics (New Haven, CT: Yale University Press, 1932)

Studies in the Problem of Sovereignty (New Haven, CT: Yale University Press, 1917)

'The Personality of Associations', *Harvard Law Review.* 29 (1915–16), 404–26

'The Responsibility of the State in England', *Harvard Law Review* 32 (1918–19), 447–72

Laski, H.J., W.I. Jennings and W.A. Robson (eds.), *A Century of Municipal Progress* (London: Allen & Unwin, 1935)

Lauterpacht, H., *Private Law Sources and Analogies of International Law (With Special Reference to International Arbitration)* (London: Longmans Green, 1927)

Lester, A., and M. Weait, 'The Use of Ministerial Powers Without Parliamentary Authority: The Ram Doctrine', *Public Law* (2003), 415–28

Lewis, J., 'The Boundary Between Voluntary and Statutory Social Service in the Late Nineteenth and Early Twentieth Centuries', *The Historical Journal* 39 (1996), 155–77.

Lindahl, H., 'Sovereignty and Representation in the European Union' in N. Walker (ed.), *Sovereignty in Transition*, (Oxford: Hart, 2003), pp. 87–114

Lindsay, A.D., 'Sovereignty', *Proceedings of the Aristotelian Society* 24 (1923–24), 235–54

Loughlin, M., *Foundations of Public Law* (Oxford University Press, 2010).

Legality and Locality: The Role of Law in Central–Local Government (Oxford: Clarendon Press, 1996)

Public Law and Political Theory (Oxford University Press, 1992)

'The Functionalist Style in Public Law', *University of Toronto Law Journal* 55 (2005), 361–403

The Idea of Public Law (Oxford University Press, 2003)

'The State, the Crown and the Law', in M. Sunkin and S. Payne (eds.), *The Nature of the Crown* (Oxford University Press, 1999) pp. 33–76

'Why the History of Administrative Law is Not Written', in D. Dyzenhaus, M. Hunt and G. Huscroft (eds.), *A Simple Common Lawyer: Essays in Honour of Michael Taggart* (Oxford: Hart, 2009), pp. 151–77

Macadam, E., *The New Philanthrophy: A Study of the Relations Between the Statutory and Voluntary Social Services* (London: Allen & Unwin, 1934)

MacCormick, N., *Institutions of Law* (Oxford University Press, 2007)

Questioning Sovereignty, (Oxford University Press, 1999)

MacDonagh, O., 'Delegated Legislation and Administrative Discretions in the 1850s: A Particular Study', *Victorian Studies* 2 (1958), 29–44

Early Victorian Government, 1830–1870 (London: Wiedenfeld and Nicolson, 1977)

'The Nineteenth-Century Revolution in Government: A Reappraisal', *The Historical Journal* 1 (1958), 52–67

Machen, A.W., 'Corporate Personality', *Harvard Law Review* 24 (1910–11), 253–67

Mack, J.A., 'Group Personality – A Footnote to Maitland', *Philosophical Quarterly* 2 (1952), 249–52

MacLeod, R.M., 'The Alkali Acts Administration, 1863–84: The Emergence of the Civil Scientist', *Victorian Studies* 9 (1965), 85–112

Maine, H. S., *Ancient Law: Its Connection with the Early History of Society, and its Relation to Modern Ideas* (London: John Murray, 1861)

Popular Government: Four Essays (New York: Holt, 1886)

Maitland, F.W., 'Body Politic', in H.A.L. Fisher (ed.), *The Collected Papers of Frederic William Maitland*, 3 vols. (Cambridge University Press, 1911), vol. III, pp. 285–303

'History of English Law', in H.M. Cam (ed.), *Selected Historical Essays of F.W. Maitland* (Cambridge University Press, 1957), pp. 97–121

'Introduction', in O. Gierke, *Political Theories of the Middle Age*, F.W. Maitland (tr.) (Cambridge University Press, 1958), pp. vii–xlv

'Moral Personality and Legal Personality' in H.A.L. Fisher (ed.), *The Collected Papers of Frederic William Maitland*, 3 vols. (Cambridge University Press, 1911), vol. III, pp. 304–20

'The Crown as Corporation', in H.A.L. Fisher (ed.), *The Collected Papers of Frederic William Maitland*, 3 vols. (Cambridge University Press, 1911), vol. III, pp. 244–70

'The Shallows and Silences of Real Life' in H.A.L. Fisher (ed.), *The Collected Papers of Frederic William Maitland*, 3 vols. (Cambridge University Press, 1911), vol I, pp. 467–79

The Constitutional History of England: A Course of Lectures Delivered by F. W. Maitland (Cambridge University Press, 1885)

The Constitutional History of England; A Course of Lectures Delivered by F. W. Maitland (Cambridge University Press, 1908)

Township and Borough: The Ford Lectures 1897, With an Appendix of Notes Relating to the History of Cambridge (Cambridge University Press, 1898)

Mali, J., 'Ernst H. Kantorowicz: History as Mythschau', *History of Political Thought* 18 (1997), 579–603

Markby, W., *Elements of Law: Considered with Reference to Principles of General Jurisprudence* (Oxford: Clarendon Press, 1871)

Marquand, D., *The Unprincipled Society: New Demands and Old Politics* (London: Jonathan Cape, 1988)

Mashaw, J.L., *Greed Chaos and Governance: Using Public Choice to Improve Public Law* (New Haven, CT: Yale University Press, 1997)

McAuslan, P., 'Administrative Law, Collective Consumption and Judicial Policy', *Modern Law Review* 46 (1983), 1–20

Public Law and Public Choice', *Modern Law Review* 51 (1988), 681–705

McBriar, A.M., *An Edwardian Mixed Doubles: The Bosanquets Versus the Webbs; A Study in British Social Policy, 1890–1929* (Oxford University Press, 1987)

McLay, G., 'The Problem With Suing Sovereigns', *Victoria University of Wellington Law Review* 41 (2010), 403–25

McLean I. and C. Foster, 'The Political Economy of Regulation: Interests, Ideology, Voters and the UK Regulation of Railways Act 1844', *Public Administration* 70 (1992), 313–31

McLean, J., 'The Crown in Contract and Administrative Law', *Oxford Journal of Legal Studies* 24 (2004), 129–154

'Public Function Tests: Bringing Back the State', in D. Dyzenhaus, M. Hunt and G. Huscroft (eds.), *A Simple Common Lawyer: Essays in Honour of Mike Taggart* (Oxford, Hart, 2009), pp. 185–207

Merrick Dodd, E., 'Dogma and Practice in the Law of Associations', *Harvard Law Review* 42 (1928–9), 977–1014

Mill, J.S., *Essays on Equality, Law and Education*, J.M. Robson (ed.) (University of Toronto Press, 1984)

On Liberty (London: J. Parker, 1959)

Millon, D., 'Theories of the Corporation', *Duke Law Journal* (1990), 201–62

Mitchell, J.D.B., 'Administrative Law and Policy Effectiveness', in J.A.G. Griffith (ed.), *From Policy to Administration: Essays in Honour of William A. Robson* (London: Allen & Unwin, 1976), pp. 174–93

The Contracts of Public Authorities; A Comparative Study (London: Bell and Sons, 1954)

Mohan, J., 'Voluntarism, Municipalism and Welfare: The Geography of Hospital Utilization in England in 1938', *Transactions of the Institute of British Geographers* 28 (2003), 56–74

Moran, M., *The British Regulatory State* (Oxford University Press, 1992)

Moravcsik, A., 'Negotiating the Single European Act: National Interests and Conventional Statecraft in the European Community', *International Organization* 45 (1991), 19–55

Morefield, J., 'Hegelian Organicism, British New Liberalism, and the Return of the Family State', *History of Political Thought* 23 (2002), 141–70

Morgan, G. H., 'Remedies Against the Crown', in G. Robinson, *Public Authorities and Legal Liability* (University of London Press, 1925)

Morris, R.J., 'Voluntary Societies and British Urban Elites, 1780–1850: An Analysis', *The Historical Journal* 26(1) (1983), 95–118

Mulgan, R., *Holding Power to Account* (New York: Palgrave Macmillan, 2003)

Mullan, D.J., *Administrative Law*, 5th edn (Toronto: Emond Montgomery, 2003)

'Administrative Law at the Margins', in M.B. Taggart, *The Province of Administrative Law* (Oxford: Hart, 1997), pp. 134–59

Novak, W., *The People's Welfare: Law and Regulation in Nineteenth-Century America* (Chapel Hill, NC: University of North Carolina Press, 1996)

O'Brien, P., 'The Political Economy of British Taxation, 1660–1815', *Economic History Review*, 41 (1988), 1–32

Ogus, A., *Regulation: Legal Form and Economic Theory* (Oxford: Hart, 2004)

Oliver, D., *Common Values and the Public Private Divide* (London: Butterworths, 1999)

'Functions of a Public Nature under the Human Rights Act', *Public Law* (2004), 329–52

'The Frontiers of the State: Public Authorities and Public Functions under the Human Rights Act', *Public Law* (2000), 476–93

Orth, J.V., 'The Trade Union Acts of 1824 and 1825: Dicey and the Relation Between Law and Opinion', *Anglo-American Law Review* 5 (1976), 131–53

Osborne, D. and T. Gaebler, *Reinventing Government* (Boston, MA: Addison Wesley, 1992)

Page, A., 'Member States, Public Undertakings and Article 90', *European Law Review* 7 (1982), 19–35

'Public Law and Economic Policy: The United Kingdom Experience', *Journal of Law and Society* 9 (1982), 225–52

Patten, A., *Hegel's Idea of Freedom* (Oxford University Press, 1999)

Pettit, P., 'Responsibility Incorporated', *Ethics* 117 (2007), 171–201

Republicanism: A Theory of Freedom and Government (Oxford University Press, 1999)

Pfander, J.E., 'Köbler v Austria: Expositional Supremacy and Member State Liability', *European Business Law Review* 17 (2006), 275–97

Phillips, M.J., 'Reappraising the Real Entity Theory of the Corporation', *Florida State University Law Review* 21 (1994), 1061–123

Pollock, F., 'Has the Common Law Received a Fiction Theory of Corporations?', *Law Quarterly Review* 27 (1911), 219–35

Poole, T., 'Between the Devil and the Deep Blue Sea: Administrative Law in the Age of Rights', in C. Harlow, L. Pearson and M. B. Taggart (eds.), *Administrative Law in a Changing State: Essays in Honour of Mark Aronson* (Oxford: Hart, 2008), pp. 15–44

Power, M., *The Risk Management of Everything: Rethinking the Politics of Uncertainty* (London: Demos, 2004)

Prest, J.M., *Liberty and Locality: Parliament, Permissive Legislation and Ratepayers' Democracies in the Nineteenth Century* (Oxford: Clarendon Press, 1990)

Prosser, T., 'Markets, Planning and Socialism', *Journal of Law and Society* 15 (1988), 42–57

The Limits of Competition Law, Markets and Public Services (Oxford University Press 2005)

Quane, H., 'The Strasbourg Jurisprudence and the Meaning of a "Public Authority" Under the Human Rights Act', *Public Law* (2006), 106–23

Randall, H., 'Personality: Human and Divine', in H. Sturt (ed.), *Personal Idealism: Philosophical Essays by Eight Members of the University of Oxford* (London: Macmillan, 1902), pp. 369–93

Raymond, R.L., 'The Genesis of the Corporation', *Harvard Law Review.* 19 (1905–6), 350–65

Raz, J., *The Authority of Law: Essays on Law and Morality* (Oxford: Clarendon Press, 1979)

Rees, R., 'Economic Aspects of Privatisation in Britain', in V. Wright (ed.), *Privatisation in Western Europe: Pressures, Problems and Paradoxes*, (New York: St Martin's Press, 1994)

Reich, C.A., 'The New Property', *Yale Law Journal* 73 (1963–4), 733–87

Rhodes, R., 'The Hollowing Out of the State: the Changing Nature of the Public Service in Britain', *Political Quarterly* 65 (1994), 138–51

Richardson, J., 'The Politics and Practice of Privatisation in Britain', in V. Wright (ed.), *Privatisation in Western Europe: Pressures, Problems and Paradoxes*, (New York: St Martin's Press, 1994)

Rishworth, P., 'New Zealand Taking Human Rights into The Private Sphere' in D. Oliver and J. Fedtke (eds.), *Human Rights in the Private Sphere: A Comparative Study* (London: Routledge-Cavendish, 2007), pp. 312–50

Rishworth, P. and J. McLean, 'Human Rights Obligations in the Private Sector: Reflections on *YL v Birmingham City Council* and the Meaning of "Public Function"', in C.F. Forsyth, M. Elliott, S. Jhaveri, M. Ramsden and A. Scully Hill (eds.), *Effective Judicial Review: A Cornerstone of Good Government* (Oxford University Press, 2010), pp. 101–19

Roberts, D., 'Tory Paternalism and Social Reform in Early Victorian England', *The American Historical Review* 63 (1958), 323–37

Robson, W.A., *Civilisation and the Growth of Law; A Study of the Relations Between Men's Ideas About the Universe and the Institutions of Law and Government* (New York: Macmillan, 1935)

Justice and Administrative Law: A Study of the British Constitution (London: Macmillan, 1928)

Justice and Administrative Law; A Study of the British Constitution, 2nd edn (London: Stevens, 1947)

Nationalized Industry and Public Ownership, 2nd edn (London: Allen & Unwin, 1962)

'The Report of the Committee on Ministers' Powers', *The Political Quarterly* 3 (1932), 346–64

Rockmore, T., *Hegel, Idealism and Analytic Philosophy* (New Haven, CT: Yale University Press, 2005)

Rumble, W.E., *Doing Austin Justice: The Reception of John Austin's Philosophy of Law in Nineteenth-Century England* (London: Continuum, 2005)

The Thought of John Austin: Jurisprudence, Colonial Reform, and the British Constitution (London: Athlone, 1985)

Runciman, D., *Pluralism and the Personality of the State* (Cambridge University Press, 1997)

Salmond, J., *Jurisprudence, or the Theory of the Law* (London: Sweet & Maxwell, 1902)

Jurisprudence, or the Theory of the Law, 2nd edn (London: Stevens and Haynes, 2nd edn, 1907)

Jurisprudence 7th edn (London: Sweet & Maxwell, 1924)

Samuel, G., 'Public and Private Law: A Private Lawyer's Response', *Modern Law Review* 46 (1983), 558–83

Sawer, G., 'Crown Liability in Tort and the Exercise of Discretions', *Res Judicatae* 5 (1951), 14–20

'Government as Personalized Legal Entity', in L.C. Webb (ed.), *Legal Personality and Political Pluralism* (Melbourne University Press, 1958), pp. 158–77

Schmitt, C., *The Concept of the Political*, G. Schwab (tr.) (University of Chicago Press, 2007)

Schneiderman, D., 'Harold Laski, Viscount Haldane, and the Law of the Canadian Constitution in the Early Twentieth Century', *University of Toronto Law Journal* 48 (1998), 521–60

Seddon, N., *Government Contracts: Federal State and Local*, 3 edn, (Annadale, New South Wales: Federation Press, 2004)

Selway, B., 'Of Kings and Officers – The Judicial Development of Public Law', *Federal Law Review* 33 (2005), 187–238

Shaw, J., 'The European Union: Discipline Building Meets Polity Building' in P. Cane and M. Tushnet (eds.), *Oxford Handbook of Legal Studies*, (Oxford University Press, 2003), pp. 325–52

Sheldrake, J., *Municipal Socialism* (Avebury: Aldershot, 1989)

Shortt, J., *Informations (Criminal and Quo Warranto), Mandamus and Prohibition* (London: Clowes, 1887)

Sidgwick, H., *The Elements of Politics*, 2nd edn (London: Macmillan, 1897)

Simhony, A., 'Rights that Bind: T.H. Green on Rights and Community' in M. Dimova-Cookson and W.J. Mander (eds.), *T.H. Green: Ethics, Metaphysics and Political Philosophy* (Oxford: Clarendon Press, 2006), pp. 236–61

Simpson, A.W.B., *In the Highest Degree Odious: Detention Without Trial in Wartime Britain* (Oxford University Press, 1992)

Human Rights and the End of Empire: Britain and the Genesis of the European Convention (Oxford University Press, 2004)

Skinner, Q., 'A Genealogy of the Modern State', *Proceedings of the British Academy* 162 (2009), 325–70

Liberty Before Liberalism (Cambridge University Press, 1997)

Smith, A., *The Wealth of Nations* (Edinburgh: Adam and Charles Black, 1850)

Smith, B., 'Legal Personality', *Yale Law Journal* 37 (1928), 283–99

Stears, M., *Progressives, Pluralists and the Problems of the State: Ideologies of Reform in the United States and Britain, 1909–1926* (Oxford University Press, 2002)

Stebbings, C., '"Officialism": Law, Bureaucracy, and Ideology in Late Victorian England', in A. Lewis and M. Lobban (eds.), *Law and History* (Oxford University Press, 2004), pp. 317–43

Stein, E., 'Lawyers, Judges and the Making of the Transnational Constitution', *American Journal of International Law* 75 (1981), 1–27

Street, H., *Government Liability: A Comparative Study* (Cambridge University Press, 1953)

Sugarman, D., 'Hart Interviewed: H.L.A. Hart in Conversation with David Sugarman,' *Journal of Law and Society* 32 (2005), 267–293

Sunkin, M. and S. Payne, *The Nature of the Crown* (Oxford University Press, 1999)

Taggart, M.B., 'From "Parliamentary Powers" to Privatization: The Chequered History of Delegated Legislation in the Twentieth Century', *University of Toronto Law Journal.* 55 (2005), 575–627

'Proportionality, Deference, Wednesbury', *New Zealand Law Review.* (2008), 423–82

'The Nature and Functions of the State,' in P. Cane and M. Tushnet (eds.), *Oxford Handbook of Legal Studies* (Oxford University Press, 2003), pp. 101–18

'The Province of Administrative Law Determined?', in M. B. Taggart (ed.), *The Province of Administrative Law* (Oxford: Hart, 1997), pp. 1–20.

Taylor, B., 'Municipal Glasgow', *The North American Review* 184 (1907), 590–603

Teubner, G., 'Juridification: Concepts, Aspects, Limits and Solutions', in G. Teubner (ed.), *Juridification of Social Spheres* (New York: Walter de Gruyter, 1987), pp. 3–48

Todd, A., *On Parliamentary Government in England: Its Origin, Development and Practical Operation* (London: Longman Green, 1867)

Torrance, J.R., 'Sir George Harrison and the Growth of Bureaucracy in the Early Nineteenth Century', *English Historical Review* 83 (1968), 52–88

Toulmin-Smith, J., *Local Self-Government and Centralization* (London: Chapman, 1851)

Twining, W.L., *General Jurisprudence: Understanding Law From a Global Perspective* (Cambridge University Press, 2009)

Globalisation and Legal Theory (London: Butterworths, 2000)

Twomey, A., 'Responsible Government and the Divisibility of the Crown', *Public Law* (2008), 742–67

Vattel, E., *The Law of Nations, or, Principles of the Law of Nature: Applied to the Conduct and Affairs of Nations and Sovereigns* (London: Robinson, 1797)

The Law of Nations, or, Principles of the Law of Nature: Applied to the Conduct and Affairs of Nations and Sovereigns, J. Chitty (tr.) (London: Sweet, 1834)

Vincent, A., 'German Philosophy and British Public Policy: Richard Burdon Haldane in Theory and Practice', *Journal of the History of Ideas* 68 (2007), 157–79

Vincent-Jones, P., *The New Public Contracting* (Oxford University Press, 2006)

Vinogradoff, P., 'Juridical Persons', *Columbia Law Review* 24 (1924), 594–604

Vinx, L., *Hans Kelsen's Pure Theory of Law: Legality and Legitimacy* (Oxford: Clarendon Press, 2007)

Wade, H.W.R., *Administrative Law* (Oxford: Clarendon Press, 1961)

Administrative Law, 2nd edn (Oxford University Press, 1967)

Towards Administrative Justice (Ann Arbor, MI: Michigan University Press, 1963)

Wade, H.W.R., and C.F. Forsyth, *Administrative Law*, 9th edn (Oxford: Clarendon Press, 2004)

Walker, N. (ed.), *Sovereignty in Transition* (Oxford: Hart Publishing, 2003)

Walker, N. and M. Loughlin, *The Paradox of Constitutionalism* (Oxford University Press, 2007)

Webb, B., *The Diary of Beatrice Webb*, N. MacKenzie and J. MacKenzie (eds.) (London: Virago, 2000)

Webb, B.P., and S. Webb, *A Constitution for the Socialist Commonwealth of Great Britain* (London: Longmans Green, 1920)

The Public Organisation of the Labour Market: Being Part Two of the Minority Report of the Poor Law Commission (London: Longmans Green, 1909)

Weinbren, D., and B. Jones, 'Getting a Grip: the Roles of Friendly Societies in Australia and Britain Reappraised', *Labour History* 88 (2005), 87–104

Westlake, J., *The Collected Papers of John Westlake on International Law*, L. Oppenheim (ed.) (Cambridge University Press, 1910).

Whiteside, N., 'Private Agencies for Public Purposes: Some New Perspectives on Policy Making in Health Insurance Between the Wars', *Journal of Social Policy* 12 (1983), 65–94

Williams, D.G.T., 'The Donoughmore Report in Retrospect', *Public Administration* 60 (1982), 273–92

Willis, J., 'Administrative Law and the British North America Act', *Harvard Law Review* 53 (1939–40), 251–81

'Parliament and the Local Authorities' in H.J. Laski, W.I. Jennings and W.A. Robson (eds.), *A Century of Municipal Progress* (London: Allen & Unwin, 1935), pp. 400–16

Willoughby, W.W., 'The Juristic Conception of the State', *American Political Science Review* 12 (1918), 192–208

Wilson, J.E., *Lighting The Town: A Study of Management in the North West Gas Industry, 1805–1880* (London: Paul Chapman, 1991)

Winkler, J., 'Law State and the Economy: The Industry Act 1975 in Context', *British Journal of Law and Society* 2(2) (1975), 103–28

Winter, C., 'Parliamentary, Ministerial, and Judicial Control of Nationalized Industries in Great Britain', *Law and Contemporary Problems* 16 (1951), 670–701

Wolff, M., 'On the Nature of Legal Persons', *Law Quarterly Review.* 54 (1938), 494–521

Wright, V., 'Industrial Privatization in Western Europe: Pressures, Problems and Paradoxes', in V. Wright (ed.), *Privatization in Western Europe: Pressures, Problems and Paradoxes* (New York: St Martin's Press, 1994), pp. 1–43

Zines, L., 'Commentary', in H.V. Evatt (ed.), *The Royal Prerogative* (North Ryde, New South Wales: Law Book Co, 1987)

INDEX

For EU product safety concerns, contact us at Calle de José Abascal, 56–1°, 28003 Madrid, Spain or eugpsr@cambridge.org.

www.ingramcontent.com/pod-product-compliance
Lightning Source LLC
LaVergne TN
LVHW011528200926
848484LV00001B/187
9781107022485